Education of Lifestyle and Lifetime Diseases

EDUCATION OF LIFESTYLE AND LIFETIME DISEASES

DR. S.L. GOEL

Advisor, Mahatma Gandhi State Institute of Public Administration, Punjab
Editor, The Indian Journal of Publitc Administration, New Delhi
Former Member of UGC, Management Board AICTE
Director, State Bank of India, Northern Region
Vice-Predident of IIPA and Emeritus Professor of Public Administration, UGC
Professor of Public Administration (Retd.)
Panjab University, Chandigarh

DEEP & DEEP PUBLICATIONS PVT. LTD.

F-159, Rajouri Garden, New Delhi-110027

EDUCATION OF LIFESTYLE AND LIFETIME DISEASES

ISBN 978-81-8450-136-0

Typeset by S.S. COMPOSERS,
3190, Mohindra Park, Shakur Basti, Delhi-110034.

Printed in India at MAYUR ENTERPRISES,
WZ Plot No. 3, Gujjar Market, Tihar Village, New Delhi-110018.

Published by DEEP & DEEP PUBLICATIONS PVT. LTD.,
F-159, Rajouri Garden, New Delhi-110027.
Phones: 25435369, 25440916
E-mail: ddpbooks@yahoo.co.in • ddpubs@gmail.com
Showroom:
2/13, Ansari Road, Daryaganj, New Delhi-110002 • Telefax: 23245122

Contents

Preface

Non-Communicable Diseases or Lifestyle Diseases or Lifetime Diseases are the creatures of our own way of living. These diseases are not infectious but self-imposed. The right quality of health education is the only answer to avoid them. These diseases are on the increase because of stresses and strains caused by Urbanization, pollution, violating laws of nature and glamour of temporary pleasures.

Most of the chronic, degenerative, non-communicable diseases are diseases of the second half of human life, and are becoming more common as people live longer in both developed and developing countries. Decreasing the incidence of death from one cause entails increasing the deaths from some other cause. We all have to die from something: our task is to increase the healthy lifespan as far as possible.

The most important non-communicable diseases are undoubtedly the cardiovascular diseases, since the total number of sufferers in both developed and developing countries is higher than the total cases of communicable disease. Next come the different malignancies gathered under the general term of cancer, followed by the non-communicable respiratory diseases, diabetes, and a number of other conditions which include hereditary ailments and the mental and neurological diseases.

Limited but Important Role of Lifestyle

We traditionally consider cardiovascular diseases, cancer, diabetes and hereditary diseases in a single group, not only because of the considerable damage they do but also because they are caused by agents of a chemical and physical nature, which influence the hereditary system or the metabolism of the body.

Certain groups of cancer can be produced by biological factors such as viruses, as well as chronic infection, and by physical factors, which set in train a cytotoxic process when they interfere with the genetic mechanism of the cells. A second group of factors acts at the level of cell regulation and produces the milieu in which the cancer cells start to multiply. There are also hereditary factors that produce a predisposition to the development of cancer.

Although sometimes called lifestyle diseases, I personally do not like to claim that such-and-such a percentage of all non-communicable diseases are lifestyle-dependent diseases and could, therefore, be completely prevented. It is very difficult to calculate this percentage because so many other factors influence the incidence of different diseases. What we can say is that most non-communicable diseases are strongly influenced by the lifestyles of different population groups. But lifestyles do not only mean bad habits or improper behaviour; they are also basic conditions of life that often do not depend on the behaviour or habits of a given individual. Quality of air, drinking-water and soil, for instance, are environmental factors which mostly depend on the behaviour of whole communities rather than individuals.

Prevention health actions are always, in the long-run, the most effective; the earlier you start treatment the better are the results. For more than a decade, WHO has been trying to develop an integrated approach to the prevention of different non-communicable diseases through early detection and treatment. It makes sense to screen a population, not for one particular disease but for all those that mostly affect people in the second half of their lives, using an integrated system of diagnosis and treatment.

The ÇINDI—Countrywide Integrated Non-communicable Disease Intervention—Programme, the Inter-Health Programme and the MONICA Programme are closely related to each other. The WHO MONICA Project (MONItoring of trends and determinants in Cardiovascular disease) is a ten-year study which began in the mid-1980s; the drive against lifestyles that are potentially harmful to health; and CINDI is rather more oriented towards the needs and problems of the developed countries, since it started in countries of Europe and the Americas which had more developed systems of public health services.

But the principle is one and the same—protecting the health of certain groups in the population, not only by detecting the diseases at an early stage but also by monitoring these groups in order to formulate the best approaches to prophylactic and treatment measures, while at the same time neutralizing the effect of the causative factors responsible for these relatively common diseases.[1]

Substance abuse has touched every corner of the world. Epidemics shift from one region to another and between different substances. New and often more harmful drugs and patterns of use are replacing traditional practices. Modern drugs of abuse are often injected, bringing the risk of HIV infection on top of drug dependence. The tobacco industry is taking advantage of the huge untapped markets of the developing world. The traditional and controlled use of alcohol in rites and ceremonies is giving way to causal drunkenness.

The problems No. longer relate to the use of only one or a few drugs. More often, users move from one drug to another and use combinations of different substances. In many societies, habit-forming exposure to tobacco, alcohol and drugs can start at a very early age, with grave consequences

1. WHO: Nikolai P. Napalkov, "Live Better—Live Longer", *World Health*, March-April, 1995, pp. 12-13.

for health in later life. Substance abuse, a major preventable cause of morbidity and mortality in most regions of the world, is thus ultimately a health issue.

The complexities and scope of drug problems require an equally complex and integrated response. We need to strike a balance in our policies, acknowledging that many psychoactive substances play an important role in our societies and in healthcare but, at the same time, they may be misused and cause considerable harm. Prevention of abuse can take the form of promoting healthy lifestyles and reducing health risks, while insisting that the rights of each individual should be respected at all times.

Considering the pervasive nature of the problem, which cuts across geographical and socio-cultural boundaries, it is essential that we involve communities and primary healthcare systems in our policies for prevention, care and rehabilitation. Communities must be prepared and equipped to treat and care for those who have already been harmed, and to confront the physical disease, mental disorders and social disruption which substance abuse entails. We need to educate communities, particularly the young, on how to cope with the risk of substance abuse and especially in a society where drugs proliferate. Such actions are possible only if political leaders, law-makers and society at large recognize the many dimensions of the drug problem and if they all work together to support the response of health ministries and professionals. In addition, of course, health policies must take into account drug issues just as drug policies must take into account and integrate health issues and approaches.[2]

So we have to try to change the beliefs, rituals and habits that now make drug use appear pleasurable, glamorous or special. Activities based on this idea are producing some very promising results in Sri Lanka. Some communities, and young people themselves, are now working to change or reverse the assumptions and practices that make alcohol, tobacco and other drugs appear great and wonderful.

A community can examine how it refers to drug use and intoxication, and how every body similes or laughs when they talk about drug use. Even the stupor caused by alcohol or heroin is referred to as being "high"!

The community has to actively contest all those words and expressions that are currently used to make drugs appear special, and replace them by words, which more accurately describe the real experience. Reversing the image also involves countering the effect of the special rituals connected with alcohol and drug use. It is often even exciting to make fun of these grand rituals surrounding drug use, and to expose them as rather silly.[3]

---

2. WHO: Editorial, "Substance Abuse is a Health Issue", *World Health*, July-August, 1995, p. 3.
3. WHO: Diyanath Samarasinghe, "Removing the Glamour," *World Health*, July-August, 1995, p. 5.

Religious festivals, rituals or ceremonies serve to mobilize the community to action, and affirm the relevance and centrality of the spiritual dimension in the lives of all. This approach has played a significant role in demystifying substance use and dependence, and encourages the notion that rehabilitation should, and does, being prior to detoxification. Medicine necessarily plays a central role in assessing health needs and providing pharmaceuticals to alleviate withdrawal symptoms.[4]

To control the tobacco epidemic in children, a two-pronged attack is necessary. Firstly, strong legislation is needed to ban all pro-tobacco propaganda aimed at converting young impressionable minds into addicts. Secondly, anti-tobacco education in schools should be made mandatory, and it should be complemented by nationwide anti-tobacco media campaigns wholeheartedly backed by the government.[5]

Accidents especially on roads take a heavy toll causing economic and human loss, which is preventable.

Accidents in developing countries have a major negative effect on social and economic development. The social and psychological effects they inflict can result in reduced productivity and even social instability. The economic losses can be both direct and indirect. The direct results take the form of losses in years of productive life, property and commodities, to which must be added the costs of insurance, prevention and medical treatment. The indirect effects may be reckoned in terms of the economic value of wasted time and ill-health, the need to compensate for lost lives, and reduced productive capacity.[6]

Seldom seen as a public health issue, violence against women is a significant cause of female morbidity and mortality around the globe. In the USA, for example, wife abuse is the leading cause of injury among women of reproductive age. Between 22% and 35% of women who visit United States emergency clinics are there for symptoms related to on-going abuse.

But women in the USA share the reality of violence with women in virtually every other culture in the world. Data from developing countries reveal that one-third to over half of women surveyed report being beaten by their partner. Not uncommonly, beatings are part of a pattern of emotional and physical abuse that escalates over time. In Papua New Guinea, 18% of all urban wives surveyed had sought hospital treatment for injuries inflicted by their husbands. A survey of one Caribbean island revealed that one in three women had been sexually abused as a child.

Wife abuse also provides the primary context for many other health problems. Again, research from the USA indicates that battered women are

4. WHO: John Howard, "Community-based Treatment", *World Health*, July-August, 1995, p. 15.
5. WHO: S.G. Vaidya, "Young Tobacco Users", *World Health*, July-August, 1995, p. 30.
6. WHO: I.G. Badran, "Accidents in the Developing World", *World Health*, January-February, 1993, p. 14.

four to five times more likely to require psychiatric treatment and five times more likely to attempt suicide than non-battered women. And they are at increased risk of alcohol abuse, drug dependence, chronic pain, and depression. In one US study of the use made of healthcare, a history of rape and/or assault was a stronger predictor of physician visits and outpatient costs than were a woman's age or other health risks such as smoking. Along with physical injury and emotional trauma, rape survivors run the risk of becoming pregnant or contracting sexually transmitted diseases, including AIDS.

Violence poses a powerful obstacle to achieving other goals that are high on the developing agenda. During pregnancy, for example, it threatens the goal of "Safe motherhood" for all women. Battered women run twice the risk of miscarriage and four times the risk of having a low-birth-weight infant.[7]

Abuse and neglect of children is an emotional crippler and disabler of both children and adults. The cost of inaction far exceeds any potential cost of prevention.[8]

As we live in the 21st century, the numbers of maltreated children continue to increase. It is clear that by paying more attention to this problem, we will have the opportunity to work on prevention just as in recent decades we have eradicated small pox and are eliminating poliomyelitis and other scourges of childhood. Abuse and neglect of children is an emotional crippler and disabler of both children and adults. The cost to society of not dealing directly with the problem far exceeds any potential cost of the prevention efforts.[9]

Daily observation and statistics confirm that adolescents and young adults, more than any other age group, are both the instigators of violent behaviour and its victims.[10]

In the aftermath of war, health workers must recognize that they have a key social role to play in reconstructing services, and that battle-related injuries and deaths are just the tip of the iceberg.

Over 21 million people died in the 150 wars that have taken place, mostly in the Third World, since the Second World War. The majority of those who died were civilians; in fact the proportion of civilian deaths to the military ones has been rising over this period and in the most recent conflicts has been well over 80%.[11]

---

7. WHO: Lori L. Heise, "Violence against Women", *World Health*, January-February 1993, p. 21.
8. WHO: Richard Krugman, "Child Abuse and Neglect", *World Health*, January-February 1993, p. 22.
9. *Ibid.*, p. 23.
10. WHO: Michel Manciaux, "Violent Youth", *World Health*, January-February 1993, p. 24.
11. WHO: Anthony Zwi and Antonio Ugalde, "Victims of War", *World Health*, January-February 1993, p. 26.

The post-war situation might, on the other hand, offer some opportunities for influencing change and ensuring that the new health sector operates equitably and efficiently. Priority issues will need to include rehabilitation services for the disabled, reconstitution of the community structures and family and other networks, and maternal and child healthcare programmes.

Health workers must recognize that—although conflict is political—they, like other development workers, have a significant social role to play, and that direct battle-related injuries and deaths are just the tip of the iceberg.[12]

The World Health Report, 2002 on Reducing risks-promoting healthy life" highlighted the fundamental role of risk factors as a cause of ill-health. Five of the top ten risk factors identified are: tobacco, alcohol, high blood pressure, high cholesterol and obesity—all major risk factors for NCDs. These risk factors are now becoming increasingly prevalent in the developing countries leading to a double burden of disease. Hence, the regional NCD surveillance programme focuses on NCD risk factors. This approach is regarded as the most feasible and appropriate way to strengthen regional health information systems and assist countries in health planning, advocacy and evaluation of NCD programme.[13]

Education is not mere acquisition of knowledge but is a process to manifest the perfection already in man. It should help a growing child to blossom into a fine flower. We want men with capital 'M' said Swami Vivekananda. For this blossoming of the child to a Man, we need man-making education. For making such Men emphasis on alround personality development and social consciousness should be laid. Then, it is not enough if our students improve their IQ levels and gather more and more information in schools and colleges but the system of education should give them an opportunity to develop their physical, mental, intellectual, emotional and spiritual dimensions (the five-fold personality development) of the build of a harmonious personality; the syllabus should be so formulated that the civic sense, patriotism, service zeal and spiritual urge (the four-fold consciousness) will emerge in our students. It is towards this goal of man-making and nation-building in our education system the present decadence of out society will vanish in future and our Bharat will regain her past glory.[14]

We suggest the following health education measures to control life style or lifetimes diseases which are a gift of modern lifestyles:

1. Exercise—Exercise is important as most of our time is spent in non-active life. Exercise of one form or the other is essential to speed up the metabolic system.

---

12. *Ibid.*, p. 27.
13. WHO SEARO: The Work of World Health, Regional Office for South-East Asia, Report of the Regional Director, 1 July 2002-03, June 2003, p. 19.
14. Yoga in Education, Vol. 1, Swamy Vivekananda Yoga Prakashana, p. V.

2. Nutrition—We should avoid fatty diet which is difficult to digest and can create many chain effects.
3. We should avoid stressful life, which is the cause of too many diseases.
4. We should keep the environment—Physical and mental healthy.
5. We should avoid the use of drugs/substances, i.e. alcohol, drugs, smoking, etc.
6. We should avoid non-peaceful life causing diseases resulting from violence.
7. We should cut speed to avoid accidents.

Scientific and technological progress all over the globe has made man highly sensitive, critical and also creative. Sharp to the core, his intellect has gained tremendous power of analysis. The left side of his brain is highly developed, helping him to unravel the subtle mysteries of nature and understand clearly the general laws of nature. Technology has helped man reap the benefits of its use. Automation and computers have brought great speed and sophistication in all our interactions. In search of happiness we are propelled by a desire to increase our living standards by acquiring more and more comfort-giving objects and experiencing sensual pleasures. To satisfy this desire we are always on the lookout to earn more and more. In the process, we have become very active and have overcome our lethargy.

Associated with this growth is the emergence of two basic challenges: pollution and stress. The challenge of pollution is being tackled effectively but not met totally. Strict pollution control measures in the industrial sectors and extensive research leading towards the use of ecologically friendly technologies have certainly yielded dividends. But on the second front, in spite of extensive research all over the globe, a decreasing quality of life, increasing health hazards, social unrest, student unrest, etc traits which are all different expressions of stress, have shown No. trend of decrease. On the contrary, over the last two decades, it is rather on the path of ascent.

The current mechanistic world-view, the matter-based approach the increased dependence on science and technology and the associated lifestyle have to undergo basic changes towards embracing a more holistic world view and a healthier and more harmonious lifestyle. Emotion training and harnessing of the will-power—the growth of the right side of the brain in general—are then the associated adjuncts for such a holistic understanding and also for a healthier and harmonious living. And that is what Yoga offers.[15]

The life of harmony can be lived by rising above our limited egocentric view of things and happenings, and expanding our mind to

15. *New Perspective in Stress Management*, Swami Vivekananda Yoga Prakashana, Bangalore, pp. 1-3.

accommodate a constant awareness of the totality of the world, the entirety of mankind and the vastness and wholeness of the universal problems. When this total and consummate perception is developed and maintained, man's individual problems sink into insignificance and absurdity.

Our life of harmony with the ampler scheme of the cosmos brings to our heart an inward peace and poise. When poise is maintained within us, problems and challenges vanish like mist before the rising sun.[16]

A man may be tossed about by uncertain storms of life but the solution to it lies in his own efforts in finding an ideal in life and then raising his personality from the level of petty emotions to the loftier heights of the chosen ideal. The secret of success in life thus lies in keeping the head above the storms of the heart. A successful man never allows his faculty of discrimination and judgment to be disturbed by the rising tides of his emotions.[17]

Chandigarh S.L. GOEL

16. Swami Chinmayananda, "*Kindle Life*", Central Chinmaya Mission Trust, Mumbai, pp. 40-41.
17. *Ibid.*, p 8.

CHAPTER I

CAUSES OF NON-COMMUNICABLE DISEASES OR LIFESTYLE DISEASES

> The creation of integrated programmes for the prevention, monitoring and treatment of non-communicable diseases is clearly of prime importance.
>
> —WHO: *E.I. Chazov*, Prevention is better, *World Health*, August 1983

1 CHAPTER

Causes of Non-Communicable Diseases or Lifestyle Diseases

> Drawing up an integrated national strategy for the prevention of non-communicable diseases is both advisable and economically justifiable. But prevention of such diseases cannot be achieved through the efforts of health officials alone. Health education has to be made accessible to the entire population, and non-health institutions and the various mass media should be mobilized to this end. Research data yielded by national as well as international studies show that early intervention can make the prevention of diseases possible.
>
> —WHO: *Muhammad Al-Khateeb*, "New Lifestyles, New Diseases", World Health Organization, July 1989

Recent social development—such as bigger incomes and greater availability of a wide variety of commodities—have led to changes in lifestyles that are on the increase because of changes in diets; people are eating more fats, carbohydrates and animal proteins; fast-food restaurants offer chicken; the intake of salt from canned food is rapidly increasing; easy transport makes for a lack of physical exercise; and stress is common in our daily life.[1]

Non-communicable diseases (NCDs), including cardiovascular diseases (CVDs), cancers, chronic pulmonary diseases, diabetes mellitus, and other chronic diseases, are assuming alarming proportions and becoming the leading causes of mortality, morbidity and disability. The situation is due to the demographic and socio-economic transformation—taking place, which, in turn, has resulted in profound lifestyle changes.

LIFESTYLE HAZARDS

It is No. exaggeration to say that the urban lifestyle which people have adopted for their personal comfort, enjoyment and well-being has been proved to be hazardous to life. Of course changes take place over time, but every change that disturbs the balanced state, which confers healthful living, ought to be compensated by a deliberate act to replace the beneficial effect, which the particular change is eliminating. For example, a farmer gets enough exercise from his occupational work and does not need additional physical exercise. If his son becomes an office worker, thus doing very little physical work, he should find time to deliberately incorporate daily physical exercise in his life. Or, if he was accustomed to eating a variety of food items from his father's produce, he now has to make a deliberate attempt to buy and eat a mixed diet.

Hiroshi Nakajima, Former, Director-General of the World Health Organization, in his Article in *World Health*, May-June 1991, rightly warns that we have to change our lifestyles in 21st Century to get good health.

Today, on the eve of the twenty-first century, we see that the world health situation is No. longer that clear-cut and simple. Many developing countries have made great progress in combating infectious diseases and malnutrition, thereby improving the length and quality of life of their people. But rapid urbanization and industrialization in those same countries, together with the adoption of modern lifestyles that adversely affect health, have brought new problems in the form of chronic non-communicable diseases. In many developing countries these "new" problems are arriving before the "old" ones are resolved, leading to a double burden of disease. At present, non-communicable diseases are responsible for 70-80% of deaths in the developed countries, and have reached the level of about 40% in the developing world.

Urban lifestyles do not necessarily have to be detrimental to the nutrition and health of people. With proper planning they could be adapted to help city dwellers to become healthier and more productive.[2]

The number of people suffering from non-communicable diseases has been increasing mainly due to increased life expectancy and lifestyle changes.[3]

The observed increase in NCDs has however not resulted in the adoption of appropriate measures to contain these diseases. This is reflected in the meager resources allocated and the limited interest of most governments in identifying and addressing public health priorities related to NCD prevention and control.[4]

At present, non-communicable diseases are the cause of 70 to 80 per cent of deaths in developed countries and of 40 to 50 per cent of deaths in developing countries. There is No. doubt that, if the trend remains the same, non-communicable diseases will play a much more important role in both societies. Cardiovascular diseases, cancer and chronic respiratory diseases take a leading role among causes of death. Cardiovascular diseases, chronic

CHART I

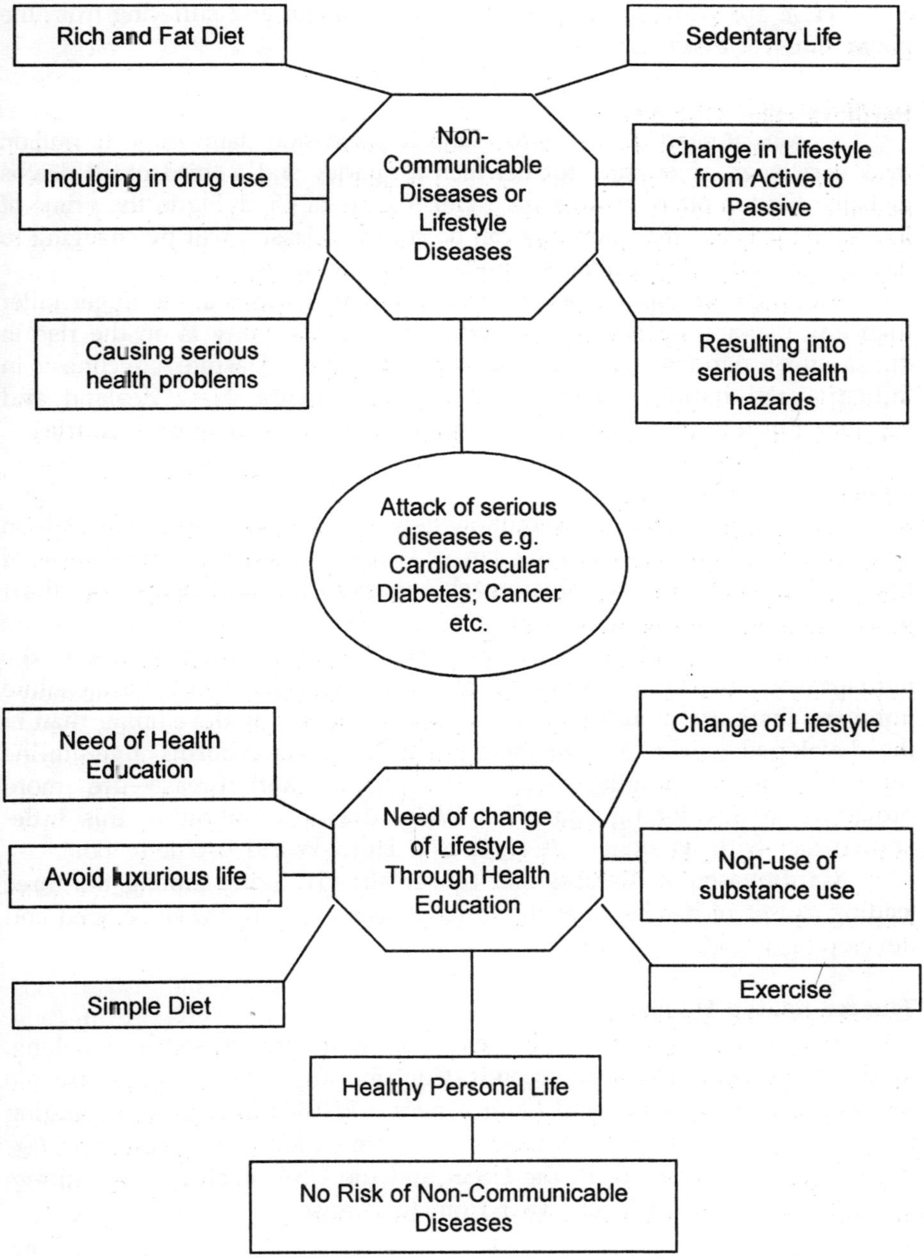

respiratory diseases, endo-crinological and gastro-intestinal complaints, osteoporosis and others are important causes of disability in invalidity.[5]

CONSEQUENCES

Here are WHO's estimates of the toll in death and suffering from the major lifestyle diseases:

Cardiovascular Diseases

Coronary heart disease, stroke and hypertension claim some 12 million lives each year, accounting for between a quarter and a third of all deaths globally. Far too often, victims are under the age of 65, dying in the prime of life. WHO believes that mortality can be cut by at least a half by changing to healthy lifestyles, thus saving six million lives every year.

Contrary to popular belief, cardiovascular diseases are a bigger killer than any major infective and parasitic disease. Mortality is on the rise in developing nations and in Eastern Europe. Despite declines in industrialized nations notably in Australia, Canada, New Zealand and Western Europe, they are still the number one killer in those countries.

Cancer

There are some seven million new cases yearly and five million deaths. All over the world, lung cancer is now the most common form of the disease, since it overtook stomach cancer in the mid-1980s. The third most common form is breast cancer.

Six to seven out of ten cancer patients die from their disease in the industrialized world, and nine out of ten in the Third World. In absolute numbers, there are more cancer cases and deaths in the developing than in the developed world. And of the eight most common forms, five-uterine cervix, stomach, mouth-pharynx, oesophagus and breast—are more prevalent in developing countries. WHO draws attention to this little-known fact with its slogan: "Cancer is a Third World problem too."

Cardiovascular diseases and cancer already figure among the three leading causes of deaths, after the teenage years, in both the developed and developing world.

Tobacco-related Diseases

Between 2.5 and 3 million deaths annually are caused by smoking, or about one death every 10 seconds. Contributing to these figures are 100 000 deaths each in Africa and Latin America; 200,000 in Asia, not counting the two most populous countries on earth—China (reporting 300,000 deaths) India 1.5 million. In the USSR and the USA, each country suffers around 400,000 deaths every year from this cause.

Osteoporosis

No. worldwide estimates are available. However, United States figures show 24 million patients in that country alone, an indication of the dimensions of a problem that is associated with increasing life-spans throughout the world.

Diabetes

WHO estimates that there are at least 50 million diabetics in the world. These persons are at high risk of hypertension and other cardiovascular diseases, as well as of kidney failure, and eye troubles including blindness.[6]

In the case of infectious diseases, it has long been recognized that an ounce of prevention is worth a pound of cure. But as regards non-communicable diseases, recourse to curative treatment and palliation has only recently been complemented by more systematic primary prevention efforts. Still, health promotion is playing an increasing role in alerting the general public to possible ways of avoiding or mitigating chronic conditions whose causes may lie in the province of unhealthy lifestyles or environments.[7]

During the first decades of WHO's existence, most of the health problems now coming under the heading of non-communicable diseases were dealt with by various expert committees within the general context of public health. The increasing importance of cancer, for instance, was first underlined by an Expert Committee on Health Statistics in 1949, while the association of diseases of the circulatory system with obesity was stressed by a joint Expert Committee on Nutrition formed by WHO and the Food and Agriculture Organization of the United Nations in 1951.

Not until the early 1970s were these ailments assembled under the umbrella of the Division of Non-communicable Diseases. Since then, there have been impressive advances in basic, pathological, clinical, epidemiological and operational research, encouraged through the expanding network of collaborating centres under WHO' aegis.

Non-communicable disease programmes now issue guidelines on classification and nomenclature, diagnostic criteria and treatment methodologies, and the norms and standards of disease management.

CAUSE AND EFFECT

Epidemiological and laboratory research has shown that there are cause-and-effect relationships between certain chronic conditions and hereditary predisposition, unhealthy lifestyles and the human environment. The new findings on the pathogenesis of these conditions have paved the way for innovative approaches to disease control.

In 1961, a WHO Expert Committee warned of the potential threat of cardiovascular disease, yet it took more than three decades to dispel the myth that these only concerned rich industrialized countries. The World Health Report, 1997 made it clear that roughly two-thirds of deaths caused worldwide by non-communicable diseases occur in developing countries and cardiovascular diseases account for nearly half of the total deaths. A decline in these diseases is apparent in some countries with established market economies and it seems possible that healthier lifestyles and improved environments are responsible.[8]

Until recently, it has been customary to pay inadequate attention to research into the primary prevention of chronic non-communicable diseases. But today, emphasis on prevention has become one of the key strategic approaches to public health.

In the economically developed society of today, it is the chronic non-specific diseases of various organs and bodily systems that are responsible for the greatest increase in morbidity and mortality, and for an appreciable loss of productivity. This drain of human resources, which also takes its toll in spiritual and material terms, stems mainly from cardiovascular diseases, malignant neoplasms, and diseases of the respiratory organs.

Medical research and the efforts of the health services were for a long time directed towards the search for better methods to diagnose and treat chronic non-communicable diseases. This led to new diagnostic equipment, many new drugs and surgical techniques, better ways of treating sufferers from myocardial infarction, localized malignant neoplasms and chronic non-specific lung diseases.

But inadequate attention was paid to research into the primary prevention of chronic non-communicable diseases. Today this has become one of the key strategic approaches to healthcare.

It would be unfair to say that nothing has been done in preventive medicine. Its importance for the development of the Soviet Union's healthcare system has long been stressed and has resulted in revolutionary improvements in the control of infectious diseases for which the primary sources and the mechanism of their action were clear. There has been great progress, for instance, in the prevention and control of rheumatic fever. As yet, however, that is the sum total of our success in preventing chronic non-communicable diseases. Until recently, morbidity from cardiovascular diseases, malignant neoplasms and diseases of the respiratory organs has steadily risen.

There are four main limiting factors, which stand in the way of practical prevention. The first is the lack of clear, scientifically based concepts of the precise causes and mechanisms of most of these diseases, whether it be atherosclerosis, stomach cancer, pulmonary emphysema or cirrhosis of the liver. Secondly, in most instances we lack precise information about the damaging effect of various environmental factors and their connection with the genetic conditioning of the pathological process.

Thirdly, we have paid inadequate attention to the moral and psychological factors, which contribute to a healthy mode of life. Indeed, scientists have still not produced a generally accepted concept of good health. Because scientific data is lacking on the possible health consequences of various aspects of life, traditions and habits, which may differ appreciably in members from different age groups, occupations and countries, we have No. precise knowledge about their positive or negative effect on the inception or cause of a pathological process, and No. criteria of assessing this influence.

The fourth and final limiting factor is that our health service institutions are only just beginning to work out and implement their strategic approaches to the primary prevention of chronic non-communicable diseases. Who actually defines the prevention of these diseases, and who then actually carries it out the specialist (whether cardiologist, oncologist, pulmonologist or gastroenterologist) or the physician in general practice (the district physician, the factory doctor or the school doctor)? And is that person the only one responsible for seeing that preventive work is effective?

Preventive medicine is a great social task, and not merely a set of problems in medical science and healthcare.[9]

The World Health Report, 2002 on "Reducing risks-promoting healthy life" highlighted the fundamental role of risk factors as a cause of ill health. Five of the top ten risk factors identified are: tobacco, alcohol, high blood pressure, high cholesterol and obesity—all major risk factors for NCDs. These risk factors are now becoming increasingly prevalent in the developing countries leading to a double burden of disease. Hence, the regional NCD surveillance programme focuses on NCD risk factors. This approach is regarded as the most feasible and appropriate way to strengthen regional health information systems and assist countries in health planning, advocacy and evaluation of NCD programme.[10]

NCDs are the leading cause of death and disability. Though disease rates from these conditions are increasing in the Region and affect all socio-economic strata of society, NCDs are not yet regarded as a high public health priority. Also, the present capacity for planning, implementing and evaluating NCD prevention and control programmes in the Region is limited and needs to be enhanced.[11]

There is a need to provide preventive measures against non-communicable diseases through effective health education.

If we summarize the range of measures for preventing chronic non-communicable diseases, they constitute a definitive code of rules of behaviour, habits and lifestyles that is essential if health is to be maintained. They amount to a set of conditions defining a healthy way of life and indicating how to keep fit and become fitter.[12]

The creation of integrated programmes for the prevention, monitoring and treatment of non-communicable diseases is clearly of prime importance. The Institute of Preventive Cardiology, forms part of the All-Union Cardiological Research Centre.[13]

Reduction of morbidity and premature mortality due to NCDs requires vigorous action and involvement of multiple sectors at all levels—from primary prevention to treatment and rehabilitation. Interventions applied during the advanced stage of the diseases usually have a limited impact and are less cost-effective. Therefore, prevention is a more feasible option of low-resource countries.[14]

Integrated Programme for Community Health in NCD

Integrated Programme for Community Health in Non-communicable diseases is essential. This combines resources and approaches currently being devoted to preventing and controlling selected diseases and related conditions; and it puts a set of preventive and other control activities under unified management in order to promote better health in whole communities. Its prime aims are:

- to reduce common risk factors in the field of smoking, alcohol consumption, bad nutritional habits, physical inactivity, high blood pressure and so on;
- to involve the entire community;
- to integrate various health promotion strategies—those aimed at high-risk groups (the elderly, children, workers, pregnant women) or at screening for early detection, of instance;
- to integrate different types of intervention—change of lifestyle, or improved healthcare or inter-sectoral action;
- and to carry out prevention and control activities through existing primary healthcare systems and other health and community structures.[15]

Management of NCDs at the PHC level needs strengthening—One of the important WHO priorities in this area is developing simple practice guidelines to help improve standards and quality of care, improve cost-effectiveness of applied interventions and reduce costs of treatment by avoiding unnecessary investigations, procedures and medication. This will also help to emphasize the importance of therapeutic education and thereby improve compliance.[16]

The results of community-based NCD prevention projects implemented in developed countries have clearly demonstrated that even modest risk factor reduction through adoption of healthy lifestyles brings a huge public health benefit. However, the evidence on feasibility and effectiveness of applying such interventions in the developing world is still missing.[17]

In the space of a few decades, there have been remarkable reductions in morbidity and mortality due to infectious and parasitic diseases in most developing countries in all regions of the world. However, other threats of health in the form of the so-called "Western degenerative" or "lifestyle" diseases are emerging at rates that far outstrip what would be expected from the fact that people are living longer.

In many developing nations, already beset with economic, social and other health problems, the rates of heart disease, diabetes and hypertension are as high as or even higher than in major developed nations. These chronic diseases impose a destructive drain on communities through their association with sickness and premature death.[18]

Primary preventive activities will focus on behavioural and structural changes related to smoking, healthy nutrition, and levels of physical activity in the community. Secondary prevention targets include improved case detection, expanded health education services, and an upgrading of follow-up and rehabilitation facilities[19] through nutrition education.

Prevention of Non-communicable Diseases Through Nutrition Education

The National Research Council of USA recommendations to lessen lifestyle diseases can be summarized as follows:

- Reduce total dietary fat intake to 30% or less of calories. Reduce saturated fatty acid intake to less than 10% of calories, and intake of cholesterol to less than 30 mg daily.
- Eat several servings every day of a combination of vegetables and fruits, especially dark green and yellow vegetables and citrus fruits.
- Increase the intake of starches and other complex carbohydrates by eating several daily servings of a combination of whole-grain breads, cereals, and legumes.
- Maintain protein intake at moderate levels.
- Balance food intake and physical activity to maintain appropriate body weight.
- For those who drink alcoholic beverages, limit consumption to the equivalent of less than one ounce of pure alcohol in a single day.
- Limit total daily intake of salt (sodium chloride) to 6 g or less.
- Maintain adequate calcium intake.
- Avoid taking (unnecessary) vitamin and mineral supplements,
- Maintain an optimal fluoride intake, particularly during periods of tooth formation and growth.

The US Surgeon General published a report on Nutrition and Health which describes the vital influence of diet on health and underscores the potential adverse consequences of certain dietary practices in relation to the major chronic diseases. Its recommendations are, in principle, quite similar to those of the NRC report. With reference to aging populations, the report states "diet, exercise, and other personal and socio-economic factors can help prolong good health for most people." It also noted that those older adults who are economically, socially and functionally disadvantaged are likely to have unique nutritional needs.

One particularly important issue raised in the Surgeon General's report is that education and counselling efforts designed to improve nutrition among consumers should give consideration to the social, cultural and psychological dimensions of food. Consumers' food preferences and habits are rooted in beliefs and customs, and are strongly influenced by such factors. Food is also a great source of pleasure in most people's lives. Education and counselling efforts must therefore consider the potential difficulties involved in changing consumer's food behaviour and attempt to overcome barriers to those changes. Practical dietary recommendations must be placed in the larger context of consumers' social and cultural frameworks, preferred types and sources of foods, and overall environmental circumstances.

DIETARY GUIDELINES

The US Departments of Agriculture and of Health and Human Services have developed practical recommendations, called the Dietary Guidelines for Americans, which are valid in many parts of the world and are summarized as:

1. Eat a Variety of Foods

Choose foods from five major food groups:

(a) Vegetables;
(b) Fruits;
(c) Breads, cereals, rice and pasta;
(d) (Skim or low-fat) milk, yoghurt and cheese; and
(e) Lean meats, poultry and fish; dried beans, peas, nuts and eggs.

2. Maintain a Health Weight

Check to see if you are a healthy weight (average range of weight related to your height). If not, set reasonable weight goals and try for long-term success through well-balanced habits of diet and exercise.

3. Choose a diet low in fat (30% of less of Calories), Saturated Fat (about 10% of Calories), and Cholesterol (300 mg or less)

Maintain a desirable level of blood cholesterol. In adults, this is under 200 mg per dl. If cholesterol levels are higher, it is recommended that appropriate medical advice is followed on diet and, if necessary, medications. Eat plenty of vegetables, fruits and whole grain products, lean meats, fish and poultry without skin, low fat and skimmed dairy products. Use fats and oils sparingly.

4. Choose a Diet with Plenty of Natural Fibre

In addition to fresh vegetables, eat more dried beans and peas, fresh and citrus fruits, whole grain breads and cereals, pastas and rice.

5. Use Sugars in Moderation:

Select food products that preferably are packaged without added sugars. Check food product ingredient lists for added sugars and avoid sucrose, brown sugar, raw sugar, honey, syrup, molasses, corn syrup and other sweeteners.

6. Use Salt and Sodium in Moderation

Use table salt sparingly if at all. Consider using foods that are naturally lower in sodium, such as fresh and frozen vegetables (rather than canned), cereals, pastas and rice cooked without salt; low-fat and skimmed milk or yoghurt rather than most cheeses; fresh lean meats, poultry, and fish rather than canned or processed items; fresh foods prepared without salt or salty condiments (like tomato sauce or soy sauce) instead of frozen dinners or packaged meals.

7. If you use Alcoholic Beverages, do so in Moderation

Women who are pregnant or trying to conceive should not drink, nor should people who intend to drive a vehicle, operate a machine, or perform an activity that requires attention and skill. Those who cannot limit their alcohol consumption should not drink.

As the world population has aged, chronic diseases have increasingly become major causes of death and disability. Many of these conditions, especially cardiovascular disease, certain forms of cancer and diabetes, can be prevented, minimized or delayed by paying attention to lifestyle behaviours, including improved diet, increased exercise and reduced tobacco consumption. As the 21st century approaches and the needs of adults, particularly older adults, are considered, preventive health practices offer considerable promise in promoting successful aging. Dietary practices which should be particularly emphasized are those that are lower in total fat intake (particularly saturated animal fat) and cholesterol; lower in salt, sugar, and alcohol; higher in complex carbohydrates, fibre, food grains and cereals, and fresh fruits and vegetables; and those that are balanced in total energy and essential nutrients.[20]

EXERCISE EDUCATION

Exercise improves health and well-being in a number of ways. Here are some of the more important effects that might be seen over a year in a sedentary person who adopts a regular programme of jogging, cycling or brisk walking, for instance. Most noticeable may be changes in body composition: body fat is progressively lost, and fat in the abdominal region is reduced. It now seems clear that fat in the tummy area is particularly related to risk of heart disease and diabetes. New converts to exercise often have to change their wardrobes because their waist size is much reduced, but it's well worth it. The exerciser becomes more fit—he or she can do more in life. Heart function changes so that more blood is pumped with each bear ("stroke volume" is increased), and the resting heart rate is reduced—both of them beneficial changes. Less well recognized is the increased diameter of the arteries supplying the heart ("coronary bore") during exertion in regular exercisers, which may help to reduce the probability of a dangerous obstruction developing in a coronary artery ("heart attack").

While all this is going on in our exercise, important events are happening in the blood. The lipoproteins-minute particles that carry fat and cholesterol about the body-change, so that the amount of the "protective" high-density lipoprotein (HDL) cholesterol increases relative to the "atherogenic" or coronary disease promoting low-density lipoprotein (LDL) cholesterol. The level of fat (triglycerides) in the blood is also dramatically decreased in our exerciser, which again is associated with a lowered risk of heart disease. The total amount of plasma in the exerciser's body increases, often by 10% or more.

The resting blood pressure and, perhaps more importantly, blood pressure during the stressful events of the day have probably dropped in our exerciser. His blood pressure will rise less in the weekly managers' meetings now that he is fit. These changes are very valuable to him, because they reduce his risk not only of heart disease, but also of stroke, where elevated blood pressure is the chief risk factor.

Adult-onset diabetes afflicts millions throughout the world. This disease is characterized by resistance to the action of insulin, abdominal obesity, high blood fat levels, low HDL cholesterol levels, and sedentariness. All of these facets of the disease are improved by regular exercise.

The health benefits of regular exercise are extensive and should compel the many sedentary citizens of the world to take action. These persons are particularly subject to heart disease, stroke, cancer, diabetes and osteoporosis.

The type of exercise chosen is important. It must challenge the heart and lungs moderately, but not necessarily strenuously. Brisk walking, jogging, swimming and cycling at a moderate pace, and soccer are examples of beneficial exercises. Bowling, golf (especially using a motorized cart), and body-building are not very helpful. Choose a sport or exercises that are convenient and enjoyable, so that you can continue with them even when you grow older. For instance, cross-country skiing is excellent for health, but is of practical use in certain parts of the world and only during the winter.

First, consider your preferences before even trying out possible sports and exercises. It is a good idea to combine this with what you must already do every day. Can you walk to work rather than ride? Or can you get off the bus several stops early and walk the rest of the way? Can you routinely walk up the stairs rather than ride the elevator in your building? Every little bit helps. Try to find a companion with similar exercise aims and capacity.

Some exercises (for instance, walking to work) can be done on a daily basis. Other sessions should be fitted into your life three to five times each week. Regular "days off" are good for many people to avoid boredom and overuse. Each session might be for 30 minutes to one hour, but this will depend on the activity. Three sessions of 20 minutes each, if more convenient, will be about equivalent to one session of an hour.

Deciding on the proper intensity of the exercise can worry many people. It is not necessary to run marathons or play squash vigorously to gain substantial health benefits. A very sedentary, overweight middle-aged person who adopts a modest waling programme probably has the most to gain. You are the best judge of intensity; aim to exercise moderately, as it feels to you. An exercise programme should be progressive. But as you get fitter you are able to achieve higher energy expenditure levels and yet still feel that you are exercising "moderately".

The adverse effects of insufficient physical activity worsen with age: heart and lung functions deteriorate, muscles mass is lost while fat is gained, and a variety of metabolic and psychological problems may begin to occur. In fact, it seems probable that part of the aging process in many societies is really the result of the progressive sedentariness that so commonly accompanies aging.

This idea is supported by studies on older athletes, who retain many of the physical attributes of the young. Runners in their sixties, for instance, have the body composition and exercise capacity of much younger (but less active) men. Research shows that a progressive programme of low-level exercise in older people can partially reverse the ravages of many sedentary years, and to some degree restore endurance capacity and muscular strength. Even small increases in strength and endurance can make a substantial difference to the quality of life in old people, for example in their ability to rise from a chair, lift objects, and walk about in the house.

Old age often brings with it arthritis and the weakened bones of osteoporosis, among other infirmities that limit the ability to exercise. Exercise programmes must therefore be carefully tailored to the abilities of elderly people, a modest increase in muscular activity often bring all that is needed for the very oldest persons.

Health agencies must recognize that regular exercise is of enormous importance to vast numbers of people. Every individual will benefit greatly in improved health by ensuring adequate regular exercise for himself and his family.[21]

PRESENT LIFE IS PROMOTING BAD HABITS: NEED OF CHANGE

Ideas are changing as way of life change. The deliberate promotion of a new wave of "convenience" foods and drinks and ideas is helping to prevent the world from eating wisely. Infant foods, powdered milk and bottled soft drinks (along with cigarettes) are gaining ground as a result of massive hard-sell advertising campaigns. As a result, a number of crucial changes have been taking place in the eating and drinking habits of the poorest people on the planet.

There has been a rapid decline in breastfeeding, which has been replaced by desperate attempts to feed children with powdered cow-milk preparations that are expensive and dangerous to prepare under the real-life conditions of developing countries.

Local unrefined food products, such as grains and fruits, are being increasingly replaced by manufactured and, often, imported products. In a poor tropical country, soft drinks, tinned fruits and tinned juices may compete successfully with fresh fruits, imported flour may replace local grain. Such imports act as a drain on the fragile national economy, and the result is that local farmers grow poorer and people eat less and less well. Imported cereals may actually be nutritionally poorer than those they replace; locally made tortillas, chapattis, local corn, breads, sorgums and legumes are giving way to European breads made with imported, over-refined, white wheat flour. Even the fad for taking manufactured vitamin pills has begun to catch on, when what is needed is more food and more of the right food.

Fortunately, food habits tend to change slowly, and there is still time to retain what is best in traditional foods, to bolster local agriculture and to improve traditional foods habits. It is certainly easier and better to build on existing food patterns than to try to impose new ones. This would also help people solve their own food problems rather than relying on others.

Education is necessary but it must be pertinent and not condescending. Poor people, rural people, illiterate mothers are not as ignorant as many urban planners believe. Once they are convinced of the sincerity of the message they will listen to better ways of using their food . . . always provided there is enough of it.

A change in the status of women may prove to be the best long-term investment in nutrition that a society can make. Young mothers No. longer subjugated by older members of the society, free to learn and to take initiatives, can be shown how to prevent deaths from diarrhoea by simple oral rehydration techniques. They can learn to feed their child in a way that will protect its health, provided they receive the right support; and they too can benefit from a better diet.

And diets can be improved without overturning all the traditional values of rural societies. Firstly, those in positions of responsibility must be clear in their own minds. What is needed is not more pill hand-outs or more pious sermons on "nutrition", but better distribution of food, a healthier agriculture to produce it and a more equitable system of distribution that makes sure everyone gets a share.

The fact that wrong ideas can be sown and take root should make us more optimistic. After all, weeds grow best in fertile soil and if wrong ideas can be sown so can right ones. Men, women and children everywhere want to be healthy. The human mind can discard ideas that are useless and acquire more positive ones that will make life easier. The world community has No. higher task than that of seeing to it that each of its members has enough food to grow up on, to live on, to furnish energy for making the world a better place.[22]

PROBLEMS FOR HEALTH EDUCATION IN CONTROLLING NON-COMMUNICABLE DISEASES

(1) Funds for Health Education for NCDs are limited.
(2) Interested programmes area wise have not been developed.
(3) All the doctors and paramedical staff have not been trained in educating the people about NCD.

(4) Health Education programme should start from childhood and adolescence.
(5) Fashion to follow new bad ideas.

It has also been shown that the roots of most diseases extend right back to childhood and adolescence, and this must be our starting point when we seek to establish the harmful action of risk factors and to devise effective countermeasures. So when the basis for prevention is the creation of conditions for a healthy mode of life, it is essential to begin in childhood and adolescence. This is why the school doctor, youth groups like the Pioneer and Komosomol organizations, the staff of schools and institutes of higher education, and the organizers of sports have a growing role to play in the prevention of chronic non-communicable disease.

In such programmes, we have to make allowances for the fact that they are intended for young people who consider themselves to be completely fit, are extremely sceptical about preventive measures, may be hostile to having to meet the medical staff, and regard their health as a deeply personal matter. It is far more difficult to work among such a population than, for example, among individuals between the ages of 40 and 50 who are aware of possible diseases, may notice early symptoms, and perhaps are already sick.

CONCLUSION

One of the paradoxes of the modern age is that, just when the world is making a concerted lunge towards industrialization and advance technology, which are universally viewed as desirable, this same "progress" appears to confront mankind with a growing number of acute public health problems.

The more roads and cars we build, the more people die prematurely in traffic accidents. The greater the earnings, the greater are the spendings on alcoholic drinks and tobacco. As medicaments and chemical products proliferate so the risks increase of accidental poisoning—particularly of children. Opportunities for better and further education have never seemed brighter, yet the sinister cult of narcotic drugs is still gaining ground among young people. And the race for ever more sources of industrial energy brings in its train increasing hazards to the ecology and to human health from fumes, pollutants, oil slicks at sea and radioactive leaks from nuclear power plants.

Is this "price of progress" an inescapable consequence? Perhaps it is not. Those countries that are regarded as industrialized are trying hard to mitigate the drawbacks and dangers, and they are alerted to potential new dangers that might threaten a man and nature. Now the writing is on the wall for the fast-developing Third World countries; many of them are already taking wise steps to avoid making the same old mistakes. Forewarned is forearmed.[23]

TABLE 1.1

A Step-wise Approach for Prevention and Control of Non-Communicable Diseases[24]

Resource	*Population approaches*		*Individual high-risk approach*
	National level	*Community level*	
Step 1: Core	WHO Framework Convention on Tobacco Control (FCTC) is ratified in the country.	Local infrastructure plans include the provision and maintenance of accessible and safe sites for physical activity (such as parks and pedestrian-only areas).	Context specific management guidelines for non-communicable diseases have been adopted and are used all healthcare levels.
	Tobacco control legislation consistent with the elements of the FCTC is enacted and enforced.	Health-promoting community projects include participatory actions to cope with the environmental factors that predispose to risk of non-communicable diseases: Inactivity, unhealthy diet, tobacco use, alcohol use, etc.	A sustainable, accessible and affordable supply of appropriate medication is assured for priority non-communicable diseases.
	A national nutrition and physical activity policy consistent with the Global Strategy is developed and endorsed at Cabinet level; sustained multi-sectoral action is evident to reduce fat intake, reduce salt (with attention to iodized salt where appropriate), and promote fruit and vegetable consumption.	Active health promotion programmes focusing on non-communicable diseases are implemented in different settings: villages, schools and workplaces.	A system exists for the consistent, high quality application of clinical guidelines and for the clinical audit of services offered.

	Health impact assessment of public policy 8 is carried out (for example: transport, urban planning, taxation, and pollution).		A system for recall of patients with diabetes and hypertension is in operation.
Step 2: Expanded	Tobacco legislation provides for incremental increases in tax on tobacco, and a proportion of the revenue is earmarked for health promotion.	Sustained, well-designed programmes are in place to promote:	Systems are in place for selective and targeted prevention aimed at high-risk populations, based on absolute levels of risk.
	Food standards legislation is enacted and enforced; it includes nutrition labeling.	• Tobacco-free lifestyles, e.g. smoke-free public places, smoke-free sports; • Healthy diets, e.g. low-cost, low-fat foods, fresh fruit and vegetables; • Physical activity, e.g. "movement" in different domains (occupational and leisure).	System are in place for selective and targeted prevention aimed at high-risk populations, based on absolute levels of risk.
Step 3: Optimal	Country standards are established that regulate marketing of unhealthy food to children. Capacity for health research is built within countries by encouraging studies on non-communicable diseases.	Recreational and fitness centres are available for community use.	Opportunistic screening, case-finding and management programmes are implemented. Support groups are fostered tobacco cessation and overweight reduction. Appropriate diagnostic and therapeutic interventions are implemented.

Adapted from: (8)

Forewarned is forearmed.[23]

Proper nutrition education to be taught in schools at all levels so that students develop the right eating habits. A great responsibility rests with primary healthcare physicians to ensure that fast-food restaurants should be instructed to serve the kind of food that contains vegetable fibers and unsaturated fats. Individuals should be encouraged to practise sports, or at least walk regularly if they are short of time for exercise. Indeed, prevention is crucial, and sound healthy practices should be well inculcated in childhood through health education.

The main issue for policy-makers, at all levels of public health in developing countries, is how to deal with the growing burden of epidemics of non-communicable diseases in the presence of persisting communicable disease epidemics. Furthermore, this challenge must be faced even where health system resources are already inadequate. Although considerable policy gains can be made very cheaply, especially intersectorally, extra provision must be found. This requires a greater share of national resources for healthcare, better use of existing resources, and new sources of funding. A special tax on tobacco products for disease prevention programmes is a readily available source of new funds for most countries.

Notes and References

1. WHO: Muhammad Al-Khateeb, "New Lifestyles, New Diseases", *World Health*, July 1989, p. 23.
2. WHO: Dinesh P. Sinha, "Diet in the cities", *World Health*, July-August 1991, p. 29.
3. Annual Report, Ministry of Health and Family Welfare, 2002-03, p. 92.
4. WHO: The Work of World Health, Regional Office for South-East Asia, Report of the Regional Director, 1 July 2002-03, June 2003, p. 19.
5. By Evgueni N. Chigan, Towards a Better and a Longer Life, *World Health*, October 1988, p. 3.
6. WHO: Nikolai Khaltaev, "Inter-Health Fights Lifestyle Diseases", May-June 1991, pp. 18-20.
7. *World Health*, 51st Year, No. 2, March-April 1998, Coping with Chronic Conditions, p. 20.
8. *Ibid.*, pp. 20-21.
9. WHO: E.I. Chazov, Prevention is Better, *World Health*, August 1983, pp 26-27.
10. WHO SEARO: The Work of World Health, Regional Office for South-East Asia, Report of the Regional Director, 1 July 2002-03, June 2003, p. 19.
11. WHO SEARO: The work of World Health, Regional Office for South-East Asia, Report of the Regional Director, 1 July 2002-03, June 2003, p. 19.
12. WHO: E.I. Chazov, Prevention is better, *World Health*, August 1983, pp. 27-28.
13. *Ibid.*, p. 26.
14. WHO SEARO: The Work of World Health, Regional Office for South-East Asia, Report of the Regional Director, 1 July 2002-03, June 2003, p. 21.
15. WHO: Evgueni N. Chigan, Towards a Better and a Longer Life, *World Health*, October 1988, p. 5.
16. WHO SEARO: The work of World Health, Regional Office for South-East Asia, Report of the Regional Director, 1 July 2002-03, June 2003, p. 23.

18. WHO: The Mauritius Non-Communicable Diseases Study Group, *World Health*, June 1989, p. 18.
19. *Ibid.*, p. 19.
20. WHO: Barbara Millen Posner and Huda Murad, "Eat Wisely to Live Longer", May-June 1991, pp. 22-24.
21. WHO: Peter D. Wood, "Exercise" May-June 1991, pp. 25-27.
22. WHO: Nedd Willard, "One Man's Meat", December 1980, p. 23.
23. WHO: The Price of Progress? June 1979, pp. 2-3.
24. The World Health Report, 2003, pp. 87 and 89.

CHAPTER 2

SMOKING

"The health consequences of ever-greater cigarette consumption could well offset all the gains made in the fields of nutrition, sanitation and control of infectious diseases."

—By *Thomas Land*, Vicious Circle,
World Health, February-March 1980

2

CHAPTER

Smoking

TOBACCO SMOKING IMPACT ON HEALTH

Tune in on Radio Singapore and you'll catch little song-folksy, lively and contemporary-called "Change Your Lifestyle". Its first verse says:

"Change your lifestyle
Make a solemn vow
Clear your lungs and feel much fitter
Stop that smoking now."

—By *Thomas Land*, Vicious Circle,
World Health, February-March 1980

Smoking can be through smoking Cigarettes or Bidi, etc. while the smoking can be smokeless as well. The term 'smokeless tobacco' is used to describe tobacco that is consumed in an unburned from. Smokeless tobàcco can be used orally or nasally. Smokeless tobacco in India is used as chewing tobacco, with or without lime. Gutkha, Khaini, Zarda are all examples of such use. Snuff is an example of the nasally used form.[1]

TOBACCO CONTROL: STRENGTHENING NATIONAL EFFORTS

The consumption of cigarettes and other tobacco products and exposure to tobacco smoke are the world's leading preventable cause of death, responsible for about 5 million deaths a year, mostly in poor countries and poor populations. Latest estimates reveal that, of the nearly 4 million men and 1 million women who died, over 2 million men and 380,000 women were in developing countries.[2] The toll will double in 20 years unless available and effective interventions are urgently and widely adopted.

Globalization of the tobacco epidemic can undermine even the best national control programme. The epidemic is being spread and reinforced worldwide by a complex mix of factors with cross-borders effects, including trade liberalisation, foreign direct investment, and other factors such as global marketing, transnational tobacco advertising, promotion and sponsorship, and the international movement of contraband and counterfeit cigarettes. Recognition of this situation led to the adoption by 192 Members States at the World Health Assembly in May 2003 of the WHO 2003 of the WHO Framework Convention on Tobacco Control (WHO FCTC). This, the first treaty negotiated under the auspices of WHO, constitutes a major turning point in tackling a major global killer: it signals a new era in global and national tobacco control activities. The FCTC is an evidence-based treaty that reaffirms the right of all people to the highest standard of health. It represents a paradigm shift in developing a regulatory strategy for addictive substances: in contrast to previous drug control treaties, the FCTC asserts the importance of demand reduction strategies as well as supply issues.

GUIDING TOBACCO CONTROL

Total tobacco consumption is on the rise. The number of smokers in the world, estimated at 1.3 billion today, is expected to rise to 1.7 billion by 2025 if the global prevalence of tobacco use remains unchanged.[3] Every second smoker will die of a tobacco-caused disease. Until recently, the global response to this major public health challenge had been inadequate.[4]

Out of the total world population of 6.2 billion, 11 million were smokers and 80 per cent to them were from developing countries. A study by the WHO showed that in India 2,220 persons were killed daily due to tobacco.

What is in Tobacco that makes it dangerous?

Tobacco contains more than 4000 chemicals, several of which can cause cancer and are dangerous to health. The most important of these chemicals are: Nicotine, Tar and Carbon Monoxide.

Nicotine

A severely addictive drug found in tobacco smoke. Nicotine increases heart rate and blood pressure and also constricts blood vessels, reducing blood flow to many organs causing problems in these organs.

Tar

Tar affects the lungs like soot in a chimney making it harder to breathe. Tar in tobacco contains dozens of chemicals that cause cancer.

Carbon Monoxide

It absorbs oxygen from the blood. The ability of blood to deliver oxygen to various body tissues is thereby reduced causing a number of problems. The gas in tobacco smoke that are inhaled by both smokers and passive smokers include nitrogen oxides, hydrogen cyanide, arsenic (white ant poison), ammonia (floor cleaner), phenol (paints), naphthalene (mothballs), cadmium (car batteries), urethane, acetone (paint stripper), carbon monoxide (car exhaust), DDT (insecticide) and butane (lighter fuel) and many others.

How many Deaths are Attributed to Tobacco Globally?

Tobacco takes heavy tolls of life. According to the World Health Organization (WHO), tobacco kills more people annually than AIDS, alcohol, other addictions (drugs) and accidents put together. This figure is expected to rise from 4.9 million at present to 10 million tobacco attributable

CHART 2.1

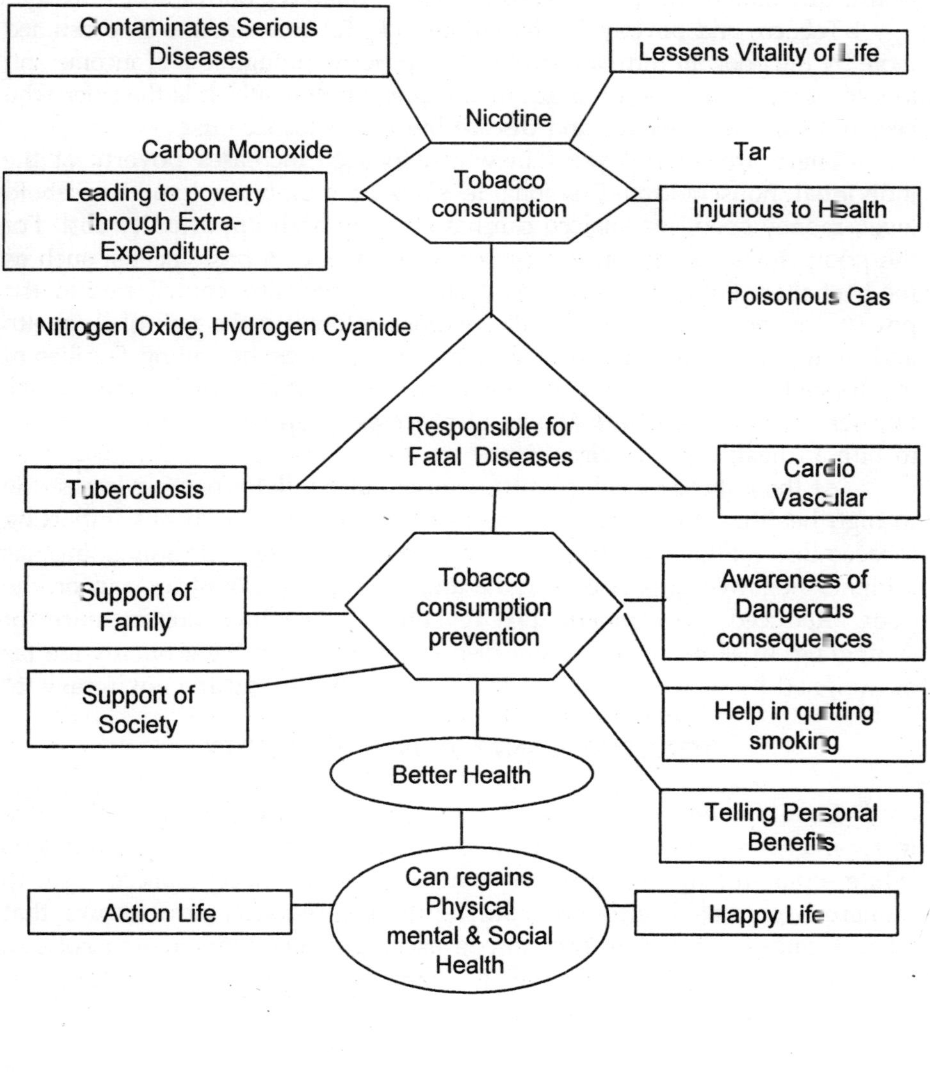

deaths per year by 2025. A recent study by WHO has cautioned that unless smoking patterns change, one billion people are expected to die from smoking habit in the 21st Century which is 10 times more than those killed by tobacco throughout the 20th Century.

How Serious is the Problem?

In India, deaths attributable to tobacco are expected to rise from 1.4% of all deaths in 1990 to 13.3% in 2020. Of 1000 teenagers smoking today, 500 will eventually die of tobacco-related diseases--250 in their middle age and 250 in their old age. Those who die earlier lose on an average 22 to 26 years of life compared to a non-smoker. Even those who die later suffer ill health due to tobacco-related diseases in the middle age. Rest 500 will have a poor quality of life. Adults who are exposed to passive smoking may die of cancers, heart attacks or lung diseases.[5]

Dr. Samlee Plianbangchang, South-East Asia, Regional Director has beautifully stated the relationship between Tobacco Control and Poverty:

Tobacco and poverty form a vicious link. Tobacco tends to be consumed more by the poor. In turn, it contributes to poverty through loss of income and loss of productivity due to ill health and premature death. It is the poor who bear most of the economic and disease burden of tobacco use.

There are several ways in which tobacco increases poverty at the individual, household and national levels. At the individual and household level, money spent on tobacco can have a very high opportunity cost. For the poor, money spent on tobacco could be spent on basic needs, such as food, shelter, education and healthcare. Tobacco also contributes to the poverty of individuals and families exposing them to the risk of ill health and premature death due to tobacco-related diseases, depriving families of much-needed income and imposing additional healthcare costs. Furthermore, tobacco cultivation and processing can cause serious damage to human health and environment.

At the national level, countries suffer substantial economic losses due to high healthcare costs, as well as lost productivity. Countries importing tobacco lose millions in precious foreign exchange. Cigarette smuggling has a higher negative impact on middle and low-income countries and on the poor. Reduced government tax revenues is another consequence of smuggling. In short, tobacco's so called contributions to the economy are far outweighed by its costs to households, public health and the environment.[6]

TOBACCO CONTROL IS A NECESSITY

Development agencies, donors and multilateral agencies are increasingly recognizing that tobacco is much more than a health issues. While epidemiological research continues to connect tobacco use to numerous serious health problems, economic research now shows that tobacco can exacerbate poverty among users, growers, workers and nations. Tobacco control, rather than being a luxury that only rich nations can afford, is now a necessity that all countries must address.

In a recent United Nations Inter-Agency Task Force on Tobacco Control, the following background observations with regard to the relationship between tobacco and development and poverty were considered.

The Commission on Macroeconomics and Health (CMH), established in 2000 by WHO's Director-General to assess the place of health in global economic development, highlighted the importance of investing in health to promote economic development and poverty reduction in particular in low-income countries. The Commission recognized that tobacco constitutes an important risk factor on the burden of disease especially for all developing countries.

The European Commission (EC) has specifically recognized tobacco as a development issue. The EC held a high-level round table on "Tobacco Control and Development Policy" in Brussels on 3-4 February 2003. During the discussions, it was stated that tobacco use is increasing in many developing countries, causing a higher death toll of tobacco-related illnesses. This poses a very heavy burden on developing countries, which are already struggling with the health impact of other communicable diseases such as HIV/AIDS, tuberculosis and malaria. The EC recognizes that tobacco production and consumption contributes to increased poverty and undermines sustainable development, and is keen to support developing countries wishing to address tobacco control, by using existing instruments of development cooperation at country level.

The Development and Assistance Committee Guidelines and Reference Series on Poverty and Health was published in 2003 in collaboration with the Organization for Economic Co-operation and Development (OECD) and the World Health Organization (WHO). The report recognized that tobacco-related diseases are strongly related to poverty. Tobacco has a profound effect on poverty and malnutrition in low-income countries. The high prevalence of tobacco use among men with little education and a low income has serious poverty implications because of the higher risk of developing dangerous diseases and dying at an early age. In order to counter the ill effects of tobacco use, especially among the poor and in low-income countries, development agencies should use policy dialogue coupled with technical and financial cooperation to support policy change.[7]

Dr. Halfdan Mahler in his article: Smoking or Health. The choice is your in *World Health*, February-March, 1980 established the relationships between smoking and diseases. To quote him.

Smoking is probably the largest single preventable cause of ill health in the world. The present increase in smoking menaces is more in most of those who live in developing countries, who are the targets of promotional drives by cigarette manufactures; there, smoking threatens to become one of tomorrow's major health hazards. In the case of developed countries, much greater and sustained efforts are required to reinforce educational and public information programmes, particularly for those most at risk such as young people. To increase awareness of this problem and its consequences and to encourage communities and nations to undertake greater efforts to reduce the smoking epidemic, WHO has selected this issue as the theme of World Health Day, 1980.

Although some scientific elements remain to be fully understood, the relationship of cigarette smoking to a variety of diseases has been clearly demonstrated. Smokings increase the risk of lung cancer, heart disease and respiratory infections of all kinds. In fact, many of the diseases associated with smoking have become current only in the last few generations, when the habit of smoking factory-made cigarettes became widespread.

The primary healthcare approach emphasizes the need for each individual to take a larger responsibility for his or her own health, and the health of family members, within the framework of active community participation. A drive to reduce smoking and particularly to prevent its spread among children and teenagers would provide a clear example of how individuals can improve their own health, with the leadership and support of national and local authorities.[8]

Tobacco kills approximately two and a half million people each year throughout the world. It is the largest single, preventable cause of death in the world today, responsible for many cancers, coronary heart disease, peripheral vascular disease, chronic bronchitis and emphysema. Taken in whatever form; it is a dangerous, expensive and addictive habit.

Contrary to popular opinion, the greatest excess mortality from tobacco is not in old age, but in productive middle life. One quarter of smokers die prematurely from the habit. This appalling statistic places tobacco in a unique risk category, far head of the risks of other consumer goods such as alcohol, sugar, cars or motorbikes.[9]

The major concern about tobacco use in the world today is the increase in developing countries. While tobacco markets are decreasing in the west at the rate of one per cent per annum, smoking is increasing in developing countries at an average of two per cent per annum. In other words, for every smoker who quits in the United States or Europe, two people start smoking in a developing country.[10]

INDIAN BURDEN

India spends about US$ 8 billion annually to treat tobacco-related diseases. An ICMR study in 2000 revealed that each patient suffering from a tobacco-related disease costs the country INR 2.5 million through direct medicine costs, absenteeism to treatment and loss of income due to premature death. With a health budget just 1% of the national budget, India finds it difficult to treat tobacco-related diseases, especially among the poor.

Bidi Workers

Tobacco industry poses an immense burden on the masses of the country in the form of various diseases and morbidity that far outweighs economic gains. Around 5 million people are directly or indirectly engaged in the Indian tobacco industry. The bidi workers form the third largest workforce in India and continue to live and work in conditions of poverty and exploitation.[11]

It remains to be seen how well we can cope with the kind of problem posed by cigarette smoking. The action taken has been of two kinds, one being health education directed towards the individual, the other being efforts to change the cigarette itself and the way it is promoted, distributed and used. These two approaches need not be alternatives. Not only can they exist side by side, they can be used to reinforce each other.

It has always been tempting for those of us in public health to wish we could "educate" people to behave the way we would like them to behave. But health education would be in a sad state if its function were to manipulate people into doing what others feel they ought to do. The real challenge is to identify the means whereby we can help people-whether children or adults--to develop the capability of understanding the issues in personal-choice health behaviour, and the capacity to make choices both in their own self-interest and in the interest of society at large.

However, if this is our goal, we must learn to accept the fact that under these conditions many thoughtful people will still make choices that they perceive as being in their own self-interest even though we deplore the choice. In that case, the best we can do is to place some boundaries to the damage to themselves and to others that may result from their choice, and then to wish them-well. Even though most people place a high value on good health, it is apt to be viewed not as a primary value-good health for its own sake-but as a value subsidiary to the attainment of other primary values.

The behavioral approach that has helped to identify the factors responsible for the complexities of the smoking problem may throw some light on how to deal with some of the other health problems that result from personal behaviour choices. Important as the smoking-related diseases are, it might be even more important to learn how to apply this knowledge to the whole range of personal-choice health behaviour problems and might take us a step closer to achieving the good health that should be everyone's right.[12]

A survey revealed the prevalence of current tobacco use to be 41% among men and 14.9% among women in Karnatka and 50% among men and 9.1% among women in Uttar Pradesh.[13]

Smoking is only a serious problem to the person whose addiction to tobacco is so strong that he cannot stop the habit form crippling his health. It is a mild flirtation to the light smoker, with little risk of disease, and an annoying pollutant to the non-smoker bystander. Only to the unborn child can it be said to be an inescapable menace. Otherwise, and on the whole, the uses to which tobacco is put today can be classed, along with the myriad excesses of human nature in seeking self-gratification in material well-being, as socially unacceptable because, on the whole, they have been found to be injurious to health. But so is drinking, eating, motoring, hang-gliding and promiscuous sex. Or so say the defenders of freedom to supply and promote tobacco, and they are many indeed, all over the world.[14]

The answer to the problem of how to diminish the effects of tobacco on ailing lungs and chests all over the world depends on the social conscience of the affluent nations.[15]

Nedd Willard in his article—Smoking—a man-made dragon observes that Lung cancer, gastro-duodenal ulcer, circulatory disorders and heart attacks, risks to the urban child: all these may stem from a single culprit—the factory-made cigarette.[16]

It is hard to give an exact picture of cigarette smokers around the world today because information is abundant in some places, almost non-existent in others, and the picture itself keeps changing. Generally speaking, people in the developing world consume far fewer cigarettes than do their counterparts in highly industrialized communities.

The United States still leads the world in cigarette consumption, with an average of over 2,700 cigarettes per person each year. Western Europe is close behind, with the figures that run from 1,000 to 2,000 cigarettes per person. In most European countries more than 50 per cent of the adult males smoke an average of 15 cigarettes a day. Women get through between 10 and 50 a day; moreover the incidence of women smoking continues to rise while that of men is beginning to show a downward trend. As more women start the habit, so the statistics show them falling victim more frequently to lung cancer and coronary heart diseases.

In Belgium, 50 per cent of the young people smoke by the age of 15. In the Federal Republic of Germany, 36 per cent of the 10 to 12 years olds are already confirmed, regular smokers. In Italy, 60 per cent of boys are cigarette users by the time they are 15. A recent survey in a Latin American city showed that 45 per cent of the men and 18 per cent of the women smoked.[17]

World Health has suggested the benefits of not smoking in the Table 2.1.

The abuse of psychoactive substances—including alcohol, tobacco and narcotic and psychotropic drugs—causes enormous damage to the health and productivity of nations. It undermines the quality of life to individuals and their families, and threatens the welfare of communities. The health consequences of abuse are also grave, and range from violence and delinquency to liver cirrhosis, brain damage and lung cancer.

Treatment of dependence on psychoactive substances is still imperfect, can take a long time and may be expensive. Its effects are all too often of short duration. Yet treatment remains a necessary part of society's response to the damage done. Sometimes it will have to be repeated; sometimes it will be discouraged by failure. Nevertheless, it must be provided to those affected, often to save their lives.[19]

In the long-run the consequences of sickness and disease, of work days lost and the drain on resources, will be far greater than the short-term

TABLE 2.1

Why you should Quit Smoking?

Risks of smoking	*Benefits of quitting*	*Low-tar, low-nicotine*	*Risks of smoking*	*Benefits of Quitting*	*Low-tar, low-nicotine*
Shortened Life Expectancy			**Cancer of Pancreas**		
Risk proportional to amount smoked. A 25-year-old person who smokes two packs a day can expect to live 8.3 years less than a non-smoking contemporary.	After 10 to 15 years ex-smoker's risk approaches that of those who never smoked.	Reduced risk of death from certain diseases suggests increased life expectancy.	Risk of fatal cancer is 2 to 5 times higher than for non-smokers.	Since risk seems related to dose, stopping smoking should reduce it.	No. identified benefit.
Lung Cancer			**Coronary Heart Disease**		
Cigarettes are major cause in both men and women. Over-all smokers risk is 10 times greater than non-smokers	After 10 to 15 years risk approached that of those who never smoked.	Filter tips reduce risk, but the risk is still 5 times that of non-smokers. Low T/N brands reduce risk to men by 20 per cent, to women by 40 per cent.	Smoking a major factor, causing 120,000 heart deaths each year.	Risk decreases sharply after one year. After 10 years risk is the same as for those who never smoked.	With low T/N brands, men have 12 per cent lower risk, women 19, than smokers of high T/N brands.
Larynx Cancer			**Bronchitis and Emphysema**		
Smoking increases risk by 2.9 to 17.7 times that of non-smokers	Gradual reduction in risk, reaching normal after 10 years.	No. identified benefit.	Smokers face 4 to 25 times greater risk of death; lung damage even in young smokers.	With weeks, cough sputum disappears. Lung function may improve; slower deterioration.	No. identified benefit.
Mouth Cancer			**Stillbirth, Low Birth Weight**		
Smokers have 3 to 10 times as many oral cancers as non-smokers. Alcohol may	Reducing or eliminating smoking/drinking lowers risk in first few years. Risk	No. identified benefit.	Smokers have more stillbirths, more low birth weight babies, and more	If smoking is stopped before fourth month of pregnancy, risk to fetus is eliminated.	No. identified benefit

act as synergist, intensifying effect.	drops to level of non-smokers in 10 to 15 years		to disease and death.		
Cancer of Oesophagus			**Peptic Ulcer**		
Smoking increases risk of fatal cancer 2 to 9 times. Alcohol acts as a synergist.	Since risk is proportional to dose, reducing or eliminating smoking/drinking should lower risk.	No. identified benefit	Smokers get more ulcers and are more likely to die from them; cure more difficult in smokers.	Ex-smokers get ulcers too, but they heal faster and more completely than smokers.	No. identified benefit
Cancer of Bladder			**Drug and Test Effects**		—
Smokers' risk is 7 to 10 times greater. Synergistic with certain occupational exposures.	Risk decreases gradually to that of non-smokers over 7 years.	No. identified benefit	Smoking changes pharmacological effects of many medicines. It changes results of diagnostic tests and increases the risk of blood clots from oral contraceptives.	Most blood factors raised by smoking return to normal. Non-smokers on birth control pill have much lower risk of hazardous clots and heart attacks.	—

Source: "Dangers of Smoking, Benefits of Quitting", prepared by the American Cancer Society. World Health Organization, September-October 1981.[18]

gains of tobacco-generated income. Developing countries still have a chance to prevent the growth of smoking. They can ensure that promoting non-smoking forms an integral part of an overall primary healthcare strategy. They can draw up widespread and well-formulated education programmes to support the health message. And they can bring in legislation to curb the promotion of tobacco. Non-governmental and voluntary organizations will be valuable allies in this battle. In particular the consumer movements that are emerging in developing countries can form the core of an anti-smoking network in support of popular initiatives for change.[20]

Most of the developing countries are not banning smoking as these countries earn revenue out of it but they do not understand that they have to pay more in terms of expenditure to control diseases borne out of smoking.

Cigarette Casualties

Tobacco growing may appear to be a painless way of extracting excise revenue but, as the consequences of smoking overtake the exercise, even countries with No. health service worth mentioning will find that they cannot escape spending the bulk of their "profits" on treating growing numbers of cigarette casualties. It is No. secret that smoking-related diseases are among those that require the most expensive care, the most sophisticated surgery. Other smoking-related ailments are among the main causes of sporadic absenteeism from work.

A notable difference between tobacco taxes in rich and poor countries is that taxes in the developed world are now nearly always applied towards efforts to curb smoking, while in the developing countries they go towards fostering the new industry.

As for the dreams of winning greater shares in the export market, this is a clear instance of the Third World coming in too late with too little. This is a highly complex manufacturing industry, practically sewn up by a very small number of buyers. The chances of developing countries selling their cigarettes to anyone but themselves are virtually nil.

On the other hand, if there is nothing to be gained by the Third World in growing tobacco and manufacturing cigarettes, at least these countries have an opportunity to achieve moderation in their smoking habits (since there does not seem to be any serious advocacy, even from bodies like WHO, for a total ban on smoking). Third World per capita consumption of cigarettes is still very low—on average about a third of consumption in the US, the Federal Republic of Germany, or Japan. Women have hardly fallen for their dubious charms yet. The techniques to combat smoking are available and the pattern of epidemics is known as is the technology for testing cigarettes.

More to the point, the smoking habit does not increase spontaneously; it has to be created. Governments could cease to encourage it, simply by controlling advertising. This costs nothing. More positively, even the most inexpensive campaign to make the public aware of the dangers of smoking must, in the circumstances, be effective.

A New International Information Order is at present emerging out of the initiatives that are thrusting forward the New International Economic Order. Cigarettes do not make economic sense to anybody but a few commercial giants. It will be interesting to see how the New International Information Order will take up the challenge of protecting developing countries from the destructive little while cylinder.[21]

The Role of Economic Consideration

Although the relationships of costs and benefits have been emphasized here, the smoking problem should not be considered solely in economic terms, since the well-being of a population can be altered in a number of ways, without necessarily affecting directly its productivity and its prosperity. As regards the question of the perceived economic benefits of tobacco-growing and cigarette smoking, there is certainly No. evidence that a non-smoking society is worse off economically than a society where smoking does take place. This statement does not imply that a country may not obtain some temporary economic or social benefits by encouraging the growing of tobacco. However, it seems likely that, in adopting such a policy, governments tend to underestimate the long-term social costs and consequences.

In summary, it would seem that society must decide mainly on the basis of medical grounds whether smoking, by a large part of the population, is acceptable. Unfortunately, the record of national governments in this respect has not been impressive. In the United States, for example, only limited actions have been taken to control tobacco smoking, whereas other substances, which may be carcinogenic in humans, such as cyclamates, have been banned. Let us hope that future years will see increased government consciousness of the need for active intervention in all circumstances that have a direct bearing on disease prevention.[22]

One day the luckless and unloved smoker may have to slink away to a small screened-off area, there to share the polluted air with other shamefaced "cranks" suffering from the same weakness.[23]

Tobacco Fine Flowers Lethal Leaves

Technology has transformed a lovely plant into a deadly weapon the machine made cigarette. The little white tube makes regular, deep, inhalation possible, and ensures that the smoker's health is chronically undermined.

Death on the Instalment Plan

Cigarette smoking causes an estimated 300,000 premature deaths in the United States from lung cancer, coronary heart disease chronic bronchitis and emphysema. Every cigarette smoked may take between five minutes and a quarter of an hour off your life-span.

Killing with Cancer

Lung cancer is a major cause of death in countries where smoking is widespread, and 90 per cent of cases occur in smokers. Smokers are five to ten times more at risk from cancer of the mouth; throat and gullet than are non-smokers. But smokers who give up the habit significantly reduce their risk of developing cancer.

A Blow to the Heart

Coronary heart disease is the leading cause of death in most developed countries, and the risk of dying from it is two to three times greater in smokers than in non-smokers.

Heavy Pollution

Tobacco smoke contains at least 1,000 constituents, many of which are known to be harmful. Non-smokers need to spend only one hour in a smoke-filled room to inhale the equivalent of one cigarette smoked "normally".

The Feminine Mistake

Women took up smoking later than men and are now beginning to pay the price. If present trends continue, lung cancer will soon be the most common form of cancer among women in the United States. Mothers to be who smoke risk having underweight, sickly babies. Women who use oral contraceptives and smoke are ten times more at risk of having a heart attack by age 50 compared to those who do not smoke.

Unsafe at any Age

One study showed that about one-third of regular smokers were found to have experimented before the age of nine. The most important factor influencing a child's smoking is whether or not his parents smoke.

New Trends

In the developed countries smoking is decreasing, with the sharpest decline occurring amongst the best educated, but more teenage girls are taking to cigarettes each year. Although those countries still lead in overall consumption tobacco, the increase in smoking around the world is sharpest in the Third World Between 1965 and 1975 smoking rose by 3.7 per cent in North America but by a staggering 33 per cent in Africa.

A Change in the Wind

Smoking has already become a minority habit in the United States, where there are now 30 million ex-smokers. Those who stop smoking enjoy better health because of it; those who don't smoke are promoting the rights of every one to enjoy clean, unpolluted air. Many countries are banning cigarette advertisements and promoting education for a smoke-free life. The goal everywhere is a healthier lifestyle. WHO's message is clear "Smoking or health: the choice is yours."[24]

Nyo Nyo Kyaing observed that:

According to 1995 global estimates, about 12% women smoked compared to 47% men. While in developed countries about 22% women smoked, in developing countries around 10% women above age 15 smoked. Although smoking prevalence in South-East Region was mostly low, the number of women using smokeless tobacco was high more than 120 million in 2000. Smokeless tobacco use was very high among Indian, Bangladeshi and rural Sri Lankan women.

When smoking amongst women was not as widespread as it is now, women were considered to be almost free from cardiovascular diseases and lung cancer. Unhappily, the situation has changed, and smoking kills over half a million women each year in the industrialized world. But it is also an increasingly important cause of ill health amongst women in developing countries.

A recent WHO Consultation on the statistical aspects of tobacco-related morality concluded that the toll that can be attributed to smoking throughout the world is 2.7 million deaths per year. It also predicted that, if current patterns of cigarette smoking continue unchanged, the global death toll from tobacco by the year 2025 may increase to eight million deaths per year. A large proportion of these will be amongst women.[25]

Smoking is Worse for Women

In addition to the problems, women who smoke have greater risk of:

- Difficulty getting pregnant (infertility);
- Miscarriage, and babies born too small or too soon;
- Problems when using birth control pills;
- Monthly bleeding that ends earlier in life (menopause);
- Weaker bones that break more easily during mid-life and old-age (osteoporosis); and
- Cancer of the cervix and womb.

A woman who is pregnant should try to avoid other people who are smoking, so that the smoke will not harm her baby.[26]

In India, the number of women using smokeless tobacco was five times higher than those who smoked. A 1997 survey in Mumbai reported 58% non-smoke tobacco use among women.

In India, an estimated 4% of all female deaths was tobacco-related. Incidence of oral sub-mucous fibrosis was high among Indian women and one-fourth of all cancers were tobacco-related.[27]

The woman who smokes risks having bad teeth, a wrinkled skin, darkened complexion, yellowing fingers and nails; yet all these are reversible if she can only stop smoking.[28]

Most pregnant women are already conscious of the dangers that smoking entails for their future child, but young mothers are less willing to give up the habit for good. The efforts of health educators should therefore be concentrated on them. When the mother eventually wants to stop her own children from falling into the toils of tobacco, her credibility will suffer if she does not live up to the non-smoking image. Doctors who smoke, it is well known, are No. longer credible when they try to stop their patients doing so, and the same is true of parents who smoke.

Protection, Education, Support

What can be done to halt and reverse the tobacco epidemic amongst women? The challenge is two-fold: to reduce the already high level of smoking among women in the industrialized world and to ensure that the low level of smoking in developing countries does not increase. In order to achieve these goals, all countries need to develop comprehensive anti-tobacco programmes, which take into account and address the needs of women. Whilst these programmes should be culture-specific and tailored to meet the local situation, experts agree that to be successful they must contain three key elements: protection, education and support.

Young girls and women need to be protected from inducements to smoke. Tobacco is a multi-national, multi-billion dollar industry. It is also an industry under threat; one quarter of its customers, in the long-term, are killed by using its product and smoking is declining in many industrialized countries. To maintain profits, tobacco companies need to ensure that at least 2.7 million new smokers, usually young people, start smoking every year. Women have been clearly identified as a key target group for tobacco advertising in both the industrialized and developing worlds. Billions of US dollars each year are spent on promoting this lethal product specifically to women. "Women only" brands, widespread advertisements depicting beautiful, glamorous, successful women smoking, free fashion goods, and the sponsorship of women's sports and events (such as tennis and fashion shows), are all part of the industry's global marketing strategy aimed at attracting and keeping women smoking.

This strategy has been highlighted by several tobacco journals, which have carried articles on "Targeting the female smoker" and suggesting that retailers should "look to the ladies". Among the 20 US magazines that received the most cigarette advertising revenue in 1985, eight were women's magazines. In the same year, a study on the cigarette advertising policies of 53 British women's magazines (read by more than half of all British women) showed that 64 percent of the magazines accepted cigarette advertising, which represented an average of seven per cent of total advertising revenue.

Research in industrialized countries has shown the subtle methods used to encourage young girls to smoke. The impact of such methods is likely to be even greater in developing countries, where young people are generally less knowledgeable about smoking hazards and may be more attracted by glamorous, affluent, desirable images of the female smoker. This is why WHO, together with other national and international health agencies, has repeatedly called for national legislation banning all forms of tobacco promotion, and for an appropriate "high price" policy, which would slow down the "enthusiasm" of young women for tobacco.

Education for Resisting the Pressures

Young girls and women have a right to be informed about the damage that smoking can do to their health. They also need to acquire skills to resist pressures to start smoking or to give it up. Several countries have developed integrated schools and preschool health education programmes which have successfully reduced girls' smoking rates; but this education should not be restricted to what happens in school. There are many other examples of effective cessation programmes in the work place and primary health centres. Unfortunately many women do not have the opportunity to be involved in such programmes, and programmes have generally been less successful with women than men. In countries where smoking has decreased, the rate of decline has been usually lower in women than men, and least amongst women with low education and income. This suggests that educational initiatives ought to be more sensitive to women's needs; they also ought to cover issues of particular significance to women—such as the gain in weight that some times occurs after they stop smoking.

They Need Educational Support

In order for women to become, and remain, non-smokers they need. Support over these difficult days when the addiction cycle is broken. Support to help them deal in other less damaging ways with the reasons that caused them to smoke. Many women use smoking as a coping strategy, for example, to create a "space" in a day filled with the stress of bringing up children and having to face different types of work, often with little social support and on a low income. Environments need to be created which enable them to break free of this health-damaging behaviour, to make the healthy choices the best choices.

Smoking amongst women has already reached epidemic proportions and will continue to escalate unless action is taken now. Delays can only cause further suffering and deaths of women; this is why WHO's new programme on tobacco or health is giving high priority to action to protect women and children.

But what can be done to tackle this problem? Community health workers can develop health education programmes for young girls. Primary care workers can ensure that all women receive information, advice and support to help them give up the habit. Governments, national and international non-governmental organizations, and WHO in particular, can act as advocates for women's health to ensure that the issue of women and tobacco is put high on the health and political agenda, by pressing for action to protect women. Strategies to this effect should involve health and educational services, community and women's organizations, the media and even the employers.

Only by exposing the previously hidden problem of women and tobacco, only by putting women in the picture, will we be able to secure major improvements in the health of women worldwide.[29]

The public authorities in many countries have already taken a clear stance in face of this problem. Anti-smoking campaigners are increasing in number. By exchanging views on the experience gained through these campaigns, we can eventually form a common front, on a global scale, to oppose the social scourge of smoking.[30]

Go shopping and you'll come across exhibit panels with graphs and illustration on the dangers of smoking displayed prominently in the lobby of the main commercial centres. Along Singapore's tree-lined streets, bright cloth streamers flutter with the same message.

To the visitor, these are very visible signs that show the island republic's determination to curb cigarette smoking. But Singaporeans have much more to reckon with. Their country is one of the few in the world with very harsh laws against the cigarette. Consider these:

- Smoking is prohibited in all buses and public vehicles. Drivers, conductors or passengers who are caught smoking are liable to fines of up to 500 Singapore dollars (US $ 230).
- Singapore's 70,000 government employees have been warned not to smoke in offices where they deal with the public.
- Doctors and hospital staff have been ordered not to smoke in wards and areas for patients.
- Teachers are not allowed to smoke in front of students or anywhere in the schools except in the staff or faculty rooms.
- Pupils caught smoking within school grounds are punished.
- Smoking is prohibited in closed auditoriums, cinemas, theatres, public lifts. Violators are liable to fines of up to 500 Singapore dollars.
- Taxi drivers can be fined up to 400 dollars if they smoke while driving with passengers.
- Food vendors in canteens or from market stalls are forbidden to smoke while handling their wares.[31]

It remains to be seen how well we can cope with the kind of problem posed by cigarette smoking. The action taken has been of two kinds, one being health education directed towards the individual, the other being efforts to change the cigarette itself and the way it is promoted, distributed and used. These two approaches need not be alternatives. Not only can they exist side by side, they can be used to reinforce each other.

It has always been tempting for those of us in public health to wish we could "educate" people to behave the way we would like them to behave. But health education would be in a sad state if its function were to manipulate people into doing what others feel they ought to do. The real challenge is to identify the means whereby we can help people—whether children or adults—to develop the capability of understanding the issues in personal-choice health behaviour, and the capacity to make choices both in their own self-interest and in the interest of society at large.

However, if this is our goal, we must learn to accept the fact that under these conditions many thoughtful people will still make choices that they perceive as being in their own self-interest even though we deplore the choice. In that case, the best we can do is to place some boundaries to the damage to themselves and to others that may result from their choice, and then to wish them well. Even though most people place a high value on good health, it is apt to be viewed not as a primary value—good health for its own sake—but as a value subsidiary to the attainment of other primary values.

The behavioural approach that has helped to identify the factors responsible for the complexities of the smoking problem may throw some light on how to deal with some of the other health problems that result from personal behaviour choices. Important as the smoking-related diseases are, it might be even more important to learn how to apply this knowledge to the whole range of personal-choice health behaviour problems and might take us a step closer to achieving the good health that should be everyone's right.[32]

How to Quit?

The American Cancer Society suggests two possible "recipes" for breaking the smoking habit. Of course, trying the suggestions from one list does not rule out those from the other list.

Recipe A:

1. Decide to smoke only once an hour; or decide to stop smoking for an entire hour, and then start lengthening that time by half hours.
2. Make it hard to get at a cigarette. Wrap up the package and put elastic bands round it. Smoke with your left hand if you usually smoke with your right.
3. Switch to a brand you don't like. Buy only one pack at a time.
4. If you always have a smoke with your coffee, switch to tea or fruit juice.
5. Do something for your body. Get back in shape. Exercise is great for relaxation.
6. Call up your friends and tell them you are going to quit.
7. If you quit for one day, you can quit for another. Try it.
8. Save all the money you would have spent on cigarettes and buy yourself something. You deserve it.
9. If you break down and have a cigarette, don't worry. Some people have several tries before they at last succeed.

Recipe B:

1. Cut out one cigarette a day.
2. Make each cigarette a special decision—and put off making the decision.
3. Don't give up cigarettes—completely. Carry one around with you in case of need. You'll find in the end you are saving it—permanently.
4. Don't quit "forever". Just stop for a day, and tomorrow try it for another day; and tomorrow, and tomorrow, and tomorrow.
5. Tell your friends and family you are quitting. A public commitment bolsters willpower.
6. Pick a Q-Day—the Day you Quit. And quit.
7. Hide all evidence of cigarettes, ashtrays and matches, so you are not reminded of the habit.
8. Lay in a supply of chewing gum; cough sweets or peanuts to nibble instead of reaching for a smoke.[33]

Educational and other activities should encourage community leaders to develop a better understanding of the complex personal, pharmacological, social and cultural consequences of drug-taking, and thus to foster new cultural attitudes towards drug use. Apart from discouraging the use cf a particular drug, it may also be possible to restrict practices that actively promote dependence-producing drugs, such as the advertising of alcoholic drinks, certain tobacco products and mood modifying pharmaceuticals.

Every thing possible should be done to alleviate environmental conditions that lead to undue stress-discrimination of various kinds, blocked opportunities at work, slum conditions, unfair business or labour practice.

Above all, however, approaches to the prevention of drug dependence should have realistic aims. Changes in cultural attitudes as well as in environmental stresses can only be brought about very slowly, and over-ambitious hopes of "eradicating" a drug problem in a short time are likely to lead to policies that are unrealistic and self-discrediting.[34]

Good Reasons for Quitting Smoking

(a) Quality Life and Better Health.
(b) Safety from non-communicable.
(c) Family members diseases would also be healthy.
(d) Children would be healthy.
(e) Money saved can be spent for good life.

The U.S. Food and Drug Administration (FDA) has approved five medications to help you quit smoking:

1. Bupropion SRs,
2. Nicotine gum,
3. Nicotine inhaler,
4. Nicotine nasal spray, and
5. Nicotine Patch.

CASE STUDIES

A group matched, case-control study was carried out at Government Medical College Hospital, Nagpur, India, to investigate the association between tobacco smoking and age-related cataract. The study included 275 male cases of age-related cataract and an equal number of controls group matched for age. Prevalence of smoking in cases and controls was calculated to be 33.4% and 15.3% respectively. A significant risk association between smoking and age-related cataract was observed (OR = 2.90, 95% CI = 1.92-4.39). The overall estimates of attributable risk proportion and population attributable risk proportion were calculated to be 0.66 (0.48-0.77) and 0.23 (0.13-0.35) respectively. Stratified analysis revealed dose and duration response relationship between tobacco smoking and age-related cataract. The current study thus identified the significant role of smoking in the outcome of age-related cataract.[35]

Policy Issues

- The government should immediately identify the harm that tobacco causes to agriculture and eventually to the net food production of the country. Provision of facilities and incentives to grow food crops would help tobacco farmers to turn away from tobacco.
- Only a handful of health and other professionals are actively engaged in tobacco prevention activities. It also seems that tobacco prevention activities take place in the main cities and are confined only to certain activities on special days, such as World No.-Tobacco Day, etc.
- Research on various aspects of tobacco use are rarely done and, as a result, issues such as the effects of tobacco advertising on various community groups, socio-cultural values attributed to tobacco chewing, the effect of tobacco cultivation, etc. are less known.
- Continuous efforts should be made to get support from experts from the fields other than medical and all available resources put together to avert this public health problem. Attention should be paid to strengthen the National Coordinating Committee on alcohol, tobacco and other substances, which can act as the main coordinating body of tobacco control activities in Sri Lanka. This Committee should have strong linkages with anti-tobacco activities in the South Asian Region.[36]

The present community-based cross-sectional study was carried out of Hanumannagar area of Nagpur City, India. A total of 1168 study subjects included 590 males (50.5%) and 578 females (49.5%). Of the females, 12.6% were using smokeless tobacco while 30.8% of the males were consuming tobacco of which 148 (25.1%) were daily tobacco chewers. With increasing age, the prevalence of tobacco chewing was found to increase whereas it decreases with the level of educational attainment. Though 82.8% of the study subjects agreed on the harmful effects of tobacco chewing on health, only 23.9% of the users were concerned about their own health. Health education and mass media should be used to control the epidemic of tobacco use.[37]

The Tobacco Tradition in India

When the Portuguese first introduced tobacco into India in the 17th century, it was credited with the qualities of calming and relaxing an individual and was also considered to be a sort of stimulant. Various cultures gradually discovered their own ways of using tobacco, and as time passed, tobacco habits became not only socially acceptable but a tradition, even playing a part in cultural rituals. The younger generation began to equate tobacco usage with adult behaviour.

Over the years, tobacco usage in India has evolved in two distinct forms, namely, chewing and smoking. Chewing is hardly a correct description of the habit because in most cases tobacco is kept in the mouth and not chewed. The practice of pan chewing is at least 2000 years old and has the sanction of ancient Indian scriptures. Basically pan is a combination of betel leaf, slaked lime (calcium hydroxide) and pieces of areca nuts, with sweetening added. Today, however, almost all the habitual chewers of pan chew it along with tobacco.

Khaini can be described as the habit of chewing tobacco without the betel leaf, and Mishri is prepared from burnt powdered tobacco. It is primarily used as a way of cleaning teeth, mostly by women.

The bidi is undoubtedly the most common and widespread smoking habit. This is a reed-like cigarette made by rolling a dried rectangular piece of temburni (Diospyros Melanoxylon) between the fingers with a small amount of tobacco into a roughly conical shape and securing the roll with a thread. Unlike a cigarette, the bidi cannot be held between the fingers for a long time, and it has to be puffed continuously, otherwise it goes out.

A chutta is a coarsely prepared cheroot, commonly smoked on the east coast of India. It is often smoked in reverse (with the burning end kept inside the mouth) especially by women. The hookli is a clay pipe smoked by men in Gujarat. In other regions, men smoke another pipe called a chillum, which is cone-shaped. In the hooka, the smoke is filtered through water kept in a bottle connected a special receptacle containing a small amount of tobacco, seasoned with molasses and topped with pieces of burning charcoal.

Today the most fashionable form of smoking is the cigarette. More than 80 brands are available but since they are generally very expensive, they are confined mainly to urban upper income people in the cities. The bidi is the village cigarette.

India ranks third in world tobacco production, and of the 250 million kilograms of tobacco per year allocated for local consumption, 73 per cent is smoked, 20 per cent is taken as snuff or rubbed on the skin

No. Health Warning

Much is known about the smoking behaviour of children in the industrialized world, but in India hardly anything on this subject is documented. But as a matter of common observation, it can be said that, since more people live in villages, more children in villages smoke. And the villager knows nothing about the hazards connected with smoking. Cigarette advertisements with the statutory health warning are not found in the village, and a bundle of bidis does not have any warning on it. Yet there is a higher risk of lung cancer for bidi smokers and also a risk of oral and pharyngeal cancers.

Among well-to-do city families, it is yet not acceptable to the Indian lifestyle that daughters and daughters-in-law should smoke, even though the men do. Away from home, in schools, colleges and other public places, young girls rarely smoke and few young boys do so although the number is on the increase. The real problem is located among the urban poor, where boys commonly start to smoke before the age of ten, and sometimes even as early as five to six years. These children smoke not so much because their friends do so, but because they constantly see their movie film heroes with a cigarette.

In the villages of Kerala State, one survey found that the main reason given for starting smoking was tooth-related problems; tobacco is believed to have magical and medicinal value incurring toothache. In Gujarat, village boys start smoking from about the age of nine. They are often sent by their fathers to buy the bidis and, if they take away a few from the bundle, the fathers do not mind.

But certain myths have grown up about smoking—that it facilitates bowel movement in the morning, helps one to concentrate at work and wards off sleep at night when it is essential to work in the fields.

A majority of young girls who smoke (backward or reverse chutta) reported that they had been advised to smoke by older women to appease "longings" during pregnancy, as a cure for anaemia and asthma, or to get relief from tooth troubles. And a belief has even grown up in the Andhra Pradesh countryside that "one should not see a non-smoker's face in the morning" as this brings ill-luck!

These observations are just examples of what is known about the dynamics of tobacco consumption in the India countryside. What certainly needs to be brought to the attention of the policy-makers is that No. awareness or knowledge exists in rural India about the ill-effects of tobacco. The responsibility for ensuring that youngsters "talk health" before they start the dangerous smoking habit rests with health workers at every level.[38]

This health problem is just too big for the medical profession alone to handle. Legislators, labour unions, citizens' groups, school teachers, journalists who work in the mass media, all of these have tasks that are just as important. Smoking concerns all of us. It is up to all of us to do something about it.[39]

Do not use your lungs as ashtrays.

Based upon discussion, observation, case studies, the author suggests the following to lessen smoking menace:

1. Teachers in schools, colleges, and Universities need be sensitized to help students addicted to smoking in leaving this bad habit.
2. Government should discourage production of cigarette of all brands as the revenue earned results into more losses if we carry out social cost/benefit analysis.

3. Government should implement the ban on smoking in letter and spirit.
4. Audio-Visual aids may be used to tell the disadvantages of smoking.
5. People suffering from cancer and other diseases should be picturized and shown to people.

As another World No.-Tobacco Day went by today the data of various surveys—conducted by authoritative agencies including WHO and released by PGI—show that the day only illuminates the threat which is getting grimmer by the year.

Prof. Savita Malhotra, who head Tobacco Cessation Clinic (TCC) at PGI, set-up at WHO's behest two years back, says over 10 per cent of students in age group of 13-15, who are at the biggest risk of turning into addicts, use tobacco. "Though people are taking the danger more seriously, its threat is also getting bigger, as more people are falling in its net."

Another startling data is that tobacco consumption, which includes smoking and chewing, in developed countries was twice of that in developing countries a few decades back.

Things are almost reverse now, as tobacco companies are luring more users in countries like India after developed countries have made their laws stringent and their natives becoming more sensitive to its dangers. A PGI release states that in some parts of Punjab almost 72 per cent of school children consume tobacco.

The best bet remains to educate people about its dangers and we are stressing it further. We are communicating with students at schools and organizing community camps to sanitize at slums, she says.

And, yes, there is a hope. The analysis of first 500 patients of TCC showed that quit rate was impressive 10 per cent while over half of them reduced tobacco consumption by half. Most of the patients were heavy smokers who suffered from other complications and were referred to from other departments.[40]

Dr. Samlee Plianbangchang suggested the following points:

(i) Behaviour change interventions should form an integral part of tobacco control efforts;
(ii) Increasing taxation on tobacco products could reduce tobacco consumption, particularly, among the poor;
(iii) Governments need to arrange alternative means of livelihood for tobacco growers;
(iv) Tobacco control should be one of the factors to be considered in poverty reduction and other development strategies;
(v) The European Union and the World Bank have pledged support for diversifying tobacco growing as well as for other tobacco control activities if these are integrated into the overall development agenda. Countries must avail of this opportunity to

mobilize the required funds for tobacco control programmes. Meanwhile, as research suggest;

(vi) Programmatic collaboration between TB and tobacco would not only reduce the death toll but would also encourage donors to support this collaborative programme in these two priority areas;

(vii) Partnership with media and civil society is important in the fight against tobacco. The media can play a vital role in influencing government policy, especially in undertaking targeted tobacco control programmes for the poor. Let us join hands to encourage countries to sign and ratify;[41] and

(viii) India enacted comprehensive tobacco legislation in May 2004, which need be strengthened.

CONCLUSION

Treatment of tobacco dependence is another possible policy measure in low-income and middle-income countries.[42] As the projections demonstrate, a mix of effective prevention and treatment measures will avert significantly more tobacco-caused deaths within the coming decades compared with prevention alone.[43] Cessation programmes for adult smokers are essential for rapid population health improvements over the next 20-30 years, since the benefits of preventing young people from taking up smoking will become apparent only after several decades. The Global Youth Tobacco Survey showed that most young smokers in the Western Pacific Region wished to stop smoking.

The delivery of cost-effective treatment of tobacco dependence in most countries is hampered by many factors, including: the lack of integration of tobacco dependence treatment into healthcare systems; lack of skills of healthcare providers; high price of nicotine replacement therapy products and cessation services; and the strict regulation of such products. Support and greater access to treatment provided through the healthcare systems will help the poor populations who are most likely to smoke.[44] All health providers must be involved, including oral health professionals who, in many countries, reach a large proportion of the healthy population. A supportive environment is essential to support smoking cessation programmes and this requires strong government action, for example, in the promotion of smoke-free environments and communication and awareness measures to reduce the social acceptability of tobacco use.[45]

One of the most advanced mixes of population-level smoking cessation initiatives is in New Zealand, where 50% of the indigenous populations are smokers.[46] Services include a national Quitline, subsidized nicotine replacement therapy, Maori-focused services including quitting support and therapy for Maori women and their families, and a hospital-based quitting service. Key factors in establishing programmes including cessation activities are media campaigns, an active tobacco control lobby, proactive policy analysts and a supportive government; tax increases also create incentives to help people to stop smoking.

The FCTC is a global response to the pandemic of tobacco-induced deaths and disease. The opening of the Convention of signature and ratification provides an unprecedented opportunity for countries to strengthen national tobacco control capacity. Success in controlling the tobacco epidemic requires continuing political engagement and additional resources at both global and national levels. The resulting improvement in health, especially of poor populations, will be a major public health achievement.[47]

A health education programme against tobacco use should be directed and information disseminated which not only makes people aware that tobacco causes oropharygeal cancer and other cancers because of the carcinogens present in it,[48] but also instills and supports the desire to stop tobacco chewing.[49]

Notes and References

1. Tobacco Facts, HRIDAY, Health Related Information Dissemination Amongst Youth, SHAN, Student Health Action Network, p. 7.
2. Ezzati M. Lopez A.D. Estimates of global mortality attributable to smoking in 2000. Lancet, 2003. 362:847-852.
3. Gundon, G.E., Boisclair, D. Past, Current and Future Trends in Tobacco Use. Washington, DC, World Bank, 2003 (HNP Discussion Paper No. 6, Economics of Tobacco Control Paper No. 6)
4. The World Health Report, 2003, pp. 91-92.
5. Tobacco Facts, HRIDAY, Health Related Information Dissemination Amongst Youth, SHAN, Student Health Action Network, pp. 1-2.
6. Dr. Samlee Plianbangchang, Life Line, WHO: Volume 1, Issue 2, Regional Office for South-East Asia, April-June 2004
7. WHO: Tobacco and Poverty, A vicious circle, *World Health*, p. 11.
8. Dr. Halfdan Mahler, Director General of the World Health Organization, World Health Day, 7 April 1980—Smoking or Health, The choice is yours!, *World Health*, Feb.-March, 1980, p. 3.
9. By Judith Mackay, The Tobacco Epidemic Spreads, *World Health*, October 1988, p. 9.
10. *Ibid.*
11. Dr. Samlee Plianbangchang, Life Line, WHO: Volume 1 issue 2, Regional Office for South-East Asia, April-June '15.
12. WHO: Behaviour and Health, *World Health*, December 1975, USA $1, p. 31.
13. Annual Report, 2002-03, "Ministry of Health and Family Welfare", GOI, p. 92.
14. WHO: Arthur Hayward-Costa, the smoker' world, *World Health*, October 1977 USA $1, p. 26.
15. *Ibid.*
16. Nedd Willard, Smoking—a man-made dragon, *World Health*, June 1979, p. 5.
17. *Ibid.*, pp. 5-7.
18. World Health Organization, September-October 1981, p. 7.
19. Norman Sartorius, Putting a higher value on health, *World Health*, June 1986, p. 2.

20. *Ibid.*, p. 7.
21. Gamini Seneviratne, Tomorrow's disaster area, World Health Organization, February-March 1980, p. 6.
22. W.F. Forbes and M.E. Thompson, The economics of tobacco, *World Health*, February-March 1980, p. 13.
23. Alastair Anderson, Slow-motion suicide, World Health, February-March 1980, p. 14.
24. *Ibid.*
25. WHO: Amanda Amos and Claire Chollat-Traquet, "Women and Tobacco", September 1995, p. 22.
26. A. August Burns, "Where Women Have No. Doctor", Published by Macmillan, 1997, p. 443.
27. Dr. Samlee Plianbangchang, Life Line, WHO: Volume 1, issue 2, Regional Office for South-East Asia, April-June 2004, pp. 13-14.
28. M.M. Arnaud, Women and Smoking, *World Health*, February-March 1980, p. 23.
29. WHO: Amanda Amos and Clare Chollat-Traquet, "Women and tobacco", September 1995, pp. 22-23.
30. M.M. Arnaud, Women and Smoking, *World Health*, February-March 1980, p. 25.
31. Jose C. Abcede, Change your lifestyle, *World Health*, February-March 1980, p. 32.
32. Daniel Horn, Why People Smoke, World Health, Behaviour and Health, December 1975, p. 31.
33. Alastair Anderson, Slow-motion suicide, *World Health*, Smoking or Health, February-March 1980, p. 17.
34. Dale C. Cameron and George M. Ling, Fool's Paradise, *World Health*, December 1975, USA $1, p. 21.
35. *Ibid.*, p. 23.
36. *Ibid.*, pp. 32-33.
37. Regional Health Forum, WHO South-East Asia Region, Vol. 3, Number 1, 1999, p. 35.
38. Mira B. Aghee, The Tobacco Tradition in India, *World Health*, January-February 1989, p. 23.
39. Nedd Willard, Smoking—a man-made dragon, *World Health*, June 1979, p. 5.
40. *Hindustan Times*, June 1, 2004.
41. Dr. Samlee Plianbangchang, Life Line, WHO: Volume 1, issue 2, April-June 2004, p. 2.
42. Curbing the epidemic: governments and the economics of tobacco control, Washington, DC, World Bank, 1999.
43. Henningfiedl, J.E., Slade, J., Tobacco-dependence medications: public health and regularity issues; *Food, Drug and Law Journal*, 1988, 53 (Suppl.):75-114.
44. Friend, K., Levy, D., Smoking treatment interventions and policies to promote their use: critical review. *Nicotine and Tobacco Research*, 2001, 3:299-310.
45. Policy recommendations for smoking cessation and treatment of tobacco dependence. Geneva, World Health Organization, 2003.
46. Price, L, Allen, M., Effective access to tobacco dependence treatment, New Zealand, Geneva, World Health Organization, 2003 (WHO/NMH/TFI/FTC/03.8).
47. The World Health Report, 2003, pp. 94-95.
48. WHO: Guidelines for controlling and monitoring the tobacco epidemic. WHO, Geneva, 1988: 1-27.
49. Regional Health Forum, WHO: South-East Asia Region, Vol. 3, Number 1, 1999, p. 39.

APPENDIX 2.1

Tobacco Increases the Poverty of Individuals and Families

Together, tobacco and poverty create a vicious circle. In most countries, tobacco use tends to be higher among the poor. Poor Families, in turn, spend a larger proportion of their income on tobacco. Money spent on tobacco cannot be spent on basic human needs such as food, shelter, education and health care. Tobacco can also worsen poverty among users and their families since tobacco users are at much higher risk of falling ill and dying prematurely of cancers, heart attacks, respiratory diseases or other tobacco-related diseases, depriving families of much-needed income and imposing additional costs for healthcare. And, although the tobacco industry provides jobs for thousands of people the vast majority employed in the tobacco sector earn very little, while the big tobacco companies reap enormous profits.

The poor and tobacco consumption:

- It is the poorer and the poorest who tend to smoke the most. Globally, 84% of smokers live in developing and transitional economy countries.[1]
- At the country level, tobacco consumption varies by socio-economic group. In many countries, at all levels of development and income, it is the poor who smoke the most and who bear most of the economic and disease burden of tobacco use.
- A study of smoking prevalence among men in Chennai (India) in 1997 shows that the highest rate is found among the illiterate population (64%). This prevalence decreases by number of years of schooling, and it decreases to about one-fifth (21%) among those with more than 12 years of schooling.[2]
- A study in the United Kingdom shows that only 10% of women and 12% of men in the highest socio-economic group are smokers while 35% of women and 40% of men in the lowest socio-economic group smoke.[3]

Diverting money tobacco

In many countries, especially in developing countries, the majority of people who use tobacco are poor and can ill-afford to spend scarce

---

1 Guindon, G.E. and Boisclair, D. Past, Current and Future Trends in Tobacco Use. HNP Discussion paper, Economics of Tobacco Control, Paper No. 6, February 2003.

2. Gajalakshmi, G.K. *et al.*, Global Patterns of Smoking and Smoking-Attributable Mortality. Tobacco Control in Developing Countries. Oxford University Press, 2000.

3. United Kingdom Department of Health. Smoking Kills: A white paper on tobacco. London: The Stationary Office. 1998. At web site: http:/ www.archive.official-documents.co.uk/document/cm41/4177/contents.htm.

household income on tobacco. Yet their addiction to nicotine drives them to spend money on tobacco, diverting critical resources that could otherwise be spent on vital necessities. In the case of the poorest, where a significant portion of their meager income is required to buy food, expenditures on tobacco may make the difference between an adequate diet and malnutrition.

- The poorest household in Bangladesh spend almost 10 times as much on tobacco as on education.[4] And at country level, over 10.5 million currently malnourished people could have an adequate diet if money spent on tobacco were spent on food instead.[5]
- Some street children and other homeless people in India spend more on tobacco than on food, education or savings.[6]
- Preliminary results from an ongoing study in three provinces of Viet Nam found that over the course of a year, smokers spent 3.6 times more on tobacco than on education; 2.5 times more for tobacco than clothes; and 1.9 times more for tobacco than for health care.[7]
- Among lower income households in Egypt, more than 10% of household expenditures went to cigarettes or other forms of tobacco.[8]
- In Morocco, in 1999, households spent nearly as much on tobacco as they did on education.[9]
- Poor, rural household in south-west China spend over 11% of their total expenditures on cigarettes.[10]

---

4. Efroymson, D. *et al.*, Hungry for Tobacco: An analysis of the economic impact of tobacco on the poor in Bangladesh. Tobacco Control 2001, 10:212-217.
5. *Ibid.*
6. Shah, S., Vaite, S. Choosing tobacco over food: daily struggles for existence among the street children of Mumbai, India, 2002; and PATH Canada and Shah, S., Vaite S. Pavement dwellers in Mumbai, India: Prioritizing tobacco over basic needs. In: Efroymson, D., ed. Tobacco and Poverty, Observations from India and Bangladesh, 2002.
7. "The Economics of Tobacco in Viet Nam: Tobacco Expenditures and their Opportunity Cost", (ongoing research project of PATH Canada, Viet Nam, funded by Research for International Tobacco Control (RITC)).
8. Nassar, H., The economics of tobacco in Egypt, A New Analysis of Demand. HNP Discussion Paper, Economics of Tobacco Control, Paper No. 8, March 2003.
9. Aloui, O., Analysis of the Economics of Tobacco in Morocco. HNP Discussion Paper. Economics of Tobacco Control, Paper No. 7, March 2003.
10. Hu T., Mao Z., Liu Y., Smoking, Standard of Living, and Poverty in China, International Development for Research Centre/Research Institute for Tobacco Control and the World Bank, forthcoming.

- In many countries, workers spend a significant portion of their salaries on tobacco. The following table shows the amount of time that workers in selected countries would have to work in order to pay for a pack of Marlboro or local brand cigarettes and the equivalent amount of time that it would take to buy bread or rice instead.[11]

Required Work Time to Buy Cigarette Pack *vs.* Bread or Rice (Selected Countries)

Country	*Marlboro*	*Local Brand*	*Bread (1 kg)*	*Rice (1 kg)*
Brazil (Rio de Janeiro)	22 min.	18 min.	52 min.	13 min.
Canada (Toronto)	21 min.	17 min.	10 min.	11 min.
Chile	38 min.	33 min.	19 min.	25 min.
China	62 min.	56 min.	103 min.	47 min.
Hungary	71 min.	54 min.	25 min.	42 min.
India	102 min.	77 min.	34 min.	79 min.
Kenya	158 min.	92 min.	64 min.	109 min.
Mexico	49 min.	40 min.	49 min.	25 min.
Poland	56 min.	40 min.	21 min.	23 min.
United Kingdom	40 min.	40 min.	6 min.	8 min.

Tobacco farming: a vicious circle of poverty and illness

Tobacco farming is extremely labour-intensive and requires expensive inputs such as fertilizers and pesticides. These products are often sold to the farmer by the tobacco industry at the start of the growing season, condemning him to a cycle of indebtedness. While the tobacco industry often boasts of the positive economic benefits of growing tobacco, it fails to mention that the overwhelming majority of the profits go to the large companies, while many tobacco farmers find themselves poor and in debt. In addition, there are many occupational hazards in the tobacco fields, from pesticide exposure to nicotine poisoning. And, while tobacco farming is not unique in its use of child labour, the particular hazards posed by tobacco cultivation place these children at increased risk of injury and illness.

- Children and adults working with tobacco often suffer from green tobacco sickness (GTS), which is caused by dermal absorption of nicotine from contact with tobacco leaves. Common symptoms include nausea, vomiting, weakness, headache and dizziness, and may also include abdominal

11. Guindon, G.E. *et al.*, Special Communication. Trends and affordability of cigarette prices: ample room for tax increased and related health gains. Tobacco Control, 2002, 11:35-43.

cramps and difficulty breathing, as well as fluctuations in blood pressure and heart rates.[12]

- In the United States of America, tobacco growers' share of each dollar spent on a pack of cigarettes dropped from US$ 0.07 in 1980 to US$ 0.02 in the late 1990s, while the companies' share rose from US$ 0.37 to US$ 0.49.[13] Meanwhile, 71% of all tobacco farmers have gross sales of less than US$ 20,000 per year and most work off-farm to supplement their income. In contrast, garbage collectors in the United States of America made an average of over US$ 29,000 in 1999.[14]
- According to a study in Brazil, tobacco requires 3000 hours of labour per hectare per year, while beans require only 298 hours and maize 265.[15]
- It would take the average tobacco farmer in Brazil around six years to earn the equivalent of what BAT's director earns in a single day, or 2140 years to earn his annual salary.[16]
- There is growing concern about the neuropsychiatry effects among tobacco workers of exposure to organophosphate pesticides, with preliminary studies indicating increased rates of depression and suicides in Brazil among tobacco farmers.[17]

---

12. Arcury, T.A. *et al.*, High levels of transdermal nicotine exposure produce green tobacco sickness in Latino farm workers. Nicotine and Tobacco Research, 2003, 5:315-321 and Ballard, T. *et al.*, Green tobacco sickness: occupational nicotine poisoning in tobacco workers. Archives of Environmental Health, 1995, 50:384-389.
13. Capehart, T. and Grise, V.N., USDA Economic Research Service. The Changing Tobacco User's Dollar. Tobacco Situation and Outlook, June 1992; Purcell, W., Who Gets the Tobacco Dollar? Tobacco Farming: Current Challenges and Future Alternatives, Southern Research Report #10, Academic Affairs Library, Centre for the Study of the American South, Spring 1998.
14. USDA Economic Research Service, Table B-1: Characteristics of Tobacco Farms, 1992. Tobacco: Situation and Outlook Report, April 1998 and U.S. Department of Labour. National Compensation.
15. Varshin, V.M. *et al.*, "fatores limitantes ao desnvolvimiento da agricultura familiar de subsistencia da Regiao Centro-sul do Parana", Iapar: Londrina, 1991, Cited in Angela Cordeiro, Francisco Marochi and Jose Maria Tardin, "A Poison Crop—Tobacco in Brazil," Pesticide Action Network Briefing Paper, June 1998.
16. Christian Aid/DESER, "Hooked on Tobacco Report, February 2002."
17. Salvi, Ron *et al.*, Neuropsychiatric evaluation in subjects chronically exposed to organophosphate pesticides. Toxicological Science, 2003, 73:267-271; and Jamal, G.A. *et al.*, A clinical neurological, neuropsychological, and neuropsychological study of sheep farmers and dippers exposed to organophosphate pesticides. Occupational and Environmental Medicine, 2002, 59:434-441; Christian Aid/ DESER. Hooked on Tobacco Report, February 2002.

APPENDIX 2.2

Tobacco Increases the Poverty of Countries

Tobacco not only impoverishes those who use it, it puts an enormous financial burden on countries. The costs of tobacco use at the national level encompass increased healthcare costs, lost productivity due to illness and early deaths, foreign exchange losses, and environmental damage. The tobacco industry's desperate attempts to stave off sensible regulation have included overstating the employment and trade benefits of tobacco to developing countries and raising the specter of massive job losses if governments move to protect public health. Yet according to the World Bank, these arguments and the data on which they are based greatly misrepresent the effects of tobacco control policies.

Increased healthcare costs and productivity losses

- Countries suffer huge economic losses due to high healthcare costs and lost productivity as a result of tobacco related illnesses and premature deaths. In high-income countries, the overall annual cost of healthcare attributed to tobacco use has been estimated at between 6% and 15% of total healthcare costs.[1]
- Between 1995 and 1999 in the United States of America, tobacco use accounted for 440,000 premature deaths annually and approximately US$ 157 billion in annual health-related economic losses: US$ 81.9 billion in mortality-related productivity losses and US$ 75.5 billion in excess medical expenditures.[2]
- In China, where tobacco use is increasing, one study from the mid-1990s estimated the direct and indirect health costs of smoking at US $ 6.5 billion per year.[3] In 1998, an estimated 514,100 people in China died prematurely from smoking-related illnesses, resting in a productivity loss of 1146 million persons years.[4]
- In Egypt, the direct annual cost of treating diseases caused by

1. Prabhat Jha, Chaloupka Fj., Curbing the epidemic: Governments and the economic of tobacco control. Washington, D.C., World Health, 1999.
2. Morbidity and Mortality Weekly Report Highlights, April 12, 2002, Vol. 51, No. 14.
3. Jin, S. *et al.* An Evaluation on Smoking-induced Health Costs in China (1988-89). Biomedical and Environmental Science, 1995, 8, 342-9.
4. Jiang, O, Jin, S. Social economic burden attributed to smoking in China, 1998. Paper presented at the National Conference on Policy Development of Tobacco Control in China in the 21st Century, Beiking, 29-31 May 2000; and Hu T.W. and Z. Mao., Effects of cigarette tax on cigarette consumption and the Chinese economy. Tobacco Control, 2002; 11: 105-08.

tobacco use is estimated at US$ 545.5 million.[5]

- If current trends persist, about 650 million people alive today will eventually be killed by tobacco,[6] half of them productive middle age, each losing 20 to 25 years of life.[7]

Falling prices and foreign exchange losses

- The massive increase in tobacco cultivation fuelled by the global expansion of the tobacco industry has resulted in worldwide oversupply of tobacco and a corresponding decline in prices. This trend accelerated between 1985 and decline, when the real price per tonne fell 37%.[8]
- Many countries are net importers of tobacco leaf and tobacco products, and lose millions of dollars each year in foreign exchange as a result. In 2002, two-thirds of 161 countries surveyed imported more tobacco leaf and tobacco products than they exported. There were 19 countries that had a negative balance of trade in tobacco products of over US$ 100 million or more, including Cambodia, Malaysia, Nigeria, the Republic of Korea, Romania, the Russian Federation and Viet Nam.[9]
- Only 17 out of 125 countries that export tobacco leaf derive more than 1% of their total export earnings from tobacco and in only five of those (the Central African Republic, Malawi, Uganda, the United Republic of Tanzania and Zimbabwe) do tobacco leaf exports account for more than 5% of total export earnings.[10]
- The only two countries worldwide that are significantly dependent on raw tobacco for their export earnings are: Malawi with 63% of export earnings and Zimbabwe, with 16%.[11]

Illicit trade

Over one quarter of exported cigarettes disappear into the illegal market. Cigarette smuggling reduces the average price that consumers pay for cigarettes thus increasing consumption. Worldwide, governments lose

---

5. Nassar, H. The economics of tobacco in Egypt, A New Analysis of Demand. HNP Discussion Paper, Economics of Tobacco Control Paper No. 8, March 2003.
6. Shaping the Future, The World Health Report, 2003.
7. Prabhat Jha, Chaloupka, Fj., Curbing the epidemic: Governments and the economics of tobacco control. Washington, D.C., World Bank, 1999.
8. Jacobs, R. *et al.*, The Supply-Side Effects of Tobacco Control Policies. In: Jha and Chaloupka eds., Tobacco Control in Developing Countries, Oxford University Press, 2000.
9. From FAO Database, http:/apps.fao.org.
10. Tobacco leaves export data from FAO statistical database (http:/apps.fao.org.) for 2002; Value of total exports by country for 2002, UNCTAD Handbook of Statistics 2003.
11. *Ibid.*

tens of billions of dollars in tax revenues every year from cigarette smuggling.[12] That the tobacco industry has been complicit in this illegal trade is suggested by recent court cases brought by Canada, the European Union and others, as well as the tobacco industry's own internal files.[13]

Employment[14]

- When people quit or smoke less, money previously spent on tobacco does not disappear-rather, it is spent on other goods and services, generating demand and new jobs across the economy.
- Countries that import substantial amounts of tobacco and cigarettes would especially benefit from falling cigarette consumption, since spending could switch to goods and service produced domestically. Bangladesh, for example, which imports nearly all of its cigarettes, would benefit tremendously if cigarette consumption fell.
- In all but a very few countries heavily dependent on tobacco farming, there would be No. net loss of jobs, and there might even be job gains, if global tobacco consumption fell. The net change in jobs would depend on whether the new patterns of spending were on goods and services produced in more or less labour-intensive ways than cigarettes.
- The manufacturing side of the tobacco industry is only a small source of jobs, as it is usually highly mechanized. In most countries tobacco manufacturing jobs account for well below 1% of total manufacturing employment. And, with the exception of a few heavily dependent countries, tobacco farming in most countries makes up a tiny proportion of employment in the agricultural sector:
    - o In China, the largest tobacco producer in the world, only about 3% of farmers grow any tobacco at all, and tobacco constitutes only about 1% of the value of all agricultural output.[15]
    - o In Brazil, another major producer, tobacco only accounts for about 1.9% of the total agricultural labour force and 0.44% of the total labour force.[16]

---

12. The Cigarette "Transit" Road to the Islamic Republic of Iran and Iraq: Illicit Tobacco Trade in the Middle East. Geneva, World Health Organization, 2003.
13. European Community *vs.* R.J. Reynolds, http:/www.yed.uscourts.gov/coi/02cv5771cmp.pdf
14 Prabhat Jha, Chaloupka Fj. Curbing the epidemic: Governments and the economics of tobacco control. Washington, D.C., World Bank, 1999.
15. Hu T. and Mao, Z. Tobacco Farming and Government Policies in China. World Bank Discussion Paper, Forthcoming.

- Current projections show that the number of smokers world wide will increase from the current 1.3 billion to more than 1.7 billion in 2025 (due in part to an increase in the global population) if the global prevalence of tobacco use (percentage of people who use tobacco) remains unchanged. Even assuming a decrease of overall prevalence at an annual rate of 1%, the number of consumers is expected to increase to 1.46 billion in 2025.[17] While future declines in consumption will clearly reduce the number of tobacco-related jobs, those jobs will be lost over decades, not overnight.

Myth and truth about tobacco employment

The tobacco industry constantly exaggerates both the number of people employed in tobacco framing and manufacturing, and the likely impact of reduced tobacco consumption on employment. The tobacco industry claims that it employs 33 million people, but this number includes farmers who grow other crops in addition to tobacco, seasonal labourers, family members and other part-time workers. The World Bank suggests that a more meaningful measure would be to use Full Time Equivalents (FTE), which would yield a number much smaller than the industry's estimates.[18]

It has also been estimated that job losses resulting from technology changes in the tobacco industry far outstrip any job losses that might result from tobacco control policies.[19]

Deforestation and other environmental damage

- Tobacco cultivation has contributed to an environmental crisis in a number of countries. In many developing countries wood is used as fuel to cure tobacco leaves and to construct curing barns. An estimated 20,000 hectares of forests and woodlands are cut down each year because of tobacco farming.[20]
- In the Southern Africa region as a whole, more than 1400 square kilometers of indigenous woodlands disappear annually to

16. Jacobs, R., *op. cit.* According to one report, Universal is conducting experiments with mechanized farming in Brazil, possibly reducing this number further (Jungbluth G. Double Whammy. Tobacco International, April 2000).
17. Guindon, G.E. and Boisclair, D., Past, Current and Future Trends in Tobacco Use. HNP Discussion Paper, Economics of Tobacco Control Paper No. 6, February 2003.
18. Campaign for Tobacco Free Kids, Barren Leaf, Golden Harvest: The Costs of Tobacco Farming, 2001.
19. Van Liemt G. The World tobacco industry: Trends and prospects. Geneva, International Labour Office, Working Paper 179, 2002.
20. Geist Hj. Global assessment of deforestation related to tobacco farming. Tobacco Control, 1999, 8:18-28.

supply fuel wood for tobacco curing, accounting for 12% of the overall annual deforestation in the region, excluding other tobacco-related uses of wood, like pole wood for constructing curing barns.[21]

- In 1995, the global tobacco industry produced an estimated 2.3 billion kilograms of manufacturing waste and 209 million kilograms of chemical wastes.[22] This does not include the enormous amount of litter caused by cigarette butts, most of which, contrary to popular belief, are not biodegradable. According to one estimate, 954 million kilograms worth of filters were produced in 1998, with many of them ending up littering the streets, waterways and parklands of countries.[23] This figure does not include cigarette packaging, lighters, matches and other waste by-products of tobacco use.

Can the damage be reversed?

The rates of deforestation due to tobacco growing and curing are high and a cause for concern. Reforestation programmes cosponsored and promoted by the tobacco industry are not enough to reverse the damage. One of the biggest tobacco companies says that in tobacco farming operations in Kenya, The company requires their contract farmers to plant 1,000 years eucalyptus trees on their lands for three consecutive years.[24] This would require 1.5 hectares, but the average Kenyan farmer has only between half and one hectare.[25] According to Samson Mwita Marwa, a tobacco farmer and former member of parliament from the Kuria district in Kenya, "BAT claims to be engaged in reforestation programmes. I have yet to see a single mature tree that BAT has planted in Kuria district. In any case, the rate of deforestation far too fast to be equal to the rate of reforestations.[26]

---

21. Geist Hj. How tobacco farming contributes to tropical deforestation. In: Abedian *et al.* eds., The Economics of Tobacco Control: Towards an Optimal Policy Mix. Cape Town, Applied Fiscal Research Centre, 1998.
22. Novotny, T.E., Zhao, F., Consumption and Production Waste: Another Externality of Tobacco Use, Tobacco Control, 1999, 8:75-80.
23. Register, K. Cigarette Butts as Litter: Toxic as well as Ugly. Underwater Naturalist: Bulletin of the American Littoral Society, Volume 25, Number 2, August 2000.
24. Simon Chapman, Tobacco and Deforestation in the Developing World, Tobacco Control, 1994; 3: 191-3.
25. Currie, K., Ray, L., Contract farmers: a case study from rural Kenya. Development Research Digest, 1983, Winter, 10, *op. cit.*, In Simon Chapman's Tobacco and Deforestation in the Developing World.
26. Testimony submitted on 17 August 2000 before the WHO public hearing on the FCTC: http://www3.who.int/whosis/fctc/Submissions/F6360629.pdf.

In the end. Where do profits go?

In 2002, Japan Tobacco, Philip Morris/Altria and BAT, the world's three largest tobacco multinationals, had combined tobacco revenues of more than US$ 212 billion. This sum is greater than the total combined GDP of Albania, Bahrain, Belize, Bolivia, Botswana, Cambodia, Cameroon, Estonia, Georgia, Ghana, Honduras, Jamaica, Jordan, Macedonia, Malawi, Malta, Moldova, Mongolia, Namibia, Nepal, Paraguay, Senegal, Tajikistan, Togo, Uganda, Zambia and Zimbabwe.[27]

27. Philip Morris/Altria, BAT and Japan Tobacco, 2002, Annual Reports, World Bank, World Development Indicators, July 2003.

Source: WHO 2004, Tobacco and Poverty: A Vicious Circle.

CHAPTER 3

DRUGS ABUSE

Young people may be given opportunities to demonstrate their creativity, energy and commitment to solving their own problems and helping to build a healthy future for the entire community in which they live.

—*Hiroshi Nakajima*

3

CHAPTER

Drugs Abuse

Substance abuse is a health issue:
We need to educate communities, particularly the young, on how to cope in a society where drugs proliferate. This is only possible if political leaders, law-makers and society at large recognize the many dimensions of the drug problem and all work together to support the response of health professionals.

—*Hiroshi Nakajima*

HISTORICAL CONTEXT OF DRUG USE IN INDIA

Heroin in Asia[1]

Asia has a history of opium production and oral consumption: Opium has been produced throughout South and Central Southeast Asia for centuries. The extracted opium from the opium poppies was fundamentally administered by smoking or inhaling and also ingested by mouth.

"Smoking or inhaling of drugs does not carry a direct risk of HIV transmission."

The changes in the production and distribution patterns have exposed new populations to opiate use, and led to the introduction of injecting drug use (drug to the availability of a high grade of heroin).

Geographically, India lies between two major areas producing opium for illegal markets:

- The South East Asian region of Thailand, Myanmar and Laos in Southeast Asia (Myanmar accounts for 70 percent of the estimated world opium poppy cultivation). The heroin produced in this region is commonly called 'Number 4' and is very pure. It is commonly injected, but it can be inhaled as well.

- The South West Asian region of Pakistan, Afghanistan, Iran and Turkey, possess the largest poppy crop in the region. The heroin from this area is commonly called 'smack' (brown sugar). It is not very pure and is most commonly inhaled, though it can also be injected.
- India is the largest producer of opium for medicinal use; some of this finds its way to the illicit drug trade, because of the potential price difference between government procurement price and the black market price. Conversion of opium to Brown Sugar is a viable and lucrative option for many, especially because it can be made quite simply.
- Asia is witnessing a major epidemic of amphetamine use, with a small percentage of amphetamine users reverting to injecting.

Different uses of Drug use in India

These substances (e.g. opium and cannabis) were used for:

Medical Purposes

"India has a vast repertoire of home remedies and folk medicine practices, which use opium and cannabis extensively. Traditional systems of medicine such as Ayurveda, Siddha, Unani or Tibbi, also use opium in the form of paste applied for headaches, toothaches, inflammation and swollen joints. Suppositories of opium were used for disorders of the pelvic region; it reduced sensibility during the advanced stages of smallpox, and prevented relapse of malaria fever and controlled diabetes."

Religion Use

Cannabis was consumed in Hindu and Sikh temples and at Mohammedan shrines; among fakirs, bhang is viewed as the giver of long life and a means of communion with divine spirit. The Prophet Mohammed (AD 570-632) did not explicitly prohibit the use of cannabis, but alcohol was not permitted; among the high caste Hindus, alcohol was prohibited, but cannabis use for festivals and ceremonies was sanctioned.

Social and Functional Uses

Various psychoactive substances were used in important social functions. The Rajputs used opium for marriage, for sealing an important business deal, to facilitate catharsis after the death of an immediate family member, for longevity and for enhancing sexual pleasure. They also used opium before engaging in battle and for sealing peace treaties.

> "Historical information indicates that on certain occasions, cultural sanction was given to drug use in different parts of the country. This persists even to this day and can be seen in Orissa, Gujarat, Karnataka, Rajasthan and Himachal Pradesh."

Injecting Drug use in India

Injecting drug use has been increasing in India since the mid-late 1980s. This increase was identified in Manipur between 1988-89, in Delhi in 1991 (Sharan Report) and Chennai (earlier Madras) in 1987 (Kumar).

The specific factors causing the diffusion of injecting drug use, however, vary from place to place. Three factors, which interact that lead to the diffusion of injecting drug use are:

- The drug supply, which is available in the area (e.g. type, quality, quantity, price and availability).
- Law enforcement activity (such as that arising from the NDSP Act, 1985 and amended in 1988 legislation).
- Characteristics of the drug users (especially their socio-economic status and rising physical tolerance[2].

DRUG DE-ADDICTION PROGRAMME

The basic role of the Ministry of Health and Family Welfare in the area of drug de-addiction is demand reduction by way of providing treatment services including preventive health and after care. The Drug De-addiction Programme of the Ministry was started in 1987-88 with the establishment of 6 De-addiction Centres in Central Institutions viz. AIIMS, New Delhi, Dr. RML Hospital, New Delhi, JIPMER, Pondicherry, PGI, Chandigarh and NIMHANS, Bangalore.

A scheme under central sector assistance to states during 1992-93 was introduced for providing an assistance of Rs. 8.00 lakhs (one time grant) to States/UT Governments towards construction of building for establishing Drug De-addiction Centres in identified Medical Colleges and District Level Hospitals. One of the essential requirements of the Scheme is that the State Government shall provide necessary land and also meet the recurring expenses towards staff, medical care, diet, maintenance, etc. The scheme, in addition to above mentioned grant, also provides grant of Rs. 2.00 lakhs (recurring grant) per annum to the Centres in North-Eastern States to meet the cost of medicines, linen, diet, etc.

Construction of New Building for Drug De-addiction Centres

A Drug De-addiction Centre under AIIMS is being established at CGO Complex, Ghaziabad (UP) at an estimated cost of Rs. 11.28 crores of which the capital cost is Rs. 9.9 crores. The present Drug De-addiction Centre, AIIMS will be shifted there after completion of construction. The construction work is in progress and is expected to be completed by March 2003. The OPD block of the Centre is scheduled to be started by the end of the current year.

A proposal for a new building for a 20-bedded Drug De-addiction Centre at Post Graduate Institute of Medical Education and Research (PGIMER), Chandigarh has been approved at a cost of Rs. 77 lakhs out of

CHART 3.1

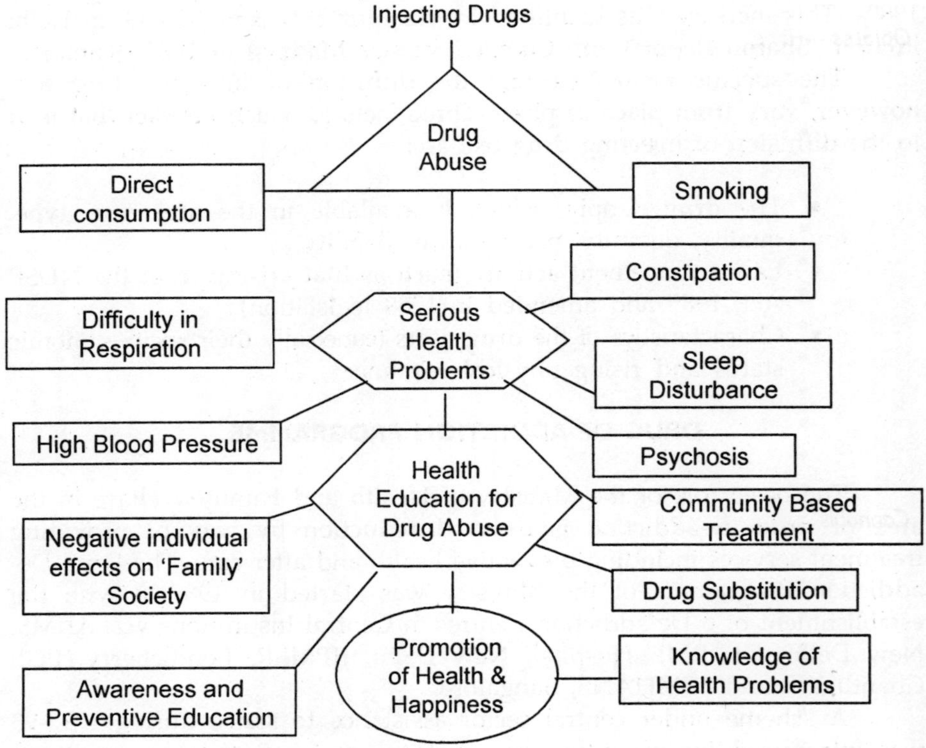

which a grant-in-aid of Rs. 45 lakhs has been released and a provision of Rs. 20.00 is available under BE 2002-03, provision for remaining amount Rs. 12.00 lakh has been proposed under Budget proposal for BE 2003-04.

The Standing Finance Committees (SFC) had approved the project for the development of an independent Drug De-addiction Centre in the premises of the NIMHANS Banglore at a total cost of Rs. 5.10 crores (Rs. 3.94 crores (Recurring) and Rs. 1.15,80 crores (Non-recurring). The period to complete the project is 5 years.

Evaluation

Under the Drug-De-addiction Programme, so far 114 Drug De-addiction Centres have been established in various States. On the request of the Ministry, WHO has provided funds for the evaluation of centres. Evaluation of the Centres is to be done (a) to assess the status of functioning of Government De-addiction centres by assessing the patient load, (b) treatment being provided, (c) availability and utilization of equipment, (d) staffing in terms of posts available and filled, (e) on-site interview, and (f) review of records of de-addiction centres. The evaluation has already started and the states of Manipur, Nagaland and Rajasthan have been covered so far by the evaluation teams of AIIMS.[3]

Dangers of Drug Abuse

Opiates—(Drugs from Opium Poppy) can cause

- Difficulty in respiration;
- Constipation;
- Loss of appetite;
- Heroin use nephropathy;
- Loss of libido;
- Impotence and sterility;
- Sleep disturbance;
- Psychiatric problems;
- Diseases associated with injecting practices;
- Diseases associated with inhaling;
- Reduction in heart rate and blood pressure; and
- Loss in immediate or short-term and long-term memory.

Cannabis

- Psychosis;
- Constipation;
- Respiratory ailments;
- Decrease in sperm count;
- Loss of memory; and
- Increase in heart rate.

Stimulants (Cocaine and Amphetamines)

- Increase blood pressure;
- Generalized fits;
- Cocaine if snorted can cause infections in the nose. The brain is an inhibitory organ. After taking any mood-altering drug the inhibitory control decreases and high-risk behaviour becomes a probability; and
- Unsafe sex is an example of high-risk behaviour, which leads to genito urinary disease (GDU) and STIs.[4]

Extent of the Problems

The magnitude and dynamics of drug abuse at the national level have not been well researched in India. This deficiency of data is contributed by the lack of resources on the one hand, and the sheer vastness of the country on the other. Cognizant of this fact and in line with its mandate, the Ministry of Social Justice and Empowerment, Government of India, and the United Office on Drugs and Crime, Regional Office for South Asia (UNODC, ROSA), jointly launched an initiative in the area of drug abuse prevention. A major outcome of this is the national report titled

'The Extent, Pattern and Trends of Drug Abuse in India—National Survey'.[5]

Much of the information on abuse of drugs in India is anecdotal and the available reports are from small-scale surveys carried out in isolated areas of the country. Rational response and national programme planning require accurate data through painstaking research from many parts of the nation. In 1999, the Ministry of Social Justice and Empowerment, Government of India, and the United Nations International Drug Control Programme, Regional Office for South Asia, decided to undertake a large-scale national survey to obtain information on extent, pattern and magnitude of drug abuse in the country. For this purpose multiple indicators and several methods to assess the situation were chosen.

The major components of this survey are National Household Survey (NHS), Drug Abuse Monitoring System (DAMS) and Rapid Assessment Survey (RAS). Additionally, focussed studies on special populations like women, rural subjects, people living in border towns and prison population have also been carried out. Finally, burden as perceived by women due to drug abuse in the family has also been enquired into.[6]

Highlights of Common Data Parameters

The data from the NHS and DAMS reflects information on the nation as a whole, while data from the remaining studies provides information on specialized sub-groups of the population and thus applies only to the population studied. Furthermore, while the data from the NHS reflects the general population, the DAMS component reflects the population seeking treatment in the organized sector and the RAS component mainly represents a street population sample. Nonetheless, there were certain common data parameters in the three major components (NHS, DAMS and RAS) and the five focussed thematic studies.

The highlights of the data on common parameters and indicators of drug abuse across various components of the project are as follows:

- Alcohol, cannabis and opiates were the commonest drugs of abuse except in the RAS where the proportion of opiate users was higher.
- Between 22 and 66 percent were poly-drug users.
- The subjects were largely male (91-100%) except the studies focusing on drug abuse among women.
- Most were in their early thirties; drug users in the NHS were older (37.9 years) and younger in the RAS (29.8 years).
- Between 51 and 76 per cent were rural subjects except for the sample in the RAS who were all from an urban background. In the Focussed Thematic Study on rural subjects all respondents were, by definition, rural.
- Between 11 and 49 per cent were unmarried.
- Between 16 and 49 percent were illiterate.

- Between 3 and 27 percent were students.
- Between 20 and 49 percent had a positive family history of drug abuse.
- The proportion of IDUs varied between 0.1 (NHS) and 43 percent (RAS).
- Buprenorphine, propoxyphene and heroin were commonly injected drugs.
- Sharing needles among IDUs was common and on average with three partners per person.
- Sex with commercial sex workers varied between 4 and 24 percent.
- Unprotected sex practices with partners other than the spouse were quite common.
- Several health hazards like weakness, cough, loss of body weight, chest infection, fever and tuberculosis were common across studies.
- Depression and anxiety were the most commonly reported psychological symptoms.
- Between 6 and 49 per cent reported drug-related arrests.
- Between 24 and 66 per cent reported drug-related violence.
- Most had not sought treatment and very few were currently undergoing treatment.
- Most drug users were earning on average about Rs. 3,000 per month.

The following important themes were evident from the survey.

Major Drugs of Abuse

The survey demonstrates that alcohol, cannabis, opium and heroin are the major drugs of abuse in the country. However, there is a difference between their relative importance, as reflected in the survey on the community (NHS) as compared with treatment seekers (DAMS).

The current prevalence rates (i.e., subjects who had used within the last one month) according to the NHS are as follows:

• Alcohol	21.4%
• Cannabis	03.0%
• Opiates	00.7%
• Any illicit drug	03.6%

Applying prevalence estimates to the population figures in 2001, based on population growth, it can be projected that in that year there were about 62.5 million alcohol users, abut 8.7 million cannabis users and about 2 million opiate users in the country. Not all of the current users were dependent users. Between 17 and 26 per cent of current users can be classified dependent users according to the WHO definition (ICD—10, see

WHO 1992). Injecting drug use (IDU) was reported (ever) by 0.1 percent of the population. Among opiate users, opium use (0.5%) was most frequently reported followed by heroin (0.2%) and other opiates (0.2%). About 0.1 percent reported had use tranquilizers (ever).

It appears that the abuse prevalence of various drugs is uneven in the country. A high level of alcohol abuse was reported from the North-East and Northern regions, high cannabis use from North-East and Eastern regions and high opiate use in North East, North and Western regions. No. meaningful relationship could be established between high drug use and the socio-economic indicators of any given state.

Data from treatment centres (DAMS) revealed that the primary drug of abuse among these subjects was: alcohol (43.9%), followed by opiates (26.0%) of which heroin was 11.1%, opium was 8.6%, other opiates were 3.7% and propoxyphene 2.6%, cannabis (11.6%), stimulants (1.8%) and others (16.7%). A few subjects reported abuse of minor tranquilizers, sedatives, barbiturates, amphetamines, inhalants and hallucinogens. Many were poly-drug users.

Drug Abuse among Women

Among drug users interviewed in the 14 urban sites of the RAS, around 8 percent were women. The numbers varied across sites. The data from the FTS on drug abuse among women showed that opiates (heroin and propoxyphene), alcohol and minor tranquilizers were the main drugs of abuse. Thirty of the 75 women drug users interviewed were IDUs. Most had been introduced to drugs at an early age (under 20 years). Another FTS reported that the burden on women due to drug abuse by their family members was significant.

Drug Abuse among Adolescents and the Youth

This survey demonstrates that drug abuse among the youth is common. Most get introduced to drugs at an early age and some continue to sue them. One major concern is the tendency of some young respondents in states like Mizoram and Manipur to inject propoxyphene. Besides being featuring in the regular treatment centres (both government and NGO), young drug users were also noted at youth organizations. Here too, some were IDUs, were sexually active, and engaging in high-risk behaviour.

Drug Abuse among the Elderly Population

The available data on drug abuse by the elderly population, though inadequate, suggests mainly the abuse of alcohol, cannabis and opium. Only a small minority (2-5%) had reported for any treatment.

Injecting Drug Use

In the NHS component, a total of 52 subjects (0.1 percent of sample population) were identified as IDUs ('had ever used'). In the DAMS component (in treatment centres), about 14 percent were IDUs ('had ever used'). In the RAS component, about 43 percent of the total sample reported IDU ('had ever used'). Common drugs of abuse by means of injecting were propoxyphene and heroin. It was observed that several high-risk behaviours like unsafe sex and sex with CSWs were associated, with injecting drug use. The sharing of needles and non-sterile equipment was extremely common in the sample studied in NHS and RAS where it varied between 58 and 97 percent.

Drug Abuse in Rural India

Information on drug abuse among the rural population in India is available from treatment centres (DAMS—rural subjects) and the special study on rural subjects (FTS). Additionally, in the NHS component, about 77 percent of the subjects interviewed were from a rural background. All three studies showed that alcohol, cannabis and opiates were the major drugs of abuse. Among opiates, the abuse of opium was more often reported. The abuse of heroin and IDU was also reported to some extent in rural India.

Drug Abuse in Border Areas

This FTS confirms a popular perception that drugs are easily available in border towns where drug abuse is marked among the local population. In these sites common drugs of abuse reported were popply husk, opium, heroin and some psychotropic substances. Most of the respondents and the key informants believed that there was a strong correlation between the availability of various drugs and the often-high level of consumption.

Treatment Seeking

Among the subjects in the DAMS component, only a minority (about 27%) reported that they had undergone treatment for drug use in the past, even though their drug habit may have existed for some years. The drug-using subjects interviewed in the NHS component reported that between 2 and 19 percent had ever taken treatment for drug dependence or associated disorders. In the RAS component too, it was observed that only a minority had ever sought treatment. The findings of the various Focussed Thematic Studies led to a similar conclusion. As a whole, only a relatively small proportion (ranging between 2-33%, depending on the survey component) had reported ever taking treatment for drug abuse. The qualitative findings of the survey demonstrate that available treatment facilities are deemed inadequate. Many users themselves appeared unaware of the treatment facilities available in their localities. Many felt that most treatment centres were understaffed, received poor funding and the skills of the service providers were low. Respondents were concerned that treatment was not free and many considered treatments cost unaffordable.

Areas of Concern

The survey notes several areas of concern, including: the practice of IDU, associated multiple high-risk behaviours, long duration of drug use, drug abuse in the rural setting, IDU among rural subjects, and finally, a significant time lag between the onset of drug dependence and subsequent treatment seeking. It was noted that overall enrolment in the treatment centres is low and the workload of many established centres appears insufficient. The report makes various recommendations regarding the need to augment treatment services.[7]

Impact of Drug Abuse

The sample (women interviewed) reported several hazards on self and the family due to drug use by their family members. These could be broadly categorized as health, economic, occupational and psychosocial problems (impact) and are listed in Table 3.1). Several health, psychological, occupational and economic problems were reported. The money spent on treatment was an additional burden for which loans had to be taken and sometimes savings were spent for day-to-day running of the household. It was also reported that a substantial number of drugs using family members were spending significant amount of their income to support drug consumption. The family environment and the relationship with the affected members were also disturbed. Neglect of children and violence was also quite common.

The subjects were asked to quantify the degree of burden (overall) on a continuum scale from 0 to 100, where 0 represented No. burden felt and 100 was the maximum possible burden. Overall, the composite burden score of 75 was reported by 64 percent.

Scheme for Prevention of Alcoholism and Substances (Drugs) Abuse

The Government believes in addressing the problem of substance abuse in its totality. This includes creating awareness, early identification, treatment and rehabilitation and sustained follow-up care. Further, the Government is of the view that substance abuse is a psychosocial medical problem which can be best addressed through community-based interventions. Hence, special emphasis has been given for involving and mobilizing the community.

Under the *Scheme for Prevention of Alcoholism and Substance (Drugs) Abuse,* implemented by the Ministry of Social Justice and Empowerment, the non-governmental organizations have been entrusted with the responsibility for delivery of services and the Ministry bears substantial financial responsibility (90% of the prescribed grant amount).

The Aims and Objectives of the Scheme for Prevention of Alcoholism and Substance Abuse are:

- To support activities of non-governmental organizations, working in the areas of prevention of addiction and rehabilitation addicts.

TABLE 3.1

Impact of Drug Use on the Subjects (% Distribution*) N=179

Items	%
Health Problems	
Aches and pain	26.5
Weight loss	29.6
Psychological Problems	
Depression	43.0
Anxiety	54.7
Sleeplessness	46.9
Neglect of self	22.9
Occupational Problems	
Neglect of work	20.1
Neglect of household work	34.6
Absence from work	22.3
Economic Problems	
Loss of income	39.7
Debts	15.6
Less money available at home	42.5
Family Environment	
Disruption of family routine	43.6
Disturbance of family celebrations	49.2
Reduced leisure time activity	51.4
Violence	
Physical	42.5
Verbal	49.7

* Since each subject could provide more than one response, the total is more than 100%.

Source: Focussed Thematic Study: Burden on Women due to Drug Abuse by Family Members.

- To create awareness and educating the people about the ill effects of alcoholism and substance abuse on the individual, the family and society at large.
- To develop culture-specific models for the prevention of addiction and treatment and rehabilitation of addicts.
- To evolve and provide a whole range of community-based services for the identification motivation, detoxification, counselling, after care and rehabilitation of addicts.
- To promote community participation and public cooperation in the reduction of demand for dependence-producing substances.
- To promote collective initiatives and self-help endeavours among individuals and groups vulnerable to addiction and considered at risk.
- To establish appropriate linkages between voluntary agencies working in the field of addiction and government organizations.

The following legal entities ***are eligible for assistance*** under the Scheme:

- A society registered under the Societies' Registration Act, 1860 (XXI of 1860) or any relevant Act of the State Governments/ Union Territory or under any State law relating to registration of charitable societies.
- A registered public Trust.
- A Company established under Section 25 of the Companies Act, 1956.
- An organization/institution fully funded or managed by Government or a local body.
- An organization or institution, which has been approved by the Ministry of Social Justice and Empowerment.

The Scheme has the ***following components for financial support:***

- Awareness and Preventive Education;
- Drug Awareness and Counselling Centres;
- Treatment-*cum*-Rehabilitation Centres;
- Workplace Prevention Programmes;
- De-addiction Camps;
- NGO Forum of Drug Abuse Prevention;
- Innovative Interventions to Strengthen Community Based Rehabilitation;
- Technical Exchange and Manpower Development;
- Surveys, Studies, Evaluation and Research;
- Any other activity considered suitable to meet the objectives of the Scheme.[8]

RESPONSE TO DRUG USE AND HIV EPIDEMIC

Prevention through Education and Awareness

It is important to know the client before developing any IEC material for distribution. Prevention messages should be based on an understanding of the living conditions of the people. In order to ensure that messages on drug use, HIV/AIDS and STD prevention are effective, a communication plan should be developed. It should include the following:

- Defining the problem (situation analysis);
- Setting the objectives;
- Identifying the target audience;
- Developing key messages;
- Pre-testing messages/materials;
- Producing and disseminating; and
- Implementing the programme.

State of Behaviour Change in an Individual

States of Change

First Phase

- Target people who are not aware of the problem.
- Suitable IEC is given and the target people become aware of the problem.
- They are now concerned that their behaviour places them at risk.

Second Phase

- They acquire knowledge about the problem.
- They are motivated to act through a perception of risks and benefits that might accrue if they adopt changes in behaviour.

Third Phase

- They are ready for action through skills acquired to enable change.
- They try new behaviour.
- They assess the efficacy of changing behaviour and, if successful the behaviour changes are sustained.

Strategies for Developing an Appropriate Awareness Programme

- Give required factual information.
- Messages should not induce fear.
- Avoid stigmatizing of any target group.
- IEC material should draw upon local customs and social practices.
- Services of former drug users should be utilized for disseminating information.
- Integrate HIV-related information in a simple and understandable manner.

The Education Packages should deal with the following issues:

- HIV/AIDS.
- Drug use and addiction.
- Sexual health, safer sexual practices and safe injecting practices.
- Highlighting treatment available in the area.
- Accessibility of the programme by street dwelling population.

The Public Health Model of prevention, which may be used to limit the dangerous consequences of drug use and HIV due to drug use.

The Public Health Model

Prevention level	*Description*	*Activities*	*Indicator*
Primary	Health promotion	Lifestyle change IEC production. Prevent activities.	Drug free lifestyle. Evidence of alternative gainful activity.
	Specific protection	Maintenance therapy/ drug substitution. Needle exchange. Condom distribution.	Behaviour modification through objectively verifiable methods or surrogates. Reduction in abscesses. Reduction in HIV/STD transmission.
Secondary	Early Diagnosis and Treatment	Improved surveillance. Capacity building in BCC. Skills in diagnosis and management of HIV cases (e.g. abscess management, opportunistic infections), Drug Overdose, STD, Detoxification, Substitution therapy.	Increased case coverage. Behaviour change. Decreased morbidity. Reduction in mortality. Better case management. Increased evidence of health seeking behaviour. Increase in voluntary testing.
	Disability	Continuum of care process. Home based care. Palliative Care Services/ Hospice.	Increased utilization of referral services. Improved care quality.
Tertiary	Rehabilitation	Psychological. Social reintegration. Programmes for widows, orphans and spouses of HIV/ AIDS infected.	Increase in numbers accepting drug free state/reduced drug use/(Recoveries). Increase in numbers opting for income generation/gainful employment/peer educator schemes. Evidence of non-discrimination. Evidence of social/employment/educational support.

Source: Ministry of Social Justice and Empowerment, GOI, New Delhi.

Intervention

An intervention must clearly define its aims and objectives on the basis of assessment of felt needs, real needs, willingness of the people to take part and resource available (persons, skills, materials,). In the contest of targeting HIV infection in drug using populations, strategies should focus on ways to prevent and reduce the incidence of HIV infection among drug using populations, particularly injecting drug-users.

Reducing the Number of Injecting Drug Users in the Populations

The size of drug using population (particularly injecting drug users) can be reduced in the following ways:

- Effective campaigns that reduce the number of people who use drugs.
- Reduce the IDU group by preventing the transition to injecting from non-injecting drug use.
- Targeting new injectors.
- Targeting intermittent injectors.
- Providing substitution and maintenance therapy.

These prevention strategies require the presence of drug treatment services, effective IEC and community outreach measures.

Reducing Transmission among Injecting Drug Users

- Drug substitution.
- Promote sterile injecting equipment.
- Providing cleaning agents and information on how and where to dispose.
- Equipment is not available (2 x 2 x 2, bleach and water cleaning).
- Condom provisions and related counselling.
- STD treatment.

Reducing Transmission from Injecting Drug Users to their Partners and the General Population

HIV epidemic among injecting drug users can be prevented, stop and even reverse by implementing programmes that:

- Provide IDUs with information on ways to prevent, stop and even reverse by infection.
- Deliver outreach services to IDUs in their own community.
- Ensure ready access to sterile injecting equipment through needle and syringe programmes and pharmacy sales.
- Encourage condom use among IDUs and ensure condoms are readily available.

- Involve IDUs in the planning and implementation of all HIV prevention activities.
- Drug Substitution.
- Promote the adoption of policies and legislation to—
  - o Create a supportive environment for implementing HIV prevention programmes.
  - o Decrease the marginalization of, and discrimination against, IDUs.

This will require quality service delivery and testing facilities along with focused IEC campaigns attuned to gender and sero-status of target groups.[9]

The concept of comprehensive HIV/AIDS care includes the following:

- Voluntary counselling and testing (VCT) facilitates an entry point in the continuum of comprehensive care. Establishing a site where, in privacy, people can come to learn and accept their HIV sero-status allows access to effective care and prevention interventions.
- Clinical management of symptomatic infection with early and appropriate diagnosis and rational treatment, nutritional support, discharge planning and referral to other service providers.
- Nursing care to relieve the physical discomfort of illness, hygiene and infection control promotion, palliative and terminal care, training of family members in home care and preventive education and condom promotion.
- Pre- and post-test counselling to help individuals make informed decisions on HIV testing. This should also include a supportive and accepting environment in which coping, behaviour change and positive living are promoted and should continue with follow-up counselling for the patient and others so identified.
- Care at home and in the community, including the training of relatives and volunteers in the provision of care, treatment of common symptoms and palliative care. Promotive of good nutrition, psychological and emotional support, spiritual support and counselling.
- Formation of community support groups to provide emotional support to PLWHAs and their care providers. Opportunities for developing income-generating projects could be explored in these groups.
- Eliminating the stigma of HIV/AIDS and developing attitudes in the community towards persons and families living with HIV/AIDS. This includes healthcare workers in both private and public health institutions.

- Social support or referral to appropriate social welfare services to meet the needs for housing, employment, legal support, and to monitor and prevent discrimination.
- Partnership-building between various providers (clinical, social, support groups) in order to be accessible through mutual referrals.[10]

The sheer numbers of people involved—particularly young people—give cause for concern. There is No. vaccine we can give to our children to protect them, and there are No. easy answers. Effective prevention requires action by the entire, including the youngsters.[11]

Kofi A. Annan, Secretary General, United Nations in his message on International Day Against Drug Abuse and Illicit Trafficking, June 26, 2004 remarked that:

One of the most damaging misconceptions about drug use is that it is a permanent problem. The truth is that treatment for drug abuse can work year's International Day against Drug Abuse and Illicit Trafficking, "Drugs: Treatment Works", aims to correct this misconception and convey the facts about drug abuse treatment, based on the latest and most reliable evidence and research.

Millions of people worldwide have been directly affected by drug problems—those who are dependent, as well as their families. Their lives have been disrupted, their health undermined, their education interrupted, their jobs lost, their families broken. People with drug-related problems and their families and friends, need to know that there is a way out, and that effective help is available in different forms, depending on the needs and situation of each individual.

Today we have a better understanding of the mechanism of dependence. We know that dependence is a chronic and, in many cases, relapsing disorder. We know that, like many other chronic disorders, there are effective interventions that can help those affected to adopt productive lifestyles, avoid and reduce physical and mental health problems, improve family relationships, regain and retain child custody, and find better housing and employment opportunities. We also know that drug abuse treatment helps communities, by reducing criminality and the risks of transmission of blood-borne infectious diseases, particularly HIV/AIDS, and by allowing them to benefit from the contributions of healthier, more productive and better integrated individuals and families.

Policy-makers need to bear in mind that treatment is a cost-effective way to tackle not only the health and social consequences of drug abuse, but also reduce the associated costs of medical care, social welfare and criminal justice interventions. The United Nations Office on Drugs and Crime has a variety of tools available at www.unodc.org to help clarify the facts about drug-abuse treatment.

On this International Day against Drug Abuse, I call on everyone to examine and take into account the strong evidence about drug-abuse treatment and its effectiveness. When treatment works, it benefits us all.

A.P.J. Abdul Kalam, H.E. President of India in his message on International Day against Drug Abuse and Illicit Trafficking, June 26, 2004 observed that:

Drug abuse adversely affects our national life, drawing the youth into crime and making them vulnerable to diseases including AIDS.

It is the responsibility of not only the government but every citizen to address this social issue. We must all work together to prevent initiation of new users and try to ensure that those who experiment with drugs do not become dependent on them. Recognizing the treatment works, dependent user must be brought into counselling, detoxification and rehabilitation programmes so that they can be helped to become socially responsible and productive members of our society, 21 per cent men are alcoholics, say UN study:

The report jointly prepared by the United Nations Office on Drugs and Crime and the Ministry of Social Justice and Empowerment has estimated that in the age group of 12 to 60 years, 21 per cent of males (62.5 million) are alcoholics, 3 per cent (8.7 million) take cannabis and 0.7 per cent of them, estimated to around 2 millions, are opium addicts.

The report indicated alarming trends of alcoholism, opium, and cannabis use among children, women, and youth in urban and rural areas.

The Indian economy will have to pay a heavy cost amounting to billions of dollars, besides social costs in near future if the government and the corporate sector fail to check the increasing use of drugs among the workers and youth.

Since India lacks any comprehensive policy to check growing drug abuse, the country may have to face fall in industrial and agricultural productivity like some of the African and some Latin American countries. The spread of AIDS in the country has already assumed alarming proportions.

"The Extent, Pattern and Trends of Drug Abuse in India" on the eve of the International Day against drug abuse and illicit trafficking, is falling today.[12]

Administration of abuse of Drugs in India

Meira Kumar, Minister of Social Justice and Empowerment, Government of India in his message on International Day against Drug Abuse and Illicit Trafficking, June 26, 2004 observed that:

The Ministry of Social Justice and Empowerment is the nodal Ministry for dealing with issues relating to substance abuse prevention. We support the efforts of Governments and voluntary organizations towards informing and educating the public about the menace of drug abuse. Many committed social activists and institutions are making a meaningful contribution in weaning away people from usage of addictive substances and alcohol and providing rehabilitation services.

Strategy of the Ministry of Social Justice and Empowerment to Prevent Drug Abuse

- Building awareness and educating people about ill effects of drug abuse;
- Dealing with the addicts through a programme of psycho-social interventions, follow-up and socio-economic integration of recovering addicts;
- Imparting drug abuse prevention and rehabilitation training to the volunteers with a view to build up an educated cadre of service providers;
- There are about 8.7 million cannabis users and 2 million opiate users; and
- Victims come from diverse socio-economic, cultural, religious and linguistic backgrounds.

Services Available for the Treatment for Drug Addicts

- Scheme for Prevention of Alcoholism and Substance (Drugs) Abuse prevention, treatment and rehabilitation services for the addicts through NGOs.
- Around 450 De-addiction Centres and Counselling Centres working all over the country.
- Around 15 Workplace Prevention Programmes have been set-up in the industries and enterprises.
- ARMADA (Association of Resource Manager Against Alcohol and Drug Abuse), an autonomous entity set-up for technical expertise and support to workplace prevention programme.
- 100 De-addiction centres empowered to provide preventive support for HIV/AIDS.
- National Centre for Drug Abuse Prevention in Delhi with eight Regional Resource and Training Centres located in different regions of the country provides services for manpower development.

Treatment Provided

- Drug Addiction is like any other medical ailment which can be treated;
- Drug addiction treatment is cost effective in reducing drug use and its associated health costs;
- Treatment is better than alternatives, such as not treating addicts or simply incarcerating addicts;
- Remaining in treatment for an adequate period of time is crucial for treatment effectiveness;

- Family and friends play crucial roles in motivating individuals; and
- Family therapy is important, especially for adolescents.

Children and Drugs

The misuse and abuse of psychoactive substances, as well as their associated health and socio-economic consequences, continue to be a major source of concern for societies in both developed and developing countries. No. society is without its mood-modifying drugs, whether they are used legally under medical supervision or illegally abused by chewing, sniffing, inhalation, swallowing, smoking or injection.

Among all the diseases of civilization, drug abuse has a history that stretches far back in time. The discovery and use of the therapeutic benefits of medicinal plants have been accompanied by their misuse—the deliberate provoking of changes in mood, thought and behaviour in order to escape environmental boredom, disquietude and stress. The problems, hazards and disabilities associated with the use of psychoactive substances are found all over the world and in all age groups—even in the new born babies of drug-addicted and alcoholic mothers.[13]

VIENNA CONFERENCE, 1987

Drug abuse presents as destructive a threat to present and future generations as the plagues, which swept many parts of the world in earlier centuries. Unless controlled, its effects could be even more insidious and devastating. In order to coordinate a concerted and determined struggle on the part of the entire world community, and International Conference on Drug Abuse and Illicit Trafficking will be held at ministerial level in June next year, at the International Centre in Vienna.

A resolution of the UN General Assembly last December strongly urged all states to summon the utmost political will to combat drug abuse and illicit trafficking by generating increased political, cultural and social awareness. It also called upon the UN, the specialized agencies and other organizations of the UN system and non-governmental organizations to give the highest attention and priority possible to international means to combat illicit production of, trafficking in, and demand for drugs.

The resolution emphasizes the need for all states to ratify the existing drug control treaties and to make serious efforts to comply with the provisions of these instruments. In convening the 1987 Vienna Conference, it urged the adoption of a comprehensive multi-disciplinary outline of future activities, which will focus on concrete and substantial issues directly relevant to the problems. The Conference will undertake an in-depth review of existing mechanisms, and will suggest governmental, inter-governmental and non-governmental objectives for combating all forms of drug abuse, drawing up strategic legislation and improving UN coordination.

At this Conference, a thorough review will be given to subjects ranging from supply of substances of abuse to a reduction in demand. WHO has a special interest in these subjects and in particular in reducing demand. The ministries of health have specific responsibilities in the area of epidemiological investigation, treatment and prevention of drug abuse[14].

Removing the Glamour

We have to try to change the beliefs, rituals and habits that now make drug use appear pleasurable, glamorous or special.[15]

Meira Kumar: Minister of Social Justice and Empowerment, Government of India, in her message on International Day against Drug Abuse and Illicit Trafficking, June 26, 2004 observed that:

The spread of drug abuse and alcoholism threatens the very fabric of our social life today. These result in a diversion of resources from the development of the children. Amongst workers there is significant fall in the productivity. Accidents in the workplace and on the roads increase. Overall, the consequences of such abuse entail a heavy loss to the society, as well as to the persons concerned.

Subbulakshmi Jagadeesan: Minister of Social Justice and Empowerment, Government of India, in her message on International Day against Drug Abuse and Illicit Trafficking, June 26, 2004 observed that:

The International Day against Drug Abuse and Illicit Trafficking is an occasion for reaffirming our resolve and commitment to ensure a society free from the curse of drug abuse and alcoholism.

Our youth and children continue to fall prey to drug abuse, thus depriving our society of a sizeable productive population. Drug abuse has emerged as a curse of the modern age where, in our zeal for scientific and technological advancement, we have moved away from traditional, social and moral values. The Ministry of Social Justice and Empowerment has been persistently striving to empower society to fight against drug abuse through prevention, treatment and rehabilitation services. This requires a massive community effort and voluntary organizations have a valuable role in developing an enabling environment.[16]

Health Education

Activities undertaken in an effort to prevent drug problems are often boring, irrelevant, impractical and ineffective. Why do they fail? Boring approaches are mostly those which set out to warn young people of the alleged dangers, harm or evil of drugs, coupled with recommendations to be good boys and girls. Young people tend to respond much better to approaches that involve them and allow them an active role.[17]

There has to be a change in the community's perception of drug use too. If the community begins to see it as rather a flat, boring and silly experience, the efforts can be successful. Eventually the community can hope to reach the stage where even habitual users recognize that they are stuck in a fixed and limited routine, and therefore less able to enjoy real life.[18]

Women and Substance Abuse

In most countries, psychoactive substance use has traditionally been a problem-affecting males. But with the rapid social and economic changes over the past few decades, there has been a dramatic increase in this problem among women in both developed and developing countries.

Women and men respond differently to alcohol and drugs, women having a lower tolerance to most substances. Since many women substance users are of childbearing age, the effects on the developing fetus are of serious concern. Especially, women and their partners should be made aware of the risks when alcohol, tobacco and other legal substances are used during pregnancy. The use of psychoactive substances facilitates the spread of HIV infection through sexual contact or needles shared by injecting drug users. In many societies drug use, drug dealing and prostitution are closely connected; consequently the women involved are at high risk of infection with HIV and other sexually transmitted diseases.

To deal with these problems the focus must be on both men and women, taking into account the effects on the family and children. Women who do not use substances can suffer from their use by a partner or other family members; for instance, a family's income for food, healthcare and education may be spent on alcohol, tobacco or drugs. Domestic violence is often associated with alcohol or other drug use.

At all levels—international, national and local—the issue of women and substance use is increasingly being recognized, as is the important role of women. Women assume the major responsibility for healthcare within the family, and are often concerned about the social and health situation in the community. Thus women, especially if training and education can be provided, are instrumental in preventing substance abuse and its potential harmful consequences.[19]

Drugs and Alcohol can be Worse for Women

In addition to the problems that anyone who misuse drugs or alcohol may suffer, women face some special health problems:

- Women who drink large amounts of alcohol or use a lot of drugs are more likely to get liver disease than men.
- Many women and girls are pushed into sex they do not want when they drink alcohol or use drugs. This may result in unwanted pregnancy, STDs, and even HIV/AIDS.
- If used during pregnancy, drugs and alcohol can cause children to be born with birth defects and mental disabilities, such as:
  - o Problems of the heart, bones, genitals, and head and face;
  - o Low birth weight;
  - o Slow growth; and
  - o Learning difficulties.

A baby can also be born dependent on drugs and suffer the same signs of withdrawal as an adult.[20]

Community-based Treatment

Special camps in India, set-up in or close to villages, are an innovative example of the community approach to alcohol or drug use problems. They show that everyone can be given access to all health services.[21]

The new concept that smoking induces nicotine dependence means that this is considered an addictive drug. This fact is gaining support from international scientific agencies. Many studies, including some, which have been concealed by the tobacco industry, show that nicotine does produce chemical reactions in the body similar to those produced by heroin or cocaine. The relapse rates of dependent persons trying in quit using nicotine, alcohol, cocaine and heroin are roughly the same; many even report that it is harder to quit tobacco than various illegal drugs.

A new study by the Center on Addiction and Substance Abuse at Columbia University in the USA confirms that nicotine is a "gateway drug" which is associated with the use of illicit substances. About 65% of cocaine users in the USA have smoked cigarettes. Adults who started to smile before the age of 15 are three times as likely to be regular hard drug users and more than twice as likely to be regular cocaine users than those who started smoking at 18 or older. Children who smoke daily are 13 times more likely to use heroin than children who smoke less often.

Anti-drug policies must be identified as part of every health strategy. Health education, public information and drug cessation programmes must work hand in hand with the legal regulation of drug production and sales and the banning of advertisement.[22]

Its three functions of teaching, research and service have to be reviewed in the light of a world blemished with gross inequalities and clamorous with need. The winds of change must blow away the cobwebs of learning for its own sake (and of course Oxford itself is changing).

I the particular field of health, teaching is vital; but it must be directed towards all categories of health workers, including those in primary healthcare, not merely towards the medical specialist. And then research too is vital; but it should seek to resolve real problems, rather than being "pure research." And the service function of a university should surely rate top priority; in any country, whether developing or developed, there are serious gaps in the public health services which can only be filled through the efforts of well-motivated people who are keen to apply their talents and their hard-earned skills to serving the community.[23]

CONCLUSION

There are No. easy answers and No. miracles can be expected. Reducing the availability of psychoactive substances by tighter controls on legal and illegal supplies is one important, but difficult, preventive measure to implement. But we cannot hope to find a total solution, solely through control. Nor will a solution be found in isolating drug abusers from society—locked away in rehabilitation centres so as not to "contaminate" others.

Effective prevention will require the input of the entire community, including young people themselves. In some countries this approach is beginning to take shape and is showing considerable promise. However, it will take time, and, more important still, it will take the commitment of people who recognize the significant contribution they can make by sharing in community participation.[24]

Manmohan Singh, Prime Minister of India, in his message on International Day against Drug Abuse and Illicit Trafficking, June 26, 2004 observed that:

Although India has made sustained economic progress in the last two decades, socio-economic conditions in some parts of the country are such that many of our young citizens have become habitual drug users. Addiction results in diversion of financial resources, loss of productivity, a diminished quality of family life and an increased risk of contracting HIV/ AIDS. The situation is exacerbated due to India's location on the trafficking routes from the Golden Triangle and the Golden Crescent.

On the occasion of the International Day against Drug Abuse and Illicit Trafficking, let us resolve to step up our efforts to reduce the supply of illicit drugs and to check the availability of dual-use prescription drugs across the counter. At the same time, we must develop an environment, which provides the youth with a sense of direction and purposefulness and enables them to participate in the task of nation building.[25]

In the area of prevention, it is now considered good practice if the focus of prevention shifts from total abstinence-oriented programmes to those, which delay the onset of drug use among young people. Rather then developing a broad programme directed towards a large section of the society, specific programmes targeting various at risk groups should be developed. Preventive programmes, which are based purely on information dissemination, are rarely successful, especially if the approach depicts exaggerated risks associated with drug use in order to frighten people into abstinence. The presentation of enhanced risks and hazards of drug abuse is often not credible, causing the messages to lose their impact. Sometimes they are even counterproductive. Research carried out in this area has shown that a less sensational scientific approach can be a more promising basis for progress. Modern preventive programmes should present accurate information and discuss the broad risk factors associated with drug abuse. Substance abuse prevention may thus be embedded within the large framework of crime prevention, safe and healthy lifestyles.

The factors that may help early initiation of treatment are: outreach programmes, reduced waiting time, case management and motivational interaction (Marlatt *et. al.*, 1997). The authors recommended less stigmatizing of users, less intensive interventions, involvement of healthcare professionals in primary care setting and a public health approach would facilitate treatment seeking and retentions in a treatment centre. The authors further stated that expanding community involvement and low threshold programmes were important. Simply increasing treatment availability may not result in improved treatment utilization.

Treatment and Education

- o Enhance treatment capacity;
- o Facilitate entry into treatment;
- o Treatment of health damage;
- o Training of peer educators; and
- o Upgrade emergency services to treat overdose.

Augmenting services is best achieved by enhanced capacity of the established centres rather than by increasing their numbers.

Notes and References

1. The information in this section has been taken from "The Manual for Reducing Drug Related Harm in Asia", pp. 13-15.
2. United Nations, Office on Drugs and Crime Regional Office for South Asia, June 2004, pp. 3-4.
3. Annual Report, 2002-03, Ministry of Health and Family Welfare, GOI, New Delhi, pp. 60-61.
4. United Nations, Office on Drugs and Crime Regional Office for South Asia, June 2004, p. 8.
5. The Extent, Pattern and Trends of Drug Abuse in India, National Survey, p. (i).
6. *Ibid.*, p. (iii).
7. *Ibid.*, pp. (vi to x).
8. A Resource Book for Implementing Agencies, June 2004, M/o Social Justice and Empowerment, GOI, pp. 6-7.
9. Drug Use and HIV/AIDS Prevention and Management, June 2004, pp. 31-35.
10. *Ibid.*, pp. 40-41.
11. Marilynn E. Katatsky, Drug abuse in the Americas, *World Health*, Alcohol and Drugs, August 1981, p. 27.
12. *The Tribune*, Chandigarh, Saturday, June 26, 2004
13. George M. Ling and Susan Boutle, Chidren and drugs, *World Health*, June 1979, p. 10.
14. Marcus Grant, Lifestyles and Health, *World Health*, June 1986, p. 21.
15. Diyanath Samarasinghe, *World Health*, 48th Year, No. 4, July-August 1995, p. 5.
16. *The Tribune*, Chandigarh, Saturday, June 26, 2004.
17. Diyanath Samarasinghe, *World Health*, 48th Year, No. 4, July-August 1995, p. 5.
18. *Ibid.*
19. WHO: Pia Bergendahl and Lee-Nah Hsu, "Women and substance abuse", July-August 1995, p. 12.
20. A. August Burns: "Where Women Have No. Doctor", 1997, p. 439.
21. WHO: John Howard, "Community-based treatment" July-August 1995, p. 12.
22. WHO: Sherif Omar, "Smoking in the Third World", July-August 1995, p. 12.
23. WHO: "Down from the Ivory Tower", April 1984, p. 16.
24. Marilynn E. Katatsky, Drug abuse in the Americas, *World Health*, Alcohol and Drugs, August 1981, p. 29.
25. *The Tribune*, Chandigarh, Saturday, June 26, 2004.

CHAPTER 4

ALCOHOL

The problem of alcohol ought not be conceived as alcoholism in the narrow medical sense—not just as the advanced case, delirium tremens, fully developed alcohol dependence, the end of the spectrum. Much rather should the focus be on alcohol-related problems, whatever form they take, whatever their degree, the whole spectrum. Alcohol problems as they affect work capacity, family adjustment, the health of the child. Alcohol problems in the shape of drunk driving, or petty crime, or violence. And problems that may come to medical attention through the primary healthcare worker, the medical assistant, the casualty department, the general medical and surgical wards. Such a broader view would offer a far more sensitive and accurate perspective on where in the community the problem really lies, where the pains in the community are really being felt. It is a perspective fully in accord with WHO's basic commitment to health as a social state, as well as a physical and mental state.

—*Griffith Edwards,* WHO: June 1979

4

CHAPTER

Alcohol

> Money spent on alcohol contributes to secondary poverty and exacerbates the risk of malnutrition in settings where living standards are already marginal. Excessive drinking may contribute to the multiple origins of ill-defined organic psychoses. Toxic substances present in certain home-brewed or home distilled beverages add to the risks. And in all this toll of alcohol-related damage, we have to get away from any habit of thinking just of the man as the casualty-rates of drinking problems among women are increasing, and among young people. It must also be remembered that excessive drinking is a great source of family disruption, quite apart from its direct impact on the individual.
>
> —*Griffith Edwards*, WHO: June 1979

THE COST OF A DRINK

It is a drug, which gives pleasure and relaxation to millions. Yet the problems posed by alcohol block social and economic development, and even threaten to overwhelm the health services.[1]

The cup that cheers can be the cup that kills. Not only alcohol addiction itself but many disabling, and some fatal, physical and psychological conditions can be attributed to excessive drinking.

In addition, alcohol-related traffic accidents account for a significant proportion among young people. Accidents at work or in the home are more frequently related to over-drinking than is widely recognized. Excessive drinking disrupts family life and can often result in violence and neglect.[2]

The use of alcohol by road users is the largest single identifiable contributory factor to road accidents, and in theory should be relatively easy to prevent. In practice, the problem is surprisingly robust and resistant to treatment, especially in the developed countries, where both drinking and driving a car are integral social features of long standing.

The developing countries may be in a much better position, and most of them have either imposed a complete ban on alcohol when driving, or have set maximum alcohol levels for drivers at about 0.8 per mill. or lower.

The experiences of the developed countries are being studied with some advantage and important lessons have been learned to benefit the Third World. During the early period of motor transport growth, the emphasis was on detection and punishment of offenders. With hindsight, it might have been more appropriate to concentrate on public health education and reinforcing of social pressures against drinking and driving.[3]

WORLD HEALTH ORGANIZATION HAS BEEN MAKING WARNINGS ABOUT VIOLENCE AND ALCOHOL

Alcohol and Heart

Alcohol is responsible for much death and sickness, quite apart from the social problems it causes. From a public health viewpoint, therefore, the importance of limiting alcohol consumption is not questioned. Recently a large number of case-control and prospective observational studies from around the world have supported the hypothesis that light-to-moderate levels of alcohol consumption result in a modest but consistent reduction in coronary heart disease. However, many of those same studies show that, with alcohol consumption levels above two drinks per day—or roughly 24 g of ethanol—there is a consistent trend for increased rates of morbidity and mortality from all cardiovascular diseases combined, including stroke, arrhythmia and hypertensive heart disease.

The protective effect of moderate alcohol consumption, as compared to abstaining altogether, is related to the modulation of several well-recognized pathogenic mechanisms that can lead to atheroma and/or thrombosis. In medical terms, there is an increase in HDL choleserol, a reduction in plasma fibrinogen concentration and decreased platelet aggregation.

Any public health recommendation that simply emphasized the positive effects of alcohol would do more harm than good. A study called INTERSALT has suggested that an increase in mean consumption of only 15 g of alcohol (about one drink) a week would be associated with a 10% increase in the prevalence of heavy drinkers. So it would be irresponsible to advocate moderate alcohol consumption as a means of preventing coronary heart disease. As a strategy for reducing heart disease it would be much better to address the most important risk factors by promoting:

- Smoking prevention;
- Healthy nutrition;
- Regular exercise; and
- Hypertension control.

Alcohol and Violence: Not only on the Roads

The connection between drunken driving and road disaster is amply supported by police reports and hospital records. But the influence of alcohol on injury and deaths extends much beyond the havoc on the roads with which drink is commonly associated.

The kind of alcohol-inflicted injuries that take place at home, at work, in schools and even on recreation fields, are poorly, if at all, documented. Yet there is enough information to indicate that it is too much drink that often triggers acts of violence, World Health Organization (WHO) experts state.

Though patchy, information from Africa, Europe, North America, and Australia, shows adequately that alcohol-related accidents are not only a significant cause of human misery, but also represent major economic losses for all countries.

Because they over-drink, the imbibers are more likely to hurt themselves by falls, by burns or scalds, more likely to over-dose on medicines, more likely to drown, or to commit homicide or suicide—in short, those under the influence are at greater risk of injury.

Both in the United Kingdom and the United States of America, experts estimate that about 45 per cent of all alcohol-related deaths are linked to accidental injuries and poisoning.

"Domestic and occupational injuries, more often than not,' are associated with over-drinking", says Mr. Marcus Grant, technical officer of WHO's programme on substance abuse.

"But because of little documentation, not much has been done anywhere in the world against these alcohol-related injuries," he adds in calling for better record keeping as a much-needed first step for preventive programmes.

There are as well a range of social problems caused by excessive drinking: martial discord, spouse and child neglect, absenteeism, and, when pay goes to drink instead of groceries and rent, even poverty.

Over the last three decades, production of alcohol has increased world-wide, in some developing countries even out-pacing population growth. Supply has created demand for wine, spirits, and particularly, beer.

While in the developed world, trends show drinking leveling out or even decreasing, in the developing world, trends are on the upswing jumping, according to WHO estimates, over recent decades by at least 500 per cent in Asia, 400 per cent in Africa and 200 per cent in Latin America.

Along with this increase, there has been a corresponding rise in alcohol-related injury, some of it intentionally inflicted, some unintentionally. And the up-trend is expected to accelerate in the years ahead.[4]

Alcohol and Women

Women react to their own alcoholism differently from men. They tend to have extreme guilt feelings and to blame themselves for their drinking

CHART 4.1

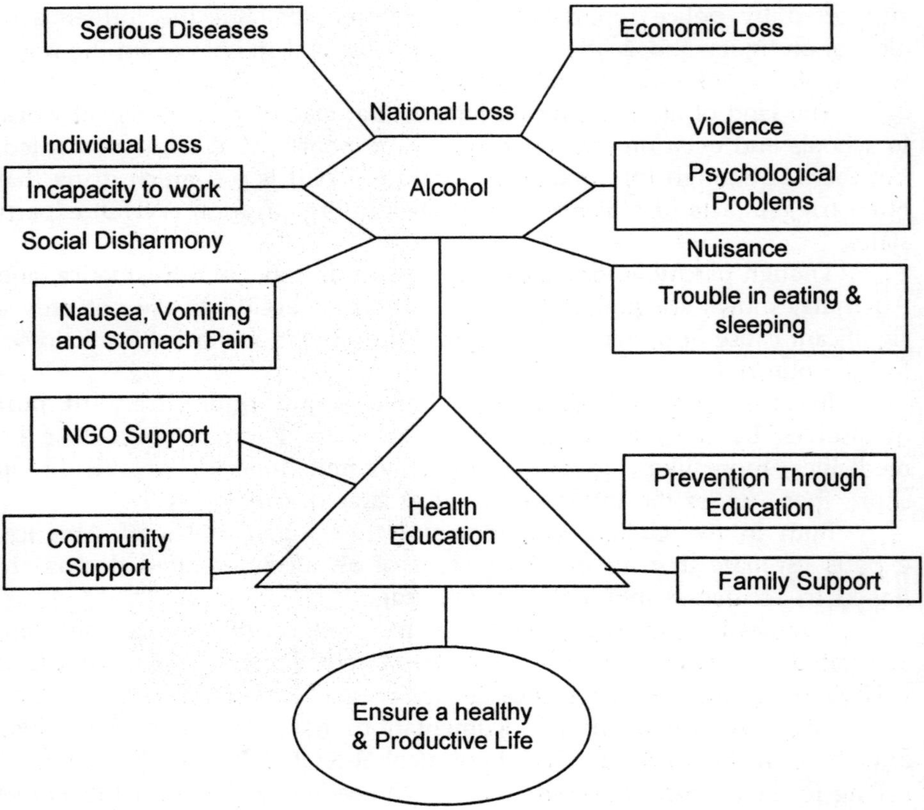

habit. Their loss of self-respect may lead them to self-destructiveness.[5]

In some industrialized countries the number of women alcoholics is estimated to equal that of men. This fact surprises many, for alcoholism is generally regarded as a male disease. In the United States alone, the number of alcoholic women is rated at about five million. However, it is not only the extent of the problem which commands urgent attention but also the fact that women alcoholics are not "just like" alcoholic men. Their drinking habits are different; society has a different reaction toward them and their rehabilitation process requires different measures.

Female alcoholism is one of the most carefully hidden problems because of the social stigma attached to it. Heavily-drinking women are looked down upon more than their male counterparts. They are regarded as irresponsible, loose persons, who ruin themselves and their families. As a result, women do not want to be identified as alcoholic, and even their relatives help them to conceal the fact in order to save the family's reputation. Families are often afraid to admit even to themselves that the problem exists—No. one likes to believe that the hand that rocks the cradle might be a shaky one.

The result of this conscious or subconscious refusal to acknowledge female alcoholism is that women are not encouraged to seek treatment. Often even physicians and psychiatrists fail to recognize alcoholism in women, misjudging the symptoms, they prescribe tranquilizers, which in turn cause an even more dangerous double addiction.[6]

There is evidence that alcoholism in women is often related to specific life situations such as a divorce, the death of a loved one or bad marital relationships.

Often it conceals the unmet and unsatisfied emotional needs of love, security, significance and a sense of belonging. The loneliness of the suburban housewife is also recognized as an inciting factor for the use of alcohol. On the other hand, the career women, who must function in a business world which is highly competitive and which considers her inferior despite her professional achievements, may compensate for feelings of unfair competition with alcohol and/or drugs. Therefore when assessing the situation one must not just ask what is wrong with the woman but, above all, what is it in her environment that makes her want to escape from the scene. A serious look at the condition of women in all countries is a necessary precondition for an adequate understanding of the problems.[7]

The African Experience

Those societies which encourage unlimited, unrestricted drinking, and which fail to provide alternatives for the functions fulfilled by alcohol, and which further fail to develop adequate means to deal humanely with individual problem drinkers, and, finally, which fail to develop programmes which would minimize the socially disruptive aspects of alcohol use, deserve the alcohol problems they get.[8]

Drinking is more common in youth. There are different factors, which motivate young people. (See Table 4.1)

The alcohol dependence syndrome is the condition, which is usually being referred to when talk is of "alcoholism" although that word has been so widely and variously employed as to have lost any generally agreed precision. It may be simpler to consider that there is a whole spectrum of possible alcohol-related disabilities (physical, social and mental), among which the alcohol dependence syndrome is one possible and rather special disability. Dependence exists in degrees, and has many cultural colourings. For any individual the disabilities may come singly (he may have crashed his car but have No. other present or incipient drinking problem), or in clusters (he may have crashed his car and lost his job because of his drinking, while a medical examination also shows that his liver is beginning to be inflamed). It is arbitrary and rather unreal to think that these disabilities for any one individual can be weighed and added up into a sort of box-score, while creating a cut-off point which defines who shall and who shall not be designated a "problem drinker" makes little sense. What is needed is a new awareness that every drink-related disability counts and is real (be it falling once downstairs, once breaking up a

TABLE 4.1

What Motivates Young People to Drink Alcohol?

Motives (Swiss children aged 12 to 16)	*Percentage of all Yes replies*					
	German-speaking		*French-speaking*		*Italian-speaking*	
Self-gratification	**56.9**		**52.00**		**65.8**	
"because I like it"	36.9	746	34.7	268	48.6	226
"because it feels good to be a little tipsy"	8.2	166	12.7	98	12.0	56
"because I am bored"	11.8	239	4.6	36	5.2	24
Symbolic participation/pressure from young people of the same age	**31.1**		**35.2**		**18.8**	
"because my friends drink too"	10.9	220	15.5	120	8.2	38
"so my friends won't think me a wet blanket"	6.5	131	7.0	54	3.1	14
"because most adults drink too"	9.2	185	6.5	50	4.3	20
"so as to mix more easily with other people"	4.5	90	6.2	48	3.2	15
Psycho-dynamic relief	**12.0**		**12.8**		**15.4**	
"to give me courage and self-confidence"	3.8	76	4.5	35	5.8	27
"to calm myself down"	5.7	116	6.1	47	7.7	36
"so I can talk more easily to people"	2.5	50	2.2	17	1.9	9
Total	100	2019	100	773	100	465

The figures in bold refer to the actual number of responses.[9]
Source: *World Health*, August 1981.

relationship, once eroding your gastric lining). We should not need a drinking problem to be large, dramatic or aggregated before we take a man's (or a woman's) drinking problems seriously.[10]

Here, in broadest outline are 12 key steps which might be seen as essential to any country's design for a national strategy to respond to alcohol-related disabilities.

1. Determine every relevant fact, compiled and collated from every possible source, on the national per capita alcohol consumption and its trends; changes in patterns of alcohol manufacture, distribution and marketing; the economic significance of alcohol production, distribution and marketing to the nation as a whole and to interested sub-groups; the who, how, why, where and when of drinking—its cultural and symbolic meaning; the description and prevalence of alcohol-related disabilities (including the dependence syndrome) in the general population and in special groups. Identify and describe all those agencies, official and unofficial organizations (medical, social, penological, etc.), which at present respond to the troubled drinker or his family at an individual level. Describe what is being done in regard to prevention, where the responsibility is

at present seen to lie, and with what level of integration. The fruits of this exercise should be a short document, which puts everything together so as to produce a live picture—a dossier, which should usefully be placed on many desks.

2. Identify the relevant data sources so that a similar exercise can be mounted at intervals, and more easily, once the systems of data gathering are made more uniform and more reliable.
3. In many countries such a review would immediately provide pointers for designing more effective and better-integrated administration of the problem at a central level. An effective national response cannot be mounted if important interests are not talking to each other
4. A determined response has to be made not only at national but also at community level. Response to alcohol-related disabilities is a prime example of a medico-social problem where the responsibility should if possible be returned to the community actually experiencing those problems, since that community is most likely to understand them.
5. Education aimed at building general awareness should start to create the climate in which many things can begin to happen. That dossier is not intended only for the Minister's desk, for the legislators, for every relevant professional group, but for people in their homes—for the drinking man and drinking woman and the mass media.
6. As a rule of thumb, if national alcohol consumption rises, national prevalence of alcohol-related disabilities will also rise. If the country has the political will to use fiscal policies for health purposes, prices may be so manipulated as to prevent undue rise in consumption, and the licensing laws may in some circumstances have their health implications.
7. Education should then aim more specifically at building a climate which is not guilt-ridden about drinking, but which decries dangerous and encourages safer drinking practices. Whether we yet know enough about such educational approaches to influence deeply symbolized cultural patterns is an open question. Talking to school children should not become a comfortable substitute for more determined action.
8. Prevention should be skillfully and purposefully aimed, with special messages and social manipulations, towards improving small identified sectors of the total problem-drunk driving for instance, the drinking problems of itinerant labourers, drinking in a particular factory or in a particular valley—rather than directing all efforts only at the general population.
9. The skills of existing agencies and organizations should be enhanced, the integration of such facilities should be encouraged, local people in the community—whether

professionally involved or not—should be appropriately trained, and trained to train others. The evolution of self-help groups should be encouraged.

10. Only exceptionally should new types of response be initiated, and whenever possible these should be built on existing patterns of community response. Erecting new and architecturally splendid in-patient facilities to treat only the advanced cases has little merit; help has to be got out into the streets and villages.
11. An essential part of ensuring a helpful response to individual need is the kind of education, which tells people what to do about their problems, gets the right time, and removes the sense of shame which so often blocks the seeking of help.
12. Investment in research is No. optional extra. For any country or community, an entirely self-regarding investigation of its own alcohol-related disabilities and responses must be the basis for continued evolution of those responses. Beyond that, every country must make a contribution to an increasingly international research effort, so that every type of science can be deployed in the attack.[11]

Throughout history, human societies have recognized certain substances of natural origin, which either offer temporarily heightened perceptions or suggest an escape route from the unpleasant features of life, whether real or imaginary. Fermented liquor from fruit or vegetables, or plant products such as opium, coca leaves, cannabis, khat and tobacco have been accepted in varying degrees as social lubricants or as private escape mechanisms.

The drinking of wine and other fermented liquors were chronicled in the earliest literature known to us. But in comparatively recent times, voices have been raised against many such substances. For instance King James I of England, around the year 1600, inveighed against tobacco. It was, he wrote, "a great contempt of God's good gifts that the sweetness of man's breath . . . shall be wilfully corrupted by this stinking smoke." For good measure, he added that the habit was "a branch of the sin of drunkenness, which is the root of all sins."

But for every such grumbler, there were scores of poets, philosophers and physicians willing to speak out in praise of drinking, smoking or chewing one or another drug. What has come more slowly to the attention of the world is the realization that these substances produce addiction, and lend themselves to abuse.[12]

Prevention Action

The international review suggests that national and worldwide programmes concerning alcohol-related problems need to be developed in a coordinated way. For the problems cannot be solved in isolation. Health, welfare, moral, educational and economic aspects all need to be taken into account, and a programme on alcohol problems needs to be situated in the general framework of a policy to promote health, welfare and development. The 1979 Expert Committee pointed out that alcoholism, "while prevalent and a matter for serious concern, constitutes only a small part of the gamut of alcohol-related problems." Aware of the "limited efficacy and high cost of the existing treatment or management of most of these problems, and their high prevalence in many parts of the world", the Committee recommended that "prevention should be given clear priority."

One of the impediments to initiating preventive action programmes can often be the lack of a suitable organization, such as a national coordinating committee, to take responsibility for promoting action. Such committees can be valuable, for example, in researching and collating information, and coordinating the different aspects of the programme.

Despite the seriousness of alcohol-related problems, there has never been any worldwide policy concerning prevention. But Joy Moser suggests that the economic aspects of the problems, including the implications of international trade in beverage alcohol and the economic consequences of alternative preventive measures, need to be approached at the international level.[13]

The government's reliance on the alcohol industry for revenue should be reconsidered, since this indirectly encourage production (and therefore the expansion of the alcohol industry).

- Control on availability should be exercised by reducing production, curbing the hours of drinking, reducing the number of outlets through restrictions in the issue of liquor licences and raising the age of eligibility to 21 years.
- Alternatives to drinking should be promoted by providing more recreational and educational activities, such as cultural dances, football, reading, home economics and so forth. In this connection, community centres in the various communities should be revamped and other social or church organizations should be encouraged to actively provide alternatives to drinking.
- Alternative, more moderate and responsible styles of drinking should be encouraged through the inculcation of values supportive of "healthy" attitudes to drinking.
- Alcohol education should be related to the experiences of the people, and undue weight should not be placed on the pathological aspects of drinking since this is likely to produce a "boomerang" effect.
- Education should be seen as a community responsibility and all community agencies—political, church and school groups, clinics, community centres and so on—should be called upon to contribute to this instructional effort.[14]

Fully aware of all the complexities of this field of studies, a British writer, Marcus Grant, tried to identify six different strategies for an educational approach to young people and alcohol.

There are:

- Promoting moderate drinking. A system of self-control should enable most adolescents to become adults on familiar terms with alcohol—but without alcohol problems.
- Reducing the reasons for resorting to alcohol and cutting down the occasions of drinking. Obviously this calls for a sound knowledge of those reasons and those occasions. Starting with situations under adult control, especially within the family, it should be possible to make young people self-reliant on their own decisions and capable of resisting the promptings of comrades of their own age. If this succeeds in developing a capacity for self-control, it may also form an element in broader programmes covering other fields of risk, such as sexual behaviour.
- Suggesting or even recommending alternatives. As Mr Grant says: "This is a more ambitious attempt to modify the existing models of cultural values, in which alcoholic drinks rate very high." This is where religious and moral considerations—whether traditional or new (to the Western world)—have a role to play, but so too have such active leisure pursuits as sport and the return to a more natural way of life, including diet.
- Limiting the harmful effects of over-drinking. The risks entailed in driving any vehicle, from a bicycle to a sports car, while under the influence of alcohol, have already been mentioned. But there are also well-known harmful effects on mental performance (in school examinations) or physical trails (in sporting events)—and perhaps less well-known effects on sexual activity.
- Encouraging youngsters to accept help in god time, and even to seek such help. "In good time" means at the moment when problems of all kinds arise as a result of excessive, repeated or prolonged drinking, followed by alcohol dependence itself.
- Trying to change the ways of speaking and behaving within the family, at school, at work and even in society itself. By spotlighting mature personalities who are capable of living without dependence on any drug, this strategy tries to promote new models precisely contrary to those offered by commercial propaganda in favour of alcohol (and tobacco), but using similar methods.
- Clearly, after considering the "why" we have to decide on the "how", and must move on from theory to practice—or better still to practices in the plural! But this involves taking very careful

account of the cultural, economic, social and even legislative context, so that the practical steps that are available are practically infinite in their variety.[15]

Overcoming Problems with Alcohol and Drugs

1. Admit you have a Problem

But I only had 3 cups . . . or was that 4? I'm not sure. You're right. May be I am drinking too much.

Stopping is often easier with the help and support of others.

2. Decide to do Something Today

I'll stop drinking so much chicha tomorrow.

It is tomorrow. Believe you can begin to quit today.

3. Stop

Or use less and then stop. Many people can stop drinking or using drugs all at once. All it takes for them is the will to stop and the belief they can do it. Others need help from a group or treatment programme like Alcoholics Anonymous (AA) that helps people with drinking or drug problems. There are AA groups in may countries. There may also be other groups or treatment programmes in your area. Most women feel more comfortable in a group with women only. If there are No. groups in your area, try starting your own group with someone who has been starting your own groups with someone who has been successful in helping people to stop drinking or using drugs.

4. If you start drinking or using drugs again, do not blame yourself

But try to stop again right away.

Physical Addiction and Withdrawal

When a person is physically addicted to alcohol or a drug and quits using it, he or she will go through a period of withdrawal. During this time his or her body must get used to being without the drug.

Alcohol Addiction and Withdrawal

After quitting drinking, it can take about 3 days for most signs of withdrawal to stop. Many people get through these days without problems. But since some people have very serious signs, it is important to have someone watch over the person and give help when needed.

- Some herbal teas can help the liver cleanse the body of poisonous effects of alcohol or dugs. A traditional healer may be able to suggest good local herbs.

Alcoholics Anonymous (AA)

To become a member of AA, a person needs only one thing: a desire to stop drinking. As a member, you will regularly meet with others who have quit drinking, in order to share your experience, strength, and hope. You will also have a sponsor—a person who has stopped drinking for a period of time, and who can give you individual support and guidance.

AA does not charge any money. It does not support or oppose any causes, or have connections to any religious or political groups. Instead, AA tries to stay free of conflict with other groups in order to fulfil its main purpose: to carry its message to the drinking person who still suffers.

Early Sings of Withdrawal

- Slight shaking;
- Nervous and irritable feelings;
- Sweating;
- Trouble in eating and sleeping;
- Aches all over the body; and
- Nausea, vomiting, stomach pain.

These signs may go away on their own, or they may get stronger. If they do, the man or woman should go to a health worker immediately. If help is far away, give his or her 10 to 20 mg of diazepam by mouth to prevent seizures. Give another 10 mg an hour later if the signs are not getting better. If you are still traveling, you can repeat the dose every 4 to 5 hours.

The following signs are an emergency. Any person with these signs must get medical help immediately.

- Mental confusion;
- Seeing strange things or hearing voices;
- Very fast heartbeat;
- Seizures; and
- When someone is addicted to alcohol, lack of alcohol in the body can cause seizures.

After you have Quit Drinking

As soon as possible, start eating foods (or drinks) with a lot of protein, vitamins, and minerals. These foods help the body heal itself: liver, yeast, breads made from whole wheat, other whole grains, beans, and dark green vegetables. If you cannot eat, vitamins may be helpful. Take a multi-vitamin or B-complex vitamin that contains folic acid.

CONCLUSION

Learning to Stay Free of Drugs and Alcohol

Once a person has overcome physical addiction, it is important to learn how to stay free of drugs and alcohol to prevent the problem from developing again. The best way to do this is to learn better skills for coping with life. This is not easy to do and will take time.

A man or woman who has misused alcohol or drugs often feels powerless and full of shame. He or she needs to learn that he or she is able to make changes to improve her life. One way to begin is to make small changes, that help prove to herself and to others that she can cope with problems.

Here are some ideas that have helped men or women build coping skills:

- Develop a network of support among those close to your and ask for help when you need it. It is much easier to think about problems and begin to solve them when you can talk and work with others.
- Try to solve one problem at a time. That way, problems will not seem so large that you cannot cope with them.
- Try to tell a friend or someone your trust about things that worry to upset you, or that make you sad or angry. You may begin to understand why you feel the way you do and what you can do to feel better.
- Work with other people on a project to improve you community. This proves to you and to others that you know how to work for change. You may also find that doing this helps you make personal changes, too.
- Meet together regularly with other people who are working to stay free of alcohol or drugs.
- If you are trying to stay free of drink or drugs, avoid places where you will feel pressure to use them. Work with others to organize social events where drugs and alcohol are not used.[16]

Notes and References

1. John Madeley, The cost of a drink, *World Health*, August 1981, p. 5.
2. John Wickett, Lifestyle and Health, *World Health*, June 1986, p. 12.
3. Alex Irving, World Health Organization, June 1986, p. 14.
4. *Swasth Hind*, March-April 1993, p. 81.
5. Eva Zabolai-Csekme, Alcohol and Women, *World Health*, August 1981, p. 9.
6. *Ibid.*
7. *Ibid.*
8. Muyunda Mwanalushi, The African experience, *World Health*, August 1981, p. 13.
9. Olivier Jeanneret, Alcohol and youth, *World Health*, August 1981, p. 18.

10. Griffith Edwards, Demon Drink, *World Health*, December 1975, USA $1, p. 12.
11. *Ibid.*, p. 15.
12. Alex Irving, World Health Organization, June 1986, p. 16.
13. John Madeley, The cost of a drink, World Health, August 1981, p. 7.
14. Muyunda Mwanalushi, The African experience, World Health, August 1981, p. 15.
15. Olivier Jeanneret, Alcohol and youth, *World Health*, August 1981, p. 18.
16. A. August Burns: Where Women Have No. Doctor, Published in 1997, pp. 440-42.

CHAPTER 5

ACCIDENTS: ROAD AND RAILWAY ACCIDENTS

The vast numbers of those maimed and killed on the roads are too often accepted fatalistically as a normal part of modern life. Yet, if traffic accidents are tackled by methods like those used against the great killing diseases, the present epidemic of road deaths can be made to diminish just as epidemics of plague and smallpox have now been almost completely eliminated every where in the world. The need is of education in general and health education in particular.

—*Leo A. Kaprio*

5

CHAPTER

Accidents: Road and Railway Accidents

PART A

ROAD ACCIDENTS

Introduction

India has a vast road network of 3.32 million km. of which the National Highways and the State Highways together account for 1,95,000 km. Though the 58,112 km. National Highway network, which is the responsibility of this Ministry, comprises only 1.75 per cent of the total length of roads, it has to carry over 40 per cent of the total traffic across the length and breadth of the country. The strain on the network is increasing everyday. The number of vehicles has been growing at a rapid pace of 12 per cent per annum over the last few years and, consequently, traffic on the roads is growing at 7-10 per cent per annum. The share of roads in total traffic has been growing from 12 per cent of freight traffic and 31.6 per cent passenger traffic in 1950-51 to a projected 65 per cent of freight traffic and 87 per cent of passenger traffic by the end of the Tenth Plan period. The rapid expansion and strengthening of the road network, therefore, is an imperative, both to provide for present and future traffic and for improved accessibility to the hinterland. In addition, road transport needs to be regulated for better energy efficiency, lesser pollution and enhanced road safety.

All this requires a massive infusion of funds. Historically, investments in roads, especially highways, was done by the government mainly because of the large volume of resources required, long gestation period of projects, uncertain returns and various associated externalities. In recent times, the massive and ever increasing resource requirements and the concern for managerial efficiency and consumer responsiveness have led to the private sector being actively involved in the development and maintenance of the National Highways. The Ministry has formulated

CHART I

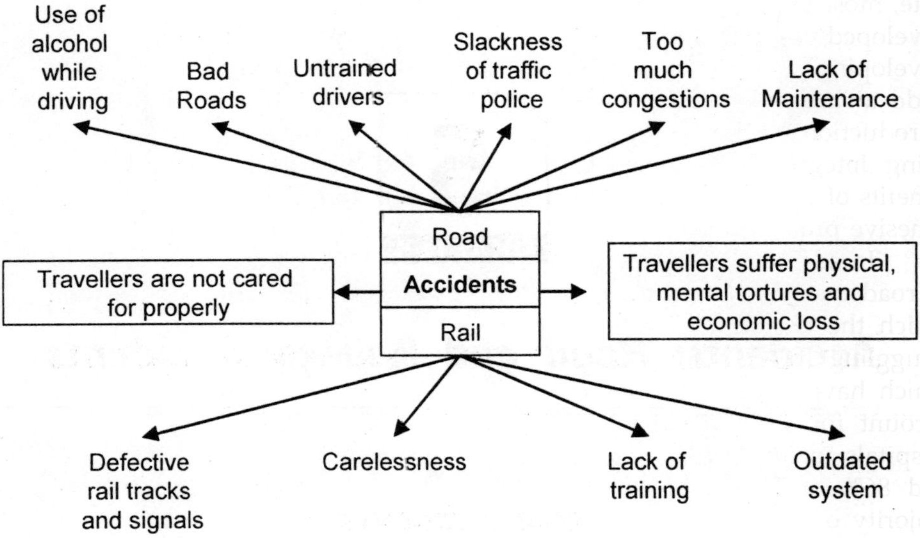

comprehensive policy guidelines to encourage private sector participation in the highway sector, besides providing several incentives such as tax exemptions and duty free import of road building equipment and machinery. Model Concession Agreements have also been finalized for major road projects.[1]

The traffic accident has come to be considered as among the deadliest of killer diseases. This disease is a problem that the motor age has created and we are sluggish in our attitude to adapt ourselves to the hazards of the motor vehicle as compared to our concern and adaptability to the maladies attached to other killer diseases.

Road Traffic Hazards: Hidden Epidemics

More than 20 million people are severely injured or killed on the world's roads each year. The burden falls most heavily on developing countries, where it will grow heavier still because of the rapid increase in the number of vehicles.

In addition to the direct costs of road injuries and deaths, the increase in the number of vehicles and reliance on certain transport policies have other serious health implications as well as wider social, economic and environmental impacts.[2] In some countries, air pollution from road transport causes even more deaths than those resulting from traffic accidents.[3] Besides the direct impacts on respiratory and heart disease, motorized transport produces around a quarter of the anthropogenic emissions of gases leading to climate change.[4] These "hidden epidemics" receive relatively little national or international attention compared with the focus on major communicable and non-communicable diseases.

To a large extent, road injuries are preventable. There are available and affordable interventions that can prevent injuries and save lives: to date, most of the evaluation of these interventions has been carried out in developed countries, and more research is needed on their effectiveness in developing countries. Renewed efforts are under way to increase world-wide awareness of the problem and its solutions and to encourage the introduction of road safety policies and practices. Several countries are using integrated strategies to deal with traffic risks and enhance the benefits of transport and land use policies to promote physical activity and cohesive projects for community development.[5]

In addition to the unacceptable human toll, the global economic cost of road crashes bas been estimated at about US$ 518 billion annually, of which the developing country share is about US$ 65 billion.[6] Countries struggling for economic development clearly cannot afford such losses, which have a significant impact on national healthcare systems. Injuries account for approximately one-third of the acute patient load in many hospitals in low-income and middle-income countries, and between 30% and 86% of all trauma admissions;[7] road traffic injuries constitute the majority of such admissions.

Although more than 3000 people are killed each day, full recognition of the scale of the problem is obscured because road crashes usually cause only a few deaths at a time and generate little press coverage, contributing to the hidden nature of the epidemic of road traffic injuries.[8]

The problem of traffic accidents is more acute in developing countries. Thus in respect of safety on roads, our own country's position is far from satisfactory. More than 60,000 human lives are lost in road accidents each year. In a study conducted in 1990 for the Planning Commission, the economic cost of a fatal accident has been placed at Rs. 2 lakhs, that of an injury accident at Rs. 1 lakh and the average cost of a minor non-injury accident, at Rs. 3,000. This should give us an idea of what kind of economic loss we are confronted with on account of road accidents each year.

Trend of Accidents in our Country

There is No. denying the fact that the number of road accidents is high. However, the rate of road accidents per ten thousand vehicles has been coming down, as can be seen from on the next page.

Road Accidents Scenario

More than Eighty Thousand people are killed and around four lakh injured in about four lakh reported road accidents in the country every year.

The Following tables on next page show the number of accidents, persons killed and injured in the country on all roads during 1997 to 2002.

The corresponding data for National Highways is as under:

A Statement showing State-wise number of accidents, persons killed and injured is at Annexure I.

Year	*Number of road accidents per 10,000 vehicles*	*Number of persons killed per 10,000 vehicles*
1970	814.42	103.50
1980	338.86	54.41
1990	147.55	28.25
1998	90.07	19.32
1999	86.12	18.27
2000	80.89	16.31
2001	73.76	14.70
2002 (P)	68.32	14.05

(P) = Provisional.
Source: Ministry of Road Transport and Highway.

Year	*No. of Accidents*	*Persons killed*	*Persons Injured*
1997	373671	76977	378361
1998	385018	79919	390674
1999	386456	81966	375051
2000	391449	78911	399265
2001	405637	80888	403751
2002	402157 (P)	82717 (P)	404829 (P)

Source: Ministry of Road Transport and Highway.

Procedure for Road Accidents Data Collection

Year	*No. of Accidents*	*Persons killed*	*Persons Injured*
1997	94014	25863	87375
1998	98690	26682	94198
1999	103839	28713	98427
2000	110508	30216	124600
2001	115824	32108	119592
2002	128632 (P)	32563 (P)	129966 (P)

(P) = Provisional.
Source: Ministry of Road Transport and Highway.

The data in respect of accidents, persons killed and injured in these accidents is initially reported to the Police. The concerned Police Stations compile the data and forward to District Headquarter who in turn forward the same to State Headquarters. The Nodal Officer of the Police Departments of the respective States compile the data for the entire States and then forward the same on annual basis (for the period covering January to December of every calendar year) to this Ministry.

Further a UN-ESCAP sponsored APRAD (Asia Pacific Road Accident Database) Project/IRAD (Indian Road Accident Database) Project is under progress, in which a 19 point accident data reporting format is under finalization on the basis of its validation through field trails and a concomitant software is to be developed. The project is expected to be completed by 2005 end.[9]

Cost of Accidents

A Working Group set-up by the Planning Commission in the year 2000 under the Chairmanship of Shri Prakash Narain, Former Chairman, Railway Board and Former Secretary, Shipping and Transport to look into road accidents, injury prevention and control had gone into the issue of social cost of accidents in our country and had estimated the cost at Rs. 55,000 crores in the year 1999-2000, which constituted 3% of the GDP for the year.

Reasons for Road Accidents

An analysis of accidents data shows that the primary causes of road accidents are driver's fault (83.5%), pedestrian fault/fault of passengers (4.7%), mechanical defect in vehicles (3%), bad roads (1.1%), bad weather (0.9%) and other factors like cattle, fallen trees, road blockage, non-functioning of signals, absence of rear reflectors/road signages, etc. (6.8%).

National Road Safety Policy

The trend of increase in the vehicle population in the country is as under:

Year	*1951*	*1961*	*1971*	*1981*	*1991*	*1996*	*2000*	*2001*	*2002*	*2003*
No. of Vehicles	306	665	1865	5391	21374	33786	48857	54991	58863	64804(P)

E = Estimated.
Source: Ministry of Road Transport and Highway.

It may be seen that the vehicle population has been steadily increasing with the trend picking up significantly since the Eighties.

Increase in vehicle population in the face of the limited road space which incidentally is used by a large variety of motorized and non-motorized traffic, has led the Government to accord a high priority to road safety. A draft Road Safety Policy was therefore prepared by the Ministry in the year 1992.

According to the available records, the draft Policy was discussed and adopted on 22.12.1994 in the fourth meeting of the National Road Safety Council, an apex level body constituted in the year 1987. A copy of the National Road Safety Policy adopted is at Annexure-II. The policy document contained the following salient points:

- Classification of the cause of accident and preventive action in terms of vehicle, driver, and engineering factors;

- List of safety features of vehicle design (e.g. safety belt, air bags, collapsible stirrings, braking performance, etc.);
- Fitness certification and maintenance of vehicles;
- Proper training and effective licensing for drivers;
- Road design and geometric improvements to compensate for inadequacies of road users;
- Warning signs for road users;
- Accidents black spot investigation and rectification through road design;
- Design of road junctions;
- Design of roads in built up and residential areas, etc.;
- Traffic guidance, road signs, speed limit posts, and other traffic control devices;
- Road pavement markings, construction of footpaths/cycle tracks, bus bays, truck parking complexes, and other way side amenities, etc.;
- Traffic education and campaign on traffic discipline—inclusion of traffic education in school curriculum, promotion of defensive driving, etc.;
- Enforcement of maximum speed limits, and campaign on helmet use and seat belt use, curbing alcohol consumption among drivers, etc.; and
- Emergency medical service with emphasis on saving the lives of victims, etc.

The original Policy draft has aimed at a target for reduction of fatalities to 25,000 and road accidents to 2 lakh before the year 2001. However, the National Road Safety Council in its fourth meeting on 22.12.1994, while adopting the Road Safety Policy stated that "target to reduce the accidents should be related to the number of vehicles and not the number of persons killed."

Action in respect of Road Safety is a continuous ongoing exercise. The Road Safety measures undertaken by the Ministry over the years are overseen by the National Road Safety Council periodically.[10] The Seventh meeting of the NRSC was held on 15.1.2004 and salient points of implementation of the decisions of the seventh meeting are placed at Annexures II.

Comparison of Accidents Data with Other Countries[11]

Road traffic fatality rates in selected countries or areas (year 2000) are as on next page.

Cities are accident-infested areas with high-risk of involvement in some sort of accident or the other. Though only about 20 to 25% of the population of the country lives in urban areas, about 75% of accidents occur in cities and towns. The big cities of our country, thus contribute the major share in road accidents. The reasons for such high rate of accidents

Country or Area	*Per 10,000 inhabitants*
Great Britain	5.9
Japan	6.8
India	**8**
Australia	9.5
European Union	11
United States of America	15.2
China	15.6
Thailand	20.09
Venezuela	22.7
El Salvador	42.2

Source: World Report on Road Traffic Injury Prevention by WHO, 2004.

are many,—including urbanization, economic growth, tremendous vehicular growth, traffic congestion, poor and inadequate enforcement of traffic rules, lack of road safety sense and so on.

The World Report on Road Traffic Injury Prevention released by the World Health Organization on the World Health Day (7th April 2004) has highlighted that nearly 12 lakh people are known to die each year in road accidents globally. Keeping in view the increasing global concerns about the growing impact of road traffic accidents, the United Nations General Assembly and the World Health Organization have declared the year 2004 as the Year of Road Safety.

In our country more than 4 lakh accidents take place and more than 80,000 persons are being killed. However, these numbers have to be seen in the socio-economic ground conditions of the country, large population as also large number of motor vehicles in the country, as compared to other countries in the world, excluding China. As per information in the Asian Development Bank website, the number of road fatalities in China has been mentioned as 1,06,000 as against 80,000 in our country (year 2001).

Study by Planning Commission

A Working Group set-up by the Planning Commission in the year 2000 under the Chairmanship of Shri Prakash Narain, former Chairman, Railway Board and former Secretary, Shipping and Transport to look into road accidents, injury prevention and control had compiled the road traffic accident statistics of different countries but had concluded that "It is difficult to make comparisons between countries because often information is not available to allow for all the difference in traffic and travel conditions. For example, it is usually not possible to quantify pedestrian exposure, and in developing countries, the data on vehicle occupancy levels and distances traveled is not usually available. For this reason it is difficult to use the indices of fatalities or injuries in relation to vehicle kilometers, in the context of international comparisons. . . . Also it should be remembered that the definition of death due to RTC (Road Traffic Crashes) varies from one country to another, even though the WHO recommended definition is "Dead within 30 days of the Accident."

Planning Commission have complied data relating to fatalities per 10,000 vehicles at 1994 levels as under:

Nigeria	*Morocco*	*China*	*India*	*Indonesia*	*Malaysia*	*Mexico*	*USA*	*Canada*	*Australia*	*Japan*
160.0	30.4	26.2	25.2	12.6	5.6	4.6	2.1	2.0	1.8	1.7

The institutional arrangement existing in the other countries on Road Safety-related issues were also considered by the Working Group. In this context the Group felt that establishment or a multi-disciplinary Government or quasi-Government Body is necessary. The Group also noted that traffic conditions in India are very different from those experienced in the Western countries. The Group felt that investment in time and effort to come up with techniques for road designs and vehicle standards that suit our conditions is very important. The Group also felt the need to set-up a National Road Safety Board at the Apex level and corresponding Boards at State Levels.

This Ministry and the NGO member of the Working Group had dissented on this last issue. It was felt that the existing National Road Safety Council should continue to be the Apex level body. It was also felt that if at all a separate agency is created then same has to necessarily consult Ministry of Road Transport and Highways in all matters. Therefore, from the point of synergy and to have the benefit of a holistic and integrate approach, such an organization should be ideally within the Ministry of Road Transport and Highways. The matter had been taken up at the Ministerial level by the Ministry with the Deputy Chairman, Planning Commission in September 2001. Finally, Deputy Chairman, Planning Commission in November 2001 agreed to with the viewpoint of Ministry of Road Transport and Highways. He suggested setting up of a Group consisting of concerned ministries and few State Governments to suggest the strengthening of the system for formulation and implementation of Road Safety-related issues.

The inter-Ministerial Advisory Group was constituted in March 2002 having representatives from Ministry of Environment and Forests, Commissioner of Railway Safety, Planning Commission, representatives of Governments of Haryana, Tamil Nadu, Delhi, IRTE and ASRTU to recommend:

- Collection and analysis of road accidents data at National and Regional levels.
- Traffic Management and Road Safety.
- Road designs and safety.
- Vehicle design and safety.
- Human Resource Development.

The Report of this Group was finalized in December 2002. The Group noted that for National Highways, the road safety measures are being incorporated in the design itself at the DPR stage. Similar standards have also been laid down for their roads. In so far as educating the public and raising their awareness on road safety are concerned, the Ministry works with the different State Governments and NGOs in areas related to:

- Refresher training for heavy vehicle drivers.
- Evacuation of accident victims from the accident spot to the nearest hospital by assisting States and NGOs with ambulances.
- Removal of vehicles involved in accidents on National Highways by providing a crane to States and NGOs.
- Checking overloading of vehicles.
- Publicity and awareness on road safety through campaigns in print and electronic media.

In addition to the above, the Group noted that Government of India also proposes to encourage the State Governments/NGOs by providing non-recurring financial assistance to set-up model driver training schools (sanctions accorded for Assam, Karnataka, West Bengal and Andhra Pradesh already). A number of NGOs and institutions are also given financial assistance for conducting two days refresher training for drivers of heavy transport vehicles in unorganized sector (as against a coverage of 15,750 during the Ninth Five Year Plan, during the first two years of the Tenth Plan, a total of 52,014 have been covered and during the Tenth Plan period, more than 1 lakh drivers are proposed to be covered).

The Group also noted that increase in the Plan allocation from Rs. 60 crores during the Ninth Five Year Plan to Rs. 210 crores during the Tenth Five Year Plan. The Group concluded that efforts of Ministry are in line with the suggestion of Planning Commission for restructuring the existing large number of small schemes into five number of core schemes for the Tenth Five Year Plan.[12]

The development increases in the two-wheeler traffic in the last decade, the inadequacy of a mass rapid transport system, a greater complexity and heterogeneity of vehicular traffic among various other factors, have all contributed to push up the number of accidents in our country. Despite the steady toll on death and injury on our roads, it often appears that most people are apathetic, often feeling that such tragedies cannot be prevented. But they can be. The problem of road safety in our country has not been approached with the same urgency and earnestness as in the more affluent countries. This, due to the fact that our limited national resources have commanded higher priorities for economic development as compared to social requirement.[13]

The costs of injuries and property damage resulting from traffic accidents are borne not only by society as a whole, but also by such groups as the insurance industry as well as by the private individual and his relatives. Some of these costs are direct, out-of-pocket expenses that can readily be identified. Other costs, however, are difficult to specify and quantify. Calculated costs of traffic injuries and property damage are therefore highly imprecise and cannot be sued as bases for determining compensation.[14]

Implications

- Nearly 10% of beds in the large hospitals of some countries are occupied by road accident victims.
- For every person killed in a road accidents, between 10 and 15 persons are seriously injured, and some 30 or 40 receive minor injuries.
- It was estimated 10 years ago in the United Kingdom that more than half the children born will sooner or later be injured in road accidents, and that one in 50 will lose his, or her, life on the roads. The situation is little better today.
- Accident surveys have shown that accident involvement per mile driven is highest in youth, falls steadily until late middle age, and rises only slightly thereafter. In the USA, drivers over 60 have an accident ratio below the average for all ages.
- Road accidents are responsible for over 30% of all deaths in the 15-25 age-group, although this is the minimum-risk age group for pedestrians. Males between 15 to 25 are many times more likely to be killed than females.
- Serious traffic infringement or careless driving was the cause of 77% of a series of 92,000 accidents resulting in injuries, according to French police statistics. Of these, 20% were due to excessive speed, 17% to refusal of priority, 11% to driving on the wrong side of the road, 10% to careless driving, and 7% to faults in overtaking.
- In all countries, deaths from road accidents are higher in males than in females.[15]

Causes of Road Accidents

Various reasons for road accidents in India are: Lack of Traffic discipline on the part of drivers and road users, phenomenal increase in the number of motor vehicles with non-corresponding increase in road capacity, mixed traffic conditions, over-speeding, overloading, drunken driving, mechanical defects in vehicles, etc. The main causes of road accidents as revealed by the accident statistics in order of decreasing severity are as shown on next page:

It is rarely possible to attribute the cause of a road accident to a single factor, but there is general agreement among experts that human factors are at the root of most motor-vehicle accidents. The behaviour of the road user and the psychological and pathological processes that influence it, must be an essential consideration in all attempts to prevent road

Reasons for Road Accidents	Percentage
(a) Fault of drivers	83.5
(b) Mechanical defects of vehicles	3.0
(c) Fault of pedestrians	2.3
(d) Fault of passengers	2.4
(e) Bad road	1.1
(f) Bad weather	0.9
(g) Other causes (cattles, fallen trees, Road Blockage Sudden failure of the vehicles ahead, Absence of Rear Reflectors, Non-functioning of Signals and Absence of Road Signages, etc.	6.8
Total	100

Source: Report of Working Group for Tenth Five Year Plan[16].

accidents. Unfortunately it is an aspect of the problem about which very little is known.

One of the difficulties in persuading road users of the importance of factors influencing their behaviour is that, in the mind of any individual, the absolute risk of his being involved in a road accident is low, even though the relative risk may be increased many times. One example is the case of a driver who has developed a perfectly false feeling of security because he has driven with a high blood-alcohol concentration many time without being involved in an accident. Yet one carefully-controlled survey has demonstrated that a driver with a blood-alcohol concentration in excess of 150 mg/100 ml increases his relative risk of accident involvement 25 times as compared with a sober driver.

It is obvious that many traffic accidents could be avoided if drivers were medically fit, psychologically alert to the risks involved in driving, and not under the influence of drugs or alcohol.[17]

Where else do you have to dodge bullock carts loaded with steel girders, scooter rickshaws, battered taxis, huge trucks loaded with gravel, passenger cars, and thousand of bicycles, not to mention a thick flood of unconcerned pedestrians? Perhaps it isn't fair to call the pedestrians unconcerned; they are just more concerned with getting where they want to go than watching out for traffic. Almost 50 per cent of the traffic fatalities in Delhi are pedestrians.[18]

A breakdown of the causes of these accidents showed that 65 per cent were the fault of the drivers, a majority of whom were either drunk or sleepy, or else suffering from physical defects which should have precluded them from driving at all. Pedestrians and animals causing traffic accidents accounted for only 20 per cent of the total, while defective vehicles caused another 6 per cent.

This confirms a WHO report two years ago, which said that human factors are exclusively responsible for about two-thirds of all traffic accidents. "Thus, technical and environmental factors alone are responsible for only a small portion of such accidents", the WHO report added.

It also pinpointed the use of alcohol and psychotropic drugs as among the most widespread causes. According to Dr Hideo Shinozaki, of WHO's Western Pacific Regional Office, "this is especially true among developed countries and the rapidly developing countries in the Region."

On the other hand, the Safety Organization of the Philippines explained that the reason for an upsurge of traffic accidents in that country is that "the number of roads being built annually is not commensurate to the number of cars produced daily."[19]

A Case Study: Road Accidents in Chandigarh

City roads becoming death traps. Every third day, a human life is lost in road accidents.

City Roads are steadily becoming accident traps, with mishaps increasing each passing day. Going by the statistics, every third day a human life is lost in a road accident in the city.

While the UT Traffic Police have succeeded in preventing fatal road accidents at particular points in the city, they could do much better. The traffic police officials, however, justify their position by blaming the increasing number of vehicles and congestion on city roads for the increasing accidents.

Till September 5 this year, 94 human lives were lost in different road accidents. These alarming figures raise some questions: Why are these fatalities not being curbed? Why the traffic police, despite their claimed efforts, have failed to check road accidents? Some answers could be found in the statistics of increasing number of vehicles as compared to the number of city residents and the increasing congestion on city roads.

It may be mentioned that Madhya Marg, extended up to Housing Board light-point, and Dakshin Marg, extended up to Airport roundabout, are the two killer stretches where the maximum number of fatal road mishaps have taken place. The Piccadilly roundabout, where four lives were lost last year, has remained fatality-free till September this year.

Hallomajra turn is another spot of concern, where over four lives were lost last year, a number that has come down to three till September this year.

The most accident-prone roads have been identified as those adjacent to peripheral colonies of the city. Roads adjoining Colony No. 5, Colony No. 4, Hallomajra village, Raipur Khurd village and the Sector 25 colony are some of the most dangerous roads in the city.

Talking to HT, SP (Traffic) A.S. Dhillon explained, "The number of vehicles in the city is increasing tremendously, leading to congestion on city roads. Whenever a fatal road accident takes place, we identify the spot; do a detailed study on why it happened and how it could be averted. We have succeeded at several points, like Piccadilly roundabout, Fun Republic turn and Modella light-point. But still a number of accidents are taking place on the inner roads of the sectors, where people drive rashly and negligently."[20]

Killer stretches	*Fatalities (Apx.) (up to August 31)*	*Mode of traveling*	*Number of victims*
Dakshin Marg		Scooterists	36
(up to Airport roundabout)	15	Pedestrians	15
Madhya Marg		Cyclists	19
(up to Housing board light point)	14	Motorcyclists	5

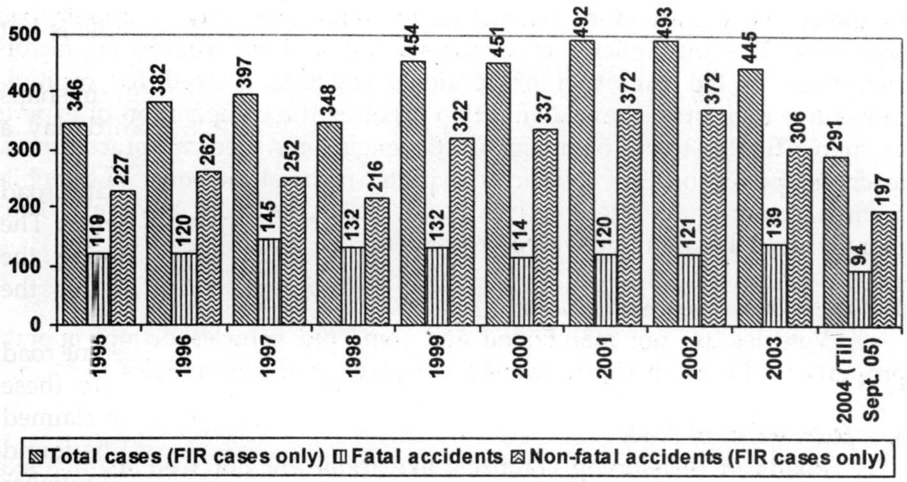

Health Education to Prevent Road Accident

I. Education in Road Safety

Education in road safety measures offer one of the most promising possibilities for accident prevention. Road Safety education is of paramount importance in today's context. It is essential that public opinion should hold widely and strongly to the view that safety is more importance than sped or added convenience. When it is safety *versus* convenience, we should learn to put safety first, even at the cost of convenience. The strengthening of public opinion in the direction of safety needs to be pressed, and pressed continuously. The creation and development of a social climate, which is conducive to the cultivation of good and sound manners, should be a natural effort for a cultured community of mature citizens. Good manners are life-savers on the road.[21]

The problems are aggravated by the migration to cities of rural populations unused to heavy city traffic and by the urban disorganization caused by the unplanned growth of these populations.

Particular stress is now placed on the need for intensified road education programmes to be organized directly by Ministries of Education and Health and indirectly through voluntary agencies. This will ensure that they reach the entire population, particularly those at risk, such as drivers of public and private vehicles, school children and so forth. In addition, several countries have run short training courses in first-aid for the police and the general public, have produced booklets and other audio-visual aids to training, and have introduced special courses for drivers and school road safety programmes.[22]

2. Education in Active Co-ordination

The prevention of mortality and injury in road accidents is essentially a public health problem. Public conscience should be developed to make every individual automatically think preventively about road accidents. The multiplicity of circumstantial and environmental factors concerned in the causation of accidents suggests a need for multiple preventive measures. Preventive action involves the co-operation of experts in many fields—town planners, traffic engineers, medical practitioners, teachers, police officers, publicity experts, medical persons, automobile manufacturers and representatives of the public as road users, etc. Thus there is need for more active co-ordination.[23]

3. Proper Maintenance of Vehicles

Vehicles are not maintained and some old vehicles do not operate properly. Delhi High Court banned the playing of old vehicles in Delhi.

4. Maintenance of Roads

Roads in developing countries like India are not well maintained. There is a need of proper maintenance.

5. Creation of Independent Authorities

Independent Bodies could be established to conduct regular safety audits of the institutions involved in road construction, traffic management, traffic law enforcement, land-use planning, public health and education.[24]

6. Education for Road Management

Poster, leaflets, films, radio and television presentations, advertisements and special campaigns will No. doubt remain an integral part of road safety activities. But the Road Safety Associations can be expected to concern themselves more directly with the behaviour of drivers and other road users, and to deal more whole-heartedly than before with education. Safety education will start, as it already does in many countries, with the very young, generally in cooperation with schools. Children need to be taught how to behave as pedestrians or cyclists in the road traffic of today. As children reach the age when they themselves may expect to be sitting behind the wheel of a motorcar, it is not enough to teach them the usual technical driving lessons should include education in safe driving habits, and should seek to develop in the pupil an attitude of concern for the safety of others.

The imparting of such basic knowledge, with it appeal to the conscience and to the public responsibility of drivers, should substantially help towards slowing down the slaughter on our streets, roads and highways.[25]

Road Safety has Three Aspects, Namely Enforcement, Engineering and Education

Enforcement

This is being done by the State Governments under the provision of Motor Vehicles Act, 1988 and Central Motor Vehicles Rules, 1989. The enforcement measures include inspections at the time of licensing/issue of permits and periodical fitness verification of the vehicles for commercial use. It is being done by the Transport Department and Police Department of the State Governments.

Engineering

Specifications/designs are constantly under review by the Ministry of Road Transport and Highways. The States are constantly being advised accordingly.

Education

Awareness is generated through various Road Safety Campaigns utilizing audio-visual and other print media and through NGOs.

Measures Taken to Reduce Accidents

The measures taken broadly fall under two categories, i.e. the Engineering measures and the Managerial measures/efforts. The Engineering measures include strengthening and widening of roads wherever necessary, improvement of road geometrics, provision of road signages, construction of bypasses, etc.

Managerial efforts include the following:

(i) Providing training to the drivers particularly in the unorganized sector.
(ii) Publicity Campaigns for awareness among the road users.
(iii) Various enforcement and regulatory measures like checking of overloading, checking of valid permit for driving transport vehicles/vehicles carrying dangerous and hazardous goods as well as personal vehicles. There is also provision under the Motor Vehicle Act for checking/certifying the periodical fitness of the transport/commercial vehicles. All these enforcement measures are being executed by the State Governments.

Highway patrolling is also one of the concepts whereby the violation of safety norms by the road users can be checked. Haryana State has launched a patrolling scheme called as Highway Patrolling Scheme under which the cranes and ambulances supplied by this Ministry are supplemented with motorcycle-based patrols, police, interceptors equipped with speed measuring devices and first-aid posts, etc. The scheme has been commended by the Asian Development Bank also and copies of the scheme have been circulated by this Ministry to all the States/UTs.

National Highway Patrolling Scheme (since Renamed as National Highway Accident Relief Service Scheme)

National Highways Patrolling Scheme was introduced in 1993-94. Under this scheme, State Governments/NGOs were provided financial assistance for purchase of crane and ambulance for clearing the accident site and evacuation of accident victims to the nearest medical center. In the year 2000-01, the scheme was renamed as National Highway Accident Relief Service Scheme, its scope extended to cover NGO's and assistance started being provided in the form of equipment. Year-wise details of cranes and ambulances sanctioned to the States/UTs/NGOs are as under:

Year	*Cranes*					*Ambulances*				
	Total No.	*NGOs*	*IG Tpt.*	*Police/ Commr.*	*SRTUs*	*Total No.*	*NGOs.*	*IG Tpt.*	*Police/ Commr.*	*SRTUs*
2000-01	—	—	—		—	41	13		—	28
2001-02	22	8		14	—	28	—		28	—
2002-03	48	8		40	—	43	8		35	—
2003-04	60	6		54	—	64*	6		58	—

* Includes 4 ambulances sanctioned for facilitating relief and safey of pilgrims at the time of Ardh Kumbh.

Public Awareness Campaigns

With a view to check the rising trend of road accidents, the Government have started a massive public awareness campaign. This includes strengthening of driver's training facilities, conducting of essay competitions among the school children, road safety marches and other publicity measures through press, radio, television, etc. Besides, certain amendments have been made in the Motor Vehicles Act, 1988 with a view to provide for stringent punishment for violation of traffic-related rules.

The year 1995 was observed as road safety year. As a continuation of the programmes undertaken in the road safety year, the public awareness campaigns have been further intensified and is being carried out throughout the country on a continuous basis through electronic media. Road safety messages in the form of cinema slides, radio jingles and T.V. interviews were carried out. Calendars and posters depicting road safety messages were distributed throughout the country. A number of hand bills/ stickers conveying road safety messages have been devised and distributed to the States and Voluntary Organizations. Road safety slogans are also painted on the buses throughout the country through State Road Transport

Undertakings. Fun game on road safety for educating the students and the general public are also being distributed throughout the country. These publicity campaigns have been appreciated by the public/various organizations. Above publicity campaigns and schemes have been appreciated by many MPs/NGOs/Commissioner, Railway Safety as also from the public including members of National Road Safety Council.

Initiatives in the Field of Driver Training

Under the Road Safety Scheme, "Refresher Training to Heavy Transport Vehicle Drivers in Unorganized Sector", financial assistance is being provided to agencies/NGOs/institutions to impart two-day refresher training to heavy vehicle drives in the unorganized sector. The scheme was started in 1997-98 and 15,750 drivers were trained during the entire Ninth Plan period. A greater emphasis has been laid on the scheme in the Tenth Plan. During the first year of the Tenth Plan (2002-03), training has been imparted to 21,999 drivers and during the year 2003-04, a total number of 30015 drivers have been trained under the scheme. It has been envisaged to cover more than 1 lakh drivers during the Tenth Five Year Plan.

Financial Assistance for Setting-up of Model Driver Training School—Salient Features

During the Ninth Five Year Plan assistance was provided to Tamil Nadu in setting-up of Driver Training School at Gummidipoondi.

During the 10th Five Year Plan, both the Ministry and Planning Commission recognized the need for setting-up of more such schools, however, an outlay of only Rs. 24 crores have been provided.

Under the scheme, the State Government/NGO would provide the land, free of cost, free from all encumbrances and also agree to bear the recurring operational and maintenance cost, while the central assistance is in nature of one time capital grant for building, driving track and teaching

(Rupees in lakhs)

	Sanctioned Cost	*(2002-03)*	*2003-04)*
1. Government of Assam	394	45	175
2. Government of Karnataka*	269	100	—
3. Government of West Bengal	328	100	175
4. The Krishna Distt. Lorry Owners' Association, Vijaywada	400	50	125
Total	**1391**	**295**	**475**

* Amount of Rs. 100 lakh released in June, 2004.

Note: Budget Provision for the year 2004-05 at BE is Rs. 6.50 crores. Proposals of assistance for Delhi, Himachal Pradesh and Kerala are being sanctioned.

equipment. The building estimates are to be based on State PWD rates or CPWD rates.

Assistance for setting up of four such schools has been accorded, all of whom would be operationalized in 2005. Details of central assistance sanctioned and released is as on previous page.

Budgetary Allocations

The budget for Road Safety programmes is being steadily increased, as under:

(Rs. in crores)

Ninth Five Year Plan		*Tenth Five Year Plan*	*2002-03*		*2003-04*		*2004-05*	
Outlay	*Exp.*	*Outlay*	*BE*	*Exp.*	*BE*	*RE*	*Exp.*	*BE*
60	43.34	210	30	29.75	40	36	35.47	44

Road Safety Related Activities by NHAI

During the preparation of the Detailed Project Report care is taken to remove back spots, improve site distances and other aspects of road safety like intersection improvements, provision of service roads, enhancement of night visibility, providing retro-reflective signs and thermoplastic lane markings, road delineators, crash barriers, crash cushions, etc.

After the completion of the project/stretches, safety audits are being conducted and wherever improvement of junctions, additional guard rails, etc. are required to be provided enhance traffic safety, the same are being carried out.

The completed stretches are put under long-term and short-term operation and maintenance contracts with the following provisions:

1. Route Patrolling

The operator is providing route patrol 24 hours per day to assist the motorists. The patrol persons are adequately trained in traffic management, road safety and in primary first-aid. One patrol vehicle is provide for approx. 50 km of road.

2. Ambulance

The operators are providing ambulances with all facilities of emergency assistance required. The ambulances have one trained nursing assistant and the driver of the ambulance have also undergone first-aid training.

3. Cranes

The operators are providing crane service for pulling and lifting of accident vehicle/break down vehicles.

4. *Highway Traffic Management System*

In certain selected stretches a Highway Traffic Management System has been provided on experimental basis wherein the entire route has been provided with emergency call boxes, which are connected to the control centre. Calls made from the call boxes are received in the control centre and immediate assistance is provided by-way-of sending the route patrol, police, ambulance, crane at the location.[26]

Injury Prevention, Safety and Treatment

Prevention, safety and treatment are the three primary aspects of a national plan to reduce road injuries. All three components need both short-term and long-term planning and surveillance to track progress and successes. Legislation and enforcement will be essential.

The first and most important objective is to prevent a crash from happening. Some countries have already made progress in prevention by separating pedestrians from cars and trucks, creating barriers and fences, building guard-rails, widening shoulders, and eliminating "black spots" where road crashes are most likely to happen. Additional successful efforts include speed control measures such as installing rumble strips and speed bumps (see Box 1), enforcing speed limits and severe laws on drinking and driving.[27]

Second, in the event of a crash, injuries can be minimized if drivers have taken safety precautions such as wearing helmets and seat belts. Crash-resistant vehicles can be built or imported with improved safety features such as rollover protection. Third, counties need effective trauma response systems in order to transport and treat victims without delay and to rehabilitate them. Rapid, efficient, emergency response systems can reduce morbidity and mortality. Quality rehabilitation care should be incorporated as part of a comprehensive plan to care for the injured.[28]

Improving road safety requires strong commitment by governments to establish, finance and sustain road safety programmes. Collaboration with other stakeholders—global, national and local—will accelerate progress and contribute to the development of more sustainable forms of public and private transport. Countries can begin with a commitment to gather more assessment data and build a comprehensive database to monitor and evaluate national plans. As the knowledge base on road traffic injuries expands, there is greater scope for collaboration between countries and across disciplines and agencies. This collaboration will be a key element in shaping a rapid response to the epidemic, especially in poorer countries, and in ensuring a reduced impact on the global environment.

Because the burden of such injuries and deaths falls disproportionately on poor countries, it is important to pursue the goal of global safety equity, in which all persons have equal access to the means of assuring safety. To achieve this, these countries will need to build infrastructure and human resource capacity, and will look to developed countries for assistance. Governments can be encouraged to view road safety and protection from injury as an important contributor to sustainable economic, social and environmental development and to mobilize the necessary forces for effective prevention of an epidemic that, while largely hidden toady, will become increasingly visible unless action is taken to control it.[29]

Box I

A Low-cost Road Safety Strategy: Speed Bumps in Ghana

Road traffic crashes are a serious problem in Ghana, where the fatality rate per 10,000 vehicles is about 30-40 times higher than that in high-income countries. As excessive speed on interurban highways and in built-up areas has been identified as one of the key factors contributing to crashes, speed bumps have been installed at some crash-prone locations on the highways, in order to lower the speed of vehicles and improve the traffic environment for other road users such as pedestrians and cyclists. Low-cost rumble strips have been installed on the main Accra-Kumasi highway at a collision hot spot. Lower vehicle speeds reduce kinetic energy (which causes injuries and deaths on impact) as well as increasing the time to collision, thereby preventing crashes.

The use of speed bumps and rumble strips has been effective on Ghanaian roads. During the 16-month period between January 2000 and April 2001, traffic crashes were reduced by 35%, fatalities by 55% and serious injuries by 76%. These speed-reducing measures also succeeded in eliminating certain kinds of crashes and improving pedestrian safety.

Legal Provision

Provisions under Motor Vehicles Act, 1988 having a Bearing on Road Safety and Amendment Proposed Therein

The important provision in the Motor Vehicles Act which have a bearing on road safety are as under:

Section 19

Power of licensing authority to disqualify from holding a driving license or to revoke such driving license. Through the proposed amendment, it is proposed to allow any officer authorized to check the driving license, to suspend the driving license on spot for a period not exceeding three months after being satisfied that the driver is under the influence of alcohol.

Section 111

Power of State Government to make rules. It is proposed to authorize the State Government to control the installation of audio-visual or audio devices in transport vehicles.

Sections 113 and 114

These prescribe the conditions for issue of permit for allowing carriage of a certain weight load by the transport vehicles and checking of the same. Through the amendment, it is proposed to curb overloading by brining the consignor of goods under the purview of the Act and also to make the weighing of overloaded vehicles mandatory.

Sections 183, 184, 192 and 192A

Section 183 prescribed penalty for driving at excessive speed, Section 184 for driving dangerously, Section 185 for driving under the influence of liquor or drugs and Section 192 for using vehicles without registration and Section 192A for using vehicles without permit.

Provisions under the Motor Vehicles Act Dealing with Compensation to Accident Victims

The Motor Vehicles Act provides for compensation to accident victims broadly under two categories.

(a) On "No. Fault" Basis

Wherein the claimant does not have to prove or establish that the death or permanent disablement in respect of which the claim has been made was due to any wrongful act or neglect or default of the owner of the vehicle or vehicles concerned of any other person.

The 'No. Fault' liability has been provided under the following Sections:

Section 140

This section provides for compensation on "No. Fault" liability for an amount of Rs. 50,000 in case of death and Rs. 25,000 in case of permanent disablement. Further, this compensation is only interim in nature as the claimant thereafter has the right to claim compensation under any other provision of the Motor Vehicles Act subject to this interim compensation being adjusted from the amount of compensation finally payable.

Section 163

Section 163 basically deals with compensation claim in case of 'hit and run' motor accident cases. Under this section the Central Government has notified the Solatium Scheme, which lays down the procedure for filing of claims, settlement/sanction of claims and payment of compensation, etc. by the Claims Inquiry Officer/Claims Settlement Officer under the scheme.

Section 163 (A)

This Section provides for payment of compensation on a pre-determined formula taking into account the income, age profile of the victim and an appropriate multiplier.

The above three Sections basically provide for compensation wherein the fault/wrongful act by the vehicle owner/insurer is not to be proved and, therefore, in such claim cases Motor Accident Claims Tribunal (MACT) is not required to determine the negligence. MACT may be required to determine the other issues like the genuineness of the claimant, the authenticity of the accident report/police report and also the insurance policy, etc.

Compensation on the basis of proving negligence/fault on the part of the driver/vehicle owner/insurer, etc.

Sections 166 and 168 of the Motor Vehicles Act

Any accident victim can file a claim under Section 166 of the Motor Vehicles Act before the MACT constituted under Section 165 and the Claims Tribunal can pass an award on the basis of this application after holding an inquiry into the claim or claims and determine the amount of compensation which appears to be just after giving an opportunity of being heard to the parties concerned.

Settlement Procedure for Awarding Compensation

Motor Accident Claims Tribunal (MACT)

Under Section 165 of the Act, these tribunals are constituted to adjudicate upon claims for compensation in respect of accidents involving death/injury arising out of use of motor vehicles or damages of properly of third party or both. The qualification prescribed for a tribunal member:

(a) is, or has been, a Judge of High Court, or
(b) is, or has been, a District Judge, or
(c) is qualified for appointment as a Judge of a High Court (or as a District Judge)

Claims for compensation can be filed in the place of accidents or in the place of residence of the claimants or the defendant or in the place where the claimant carries on business.

Section 166 of the Act provides for the procedure for filling of application for compensation.

Section 168 provides for the procedure to be followed by the Claims Tribunal for passing award in respect of such claims.

Section 169 prescribed that the Claims Tribunal shall be deemed to be a Civil Court for the purposes of these sections as well as chapter XXVI of the Code of Criminal Procedure.

Section 173 provides for appeals in case of any claimant who is aggrieved by an award of a Claims Tribunal. It also further provides that No. appeal shall lie against any award of a Claims Tribunal if the amount in dispute is less than Rs. 10,000.

Amount of Compensation under Motor Vehicles Act to Road Accident Victims/their Family Members

For the first time in India, in the year 1982 the concept of payment of compensation on 'No. Fault Liability' was brought into force with effect from 1.10.1982. Under this principle, a fixed sum of Rs. 15,000 in case of death and a sum of Rs. 7,500 in case of permanent disablement was provided for payment as compensation without pleading the fault, etc. This was a sort of interim payment and was subject to adjustment from the final amount of compensation. This amount has been raised over the years as under:

Structured Compensation

A new scheme of payment of compensation on the basis of a predetermined formula (taking into account the age and income of the victim) has been introduced. The compensation amount is decided based on a multiplier according to the age of the victim, annual income as per the second schedule to the Motor Vehicles Act. The compensation amount ranges from minimum of Rs. 50,000 to maximum of Rs. 8.00 lakhs. As per this scheme also the claimants shall not be required to plead or establish that the death or permanent disablement in respect of which the claim had been made was due to any wrongful act or neglect or default of the owner or owners of the vehicle.

Interim Compensation

(Amount in Rs.)

Year	*October 1982*	*October 1988*	*August 1994*
Amount of compensation in case of death	15,000	25,000	50,000
Amount of compensation in case of permanent disability	7,500	12,000	25,000

Compensation in Case of Hit and Run Motor Accidents

Sections 161 and 163 of the Motor Vehicles Act provides for compensation in case of Hit and Run motor accidents. The victim get compensation in case of Hit and Run motor accidents ranges from Rs. 12,500 in case of permanent disability to Rs. 25,000 in case of death. Government of India have also formulated the Solatium Scheme under this Section. The time limit for filling the application under the Solatium Scheme has also been removed.

Compensation on the Basis of Proving Negligence/Fault on the Part of the Driver/Vehicle Owner/Insurer

In addition to the fixed amount of interim compensation, the claimant can either file a claim for compensation on No.-fault basis (under Section 163A of the Motor Vehicles Act) or under Section 166 of the Motor Vehicles

Act where under this, he has to prove the negligence/fault on the part of the Driver/Vehicle Owner/Insurer on the basis of which the Motor Accident Claims Tribunal can pass an after holding an inquiry into the claim or claims.

Provision for Mandatory Insurance Cover

Section 146 of the Motor Vehicles Act provides that No. person shall use except as a passenger, a motor vehicle in a public place unless the vehicle is insured at least in respect of damage to any property of a third party.

The word accident has not been defined in the Motor Vehicles Act but in the Public Insurance Liability Act it has been elaborately defined and according to 1992 Amendment of the Public Liability Insurance Act 'accident' means unintended occurrence while handling any hazardous substance resulting to continuous or intermittent or repeated exposure to death of, or injury to any person or damage to any property but does not include an accident by reason only of war or radio-activity. Because of this definition now it has been made compulsory even under the provision of the Motor Vehicles Act, for the vehicle carrying dangerous or hazardous goods to take a policy under the Public Liability Insurance Act also.

Difficulties Faced/Anomalies Noticed and Steps Taken to Streamline The Procedure of Settlement of the Claims

Amendments already made

In 1988 Act another significant change made was with regard to amendment of the definition of the word 'property' under Section 145 (e). Prior to 1988 amendment the word 'property' included roads, bridges, culverts, causeways, trees posts and milestones whereas under the 1988 Act this was modified to include goods carried in the motor vehicles. The inclusion of the words 'goods carried in the vehicle' made a wider implication and covered the risk of the owner of the goods in case the goods also get damaged in any accident.

Certain other important amendments like substitution of the word 'insurer' by the word 'person' have been made under the 1988 Act.

Under the 1939 Act, in the event of transfer of the vehicle, the transferor had to first apply for the transfer of insurance certificate. This led to many cases where there was No. clear person to own the liability. Therefore, in the new Act of 1988, it was provided that the certificate of insurance and the policy described in the certificate shall be deemed to have been transferred in favour of person to whom the motor vehicle is transferred with effect from the date of its transfer.

Under the 1988 Act time a limit was prescribed for filling of applications for claimants. After the coming into force of 1988 Act, however, there were various representations against this time limit and through the 1994 amendment this time limit has been removed.

Amendment Proposed

Certain amendments have been further envisaged to simplify the procedure in order to reduce the number of litigations before the MACTs as at present.

The current provisions under Section 163(A) is proposed to be rationalized for the amount of compensation based on age and income of the victims. Further, a maximum cap of Rs. 10.00 lakh and a minimum amount of Rs. 50,000 for the compensation payable for permanent total disablement has been proposed.

It is also proposed to be made clear under the Act that if any claimant accepts the claim under Section 163(A) on "No. Fault Principle", he shall be debarred from filling any further claim before the MACT.

Further, if any claimant is desirous of filling a claim application for an amount beyond Rs. 10 lakh, he can do so by filling a suit in Civil Court only.

In view of the above, it is envisaged that after the proposed amendments are brought into force, the question of compensation on the basis of fault/negligence will go out of the purview of the MACTs and will be dealt with only in Civil Courts. Further, since the amount of compensation has been enhanced up to Rs. 10 lakh under the structured compensation formula and is to be awarded on "No. Fault Principle" basis, it is felt that most of the claimants will claim compensation under this instead of filling suit before the Civil Court.

The matter is at an advance stage of examination in Ministry of Law.[30]

It is necessary to increase community awareness of the key problems and to provide opportunities for wider participation in decision-making if road safety is to obtain an adequate share of resources.[31]

A Social Scourge

Africa's young nations realize that responsibility for preventing accidents rests not just with police or local authorities but with the whole community.[32]

Principles of Safety Education on the Road

Some fundamental traffic tips for road safety are:

1. Keep to the left, allow traffic in the opposite direction to pass you on the right.
2. Overtake only on the right.
3. Overtaking on the left is permitted only when the car in front is about to turn right.
4. Overtaking is not permissible, if it is likely to cause inconvenience or danger to the other traffic or where the road ahead is not visible.
5. When being overtaken or passed by another vehicle do not

increase your speed or try and prevent the other vehicle from passing you.

6. Slow down when approaching intersections, road junctions or road corners. Enter the intersection of junction, if it does not endanger anyone.
7. When entering a main road from a junction give way to the vehicles proceeding along the main road. Give way to all traffic approaching the intersection on your right hand. If there is a "Dead slow-major road ahead" sign, yield right of way to the vehicles on your left also.
8. Drive slowly when passing a procession or when passing road repairs. In any case, your speed should not exceed 25 km p.h.
9. When turning to the left, drive close to the left hand side of the road.
10. When turning to the right draw to the centre of the road, stop, if necessary, at the intersection, then move to the left hand side of the road you are about to enter.

Besides, the emphasis should be placed on the following target groups:

- School children need to the imparted road safety education specifying the various safety measures to be adopted while on the road.
- Motorists should be constantly reminded of the need to take special care of children on the roads, near the schools, etc.
- Several measures to enforce the use of zebra crossing by the pedestrians should be initiated and motorists have to be told to give right of way to pedestrians. There is a need to enforce a sense of discipline on the pedestrians.

The Government of India and State Government have undertaken the programmes of road safety. Some progress has been achieved and the rate of accidents has started slowing down during the last couple of years. The objective is to reduce the number of fatalities to 25,000 and the number of accidents to be brought down to 2 lakh per year by the year 2000. It is certain that with the active involvement of the public this target can be achieved[33].

A.S. Prashar in his press note: "No. agency for road safety engineering in India: Experts", in the *Daily Tribune* dated July 25, 2004 stated that:

Mr. Rohit Baluja, President of the Institute of Road Traffic Education, a premier New Delhi-based non-government organization engaged in sensitizing and educating the people, private and public sector organizations and government authorities about the growing menace of road accidents in the country and the ways to control it.

An estimated 1.4 million serious road accidents take place in India every year in which nearly 90,000 persons perish while about 15 lakh others suffer serious injuries; but surprisingly, there is No. single agency responsible for road safety engineering, enforcement and education in the country.

The biggest problem is that traffic management has not been defined in India. Therefore, there is nobody who is responsible for road safety engineering, enforcement and education. You go to any country of the world and you will find that all movement on the roads is governed by the civic authorities. But here in India, every thing is put in the lap of the traffic police.

The police is sometimes forced to dabble in such areas in which it has No. expertise. Traffic police has done a wonderful job by taking over the job of others but there are bound to be problems. How can it be expected to indulge in traffic engineering—a field in which it has neither the expertise nor capability?

A traffic-engineering department should be created in the civic bodies, proper training of drivers, especially of heavy vehicles should be undertaken. It must be borne in mind that heavy vehicles are responsible for 50 per cent of the serious accidents taking place on the roads of the country. There should be a traffic transportation plan by which movement of traffic on roads may be optimized.

Integrating Road Safety with Broader Policies

In most countries, the most insidious impact of road transport is air pollution, which causes public concern in both rich and poor countries. Estimates of the impact of air pollution on health indicate that this concern is justified. In Austria, France and Switzerland the number of deaths related to air pollution from traffic is twice the number of deaths from traffic accidents.[34] In addition, gases that cause climate change—quarter of which come from transport[35]—are expected to contribute to extreme weather events including floods and droughts, and changes in the habitat of disease vectors such as mosquitoes, with major health consequences.[36]

Current transport patterns have many other consequences to health,[37] including pervasive annoyance induced by traffic noise; adverse effects on rates of cardiovascular disease, diabetes, obesity and some cancers by discouraging the use of safe cycling and walking for transport[38]; and constraints on the development of neighbourhood support networks.

These consequences have a disproportionally adverse effect on the urban poor, because urban areas have higher levels of pollution and often provide fewer options for physical activity.[39]

Policies[40] adopted to reduce traffic-related air pollution do not usually consider the other health impacts of traffic such as traffic crash and injure, and *vice versa*.[41] Health systems have an important role to play in the development of integrated transport strategies that take account of all relevant health impacts.[42] Health impact assessment tools[43] can be used to help visualize the expected health implications of transport policies and make suggestions on how they can be modified to maximize overall health benefits and minimize health inequalities.[44]

CONCLUSION

Some of the important steps being taken by the Government besides highway design to check the road accidents in the country are as under:

(1) Assistance for setting up of Driving Training Schools.
(2) Provision of refresher training to drivers of heavy motor vehicles.
(3) Publicity campaign on road awareness through audio-visual-print media.
(4) Grants-in-aid to voluntary organizations for administering road safety programme.
(5) Encouraging use of simulators in driver's training.
(6) Institution of National Award for voluntary organizations/individuals for outstanding work in the field of road safety.
(7) Organizing All India Essay Competition on road safety for school children with a view to create awareness.
(8) Tightening of fitness norms of transport vehicles.
(9) Widening/improvements of roads, etc.

PART B

RAILWAY ACCIDENTS AND SECURELY

Indian Railways (IR) is the principal mode of transport of the country. For the last more than 150 years, IR has played a vital role in the overall development of the country and national integration. The growth of IR is closely linked with the economic, agricultural and industrial development of the nation. With a modest beginning in 1853 with just 34 kms., IR has today growth to a national network of 63,122 route kms., moving on an average, 1.42 million tonnes of freight and 13.6 million passengers per day. IR has also absorbed advances in Railway technology in tune with the requirement of moving large volumes of freight and passenger traffic.

The network is a multi-gauge system consisting of Broad, Metre and Narrow Gauges totaling 109,221 track kms. Gauge-wise breakup and route length under each zone as on 31st March, 2003 are as on next page.

IR has since recognized its Zones. Five New Zones, viz. East Coast Railway, Bhubaneswar, North Central Railway, Allahabad, South East Central Railway, Bilaspur, South Western Railway, Hubli and West Central Railway, Jabalpur have become functional from 1st April, 2003. Along with the reorganization of the zones, eight new Railway Divisions, viz. Agra on

Gauge	*Route (kms.)*	*Running track (kms.)*	*Total track (kms.)*
Broad Gauge (1676 mm)	45,622	64,461	87,889
Metre Gauge (100 mm)	14,364	14,859	17,848
Narrow Gauge (762 mm and 610 mm)	3,136	3,172	3,484
Total	63,122	82,492	109,221

Zones	*Headquarter*	*Route (kms.)*
Central	Mumbai	7,151
Eastern	Kolkata	2,382
East Central #	Hajipur	3,471
Northern	New Delhi	7,672
North Eastern	Gorakhpur	3,446
Northeast Frontier	Maligaon (Gowahati)	3,951
North Western #	Jaipur	6,850
Southern	Chennai	7,193
South Central	Secunderabad	7,167
South Eastern	Kolkata	7,305
Western	Mumbai	6,534
Total		63,122

#Operationalised w.e.f. 01-10-2002.

North Central Railway, Ahmedabad on Western Railway, Guntur and Nanded on South Central Railway, Pune on Central Railway, Raipur on South East Central Railway, Ranchi on South Eastern Railway and Rangiya on North-East Frontier Railway have also become operational from 1st April, 2003.

Track and Bridges

IR's route length stretches to 63,122 kms. with running track of 82,492 kms. Total track including yards, sidings, etc. stands at 109,221 kms. The table below compares the network at the end of 2002-03 with earlier years shown on next page.

Table on the next page shows route kms. of Railway lines in various States/Unions Territories at the end of 2002-03.

New Lines

During the year 2003-04, 178 kms. of new lines were constructed as indicated below:

Year	Total route kms.		Running track kms.		Total track kms.*	
	Electrical	Total	Electrical	Total	Electrical	Total
1950-51	388	53,596	937	59,315	1,253	77,609
1960-61	748	56,247	1,752	63,602	2,259	83,706
1970-71	3,706	59,790	7,447	71,669	9,586	98,546
1980-81	5,345	61,240	10,474	75,860	13,448	104,480
1990-91	9,968	62,367	18,954	78,607	25,305	108,858
1998-99	13,765	62,809	25,773	81,512	34,110	108,413
1999-00	14,261	62,759	26,809	81,252	35,120	107,969
2000-01	14,856	63,028	27,937	81,865	36,950	108,706
2001-02	15,994	63,140	29,567	82,354	39,030	109,227
2002-03	16,272	63,122	29,974	82,492	39,358	109,221

* Includes track in yards, sidings, crossing, at stations, etc.

States/UTs	*Route kms.*
Andhra Pradesh	5,197
Arunachal Pradesh	1
Assam	2,516
Bihar	3,224
Chhatisgarh	1,180
Delhi	200
Goa	69
Gujarat	5,285
Haryana	1,554
Himachal Pradesh	269
Jammu and Kashmir	96
Jharkhand	1,798
Karnataka	2,974
Kerala	1,050
Madhya Pradesh	4,825
Maharashtra	5,450
Manipur	1
Mizoram	2
Nagaland	13
Orissa	2,324
Punjab	2,102
Rajasthan	5,900
Tamil Nadu	4,184
Tripura	65
Uttaranchal	345
Uttar Pradesh	8,799
West Bengal	3,680
Union Territories	
Chandigarh	8
Pondicherry	11
Total	63,122

Note: Remaining States/Union Territories have No. railway line.

Gauge Conversion

In 2002-03, a total 830 kms. of track was converted from MG to BG.

Railway	*Section*	*Length (kms.)*
East Central	Fatuha-Islampur	42
North Eastern	Duranudha-Maharajganj	5
	Katra-Faizabad	9
Northeast Frontier	Buniadpur-Mallikpur	32
	Kumarghat-Manu	21
South Central	Yermaras-Krishna	15
South Eastern	Bajkul-Nachinda	18
	Jaroli-Keonjhar (part)	36
Total		178

Doubling

Double/multiple lines totaling 194 kms. were completed in 2002-03.

Gauge-wise Analysis

Broad Gauge, although forming 72.3% of the route, generated 99.2% of the freight output (NTKms) and 93.2% of the passenger output (Pkms.). Metre Gauge, with 22.7% of the route, generated 0.78% of freight output and 6.7% of the passenger output.

Route length as on 31.03.2003 in each gauge indicating double/ multiple line, single line and electrified route, is given below:

Gauge	*Single line*			*Double/multiple line*			*Grand*
	Electrified	*Non-Electrified*	*Total*	*Electrified*	*Non-Electrified*	*Total*	*Total*
Broad (1676 mm)	3,743	25,741	29,484	12,369	3,769	16,136	45,622
Metre (1000 mm)	104	14,180	14,284	56	24	80	14,364
Narrow (762 mm/610 mm)	—	3,136	3,136	—	—	—	3,136
Total	3,847	43,057	46,904	12,425	3,793	16,218	63,122

Almost all the double/multiple track sections and electrified routes are Broad Gauge. Metre and Narrow Gauges are mostly single line and non-electrified. From 1950-51 to 2002-03, traffic density (million GTKms. per running track km.) has increased from 4.29 to 16.85 on BG.

Track

The Railway Safety Review Committee in their Report (August 1999) had recommended that, in the interest of railway safety, the Central Government should provide a one time grant to the Railways so that the arrears in the renewal of track, bridges, rolling stock and signaling year are wiped out within a time span of years. This recommendation has since been accepted and a non-lapsable Special Railway Safety Fund (SRSF) amounting to Rs. 17,000 crore for liquidating arrears of replacement of assets has been set-up in 2001-02.

The year-wise track renewal done and expenditure incurred thereon during the IXth Plan (1997-2002) and in the first year of Xth Plan are as under:

Year	*Achievement (in kms)*	*Gross Expenditure (Rs. in crores)*
1997-98	2,950	1,805.23
1998-99	2,967	1,802.57
1999-00	3,006	2,042.00
2000-01	3,250	2,244.65
2001-02	3,620	2,475.32
2002-03	4,776	3,297.69

During the year, 65,638 kms. of mechanized tamping was completed over the IR network. Also 1,382 kms. of track renewal was carried out by machines. High output Tampers for straight track and Unimats for Turnouts are being used for tamping purpose. Similarly, various types of Ballast Cleaning Machines are being used to improve drainage of track and for deep screening of different portions of track. Dynamic Track Stabilizers and Ballast Regulators are also being used to improve the retentivity of packing by tampers. Unimats machines are used for the purpose of tamping points and crossings. 37,444 Turnouts were tamped with these machines in 2002-03. Also, T-28 machines are being used for laying concrete sleepers under Turnouts. During the year, 771 concrete sleeper Turnouts were laid with the help of machines. Track Recording Cars (TRC) are being further upgraded by providing contact less sensors. This will add to the reliability of Track Recording Car results even at higher speeds. With the help of TRC, 150,051 kms. of track recording was carried out during 2002-03.

Track Modernization

Track modernization involves upgradation of track structure at the time of renewals. Wooden, steel and CST-9 sleepers are replaced with pre-stressed concrete (PSC) sleepers. On sections with heavy traffic density, rails of 52 kg./60 kg. 90 UTS are used in place of 90 R, 72 UTS rails. Similarly, welded rails are used instead of rails with fish plate joints. During the year, 44,788 kms. of track was laid with PSC sleepers and 14, kms. with 52 kg./ 60 kg. rails. As on 31.3.2003, on the broad gauge track of IR, 71% of the length is covered by long welded rails, 75% with PSC sleepers and 61% with 52 kg./60 kg. 90 UTS rails.

Welded Rails

On most of the important routes, rails have been welded into continuous lengths—station and smaller lengths of 2 to 3 kms. as well. On the other routes, short-welded rails of 39 m. length and single rails are adopted. As on 31.03.2003 total length of welded track on IR was 59,482

Traffic Density

Million GTKMS

Per Running Track KM

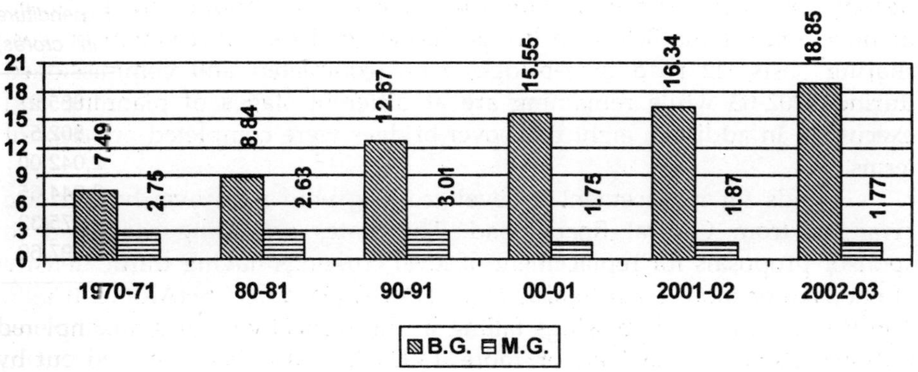

Track Renewals Per Annum

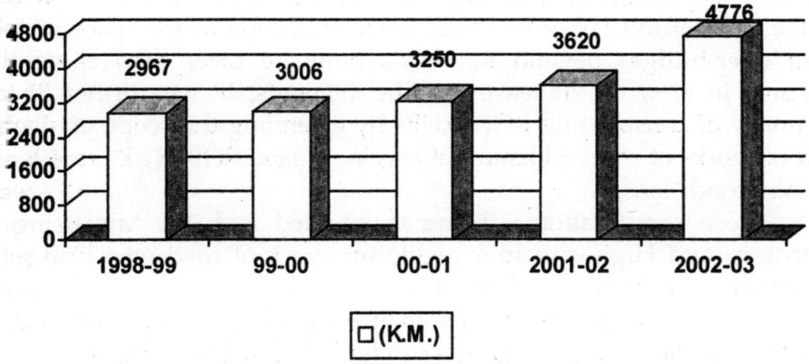

kms. out of which 44,788 kms. was with long and continuous welded rails and 14,694 kms. was with short-welded rails.

Concrete Sleepers

Prestressed concrete sleepers are most economical and technically best suited for high speed and heavy density traffic. Adequate capacity has been developed for the production of these sleepers to meet the full requirement of IR. During 2002-03, 82.85 lakh concrete line sleepers (highest ever production) and 2,741 sets of concrete turnout sleepers were produced. Intake of wooden sleepers for main line has been completely stopped and emphasis is being laid on using more and more concrete sleepers on turnouts.

Bridges

IR has 119,984 bridges, out of which 656 are important, 9,792 are major and 109,627 are minor bridges. In 2002-03, 1,151 bridges, including 343 distressed bridges, were rehabilitated/rebuilt.

To ensure smooth and safe running of trains and facilitate road users to make a safe crossing, the existing level crossings having heavy traffic density are being replaced with road over/under bridges in a phased manner. Out of the 368 such bridges sanctioned for construction on cost sharing basis, 22 road over-bridges were completed and commissioned during 2002-03 while remaining are at different stages of planning and execution. In addition, eight road over-bridges were completed on 'deposit terms'.

Funds for replacement of level crossing with road over-bridges are arranged from Central Road Fund. The States are being requested to sponsor proposals for replacement of level crossings having traffic density of one lakh or more Train Vehicle Units (TVUs) ON COST SHARING BASIS. The list of each level crossings falling in the respective States and having traffic density of one lakh or more TVUs has also been sent to them. Response received from some of the states is not much encouraging. Meanwhile, Railways are concentrating on completing the on-going works expeditiously. State Governments have also been permitted to collect funds in the form of toll tax or by commercial utilization of the space underneath road over-bridges beyond Railway's limits to meet their share of cost. Keeping in view the increasing traffic demands, IR has further liberalized its policy of constructing ROR/RUBs by extending the scope of sharing the cost of works of even widening of existing 2 lane ROB/RUBs to 4 land with certain conditions.

Close coordination is being maintained with the Ministry of Road Transport and Highways to expedite the work of road over-bridges being constructed on National Highways.

In addition, private entrepreneurs are being encouraged to invest in construction of road over-bridges/under-bridges. This scheme is known as BOT (Build, Operate and Transfer) and is attracting more and more entrepreneurs. During the year, out of the 67 works under this scheme, 14 were completed.

Level Crossings

As on March 31, 2003, IR maintained 37,423 level crossings out of which 16,741 had gate-keepers. IR has since decided to man vulnerable unmanned level crossings based on the traffic volume and visibility conditions.

Safety

During 2002-03, there were 349 consequential train accidents as compared to 413 in 2001-02. These exclude 2 accidents during accidents per million train kms., an important index of safety, on IR dropped from 0.55 in 2001-02 to 0.44 in 2002-03. Comparative position of train accidents during the last five years is as on next page.

Year	Collisions	Derailments	Level Crossing accidents	Fire in trains	Misc. Accidents	Total	Train accidents per million train kms.@
1998-99	24	292	67	5	—	388*	0.56
1999-00	20	325	93	21	—	459+	0.64
2000-01	20	344	83	15	2	464+	0.64
2001-02	30	279	88	8	8	413+	0.55
2002-03	16	216	96	14	7	349**	0.44

* Excludes 1 accidents on Metro Railway and 3 accidents on Konkan Railway.

\+ Excludes 9 accidents in 1998-99, 4 accidents in 1999-2000, 9 accidents in 2000-01 and 1 accident in 2001-02 on Konkan Railway.

@ Excludes Metro Railway and Konkan Railway.

** Excludes 1 accident on Konkan Railway.

Causalities and Compensation

The number of passengers injured or killed in train accidents and compensation paid from 1998-99 onwards, is as under:

Year	Number of Passengers		Casualties per million passengers carried	Compensation paid (Rs. in lakhs)
	Killed	Injured		
1998-99	280	615	0.06	489.65
1999-00	338	716	0.22	1,095.64
2000-01	55	281	0.01	886.07
2001-02	85	565	0.02	482.46
2002-03	157	658	0.03	489.19

Notes: (i) The above figures are excluding Konkan and Metro Railways.

(ii) Compensation paid during a year relates to the cases settled and not to accidents/casualties during the year.

Causes of Train Accidents

Out of 349 train accidents, which occurred on IR during 2002-03, 87.11% were due to human failure, including 53.30% due to the failure of railway staff and 33.81% due to persons other than Railway staff. Equipment failure was the cause of 5.16% of the accidents. 10 (2.87%) accidents were due to sabotage and 13 on account of incidental factors. Exact causes could not be established in 2 accidents.

Damage to Railway Property

The cost of damage to railway property and duration of interruption to through communication caused by consequential train accidents during 2001-02 and 2002-03 were as on next page.

Year	*Cost of Damage*		*Interruption to through communication (hours)*
	Rolling stock inclusive of engines (Rs. in lakhs)	*Permanent way (Rs. in lakhs)*	
2001-02	3,082.0	1,643.0	3,173
2002-03	3,297.7	759.0	2,363

Note: These figures excluded Konkan and Metro Railways. These are also exclusive of miscellaneous accidents and equipment failure.

Safety Measures

Some of the steps taken to avoid accidents are detailed below:

(i) A non-lapsable Special Railway Safety Fund (SRSF) of Rs. 17,000 crores has been set-up to wipe out the arrears of replacement of over-aged assets like track, bridges, rolling stock, and signaling gears within a fixed time frame of six years. The fund has been operational since October 2001.

(ii) Extended filed trails of prototype Anti Collision Device (ACD) have been successfully completed on Northern Railway. Works of provision of ACD covering about 3,500 route kms. on Northeast Frontier, South, South Central, South Western, and Northern Railways have been sanctioned. ACD survey for 10,000 route kms. has also been sanctioned.

(iii) Fouling Mark to Fouling Mark track circuiting on entire 'A', 'B', 'C', 'D' and 'D' Spl. Routes, where maximum permissible speed is more than 75 kmph, has been completed.

(iv) Auxiliary Warning System has been working on Mumbai suburban sections.

(v) Last vehicle check by Axle Counter has been introduced on over 222 block sections and is being progressively added.

(vi) To meet the situation arising out of track stresses and fatigue, up-gradation of track structure, whenever called for, is undertaken on a planned basis by utilization of 60 kg. rails on concrete sleepers. The specifications of rail steel have been up-graded and are in conformity with the International Union of Railways (UIC) specifications.

(vii) For improving maintenance and better asset reliability, Railways are continuing to eliminate fish-plated joints on tracks by welding rails to convert all single rails into long welded rails to the extent possible. During relaying/construction of new lines/ gauge conversion, long welded rails are laid on concrete sleepers to the extent possible. Turnouts are also being improved systematically.

(viii) "Quality Management Systems" have been developed and implemented as per the ISO 9001 quality standards in all the

Production Units, majority of the workshops and some of the sheds/depots. All other important manufacturing/repair units have also been advised to develop and implement Quality Management Systems. Ultrasonic testing equipment is being used for detection of flaws in the axles.

(ix) There has been progressive increase in the use of tie tamping and ballast cleaning machines for track maintenance. Also, sophisticated Track Recording Cars, Ultrasonic Flaw Detectors, Self Propelled Ultrasonic Rail Testing Cars, Oscillograph Cars and Portable Accelerometers are being used progressively.

(x) Track renewals are carried out whenever they become due for renewal.

(xi) Modern bridge inspection and management system is being adopted, which will involve non-destructive testing techniques, under water inspections, fibre composite wrapping, mapping hidden foundations and integrity testing, etc.

(xii) Intensive patrolling of railway track is carried out at vulnerable locations during monsoon, summer and winter.

(xiii) Interlocking of level crossing gates and provision of telephones at manned level crossings are some of the other safety aids being installed.

(xiv) New technological inputs like solid state interlocking, digital axle counter, high performance point machines, etc. are being progressively introduced for enhance safety and reliability of signaling systems.

(xv) Walkie-talkie sets have been provided to drivers and guards of all trains for faster communication. Guards and drivers are also being progressively provided with LED based electronic flashing lamps and hand signal lamps having better visibility than the conventional kerosene-lit signal lamps.

(xvi) Training facilities for drivers, guards and staff connected with train operation have been modernized, including use of Simulators for training of drivers. Rs. 73 crores have been provided under SRSF for upgradation of Training Institutes.

(xvii) Performance of the staff connected with train operation is being constantly monitored and those found deficient, are sent for crash training courses.

(xviii) Periodical Safety Audit of different divisions by multi-disciplinary teams has been introduced. Inter-Railway inspections and inspections by Railway Board teams have also been introduced.

(xix) Drivers are given breathalyzer tests to check for alcohol consumption, while signing on and surprise checks en-route are also undertaken to identify defaulters.

(xx) Emphasis is given on surprise inspections and ambush checks. Night inspections are conducted regularly to eradicate adoption of short-cut methods and those found to be slack, are taken up.

(xxi) With the revamping of Railway Recruitment Boards (RRBs), quality of staff being selected through RRBs has substantially improved.

(xxii) Use of fire retardant materials for coach furnishings is adopted.

(xxiii) Fire resistant PVC flooring, interior paneling, ceiling upholstery, etc. is being used.

(xxiv) Improvement in materials used in electrical fittings, fixtures such as MCB, light fittings, terminal boards, connector, etc. has been undertaken.

(xxv) Intensive publicity campaigns are undertaken to prevent the traveling public from carriage of inflammable goods.

Security

Maintenance of law and order and providing security to traveling passengers and their belongings are the responsibility of the State Governments, which they discharge through the Government Railway Police (GRP). IR bears 50% of the expenditure on the GRP incurred by each State.

Steps like provision of luggage chains underneath the lower berths to secure the luggage by passengers, closing of vestibules during night in the trains, etc. have proved effective in checking crime in trains. Facilities have also been provided to passengers to lodge their FIRs in the running trains.

The Railway Protection Force (RPF) discharges the responsibility of providing protection to Railway property, which includes both Railway's vital installations and the booked consignments.

RPF has been fighting an unrelenting battle against criminals preying on Railway property. As a result, the crime position on the Railways has been considerably under control.

Comparative position of crime against Railway property during 2002-03 *vis-a-vis* 2001-02, is as follows:

Year/Type	*No. of cases registered*	*No. of persons arrested*	*Value of Property (Rs. in lakhs)*	
			Stolen	*Recovered*
Railway materials and fittings				
2001-02	10,780	5,560	355.06	235.44
2002-03	10,040	5,666	230.29	135.60
Booked consignments				
2001-02	2,556	1,274	286.00	84.86
2002-03	2,429	1,228	158.53	52.20

Encounters with Criminals

While protecting Railway property during 2002-03, RPF personnel faced armed encounters with criminals on nine occasions in which four criminals were killed and two injured. In these encounters, four RFP personnel lost their lives and one was injured.

Railway travel has become risk and need more safety especially for women and children.[45]

Issues and Problems

Railway accidents are a pathetic scene involving passengers visiting palace on different minions. Causing psychological, economic, health, social and many others related problems. It has been seen that there is very less co-operation from Railway staff because of their apathetic and bureaucratic attitude. They come into action very late when large part of the damages has already been done. There is very less co-operation from state and local government resulting into chaos. There is lot of ornamental activities but real help is the last to be given. What is needed is to specify clearly the responsibility of all railways staff, State Government, Local Governments towards taking prompt mitigation measures.

Notes and References

1. Annual Report, 2003-04, M/o Road Transport and Highways, GOI, New Delhi, p. 5.
2. Dora, C., Philips M. Transport, environment and health. Copenhagen, World Health Organization Regional Office for Europe, 2000 (WHO Regional Publications, European Series, No. 89; http://www.euro.who.int/transport/publications_1, accessed 23 September 2003).
3. Kunzli, N. *et al.*, Public health impacts of outdoor and traffic-related air pollution; a European assessment, Lancet, 2000, 356:795-801 (http://www.euro.who.int/transport/HIA/20021107_3, accessed 23 Sept. 2003).
4. Metz, B. *et al.*, eds., Climate change 2001. Mitigation, Cambridge, Cambridge University Press for the Intergovernmental Panel on Climate Change (IPCC), 2001.
5. Dora, C., Racioppi, F., Including health in transport policy agendas: the role of health impact assessment analyses and procedures in the European experience. *Bulletin of the World Health Organization*, 2003, 81:399-403.
6. Jacobs, G., Aaron-Thomas, A., Astrop, A., Estimating global road fatalities. London, Transport Research Laboratory, 2000 (TRL Report No. 445).
7. Odero, W., Garner, P., Zwi, A., Road traffic injuries in developing countries: a comprehensive review of epidemiological studies. Tropical Medicine and International Health, 1997; 2: 445-60.
8. WHO: The World Health Report, 2003, Geneva, pp. 95-96.
9. Lok Sabha, Ministry of Road Transport and Highways, GOI, pp. 5-7.
10. *Ibid.*, pp. 2-5.
11. *Ibid.*, pp. 5.
12. Lok Sabah, M/o Road Transport and Highways, GOI, pp. 1-5.
13. Maxwell, Pereira, *Swasth Hind*, New Delhi, CHEB, March-April, 1993, World Health Day Number, p. 64.
14. WHO: Interview with Rune Andreasson, *World Health*, October 1975, p. 9.
15. WHO: LEO A. Kaprio, Death on the Road, October 1975, p. 9.
16. Lok Sabha, M/o Road Transport and Highways, GOI, pp. 7-8.
17. WHO: LEO A. Kaprio, Death on the Road, October 1975, p. 9.
18. WHO: A lack of discipline, October 1975, p. 26.
19. WHO: Adlai, J. Amor, "Killers on the road", *World Health*, June 1979, p. 20.

20. Varinder Bhatia, *Hindustan Times*, September 6, 2004.
21. *Swasth Hind*: March-April 1993, p. 65.
22. WHO: "The Americas, Road Sense", October 1975, p. 20.
23. *Swasth Hind*: March-April 1993, p. 65.
24. *Ibid.*, p. 69.
25. WHO: A social scourge, October 1975, p. 14.
26. Lok Sabha: M/o Road Transport and Highways, GOI, pp. 8-15.
27. Forjuoh S. Traffic-related injury prevention interventions for low income countries. Injury Control and Safety Promotion, 2003, 10:109-118.
28. Mock, C., Arriola-Rias, C., Quansah, R., Strengthening care for injured persons in less developed countries: a case study of Ghana and Mexico. Injury Control and Safety Promotion, 2003 10:45-51.
29. The World Health Report, 2003, pp. 98-99.
30. Lok Sabha, M/o Road Transport and Highways, GOI, pp. 15-23.
31. *Swasth Hind*: March—April 1993, p. 68.
32. WHO: A social scourge, October 1975, p. 14.
33. *Swasth Hind*: March-April 1993, p. 59
34. Kunzli, N. *et al.*, Public health impacts of outdoor and traffic-related air pollution; a European assessment, Lancet, 2000, 356:795-801 (http://www.euro.who.int/transport/HIA/20021107_3, accessed 23 Sept. 2003).
35. Metz, B. *et al.*, eds. Climate change 2001. Mitigation, Cambridge, Cambridge University Press for the Intergovernmental Panel on Climate Change (IPCC), 2001.
36. McMichael, A. *et al.*, eds. Climate change and human health: risks and responses. Geneva, World Health Organization, 2003.
37. Dora, C., Philips, M., Transport, environment and health. Copenhagen, World Health Organization Regional Office for Europe, 2000 (WHO Regional Publications, European Series, No. 89; http://www.euro.who.int/transport/publications_1, accessed 23 September 2003).
38. Racioppi, F. *et al.*, A physical active life through everyday transport: with a special focus on children and older people,. Copenhagen, World Health Organization Regional Office for Europe, 2002 (http://www.euro.int/document/e75662.pdf, accessed 15 September 2003.)
39. Road Transport and Health, London, British Medical Association, 1997.
40. The World Health Report, 2003, pp. 99-100.
41. Tiwari, G., Transport and land-use policies in Delhi. Bulletin of the World Health Organization, 2003, 81:444-450.
42. Dora, C., Racioppi, F., Including health in transport policy agendas: the role of health impact assessment analyses and procedures in the European experience. *Bulletin of the World Health Organization*, 2003, 81:399-403.
43. The World Health Report, 2002—Reducing risks, promoting healthy life. Geneva, World Health Organization, 2002.
44. Berensson, K., Millar, S., Focusing on health-HIA, How can the health impact of policy decisions be assessed: (http://www.who.int/hia/tools/toolkit/whoia038/en/, accessed 23 September 2003.)
45. Annual Report, Ministry of Railway, 2002-03.

ANNEXURE I

Total Number of Accidents on all Roads and National Highways

Sl. No.	States/UTs	Total No. of Accidents			Accidents on N.H.		
		2000	2001	2002 (P)	2000	2001	2002 (P)
1.	Andhra Pradesh	25398	30031	27634	7203	9096	8185
2.	Arunachal Pradesh	252	264	244	70	93	78
3.	Assam	2492	2516	2625	1889	1927	1928
4.	Bihar	4397	2873	N. A.	2127	1167	N. A.
5.	Chhattisgarh	6913	8751	8664	2096	2597	5531
6.	Goa	2961	2818	3419	1091	1149	1404
7.	Gujarat	36029	32523	31735	8113	6738	7239
8.	Haryana	8206	8393	8748	2765	3033	2315
9.	Himachal Pradesh	2039	2371	2524	709	898	1047
10.	Jammu and Kashmir	4598	4610	5394	2328	536	2141
11.	Jharkhand	3763	4028	4711	1419	1392	1817
12.	Karnataka	32397	33000	35784	9605	9906	10246
13.	Kerala	37072	38361	38762	8512	10095	10840
14.	Madhya Pradesh	23805	26239	26929	5611	6136	7347
15.	Maharashtra	71550	74521	66876	16150	14576	13717
16.	Manipur	506	409	520	217	208	263
17.	Meghalaya	392	600	172	186	370	113
18.	Mizoram	72	83	96	31	52	54
19.	Nagaland	79	102	84	35	54	29
20.	Orissa	6611	6405	6848	2784	2940	2920
21.	Punjab	3876	4171	4692	1268	1329	1588
22.	Rajasthan	19932	19999	20571	6718	7465	7214
23.	Sikkim	94	109	228	29	43	109
24.	Tamil Nadu	48923	51978	35503	18615	19881	22091
25.	Tripura	524	544	624	184	202	164
26.	Uttaranchal	877	1061	1117	236	469	542
27.	Uttar Pradesh	16644	20473	20684	6198	7914	7849
28.	West Bengal	18979	16954	17974	2443	3795	10002
UTs							
1.	Andaman and Nicobar Islands	158	181	168	0	0	0
2.	Chandigarh	455	492	494	62	45	99
3.	Dadra and Nagar Haveli	84	88	80	0	0	0
4.	Daman and Diu	66	53	68	0	0	0
5.	Delhi	10245	9344	8699	1277	1123	1030
6.	Lakshadweep	6	6	3	0	0	0
7.	Pondicherry	1054	1286	1484	537	595	730
	Total (States + UTs)	391449	405637	402158	110508	115824	128632

P = Provisional

Source: Ministry of Road Transport and Highways, GOI, 2003-04.

ANNEXURE I *(Contd.)*

Number of Persons Killed in Road Accidents

Sl. No.	*States/UTs*	*Total No. of Accidents*			*Accidents on N.H.*		
		2000	*2001*	*2002 (P)*	*2000*	*2001*	*2002 (P)*
1.	Andhra Pradesh	7615	8428	7517	2539	3036	2195
2.	Arunachal Pradesh	89	71	102	11	23	34
3.	Assam	1032	1021	1023	808	824	879
4.	Bihar	1452	1043	N. A.	727	442	N.A.
5.	Chhattisgarh	1102	10958	1620	363	382	670
6.	Goa	231	234	260	110	112	121
7.	Gujarat	5590	4502	5094	1973	1275	1561
8.	Haryana	2941	2911	2987	1150	1178	1070
9.	Himachal Pradesh	755	756	802	159	273	299
10.	Jammu and Kashmir	729	770	872	320	145	353
11.	Jharkhand	1244	1686	1746	493	677	731
12.	Karnataka	5655	5805	6366	2185	2283	2430
13.	Kerala	2710	2674	2792	945	1114	1148
14.	Madhya Pradesh	3810	3865	4141	1266	1139	1389
15.	Maharashtra	9840	9769	9523	3445	3383	3062
16.	Manipur	131	89	120	56	45	50
17.	Meghalaya	145	174	104	66	101	64
18.	Mizoram	62	65	50	33	43	29
19.	Nagaland	57	53	44	33	23	20
20.	Orissa	1949	1933	2220	951	972	1100
21.	Punjab	2406	2690	2638	823	924	1019
22.	Rajasthan	5388	5187	5535	2312	2455	2535
23.	Sikkim	40	50	55	8	11	27
24.	Tamil Nadu	9300	9571	9939	4362	4407	4793
25.	Tripura	125	175	157	41	74	38
26.	Uttaranchal	556	704	705	142	321	376
27.	Uttar Pradesh	8187	9654	9726	3418	3666	3758
28.	West Bengal	3428	3712	4510	1026	2421	2435
UTs							
1.	Andaman and Nicobar Islands	24	17	21	0	0	0
2.	Chandigarh	126	118	110	22	9	22
3.	Dadra and Nagar Haveli	32	40	32	0	0	0
4.	Daman and Diu	20	13	18	0	0	0
5.	Delhi	1989	1842	1696	330	268	251
6.	Lakshadweep	0	1	0	0	0	0
7.	Pondicherry	151	170	192	99	82	104
	Total (States + UTs)	78911	80888	82717	30216	32108	32563

P = Provisional.
Source: Ministry of Road Transport and Highways, GOI, 2003-04.

ANNEXURE I *(Contd.)*

Number of Persons Injured in Road Accidents

Sl. No.	*States/UTs*	*Total No. of Accidents*			*Accidents on N.H.*		
		2000	*2001*	*2002 (P)*	*2000*	*2001*	*2002 (P)*
1.	Andhra Pradesh	31268	37471	22112	8590	10758	6650
2.	Arunachal Pradesh	407	381	312	115	90	77
3.	Assam	4093	3744	3843	3329	3016	2699
4.	Bihar	2804	N.A.	N.A.	1299	N.A.	N.A.
5.	Chhattisgarh	6670	8009	7461	1792	1746	2674
6.	Goa	1973	2164	2633	717	681	1099
7.	Gujarat	38909	32508	34415	15249	7112	7317
8.	Haryana	8695	8289	8321	3153	2606	1855
9.	Himachal Pradesh	3645	4029	4009	1157	1528	1647
10.	Jammu and Kashmir	5342	6010	7186	2904	1385	2817
11.	Jharkhand	2747	3578	4201	1263	1350	1647
12.	Karnataka	38532	42196	45769	11431	12482	14163
13.	Kerala	49403	49675	494460	11801	13413	13863
14.	Madhya Pradesh	26247	27401	29780	6236	6009	8011
15.	Maharashtra	49723	49340	48377	12266	12559	11759
16.	Manipur	827	846	914	363	368	465
17.	Meghalaya	426	349	303	129	245	201
18.	Mizoram	99	38	184	31	25	105
19.	Nagaland	126	184	76	70	105	20
20.	Orissa	8924	8314	9678	3474	3409	3822
21.	Punjab	3165	3390	3932	1020	1084	1325
22.	Rajasthan	25434	25994	27119	8341	9621	10078
23.	Sikkim	265	221	321	96	91	143
24.	Tamil Nadu	53406	52922	55130	20146	19494	22963
25.	Tripura	864	949	708	297	279	201
26.	Uttaranchal	860	1148	1255	203	456	548
27.	Uttar Pradesh	12055	13256	13152	4362	4702	4616
28.	West Bengal	11587	10625	13800	3142	3348	7474
UTs							
1.	Andaman and Nicobar Islands	220	230	243	0	0	0
2.	Chandigarh	434	495	469	59	45	86
3.	Dadra and Nagar Haveli	108	117	99	0	0	0
4.	Daman and Diu	73	42	61	0	0	0
5.	Delhi	8771	8449	7929	1013	980	873
6.	Lakshadweep	8	6	6	0	0	0
7.	Pondicherry	1155	1381	1571	552	605	768
	Total (States + UTs)	399265	403751	404829	124600	119592	129966

P = Provisional.

Source: Ministry of Road Transport and Highways, GOI, 2003-04.

Annexure II

National Road Safety Policy

Introduction

1. About 57,000 persons are killed in road accidents in India every year. There are more than 3 lakh reported road accidents in 1991. The total economics loss to society in account of road accidents is estimated at over Rs. 5000 crore. The road accidents statistics gives No. indication of their social costs especially in terms of the loss of bread-winner or continued personal injury and trauma. Table 5.1 gives the details of road accidents statistics of the country as a whole. Table 5.2 gives the State-wise details for the year 1991.

Table 5.1

Road Accidents in India

Year	*No. of registered Motor Vehicles (in thousand)*	*No. of Accidents (in thousand)*	*No. of Accidents per 1000 vehicles*	*(in thousand)* No. of persons killed	No. of persons injured	Total (6+7)
1	*2*	*3*	*4*	*5*	*6*	*7*
1970	1401	114.1	81.37	14.5	70.1	84.6
1971	1865	120.2	64.34	15.0	70.7	85.7
1972	2045	122.3	59.66	16.1	76.4	92.5
1973	2109	121.6	57.85	17.6	79.3	96.9
1974	2327	114.3	48.99	17.3	76.7	94.0
1975	2472	116.8	47.33	16.9	77.0	93.9
1976	2700	124.7	46.30	17.8	82.5	100.3
1977	3260	135.4	41.41	20.1	95.6	115.7
1978	3614	146.3	40.40	21.8	99.5	121.3
1979	4059	144.4	35.48	22.6	102.9	125.5
1980	4514	153.2	33.89	24.6	109.1	133.7
1981	5173	161.2	31.12	28.4	114.0	142.4
1982	5844	166.2	28.40	30.7	126.0	156.7
1983	6905	177.0	25.63	32.8	134.1	166.9
1984	7783	195.0	25.05	35.1	156.2	191.3
1985	9097	207.0	22.75	39.2	163.4	202.6
1986	10490	215.5	20.54	40.0	176.4	216.5
1987	12539	234.0	18.66	44.4	189.0	234.2
1988	14733	246.7	16.74	46.6	214.8	262.0
1989	16920	270.0	15.96	50.7	229.7	279.4
1990	19177	282.6	14.76	54.1	244.1	298.2
1991	21310	294.0 (P)	13.80	56.5	255.3	311.8

TABLE 5.2

State-wise Road Accident (for the year 1991)

Sl. No.	*States/UTs*	*Accidents*	*Persons Killed*	*Persons Injured*
1.	Andhra Pradesh	17633	5598	17545
2.	Arunachal Pradesh	213	83	428
3.	Assam	1899	867	2589
4.	Bihar	9776	2304	2067
5.	Goa	2418	177	1683
6.	Gujarat	27140	3979	25673
7.	Haryana	4867	1916	4452
8.	Himachal Pradesh	1269	414	2308
9.	Jammu and Kashmir	245	392	2504
10.	Karnataka	22438	3979	25938
11.	Kerala	23985	1803	31831
12.	Madhya Pradesh	26406	3398	22065
13.	Maharashtra	58378	6160	34943
14.	Manipur	393	111	506
15.	Meghalaya	550	129	589
16.	Mizoram	87	29	99
17.	Nagaland	111	57	118
18.	Orissa	6177	1330	6859
19.	Punjab	1581	1141	1322
20.	Rajasthan	11046	3736	12550
21.	Sikkim	137	34	239
22.	Tamil Nadu	32522	6406	29538
23.	Tripura	371	95	665
24.	Uttar Pradesh	16864	7806	12870
25.	West Bengal	16041	2559	7048
Union Territories				
1.	Andaman and Nicobar Islands	86	5	135
2.	Chandigarh	277	72	155
3.	Dadra and Nagar Haveli	50	11	61
4.	Daman and Diu	67	7	88
5.	Delhi	8065	1820	7883
6.	Lakshadweep	Nil	Nil	Nil
7.	Pondicherry	724	107	633
	Total (States + UTs)	294022	56525	255384

Road accidents are on the increase and the cost to the Nation immense. However, since these occur at different locations and throughout the year, their total economic impact is yet to be appreciated.

3. Realizing the problem of mounting number of road accidents, a special meeting of the Transport Ministers of all State Governments and UTs was held in 1982, which, *inter-alia*, recommended for setting up of a

National Road Safety Council, as well as a Directorate of Road Safety in the Ministry of Surface Transport. The recommendations of the special meeting of the Transport Ministers were considered by the Government. A Road Safety Cell was set-up in 1987. The Cell was expected to collect, compile and analysis—accidents in the country. As per recommendations of the Council and suggestions received by the number of steps have been/are taken to spread road safety culture in the country.

4. Recent studies indicate that road safety policy should take into account the physiological and psychological limitations of humans as road users, see risks perception and acceptance and limited preparation for safe behaviour on the road, etc. Road sense and knowledge of traffic rules and regulations are not in themselves sufficient to ensure acceptable behaviour on the road. Difference between wing what is right and doing what they can get away with are very great among individual road users – chances of being caught are very small.

5. Until a few years ago, the problem of road safety was tackled from the standpoint of overemphasizing the human factor. In other words, an accident was considered to be the result of a failure to obey the rules. Due to this approach, inadequate attention was paid to an improvement of situational factor, such as the effective design of the road and its environment.

6. Our efforts should actually be directed towards interrupting the course of events which result in an accident when they combine and interact in a concrete situation; a combination of human factors and situational factors. If only one of these influential factors can be changed, then the chances of an accident occurring can be very much reduced. It is often a case of human error in a specific situation.

7. The avoidance of critical combinations of circumstances, which lead to an accident, is equivalent risk management. This is analogous to the prevention of industrial injuries, in which in addition to the human factor itself in terms of training, motivation, etc., adaptation of the working environment to compensate for the shortcomings in human behaviour, i.e., the ergonomic approach is a prime consideration.

8. In addition to measures in the fields of road safety training and education and driving instructions opt provide additional knowledge, experience, road sense, motivation to improve driving behaviour, traffic regulations, appropriate traffic monitoring, traffic law enforcement, the ways of dealing with traffic offences and improvement of both active and passive vehicle safety, sufficient attention must also be paid to the road infrastructure and town and country planning. The design of new roads and reconstruction of existing road systems must compensate for the inadequacies of road users.

9. The often unfair or incorrect way in which the most complicated and most variable of all the factors, humans themselves, are treated is strongly influenced by the other factors which in a way provoke a specific type of behaviour on the road. The physical characteristics of the traffic

situation provoke a certain type of behaviour, while people are also further influenced by the behaviour of other road users, i.e. fast cars, fleeting contact and anonymity of the road users, without any framework for enforcing informal social rules of behaviour. Behaviour modification strategies, which disregard the social and physical context, also disregard important causes of the particular type of behaviour in many situations the conditions are insufficient to ensure voluntary observance of road behaviour standards.

10. The rise in the volume of road traffic, which is a part of the economic development of the country, brings in its wake the attendant problems of road accidents. The causes of road accidents could be broadly classified into the following categories.

'Vehicle' Factor

11. Motor Vehicle, a major factor in road accidents, is also being accorded attention in design. It is a fairly complicated engineering machine which must always be maintained in proper condition to prevent accidents due to malfunctioning of critical parts. Stricter checking by Transport Authorities is being stressed since vehicle maintenance, inspection and usage are important from safety considerations.

12. In India, majority of vehicles are manufactured indigenously and potential for improved road safety through better vehicle engineering designs is possible. Bio-mechanical and orgonometric considerations in vehicle design are very important.

13. The in-built safety features advocated for vehicle design are:

(i) Cars: Safety belts, air bags, collapsible streeing colums, laminated safety glass for wind shield, improved instrument panel and lighting system, wing mirror.

(ii) Commercial Vehicles: Collapsible steering column, wing mirrors, wind shield of laminated safety glass variety, dual-line brake system, exhaust breaks and power steering for hill areas operation, improved design for wiper blades and headlights, automatic dippers, reflex reflectors, reflectorized number plate, hazard warners for break-down movement, improved design of cab and other devices for driving comfort.

(iii) Motor cycles and scooters: Reflex reflectors, direction signals, stop light, improved design for new view mirrors, roll-over bars, chain guards, handle bar grips, lighting system, telescopic front forks, braking system, increased wheel size.

(iv) Three-wheelers tempos and cycle rickshaws: Rear view mirrors and side mirror lights.

(v) Slow moving vehicles: Cat's eye reflectors on all slow vehicles including cycles, Animal carts to be provided with suitable brakes and night-lamps for cycle.

14. Vehicle being complex mechanism needs periodic checking and replacement of warm-out parts. A general maintenance awareness among the users is therefore required to be created.

15. A systematic maintenance education programme should be launched by the manufactures' and operators' associations with the Government support. Simple brief literature on maintenance norms should be supplied with every vehicle at the time of delivery. Adequate repair facilities need to be provided along highways as regular intervals. Legislative measures to prevent large-scale production of substandard parts are also needed.

16. Another area requiring more attention is issue of vehicle fitness certificates. Presently, the transport authorities do not subject the vehicles to a thorough checking for detecting deficiencies as in the developed countries. The inspection wing of the State Transport Departments needs to be appropriately strengthened for effective results. Vehicle testing equipment is proposed to be imported on an experimental measure. Side by side a checklist for vehicle inspection has been prepared for a thorough inspection of engine condition, braking system, steering mechanism, tyres, accessories. Surprise checks for vehicle fitness would also go along way in ensuring preventive maintenance of vehicles. This could be more frequent for trucks and buses. The use of bald tyres begin unsafe, minimum tread depth can be stipulated and enforced strictly.

17. Better visibility of vehicles at night is also important.

18. As measure of caution, it may however be added that though improvements of the dynamic qualities of the vehicles (road holding, brakes . . .) are often misuses by the drivers and lead to an increase in speed and a shift of the risk limits, they have however a positive effect on the outcome of an incident situation during an emergency moan oeuvre.

19. Improvements to vehicles have had a positive effect on the occurrence of incidents and their outcome, because the road user has fewer degrees of freedom during an emergency man oeuvre and improved vehicle characteristics can precisely compensate for this. The improved braking performance of today's motorcars has improved the outcome of emergency stops at low speeds.

20. Improvements in vehicles design and various hazard protection measures designed to reduce the effect of the collisions have contributed to significant reduction in the chance of a collision resulting in a fatality. It is fairly easy to intervene at this stage of the accident process, because humans cannot easily compensate by their behaviour for the effects of certain improvements such as cage construction and crumple zones in vehicle construction, safety belts, etc. However, the collision speed of vehicles on roads outside built-up areas has increased significantly. Although the ability of motorcars to resist damage on collision has increased, it still leaves much to be desired. There is still very little protection along the sides of motor cars and a side on collision, as in a collision with another vehicle crossing its path, leaving the road on a bend

at speed and collisions with other objects not designed for impact, can result in serious injury or even fatalities.

'Driver' Factor

21. Accident studies, the world over have clearly established that the vehicle driver is a very important factor in a road accident. Quality of drivers has, therefore, gained special significance. Proper training and effective are two basic pre-requisites of a quality driver. Ironically, the majority of drivers in our country have hardly any formal training. Out of about 350 lakhs persons engaged in driving different kinds of motorized vehicles, about 20 lakh persons are deployed in heavy transport vehicles. Licensing and training of such drivers, therefore, needs special attention.

22. Participation in the traffic scene demands from the road user a great capacity for recognizing that a specific traffic situation is about to occur and predicting how that situation will develop. The various components of the road, route, shape, technical equipment, signboards, etc. must constitute cohesive entity that the road user can allow clearly recognizable and predictable situations to develop which can be anticipated. The road user constructs a certain pattern of expectations both from the observations made at the time and from experiences in past situations. In order to achieve safe and smooth traffic flow, it is essential that the changes in the road and traffic picture seen by the road user agree with his pattern of expectations so that the desired behaviour on the road is actually produced in real situations. Since road users often use danger-compensating behaviour, the danger viewed subjectively should be greater than that viewed objectively. If this is not the case, then road users must be provided with additional warning signs.

23. If all possible, a connection must be found between the natural behaviour of road users and what they experience in an acceptable and logical fashion. This requires a great deal of knowledge of the way in which people process information and react to specific traffic situations. Discontinuities in the roadway such as junctions, forks, bends, road works, etc. can cause a road user to form incorrect expectations and thus led him or her to unconsciously adopt unsafe behaviour on the road. On the other hand, discontinuities in the road picture can also be desirable as a means of increasing alertness, for example, at junctions or in town centres, etc. although here they must be more greatly accentuated.

24. Prevailing system of issue of driving licences has been subject matter of criticism. In particular, the manner of testing of driving skill. Important aspects of road safety, knowledge of traffic rules and regulations and road signs, punishment to drivers violating speed limits, driving under the influence of liquor, the elementary mechanism of vehicle and driver fitness are to be stressed. Suitable provisions have been made in the recently amended Motor Vehicle Act. The system of issuing driving licence has to be reviewed and made more strict, so that only persons with adequate driving skills and knowledge of traffic regulations/road behaviour are given driving licences.

Engineering Factor

25. Road design must compensate for the inadequacies of road users, presenters of judgments and allow for the fact that the external appearance of the road and road environment exerts a profound influence on behaviour on the road.

- Road traffic installations much engender the appropriate behaviour in drivers and keep them on the right track: thus the path or route, width and verges of the road determine the speed of the vehicle.
- The design of roads involves constantly examining the problem from the viewpoint of road users, analyzing their individual tasks and viewing the situation through the eyes of inexperienced and slightly confused road user unfamiliar with the local situation, whether pedestrian, cyclist, motorist or lorry driver.
- In the event of recurrent accidents at a particular locality, known as an accident black spot, road and traffic engineers are also under an obligation to investigate the extent to which actual road design and the local situation contribute to or are responsible for this phenomenon. Traffic engineers may not just dismiss the problem by asserting that road users are solely to blame. The cause of an accident is too often merely seen as illegal behaviour on the road. Provision of warnings for the road user before an accident black spot is not only inadequate but also provides No. fundamental solution to the problem itself. Infrastructure measures must also be taken in dangerous situation.

26. Modification of roads and junctions to accommodate the capacities and limitations of road users has a significant positive effect on road safety. However, the increasing speed of motor vehicle is a disturbing development in the area of road traffic.

- Faster speeds have extremely negative consequences outside built-up areas, especially on major roads, where many sometimes-unexpected events take place.
- Within built-up areas and residential areas, attention should be drawn away from the interests of mortised traffic and focused instead on the interests of the local residents to improve their quality of life. However, this must involve a distinction between main traffic arteries and other roads.
- The increasing use of microelectronics in traffic engineering and the car itself can increase road safety.
- Most attention is focused on traffic guidance (information, route planning, auto-navigation), traffic management, incident

detection (accident, traffic-jam, fog, glazed frost), obstacle signaling, communication, defective car components indication, built-in speed limitation.

27. Road markings are excellent reference points for determining individual position, the course, position and speed of other vehicles and the positions of obstacles on and beside the road. Because road markings are not always clearly visible in rainy or twilight conditions, etc., additional vertical indications are also required. Vertical indications such as tree and shrub plantations are also desirable to create an effect of spatial guidance.

28. Lack of detailed attention to traffic provisions often causes undesirable behaviour on the road.

29. Engineering measures are an important input for highway safety. It comes into play at two levels—Macro level and Micro level. By macro-level, is meant urban and rural road network planning. The absence of proper planning of transport corridors would invariably stain the network to the extent that there would be sharp increase in accidents or traffic flow would be at crawl speeds. The in-built geometric incapability of the road network particularly in the core areas of cities make it impossible to undertake any meaningful improvements later. Thus macro-level planning has a long-term effect on safety and must be given as much care as design of details in a highway. At micro level, the spots, which are accident-prone are identified and suitable traffic engineering improvements undertaken. While designing facility, all relevant physical features designed keeping in view the safety requirements so that they are driver forgiving and of self-enforcement nature. Apart from road engineering, traffic and travel management measures have also to be undertaken.

30. For determing effective and low cost solutions particularly for micro-level safety-oriented highway engineering measures creation of traffic engineering cells in the State's Public Works Departments is a step in the right direction. We have such cells in fifteen States by now.

31. The critical requirements from engineering angle are:

(i) Installation of road signs, speed limit posts and other traffic control devices including delineators.
(ii) Road pavement markings.
(iii) Geometric improvements of hazardous alignment sections.
(iv) Proper junction designs and signal timings.
(v) Planning for footpaths, cycle tracks for pedestrians and cyclists and facilities for their crossing the heavily trafficked roads in urban areas and other segregation measures.
(vi) Provision of bus bays, wayside amenities, truck parking complexes at suitable locations.
(vii) Provision of guard rails where necessary.

32. A more serious phenomenon-gripping the highway today is the ribbon development and encroachments particularly near the urban fringes

and lack of access control. Apart from environmental degradation, the carriageway is eroded and free flow obstructed. Remedy lies in constructing parallel service roads and full development of cross-section in the available right of way but more lasting solution would be by effective land use policy and travel management measures. Steps are underway to prescribe a minimum green buffer along critical corridors near urban areas.

33. In urban areas, a demand is growing among traffic police departments, that plans for improvements of highways be shown to them to ensure that these are functional from the point of view of traffic operation and road safety. There is a merit in such a demand and it is an indicator of the concern for road safety and need for an inter-disciplinary joint efforts to fight the accident menace.

34. Increasingly the dimensions of traffic infrastructure components such as junctions, traffic lanes, etc. results in complexity and a poor understanding of the situation. The task of drivers becomes more difficult, with uncertainly not only of the individual road user's behaviour but also of the position and course of other road users. It has been observed that large-scale junctions with many individual design elements for optimum traffic flow demonstrate unsafe traffic side effects. In contrast to this, more compact junctions which have been less emphatically designed for the fastest possible traffic flow often appear much safer because they demand a greater level of concentration and more appropriate behaviour from the road user. Road markings can be sued to restrict the road space available to an individual road user, thus reducing the complexity of the junction. However, all modification must always be tested before being introduced on a permanent basis.

35. The interaction between road users has a much greater significance for safer and smoother traffic flow than the behaviour of an individual road user at a junction, the intersection of two or more traffic streams. The shape of the junction, its associated equipment and local characteristics must be carefully coordinated in order to bring about the desired behaviour at and in the vicinity of the junction. Roundabouts can function extremely well in certain areas.

36. Road signs on, above and at the side of the road used to provide information relating to direction and position on the road, warnings, traffic guidance and safety must be relevant, visible, timely, unambiguous and most importantly, consistent in a given situation. Recognizability of this type of information is important to correct anticipation.

37. An essential condition for road safety is the provision of sufficient information. However, too many indications and signs in one place should also be avoided, because the driver has insufficient time to process the information given. Also, the information must be capable of being observed in unfavourable conditions such as rain, fog, inadequate lighting, etc. Road signs indicating direction for the road user must be visible, conspicuous and legible. Road users using an unfamiliar road have the greatest need for information.

38. Road marking are an integral part of road design. In many existing situations they can be used to correct and incorrect shape. They accentuate any discontinuities, increase the recognizability of decision points and fulfil a purpose with regard to desired road behaviour.

39. Correct perception and correct judgment are the two primary measures for avoiding road accidents at the pre-crash stage and these must be learnt and understood well by every individual road user. Traffic education is the only tool for imparting this skill. Actually traffic education also makes the task of enforcement easier and more fruitful. Standard of training in the driver training schools presently operating in the country need to be upgraded.

40. Traffic education is not a one-time exercise. A sustained campaign on traffic discipline is required T.V., Press and Cinema are being utilized presently but we still have a long way to go.

41. There is need to introduce graded traffic education in school curriculum. Pedestrians and cyclists also need exposure to correct norms of behaviour on road. Voluntary organizations are coming forward. They need encouragement and recognition. For this purpose, the Ministry of Surface Transport have already announced a scheme for providing grant-in-aid to voluntary organizations engaged in the field of road safety. State Governments should also encourage voluntary organizations in a similar manner. Through them, propaganda and publicity campaigns are being mounted. The Police Departments need to be allotted specific funds in urban areas for safety campaign and sustained education programmes to improve discipline among pedestrians, cyclists and road users.

42. The control of the negative consequences of the increasing (auto) mobility represents one of the greatest challenges of our society.

43. The traffic and transport aspect will have to become of greater importance within the environment policy.

Special campaign in the following area will have to be undertaken:

- information towards specific target groups;
- fight against alcohol in traffic;
- information for the promotion of defensive driving and traffic control aimed at dangerous and anti-social behaviour;
- enforcement of maximum speed limits on national highways;
- increased risk of being caught and adjustment of legal proceedings (among others, use of electronic devices; driver's license with marks);
- promotion of the use of seat belts and helmets;
- training and follow-up of novice (young) drivers and motor cyclists;
- analysis of accidents with heavy vehicles;
- extra attention for fragile road users, pedestrians, cyclists, children elderly;
- cooperation of companies for motivation of personnel;

- coordination and organizational cooperation between ministries, consideration of road safety by other governmental actions; and
- promotion of State and Municipal Road Safety Programmes.

44. It is important that one realizes that (lack of) safety is nearly always related to speed.

Emergency Medical Service

45. The post-crash phase of a road traffic accident envisages the prompt handling of a crash victim. Unfortunately, a traffic accident victim does not get proper attention from the fellow road-users nor from the public for fear to being harassed by the Police authorities. The Supreme Court have already laid down guidelines in this regard. Suitable amendments to the MV Act, 1988 making it mandatory for drivers to provide assistance and take victims of road accidents to the nearest medical centre are being processed. Due to lack of prompt handling and transportation and inadequate first-aid facilities, numerous lives are either lost of result in permanently disability. According to some estimates, about 30 per cent of the fatalities in road accidents are due to delayed arrival of the patients to the hospitals.

46. Another vital component in the accident emergency measures is the prompt and efficient transport of accident victims. This can be achieved in may ways:

- Organizing Central ambulance service in cities as well as for rural areas.
- Giving cash incentives to auto rickshaw, taxi or other motor vehicle drivers and members of public who escort the accident victims to nearest hospital.
- Providing adequate first-aid equipment and training to police personnel on patrol duty.
- Absolutely No. harassment to person escorting an accident victim
- Making adequate provisions in law that No. private medical practitioner or a nursing home will refuse to treat an accident victim for want of money. For this purpose adequate provisions should be made for awarding prompt compensation to such medical institutions/practitions.

NATIONAL ROAD SAFETY STRATEGY

A National Road Safety Strategy has to be formulated to reduce accidents during the 1990s and into the early years of the 21st Century. The initial target is to reduce that total number of fatalities in road accidents to 25,000 by the year 2001 A. D. and the total number of accidents to 2 lakh within the same period. The fundamental aim of our road safety should be to save lives and reduce serious and debilitating injuries, loss of quality of life and opportunity that results from road accidents.

Overall National Goals

(i) To achieve a reduction of fatalities in road accidents to 25,000 and road accidents to 2 lakhs before the year 2001.

(ii) To take advantage of the major developments of technology, both domestic and international, which would help to reduce the frequency and severity of road accidents by the year 2001.

(iii) To ensure that by 2001, the behaviour of all road users would be improved to the extents that enforcement action is to be directed to only a small but specific segment of the population.

(iv) To take steps to incorporate Road Safety objectives to be incorporated in Central and State National Health, Education, Industry, Urban Development, I and B, and Home Department programmes by 31st December, 1994.

(v) All Governments and other agencies would by 31st December, 1993, prepare individual strategies and action plans aimed at progressively reducing the level of road accidents through the 1990s.

The basic elements of the implementation of the road safety strategy should in—

- Continued reduction in road fatalities and serious injuries,
- Safer road and vehicles,
- Protection of vulnerable road users,
- Better driver education,
- High Level of Safety Education in schools,
- Traffic calming especially in residential areas,
- Improved heavy vehicle safety,
- Improve public transport,
- Less Government and more-self regulation,
- Coordination between Centre and States/UTs and between police, health professionals and other service groups,
- Improved infrastructure for transport operations,
- Greater community involvement, and
- Improved trauma management.

Each one of these would need to be broken down into sectoral strategies and programmes of action drawn up.

Recommendation of National Road Safety Council

In the light of the foregoing, the recommendations of the National Road Safety Council are sought on the following:

(a) To bring down the number of fatalities in road accidents to 25,000 and to reduce the number of accidents to 2 lakhs by the year 2001 AD based on the strategy indicated above. Annual targets of reduction to be laid down and communicated to the State Government.

(b) Request Central/State Government to draw up specific programmes for construction of safer roads as indicated.

(c) To recommend to Ministry of Surface Transport/Ministry of Industry to take specification for the production of safer vehicles.

(d) To recommend to the State Transport and Police Departments to take specific steps for the protection of the vulnerable road users such as two-wheeler riders, pedestrians, cyclists, etc.

(e) To recommended to all Transport Departments to improve the quality of driver education and training and stricter control over the issue of driving licences.

(f) To recommend to the Ministry of Human Resources Development in include road safety in the curricula of schools.

(g) To request all State Governments to take special steps for traffic calming as indicated, especially in the residential areas.

(h) To recommend to all State Governments to provide for and/or operate improved public transport systems. For this, suitable fiscal incentives for public transport and dis-incentives for personalized vehicles should be approved.

(i) Recommend to State Governments to ensure better coordination between States as well within a State between police, health professional, local bodies, voluntary organizations, etc. in implementation of road safety programmes.

(j) To recommend to Ministry of the Home Affairs to amend IPC to charge drivers involved in fatal accidents (caused due to negligence or rashness) under Sections 302, 303 and 304 of the IPC and if the driver is found to be deficient in driving, to take such steps as would put the testing authority also in trial for abetment of the offence.

(k) To draw up specific programmes for greater community involvement in implementing the road safety programmes drawn up.

(l) To request the State Government/health professionals and voluntary organizations for improved trauma care to reduce fatalities.

(m) To request the Ministry of Surface Transport to set-up a National Institute for Transport and Safety Research, which would conduct, detailed studies on road safety.

(n) To activate the National Institute of Road Safety with a view to improving driver training and quality of driving skills in the country.

(o) To examine the feasibility/desirability of enacting a separate Road Safety Act in order to consolidate all pieces of legislations concerning road safety at one place and make it comprehensive on the lines of such legislation in other countries.

(p) To recommend to the State Governments for strict enforcement of fitness of motor vehicles and their continued monitoring.

(q) To provide for deterrent punishment in the Motor Vehicles Act for serious traffic violations like drunken driving, driving under the influence of drugs, rash and negligent driving, crossing of red lights, etc.

To ensure that the programmes to meet the recommendations are implemented in a systematic and time bound manner, it is suggested that a Standing Committee of 10 persons from the Council be constituted. The Standing Committee would meet atleast once in a quarter and monitor the progress of action and submit half yearly reports to the Chairman of the National Road Safety Council. These reports would also be discussed at subsequent meetings of the National Road Safety Council.

Recommendation of National Road Safety Council

Sr. No.	*Action Point*	*Action Taken*
1.	The construction of speed breakers be done wherever required, in the basis of guidelines issued by the Ministry.	All States and UTs addressed on 12th Feb., 2004 and reminded in 14th, June, 2004
2.	The NRSC complimented the Ministry regarding the measures taken relating to inclusion of road safety as a part of the school educational curriculum and desired that NCERT may be approached once again to corporate a chapter on road safety at primary level also.	NCERT who had included a chapter in Class VII (Social Science) have been asked to do at primary level also. Further the Chief Secretaries of all the states requested by Secretary (RT and H) on 30.10.2002 followed by letter to take similar action in respect of syllabus prepared by State Board/SCERT.
3.	To amend the Motor Vehicles Act, 1988 for increasing the minimum period of driving experience of light commercial vehicles before a licence to drive heavy commercial vehicles is granted.	Proposal for amendment of MV Act in Ministry of Law.
4.	To stop plying of "Jugadh" vehicles (Improvised vehicles) in the State. The Haryana representative informed that the Hon'ble High Court of Haryana and Punjab had issued similar directions in the matter to the States of Haryana and Punjab and the U.T. of Chandigarh. The NRSC felt that all the States and UTs should consider similar measures.	All States and UTs addressed on 12th Feb., 2004 and reminded on 14th June, 2004.
5.	Regarding interceptors, video cameras, etc., in the context of the Pilot Project taken up in Goa and Uttaranchal Pradesh, the	Details circulated on 11th Feb., 2004 and again on 14.6.2004.

meeting was informed that details which had already been circulated on 15.7.2003, shall be re-circulated, to enable the States/UTs to take up similar projects.	
6. Strict enforcement of rules regarding the wearing of seat belts, use of dippers on highways, as also the use of reflector/red tape on the year of motor vehicles, trailers and trolleys.	All States and UTs addressed on 12th Feb., 2004 and reminded on 14th June, 2004.
7. It generate from fines on account of violations of traffic rules for road safety be earmarked for carrying out road safety activities. The Government of Kerala is to furnish details about initiative taken by them in this regard, which could be circulated to all States/UTs.	Government of Kerala have informed that they have prepared a draft legislation which is awaiting the approval of the Legislative Assembly.
8. The NRSC noted that Haryana Government had taken certain proactive measures relating to approach roads merging with National Highways, which, together with measures stipulated under IRC code of practice, had helped in reducing accidents. The Haryana representative assured that relevant details would be supplied to the Ministry, who could then circulate the same total the States/UTs.	The relevant details have been obtained and circulated to all States/UTs on 18th March, 2004 and again on 14th July, 2004.
9. A certain percentage of the Cess Fund was being provided to the Railways for construction of ROBs/RUBs, etc. While the portion over rail tracks is	Same is already a part of Railways Manual. Railways have been addressed on 12th Feb., 2004 and reminded on 11th June, 2004.

constructed by the Railways, building the approaches were the responsibility of the State Governments. The NRSC recommended that the busier railway crossings be provided with ROBs/RUBs at an early date. Similarly, appropriate signages on unmanned crossing which were about 22,000 in number be expeditiously provided by the Railway Authorities in consultation with State PWDs/other State Authorities.	
10. State Authorities would strictly enforce the provisions of CMVR in respect of regulation and control of the numerous driver training schools. The testing of driving skills of drivers shall be carried out properly at the time of issuance/renewal of driving licenses	All States and UTs addressed on 12th Feb., 2004 and reminded on 14th June, 2004. Further refresher training of drivers of transport vehicles in un-organized sector is being strengthened.
11. During the construction stage of a road, precautions relating to dumping of construction material/debris must be observed and, after construction of the road, the removal of left over material and debris must be ensured in accordance with the instructions circulated by the Ministry in 2001. It was noted that in so far as National Highways were concerned, such precautions were now a part of the Standard Contract Document itself.	All States and UTs addressed on 12th Feb., 2004 and reminded on 14th June, 2004.
12. The Council also felt that RTO Offices should not be located on the National Highways as it often leads to congestion and traffic hazards.	All States and UTs addressed on 12th Feb., 2004 and reminded on 14th June, 2004.

13. On the question of overloading, there was unanimity that overloading was a result of collusion between the Consignor, the Booking Agent, the Transporter and the Enforcement machinery. An overloaded vehicle not only endangers itself and the other road users but also causes enormous damage to the road infrastructure. A point was made that the manufacture of trucks carrying a payload much higher than the prescribed GVW norms also encourages overloading. It was also mentioned that at times the tyre manufactures contribute to overloading by advertising that their tyres were capable of carrying loads in excess of the payloads prescribed. The Council desired that Chairman CMVR TSC should examine this aspect.	(a) States have been advised on 3.10.2004 to take enforcement measures. Further central assistance to 7 States, namely, Chattisgarh, Gujarat, Haryana, M.P., Orissa, Rajasthan and U.P. who had issued special tokens/ passes which facilitated overloading, was stopped in 2003-04 till said tokens/passes were withdrawn. Same has been done by all the 7 States during 2003-04 itself. (b) Load rating per axle have been prescribed based on road design specifications which are of the order of about 10.2 tons per rear axle, which is broadly in harmony with the permissible axle loads in other countries. Even if a truck manufactured by the OEM is capable of higher payload, the certification of the truck is done by the testing agency based on approved axle loads prescribed. Any overloading is therefore a problem of enforcement. (c) Tyres specifications are being brought under purview of CMVR in consultation with the tyre manufactures.
14. The NRSC unanimously agreed that licenses for liquor vends should not be given along National Highways.	All States and UTs addressed on 12th Feb., 2004 and reminded on 14th June, 2004.

RAISING AWARENESS ABOUT ROAD SAFETY ISSUES

Current Status

It has been experienced all over the world that the countries which are undergoing increasing and rapid motorization face proportionately higher number of road accidents.

At the earliest stages of road safety development, little or No. safety awareness may exist and efforts will first need to be made to enhance the awareness of key decision-makers to the scale and nature of the problem and the actions that are necessary to alleviate the situation.

The situation in India is somewhat better than a country, which may be at the earliest stage of safety development but still far less satisfactory than those countries, which have proven records of road safety improvements.

However, in India the situation varies from state to state and within a state from district to district and within a district from one department to another and within a department from one officer to another.

Policy Statement

The government will make increased efforts to promote awareness about the seriousness of the road accident problem, its social and economic implications and the necessity to curb the rising menace of road accidents. This will facilitate various stakeholders to play their rightful role in promoting road safety.

Strategies to Implement the Policy

1.1 Raising awareness among key decision-makers and stakeholders to facilitate them for planning and promoting road safety.

1.2 Raising awareness about the gravity of road safety issues among all citizens of the country to enable them to treat it as an important national problem.

1.3 To enlighten various road user groups with respect to their rôles and responsibilities.

PROVIDING ENABLING LEGAL INSTITUTIONAL AND FINANCIAL ENVIRONMENT FOR ROAD SAFETY

Current Status

Road Safety is a complex process involving different sectors of the economy and various elements of the society. The responsibility for improving the safety on the roads and reducing accidents is shared by private agencies at National, State and Local Levels.

To function smoothly there must be proper legal, institutional and financial environments.

The authority, responsibility and accountability of various stakeholders must be made clear and proper coordination between agencies should be developed at National, Regional and Local Levels.

Road safety is a highly cost effective activity involving the saving of human lives and the reduction of economic losses.

Policy Statement

The government will clarify the institutional responsibilities of the various stakeholders of road safety and take appropriate measures to ensure that the required legal, institutional and financial environment for road safety is put in place. The reforms in these areas would take into account an active and extensive participation of the community at large and of private and business sector as well as of NGOs.

Strategies to Implement the Policy

2.1 To create enabling legal framework for road safety at various levels.

2.2 To create enabling institutional framework for managing road safety.

2.3 To create enabling financial framework for road safety.

ROAD SAFETY INFORMATICS DATABASE

Current Status

Detailed analysis of road accidents are essential if the causes of the accidents are to be fully understood. At the present time the police prepare a report for the accidents that they are aware of. The accident report requires the precise location of the accident, details of the people involved in the accident, details of vehicles involved in the accident, details of the road network at and near to the location of the accident, conditions at the time of the accident, e.g. weather, road surface.

This daunting task would be that much easier if the details of the vehicles stored on the vehicle register, details of the drivers stored on the license register and road details stored on digital plans and maps were readily accessible.

If these basic data could be brought together in a comprehensive database, the police report could give more attention to the causes of the accident.

Policy Statement

The government will significantly increase help and assistance to set-up data collection and analysis systems in states, union territories, districts, metropolitan cities and major highway networks as the components of a national road safety information system.

Strategies to Implement the Policy

3.1 Improve the reporting of important details at the scene of accident shortly after the occurrence of the accident.

3.2 Improve the storage and accessibility of all data relevant to an accident such as vehicles involved, road environment, etc.

3.3 Development of a comprehensive road safety information database needed for operating effective safety management systems/programmes at National, State and City levels.

SAFER ROAD INFRASTRUCTURE

Current Status

Road infrastructure has a strong influence on the perception of drivers, including their understanding of the way the road operates and consequently their behaviour. Depending on its design a road may encourage people to drive too fast or without the driver being consciously aware of it, cause him to drive slowly.

In India traffic engineering measures are often haphazard and inadequate and thus not effective in tackling road safety problems. Road marking and traffic signage are often not properly implemented and usually are not properly maintained.

With present emphasis placed on the development of transportation by both central and state governments, with the construction of road networks and highways, it becomes imperative that the safety of road infrastructure is not compromised for the sake of quantity.

Policy Statement

The government will undertake additional steps to promote road safety practice at national, state and local levels. Safety conscious planning and design of roads and road networks will be encouraged whilst undertaking new as well as up-gradation and rehabilitation road schemes through application of road safety audits. Continuing application of ITS to achieve safe and efficient transport system will be encouraged.

Strategies to Implement the Policy

4.1 Require all proposed new and rehabilitation road schemes to be checked from a safety perspective for all types of road users during the planning and designing stages through Road Safety Audit and adopt accident reduction strategies for existing roads through black spot improvement programmes.

4.2 Review design standards, codes, guidelines, recommended practices, access control and development control procedures to ensure best global practices for road safety are incorporated wherever appropriate.

4.3 To facilitate quality improvement of practicing highway engineers on various road safety aspects through training and dissemination of appropriate road safety knowledge.

SAFER VEHICLES

Current Status

During the last 25 year, numerous improvements to vehicle safety have been made as a result of research. Without vehicle construction regulations governing safety standards for systems such as braking, lightening, signaling, there can be little control over the general safety of country's vehicle fleet.

In India, vehicle safety standards are specified in Rules 93 to 127 of the Central Motor Vehicles Rules (1989) but these norms are hardly followed.

Old vehicles, which have low safety standards, continue to be used.

For many vehicle owners the statutory periodic inspection is considered a troublesome imposition rather than an important "health", check on their vehicles. Furthermore the State Road Transport Authorities lack manpower and equipment to undertake task of vehicle inspection in a comprehensive way.

Policy Statement

The government will steps to increase the effectiveness of the control of vehicle design, construction, operation and maintenance standards and the means by which it can be assured in order to minimize adverse safety and environment effects of vehicle operation on road users and infrastructure.

Strategies to Implement the Policy

5.1 To promote safety conscious design of vehicles to ensure safe transport for passengers, drivers and other road users.

5.2 To promote the statutory periodic inspection as on essential check on the road worthiness of all vehicles.

5.3 To minimize contribution of vehicle conditions on roads and road users.

SAFE DRIVERS

Current Status

Motor vehicles should be driven only by those people who have appropriate license. Driving licenses can be issued only to people who have reached prescribed age, are physically and psychologically able to drive a motor vehicle, have gone through the prescribed education and training, have demonstrated ability to drive motor vehicles and have fulfilled other conditions as prescribed for driving particular groups or types of motor vehicles. The driver licensing laws are not uniform and in many instances they are quite lenient. No. rigorous standard driving test is given. At present often less than five minutes are devoted to test the ability of a driver.

Lack of lane discipline and consideration for pedestrians and other, vulnerable road users, violation of traffic rules and regulation are just some of the faulty driving traits of many Indian drivers today.

Policy Statement

The government will increase its assistance to the provision of infrastructure and tools for setting up of proper driver training. Testing and evaluation systems would be developed and made available all over the country to provide uniformity in driver training and licensing procedures, as well as providing information about all drivers.

Strategies to Implement the Policy

6.1 To facilitate the development of systems, which ensure that only safe and competent new drivers are permitted to use the roads.

6.2 To improve the manpower both quantitatively and qualitatively, to test and evaluate the driving ability of all license applicants.

6.3 To qualitatively improve the safety performance of the existing identified driver groups contributing to road safety problems.

SAFETY FOR VULNERABLE ROAD USERS

Current Status

The road users found most vulnerable on Indian roads from a road safety point of view are pedestrians, bicyclists and motorized two-wheelers.

Special provisions for people on foot include regulations for pedestrian crossings, which give legal precedence to pedestrians. However, it is the pedestrians seeking to protect their lives, who almost invariable give way to motor vehicles.

Another set of vulnerable road users are the non-motorized handcarts, cycle rickshaws, animal drawn carts, etc. In India, there is high degree of heterogeneity of traffic and No. segregation of motorized and non-motorized traffic in roads. This often leads to increased conflicts between them and thus reduced safety.

There is No. appropriate legislation to govern the behaviour of pedestrians and non-motorized traffic on the roads.

Policy Statement

The design and constriction of all road facilities will take into account of the needs of vulnerable and physically disadvantaged in an adequate and equitable manner. The Government will seek to identify current 'best practices' in this area and disseminate widely to town planners, architects, highway and traffic engineers.

Strategies to Implement the Policy

7.1 Recognize Vulnerable Road Users as equally important elements as the motorized vehicle in the planning, designing, construction and operation of roads and to provide for their special needs and requirements.

7.2 Top update existing and develop new warrants, standards, guidelines and recommended practices for guidance to professionals to facilitate safe accommodation of VRUs.

7.3 To encourage NGOs to work with Vulnerable Road Users, to increase their awareness of the dangers from vehicle traffic.

ROAD TRAFFIC SAFETY EDUCATION AND TRAINING

Current Status

In India, like in many developing countries, the lack of knowledge of road safety rules among the population at large is a major factor contributing to the non-observance of such rules in practice. This in turn leads to unsafe road user behaviour and habits.

In many areas road safety education and training facilities are not satisfactory. There are some private organizations with the association of voluntary organizations are imparting such training to their employees.

The school curricula in India hardly include a section on road safety. It is only in recent times that the traffic police personnel of some cities have been assigned the job for imparting road safety education to children.

Policy Statement

Road safety knowledge and awareness will be created amongst the population through education, training and publicity campaigns. Road safety education will focus on school children and college going students, while road safety publicity campaigns will be used to propagate good road safety practice among the community. The government will encourage all professionals undertaking road design, road construction, road network management, traffic management and law enforcement to attain adequate knowledge of road safety issues.

Strategies to Implement the Policy

8.1 Development of formal and informal road safety education systems and learning aids for children of various age groups.

8.2 To develop and implement road safety publicity campaigns for various target groups as per their respective requirements. Also Planning and implementing community based road safety programmes to engage local as well as non-governmental partners in the areas of road traffic safety that most affect their daily lives.

8.3 Planning, designing and implementing training programmes for various specific, professional groups having responsibility of road safety management tasks, e.g. Traffic Personnel, Highway Engineers, School Teachers, Town Planners, NGOs, etc.

TRAFFIC ENFORCEMENT

Current Status

Enforcement of traffic legislation is aimed at controlling road user behaviour by preventive, persuasive and punitive methods in order to effect the safe and efficient movement of people and goods. The primary objective of traffic law enforcement is the creating of a deterrent to violators and potential violators of traffic laws and raise the level of compliance among all drivers and road users. In recent years the amount of traffic has increase substantially but the number of traffic police and regional transport officers has not increased proportionately. The consequences are that the quality of enforcement has deteriorated.

The enforcement agencies face many practical problems like low priorities being assigned to traffic police departments, inadequacy of funds and lack of coordination among different supporting agencies.

Policy Statement

The government will seek appropriate measures to assist various state and other governments to improve the quality of their traffic enforcement agencies. Government will actively encourage the establishment and strengthening of Highway Patrol forces on National and State Highways taking the help of the State Government and Union Territories as appropriate.

Strategies to Implement the Policy

9.1 To undertake appropriate steps to upgrade the state transport departments, to bring their driver testing and vehicle testing to the required standards.

9.2 To undertake appropriate steps to ensure the traffic police departments are adequately manned, trained and equipped to carry out their function ensuring safe road use and orderly traffic flow.

9.3 To set-up a national level Traffic Police Training Institute to serve, motivate and provide incentive and necessary help to each State to set-up modern police training schools within their jurisdiction.

EMERGENCY MEDICAL SERVICES FOR ROAD ACCIDENT

Current Status

In the more developed countries the response of ambulances and the like to reach the scene of an accident are short and many lives are saved as a result.

In India, the average response time is much longer with the consequence that some lives are lost that with a quicker response time might have been saved.

However response time is not the only important factor. The quality of post-accident treatment also has a bearing on whether or not an accident victim lives or dies. In some areas, Highway Patrol and Traffic Aid Posts have been introduced to improve response time and quality of treatment.

To achieve quick response time and prompt high quality medical attention requires a higher degree of co-ordination between the many agencies involved.

Policy Statement

The government will strive to achieve its target that all persons involved in road accidents benefit from speedy and effective trauma care and health management. The essential functions of such a service would include the provision of rescue operation including pre-medical care and first-aid at the site of an accident, the transport of the victim from accident site to an appropriate hospital and the subsequent provision of more definitive treatment.

Strategies to Implement the Policy

10.1 To improve communications with police and emergency services as a means to reduce response times and to assist in planning and implementation of Highway Patrol and Traffic Aid Post Scheme.

10.2 To train police, fire and other emergency service personnel such as those on ambulances and paramedics in basic first-aid for accident victims.

10.3 To develop local and regional trauma plans based on study of post-accident assistance and consequence for road traffic accident casualties.

TRAFFIC ENFORCEMENT

Current Status

Road Safety research is needed to clarify the current situation in terms of priorities and problem areas.

Accurate and comprehensive accidents data is required to provide a base comparison for identifying problems evaluation changes and asserting the effectiveness of any countermeasures adopted.

A particular deficiency is the lack of research in the field of the development monitoring of low cost engineering measures. With such development immediate improvements can be implemented at the known hazardous locations.

The dissemination of information on road safety matters amongst professionals and others in the field is very poor.

Policy Statement

Government will bring together the current road research activities under an umbrella and formulate a comprehensive programme of road safety research. Priority areas will be encouraged by increased funding. Government will disseminate the result of research and identified examples of good practice to professionals working in the field through publications, training, conferences and workshops.

Strategies to Implement the Policy

11.1 To set-up a system for identifying new areas for research and for extension to ongoing research projects that are likely to be most rewarding.

11.2 To develop arrangements for the allocation of funds for research projects to be carried out by Research Institutes, Universities, NGOs.

11.3 To consolidate the results already available from research projects and resource material for widespread dissemination among road safety professionals.

CHAPTER 6

RADIATION AND RADIATION EDUCATION

Radiology in the Next Hundred Years

"To be able to prosper in the future, medical imaging must continue to decrease in invasiveness, increase insensitivity and specificity and—more than anything else—remain affordable and patient-friendly."

—*Alexander R. Margulis*
World Health Organization, May-June 1995

6

CHAPTER

Radiation and Radiation Education

Protection Against Radiation in Medicine

The protection of patients is the area in which the greatest reductions in human exposure to radiation can be made by improving the quality of equipment and practices and raising the standard of justification for procedures.

—*Cesar F. Arias and Jorge J. Skvarca,*
World Health Organization, May-June 1995

Human beings have been exposed to natural radiation throughout their existence and their evolution. This exposure from natural sources is unavoidable and represents a permanent factor of everyday life. The radiation originates from cosmic rays, soil, water, food and air; apart from external exposure, there are some natural internal radiation sources, such as radioactive potassium in the blood.

MAIN SOURCES OF RADIATION

1. Multiple exposure photograph of a total eclipse of the sun. Some 37 per cent of the total radiation we receive in a lifetime come from cosmic rays and the irradiated soil.
2. The second largest dose, 28 per cent, comes from the building materials in our homes.
3. The water we drink, food we eat and air we breathe add a further 16 per cent.
4. Diagnostic X-ray examinations are commonplace for millions of people around the world, and play a valuable role in tracking down diseases such as tuberculosis. But they can account for another 12 per cent of our total radiation dose.
5. Daily viewing of colour television can make as much as four per

cent contribution. Other household sources of radiation include watches with luminous dials and chinaware.

6. A further two per cent may be added by air travel at high altitudes—a two-way transatlantic flight, for instance. (Jet airliners have opened up new horizons for travelers, but have also severely boosted noise-levels near airports.)
7. Finally, people living in the area of nuclear power plants might receive 0.6 per cent exposure over and above the general population radiation dose.[1]

As a result of technological and scientific developments, new sources of radiation have been added, such as nuclear power production, artificial radio-isotopes and radiation-emitting equipment, while thousands of curies of radio-isotopes are today carried by air and sea, by train and car to their users in industry, mineral resources exploration, agriculture and medicine. (Named after Marie Curie, 1867-1934, the Polish-born discoverer of radium, the curie is the unit used to measure radioactivity).

Radio-isotopes and other sources of radiation are used in hospitals for diagnosis and treatment. In industrialized countries, one in every four patients undergoes diagnostic procedure involving radio-isotopes, and almost the entire population is exposed to X-ray examinations.

Of the total radiation to which a population is exposed, some 37 per cent is due to cosmic rays and terrestrial radiation, 28 per cent comes from building materials in houses, 16 per cent from food, water and air, and 12 per cent from diagnostic X-ray examinations. An additional 2 per cent could be added by air travel, (by transatlantic flights, for instance), and daily viewing of colour television could make a 4 per cent contribution. People living in the area of nuclear power plants might receive 0.6 per cent exposure over and above the general population radiation dose.

A part from natural radiation, the exposure rates were drastically increased on a global scale by nuclear weapon tests which resulted mostly in the cumulative deposit of strontium 90, and the levels of radiation exposure are still much higher than before these tests. This is why public health concern still exists in this field; in May 1973 the World Health Assembly passed a resolution calling for the prohibition of all nuclear weapon tests, and the WHO's Regional Committee for Africa passed a similar resolution four years later.[2]

WHO AND RADIATION MEDICINE

Based upon the epidemiological situation and the expected healthcare that will be needed for most of the population, the types of X-ray examination most likely to be needed by small rural and district hospitals throughout the developing world are those of the chest, skeleton (including the head), abdomen and soft tissue.

CHART 6.1

Harmful for Health

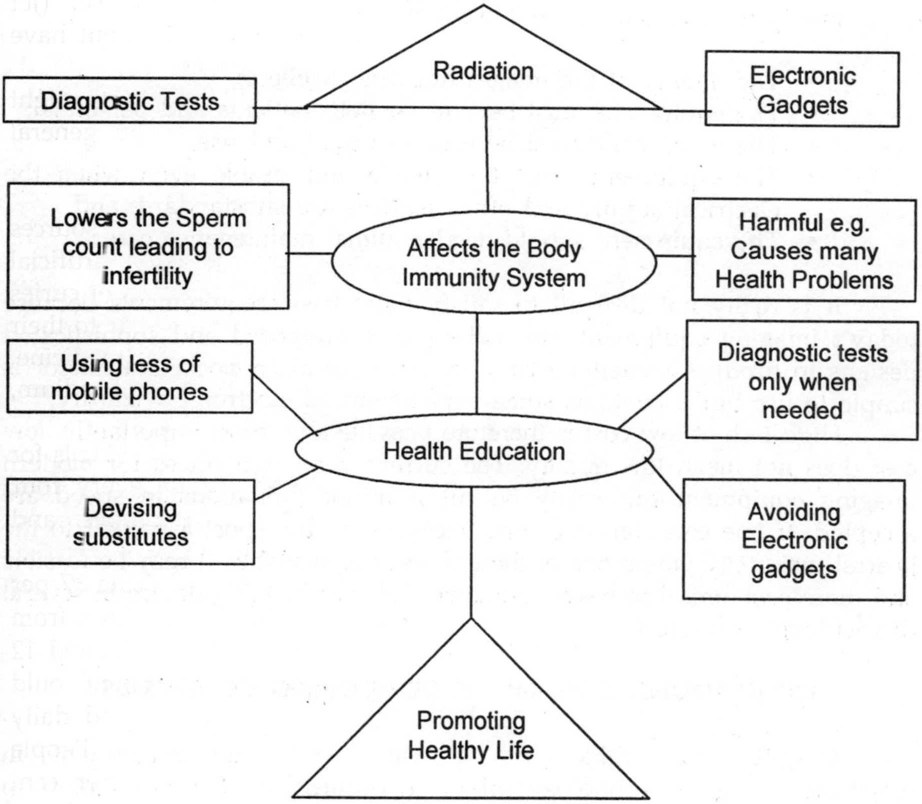

- Diagnostic imaging is involved in many crucial medical decisions, but only about one-third of the world's population has access to even the most essential services and the quality is often questionable.
- Radiation therapy is required for more than one-half of all cancer patients, yet the necessary technology for treatment, including accurate dose delivery, is often lacking.
- Radiation protection and safety are absolutely essential, because more than 95% of all man-made ionizing radiation exposures are caused by medical use.[3]

A hundred years of X-ray science have made medical imaging a vital part of modern medicine. The next hundred years will No. doubt produce still further technical advances in radiology. But it will still take the trained eye and educated mind of the physician radiologist to apply this technology to each patient's health problems.[4]

It is difficult to choose equipment because there are so many alternatives but WHO has, with the advice of a group of experts, laid down some basic criteria to simplify the choices.

Five principles must be followed:

- The quality of the images must be excellent;
- The equipment must be safe for both patients and personnel;
- The equipment must be easy to install and use;
- The equipment must be reliable and usable even when the electrical supply and other services are substandard; and
- The equipment should need minimal maintenance care.

It is really not difficult to satisfy these basic requirements because today's imaging equipment can make use of advanced and sophisticated designs to produce something easy to use; after all, a pocket calculator is simple to use but it contains some very advanced electronic wizardry.[5]

High tech at low cost is therefore possible and, most importantly, low cost does not mean low quality. The current very high prices for modern imaging equipment can easily be cut if minor limitations in speed are accepted. If one considers the time necessary to transport a patient to the nearest major city where one of these devices is available, it may be feasible and more economical to have a somewhat slower imaging device in several district-level hospitals.[6]

ULTRASOUND IMAGING IN DEVELOPING COUNTRIES

Despite considerable and growing worldwide investment in diagnostic imaging technology, about two-thirds of the population in developing countries do not have access to even the most basic X-ray or ultrasound diagnostic services.[7]

It would not be an exaggeration to say that ultrasound has revolutionized medical practice in terms of providing easier access and increased quality of diagnostic service for patients. However, much work is still needed to make this useful technology accessible to all who could benefit from it.[8]

Radiotherapy: Still Young after almost a Hundred Years

Past achievements and future expectations are based on three disciplines—

- Clinical medicine and a century's experience in the use of (a) external radiotherapy, nowadays increasingly by means of photon and electron linear accelerators; and (b) brachytherapy (curietherapy), which is internal radiotherapy by means of radioactive sources placed in tissues or natural cavities for periods ranging from a few minutes to a few days.

- Radiophysics, which makes it possible to measure the exact amount of radiation delivered to the patient (the dose) and to distribute it effectively so as to destroy cancerous tissue whilst preserving healthy tissue.
- Radiobiology, which continues to improve our understanding of how radiation works and makes a major contribution to the effectiveness with which it is used on both normal and diseased tissues.[9]

Protection against Radiation

The Second International Congress of Radiology, held in Paris in 1928, recommended the establishment of an international organization to study the question of protection against radiation. This was the origin of the International Commission on Radiological Protection (ICRP). The ICRP has produced about 70 publications and its recommendations have been followed by most countries, as well as by various international organizations such as WHO and the International Atomic Energy Agency (IAEA).

In 1990 the Commission published ICRP Publication 60, which provided an update on radiobiology and the current conceptual framework for radiation protection. The following points from this publication give an indication of its basic philosophy:

- Every exposure to radiation may have detrimental effects on human health, since the carcinogenic effect of radiation cannot be completely avoided.
- No. practice involving exposures to radiation should be adopted unless it produces sufficient benefit to the exposed individuals or to society to offset the radiation detriment it causes.
- Dose limits, defined as a level of dose above which the consequences for the individual would be widely regarded as unacceptable, are set as follows; occupational exposure should not exceed 20mSv per year and No. member of the public should receive more than 1mSv per year. The risk of accidents must be considered.
- All exposure should be kept as low as reasonably achievable. Protection against radiation is a matter of professional culture, and national regulatory authorities work to promote appropriate attitudes as well as compliance with the rules. To provide them with the necessary information for doing this, the International Basic Safety Standards for Protection Against Ionizing Radiation and for the Safety of Radiation Sources were prepared jointly by FAO, IAEA, ILO, the Nuclear Energy Agency (NEA) of OECD, the Pan American Health Organization (PAHO) and WHO. WHO also works with countries to improve standards through training and consultation on the procurement and use of equipment.

Medical establishments are the most numerous and widespread source of radiation in any country, and because their activities are mainly beneficial, the risks involved are often ignored. This makes the promotion of proper protection a difficult task. In the case of a patient's exposure, the risks and the benefits apply to the same person, and must be carefully weighed against each other by the physician responsible. Dosage must be limited to what is strictly necessary; limits have not been set because they depend on the possible benefits, but reference levels are being suggested for use in radiology and nuclear medicine as a means of judging the quality of equipment and procedures.

The protection of patients is now receiving particular attention, as it is the area in which the greatest reductions in humane exposure to radiation can be made. The global collective dose received by patients from diagnostic radiology is 5000 times greater than the dose received by the world's population from nuclear power production. A significant part of that dose could be avoided without loss of health benefits by improving the quality of equipment and practices and raising the standard of justification for procedures. To prevent accidents where radiation is used for medical purposes, safety measures have to be adopted in the design, installation, use, repair and eventual disposal of equipment.[10]

CONCLUSION

The message should be clear to all. The most insidious agent for disease today is ourselves, the only truly effective treatment is awareness and prevention, and the only valid prevention is to make positive changes in lifestyles. This is an ethical responsibility for the entire community. To make one's own health someone else's duty is unfair to the society of which we all form a part. Doctors must practice not only the science of healthcare but also the art of compassion, taking into account availability, accessibility and affordability. The medical care system with all its sophisticated gadgetry has, in the end, less impact on health than individual behaviour, lifestyle and environmental factors.[11]

The pool of knowledge available should be included in courses on radiation hygiene for the medical profession. Thus, general practitioners should be informed about the possible health consequences of radiation exposure in all fields of human activities. This in turn would serve to stimulate the development of protective and preventive activities.

The task of the public health authorities is to keep the public currently and fully informed on the likely health consequence of various uses of radiation. These authorities can also be expected to participate in disseminating this information and establishing contacts with the general public in order to assure adequate health protection for all.[12]

Notes and References

1. WHO: E.I. Komarov, Radiation in daily life, *World Health*, June 1979, pp. 27-28.
2. E.I. Komarov, Radiation in daily life, *World Health*, June 1979, p. 26.
3. Gerald P. Hanson and Vladimir Volodin, *World Health*, X-rays 1895-1995, Radioactivity 1896-1996, 48th year, No. 3, May-June 1995, p. 6.
4. Lenny, K.A. Tan, *World Health*, X-rays 1895-1995, Radioactivity 1896-1996, 48th year, No. 3, May-June 1995, p. 9.
5. Philip, E.S. Palmer and Thure Holm, *World Health*, X-rays 1895-1995, Radioactivity 1896-1996, 48th year, No. 3, May-June 1995, p. 12.
6. Peter E. Peters and Horst Lenzen, *World Health*, X-rays 1895-1995, Radioactivity 1896-1996, 48th year, No. 3, May-June 1995, p. 15.
7. Hassen A. Gharbi and M.W. Wachira, *World Health*, X-rays 1895-1995, Radioactivity 1896-1996, 48th year, No. 3, May-June 1995, p. 16.
8. *Ibid.*, p. 17.
9. Jean-Claude Horiot and Suzanne Naudy, *World Health*, X-rays 1895-1995, Radioactivity 1896-1996, 48th year, No. 3, May-June 1995, p. 20.
10. Cesar F. Arias and Jorge J. Skvarca, *World Health*, X-rays 1895-1995, Radioactivity 1896-1996, 48th year, No. 3, May-June 1995, pp. 24-25.
11. Sneh Bhargava, *World Health*, X-rays 1895-1995, Radioactivity 1896-1996, 48th year, No. 3, May-June 1995, p. 29.
12. E.I. Komarov, Radiation in daily life, *World Health*, June 1979, p. 29.

CHAPTER 7

VIOLENCE: WITH SPECIAL REFERENCES TO VIOLENCE AGAINST WOMEN

> "We have closed the doors of opportunity to many of them (women) in many areas of our economic, social, political and cultural life; we have not enabled our sisters and daughters to develop to their full potential. . . . The empowerment of women in India's empowerment."
>
> —*Atal Bihari Vajpayee*
>
> Former Prime Minsiter of India

7

CHAPTER

Violence:
With Special Reference to Violence against Women

"It is important to walk a mile in another person's shoes. As it is possible to grow up in the same family, neighbourhood, school etc. and yet have totally different experiences depending on whether you are a man or a woman. The way to resolve differences therefore is not to suppress those who are different but to notice them and not try to see our reflection in them."
Justice L'Heureux Dube, Supreme Court of Canada.

PHYSICAL VIOLENCE: PRESENT CONCERN

Although the dictionary meaning of the word "Violence" is "Swift and intense force; injury", the term is now used in a broader sense in physical, mental (psychological) and social contexts. Unlike negligence, which is regarded as an act of "Commission." It has its wide repercussions on all aspects of life, including health of the people, actively or passively involved in it. For example, during riots, not only the active participants or propagators suffer from injuries and may succumb but even the non-participants, the accidental victims meet the same fate. Besides disrupting the social life, it imposes a tremendous load on existing medical and health services too. It diverts, for example, the existing hospital services for tackling the medical emergencies consequent on it, thus depriving the other needy persons of these facilities particularly when curfew continues to be imposed for long durations as a precautionary measure. Special "high risk" groups, e.g., seriously/critically ill individuals and those in need of urgent healthcare, have to unnecessarily suffer during such periods for No. fault on their part.[1]

At least three and a half million people on our planet die every year as a result of injuries caused by accidental or intentional violence. Whether on the roads, at home, at work or at play, the risks of injury to individuals have been neglected for too long, and the need to prevent and reduce them has so far received little public attention.

Today, public health is improving in may countries, and life expectancy at birth is increasing everywhere. It is therefore less acceptable than ever before that so many people should meet a violent and premature deaths, or that millions of others should become permanently handicapped. More than half the deaths of young people are due to injuries, and injuries represent the main cause of potential years of life lost.

As a result of negligence, indifference or foul play, millions of people each year require medical care after accidents or acts of physical violence. At a time when economic crises are jeopardizing efforts to improve the health of mankind, injuries of all kinds cost the world community almost US $ 500 thousand million a year in medical care and lost productivity.[2]

Violence is a universal scourge of humanity, IN TIME AS WELL AS IN SPACE. In a time sense, because it has always been—and still is —the Number One reason for people to die at too young an age. In a spatial sense, because it pervades all societies, whatever their level of development.

Violence can be intentional—occurring to the individual, within the family or within the community; or it can take the form of a commonplace accident attributed to chance or—as so often happens— blamed on "bad luck." Unformately, some people may regard violence as both necessary and justified. What is more, it lurks deep within everyone, ready to surge up from our subconscious for reasons that are sometimes trivial.

This is why violence formed the theme for World Health Day, 7 April 1993. It is a complex and sensitive subject, but its complexity hardly justifies society's inaction on the grounds that taking action might be too costly—when the consequences of inaction are death or mutilation for individuals, families or entire communities, and mental scarring of persons close to the victims. Physical mutilation is far from being the only outcome of violence; it is often only the forerunner of deep psychological trauma. So such terms as violence, injury and accidents are No. longer neutral if we eliminate change or irresponsibility.

Accidents and, to a lesser degree, violence in general have long been seen as a matter for the police to deal with rather than health professionals. Today it is absolutely vital to make everyone aware that violence and injury are preventable.

Among the issues of *World Health*, several try to show that our day-to-day safety does not depend on chance or fatality; they underline that mankind has the necessary knowledge to overcome dangerous situations and that, provided we apply that knowledge correctly, accidents can become No. more than occasional incidents.

Some look at the more hidden aspects of violence: abuse of children within the family, violence towards women or the elderly—expression of an outmoded law that the strongest survive. The message which comes out clearly from the mere reporting of such situations is that the phenomenon-of violence is a public as there is an epidemiology of poliomyelitis, and that by learning to understand the causes or effects of violence we can little by little arrive at ways to prevent it. Any discussion of the means of prevention should think of violence in terms of health rather than of penal codes and punishment. The important thing is for a dialogue to be established, as a precursor to the study of solutions.

The growing complexity of technology and social organization in industrialized societies and the chronic poverty in other parts of the world are both accompanied by a greater vulnerability. Violence forms one part of that complexity and is one expression of that vulnerability. The time is ripe to examine its effects on health and to take measures to limit the harmful consequences.[3]

Agriculture-related injuries in our villages amounted to about 20 minor and three moderate-to-serious injuries per thousand people every year. This obviously means that in a country like India agriculture-related serious injuries and deaths would be in the region of 5 million and half-a-million respectively. Most of the minor injuries are due to hand tools.

Women and children were also found to be victims of injuries with agricultural equipment. Women and older children work alongside men in many agricultural activities, while young children get injured because they play with equipment, which is placed or stored around their homes. In these villages, children often got their fingers amputated while playing with fodder-cutting machines, and some women got their hands crushed while feeding grass into the machines. Threshing machines are also responsible for many hand-crush injuries.

A detailed examination of the conditions under which these accidents took place makes it very clear that, though the farm workers are very often aware of the hazardous nature of their machinery, they still end up being involved in accidents. This is why it is very important for safety features to be built-in when these machines are designed. The designer also has to take into account the realities of local life. For example, tractors are regularly used for transporting people, children play with equipment when not in use, and machines are dismantled and repaired on farms.

Our experience shows that it is possible to design inexpensive and practical safety features for farm machinery. To be acceptable, such safety equipment must not make the operation of the equipment more cumbersome or less efficient. It is best if these safety guards are permanently fixed on the machines.[4]

In consultation with farmers, artisans, engineers and product designers we were able to make fodder-cutting machines much safer without increasing the cost significantly. This has been done by incorporating a warning roller before the crushing mechanism and attaching a blade guard, which pushes children's hands away before the blade can touch the fingers. Over a hundred farmers in this area have now fitted these devices to their machines.

Similar improvements to equipment such as threshers, tillers and harrows can make farming a much safer occupation. But many more professionals will have to be involved and many more people will have to take up such work seriously. Otherwise the unnecessary maiming and killing of millions of farmers and their families will continue around the world.[5]

As for occupational accidents, it is recognized that 70% of them are due to human error, which can be avoided by training and constantly drawing attention to the risks. An unsafe work environment accounts for 30% of cases; it is essential to introduce safe equipment and No. hazardous chemicals, and to improve work conditions. The best precaution would be to use only technologies with built-in safety measures.[6]

One of the tragedies of modern-day society is the extent to which we are confronted with violence. Violence exists throughout the world and takes many forms, but one of the most shocking and insidious forms of violence is that which affects girls and women.

Violence against women must be seen in its broadest sense. Violence not only refers to the physical and mental abuse to which women are subjected. It also refers to the hidden violence that women face when they are discriminated against or denied basic human rights such as education, food, medical care, and a safe environment in which to live.

Violence affects women thoughout their entire life span from the in utero period right through to old-age. In some instances, the capacity to determine the sex of a child before it is born has been used to prevent the birth of girl children. In other cases, girls have been subjected to differential feeding practices, which may affect their physical and mental well-being for the rest of their lives. Discriminatory practices in childrearing, such as keeping girl children away from school to work in the home, can be seen as a form of violence which may be detrimental to the girls' own health and that of their future children.

Within the family structure many women across societies suffer various types of abuse at the hands of their partners. Elderly women, too, are often the victims of mental and physical abuse within the confines of their family, or through the neglect and disinterest shown to them by society as a whole.

When a woman works outside her home she may encounter different forms of violence, from the lack of security on the streets to the overt or hidden violence and discrimination she faces in her place or work. Too often women are afraid to speak out against violence or abuse in the workplace for fear of losing their position.

These are but a few examples of the daily violence women and girls experience, and which result from the status they are accorded in society. All forms of violence against women represent an abuse of human rights.

We must not allow these violations of human rights to go unrecognized and unchallenged. We must open our eyes to all forms of violence against women and combat them on all fronts: behind the doors of family homes; in the community; on the streets of our villages and towns; at work and in the political and economic institutions that govern our societies. Let us use the occasion of World Health Day, 1993 to speak out strongly against this abuse of human rights and take strong measures to put an end to all forms of violence against women.[7]

Over 21 million people died in the 150 wars that have taken place, mostly in the Third World, since the Second World War. The majority of those who died were civilians; in fact the proportion of civilian deaths to the military ones has been rising over this period and in the most recent conflicts has been well over 80%.[8]

The consequences of armed conflict on a population's health are so drastic that the international community must look beyond the effects of war and examine its root causes. This will call for simultaneous action at several levels:

- Doing every thing possible to settle political and economic differences by means other than violence.
- Insisting on respect for the Geneva Convention's rules governing the protection of non-combatants, which 174 signatory governments have accepted.
- Training the civilian and military health services to cope with a sudden influx of injured and to ensure their speedy transport to first-aid stations.
- Teaching as widely as possible the principles of first-aid and wartime surgery.
- Rehabilitating those very seriously injured in war so as to reintegrate them into society and restore their dignity and self-reliance.

Only by taking this global approach to the problem shall we be able to combat that most murderous of human scourges—collective violence and war.[9]

The root cause behind large-scale physical violence is the social discontentment/disharmony among various population groups/communities. Besides these, political rivalries, religious and ethnic conflicts have also been responsible for its genesis as is evident from the past and current global scenario in many parts of the world. Eruption of violence (date and time) remains unpredictable in most cases where it is of sudden onset, although in certain situations such as ongoing rivalry/conflict, it may be anticipated with high degree of certainty. However, in order to tackle the situation and its consequences effectively, adequate prior preparation on all fronts, including medical and health, is required. It therefore, calls for keeping an adequate vigilance at all times and at all places, playing particular attention to those areas/regions which have already been recognized as "violence prone" in the light of past experience. It also calls for an effective monitoring/information system for timely warning to all concerned—including medical and health authorities—about its anticipated/actual eruption and subsequent progress. Police/intelligence department should be competent to play this role and bear this responsibility. This is one area where inter-sectoral cooperation is of crucial importance.

Suggestions

A. To believe in the maxim "love one another" and other basic ethical tenets of the world's religious philosophies and a belief in the worth of an individual and of human survival.

B. To believe, in the present context, that recourse to violence of any kind is not the answer to sort out disputes of various nature, at various levels since violence is not only an anti-social but an inhuman act. History has made it amply clear that the final outcome of violence is always unpredictable. The need of the hour is therefore to settle all disputes and rivalries in a peaceful manner, in a humane way, through talks/negotiations across the table, rather than resort to violence.

C. Not to fall prey to alcoholism which is also associated with automobile accidents and violence. In the USA, it was found associated with over 50% of all deaths and major injuries due to automobile accidents, about 50% all murders, 40% of all assaults, 35% or more of all rapes and 30% of all suicides. About 1 out of every 3 arrests in US results from abuse of alcohol. Due to rising trend of alcoholism among teenagers during 1970s, it was called the "teenage tragedy of the seventies."

Teachers' role is important in preaching non-violence to their students. They should however practice what they teach and never resort to violence in any form as punishment to a student at fault.

The United Nations observed 1986 as the International year of peace. There is a perpetual necessity of having similar campaigns and observe "International Year/Decade of Non-violence." Public opinion should also be mobilized through the UN in the endeavour to put an end to all types of conflicts, wars and building up of nuclear and biochemical arsenals. Lastly, it is worthwhile to recollect what late John F. Kennedy had to say in this respect. . . . "Each man can make a difference, and each man should try."[10]

A safe life is the basic right of everyone. Safe life leads to a longer and more productive safe community. Safe community can participate in injury reduction programmes. Community participation can be sought at:

(i) Workplaces through labour unions minimizing or preventing hazards at workplaces by providing better amenities to the workers;

(ii) Academic institutions, students and faculty participations through curricular development and providing safer environment; and

(iii) Religious functions through free talks by religious leaders and people to come forward and participate in safety programme in day-to-day life supported by media in the form of newspapers, radio, T.V. and published material.

Violence against women occurs in every country and in every social and economic class, wife-beating is considered a man's right. All too often, routine beating and rape of women and girls are considered "private matters" that do not concern others—whether the legal authorities or health personnel."[11]

In today's world, violence against women constitutes a major public health problem. In the US, nearly two million women a year are beaten in their homes and it is a fair assumption that many more such cases go unreported. Cases of rape are even more numerous and even less frequently reported; it has crimes, since frequently it is not socially or culturally acceptable for women to reveal that they have been beaten or raped, nor are such revelations recognized.

Although our studies do not prove that men who watched sexually violent films will commit rape as a result, they do show that these men will find rape and violence against women more acceptable. As men, husbands and fathers ourselves, we are personally and morally deeply offended by media depictions of women that lead to such attitudes. We hope that film-makers everywhere—for this problem is in No. way confined to the United States or even to the "western" world—will recognized the damaging effects that such films have on society in general and on women in particular, and will begin to show themselves capable of exercising a greater degree of social responsibility'.[12]

Gender-based violence has only recently emerged as a global issue extending across regional, social, cultural and economic boundaries. As a near universal phenomenon, gender-based violence threatens the well-being, rights and dignity of women. [Fischback, 1997] Violence against women is being documented across cultures and nations. The United States, where the feminist movement had opportunity to flourish has not even ratified the CEDAW. According to state statistics, about 18% of women are being sexually abused in the U.S. The condition in other developed countries is not any better. The UN Rapporteur on violence against women regretted that even countries such as Denmark, Germany, Spain, Switzerland, the United Kingdom, among others, could not provide accurate documentation and statistics on domestic violence (United Nations, 1999). The Available data on wife abuse is even more appalling. In the U.S., The Department of Justice reported that, every year, 3-4 million women are battered by their husbands or partners (UN, 1999). Even in Sweden which ranks high in the gender-related index, 66 percent of the 18,650 reported cases of violence on women in 1996 were of domestic assault. Further 45 percent of 681 offences of homicide recorded in England and Wales in 1996 were cases of homicides in which women were killed by current or former spouses or lovers (UN, 1999).

Women victims needed to be treated with sensitivity. Victims of sexual violence suffered from a sense of shame, self-guilt, fear and feel humiliated, abandoned, traumatised and stigmatised. In case of domestic violence, offences were committed in the privacy of the home, by a person on whom the women were emotionally and economically dependent. Moreover even though she was a victim, she was compelled to live with the assaulter, as she had No. other alternative. In such cases, the role of the police was not one of an interrogator but of a facilitator and emphathiser.[13]

In recent years, the issue of violence against women has been recognised as a basic human rights issue and the elimination of gender-based violence has been seen as central to equality, development and peace. Violence against women includes not only physical violence, but also sexual, psychological and emotional abuse. Many forms of violence are not even recognised as such and are ignored, condoned or justified, by involving religious, cultural or traditional beliefs. There is increasing evidence to show that women regardless of age, educational level, class, caste, community and family living arrangement, are vulnerable to violence. They face violence both inside and outside the family, at all stages of their lives. Official statistics show that there has been a dramatic increase in the number of reported crimes against women over the last decade. Between 1980 and 1990, there was an increase of nearly 74 percent in crimes against women, with rape, molestation and torture by husbands and in-laws showing the highest rate of growth. The National Crime Records Bureau reported in 1998 that the growth rate of crimes against women would be higher than the population growth rate by 2010 (Sen and Shivkumar, 2001).[14]

Inspite of plethora of agencies and large number of laws to make the life of women decent, yet we do not find any newspaper or T.V. or Radio not narrating the one form or the other of violence against women. The violence is more prevalent in rural areas, urban slums and backward areas. Before, we discuss the methods of containment of violence against women, let us discuss its meaning and the various forms in which it is exhibited.

MEANING AND SCOPE

According to the United Nations, violence against women consists of "any act of gender-based violence that results in, or is likely to result in, physical, sexual or psychological harm or suffering to women, including threats of such acts, coercion or arbitrary deprivation of liberty, whether occurring in public or private life. Violence against women shall be understood to encompass but not be limited to: physical, sexual and psychological violence occurring in the family and in the community, including battering, sexual abuse of female children, dowry-related violence,

CHART 7.1

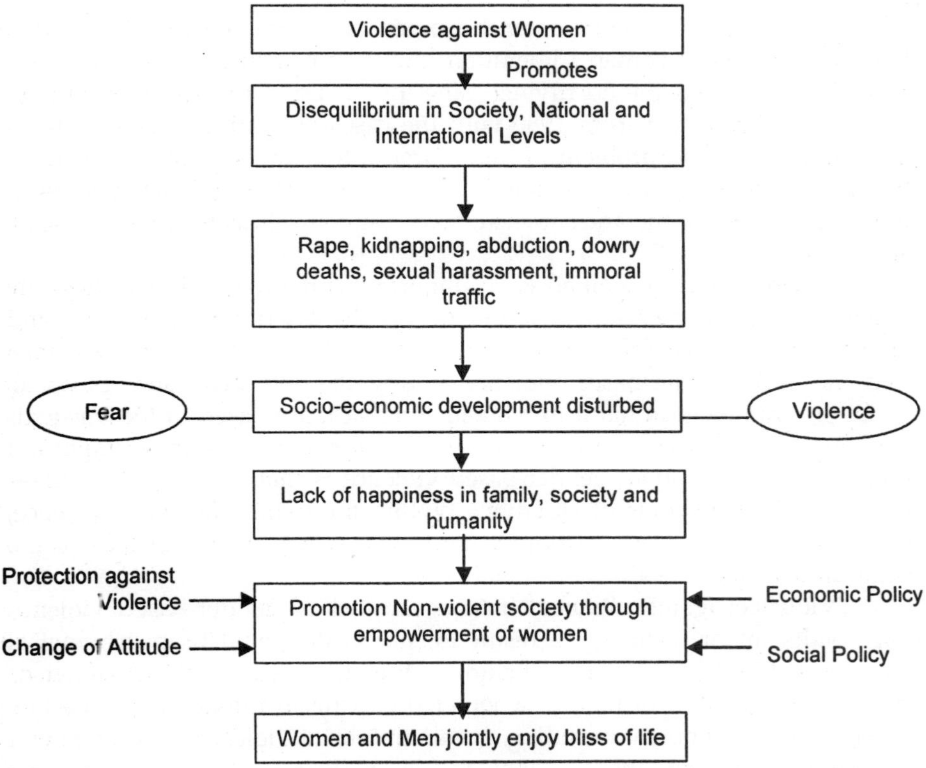

marital rape, female genital mutilation and other traditional practices harmful to women, non-spousal violence, violence related to exploitation, sexual harassment and intimidation at work, in educational institutions and elsewhere, trafficking in women, forced prostitution, and violence perpetrated or condoned by the State."

Violence against women is viewed as one of the most crucial societal mechanism by which women are forced into a subordinate position. It is a manifestation of unequal power relation, which has led to man's domination over and discrimination against woman.

Violence is defined as a physical act of aggression of one individual or group against another or others. Violence results in or is likely to result in physical, sexual, psychological harm or suffering. This also includes the threat of such act, coercion or arbitrary deprivation of liberty in public or private life and violation of human rights of women in situation of armed conflicts.

While the basic reason for violence against women is their inferior status in a male dominated society educationally, economically, politically and socially, there are other factors too. The increasing criminalisation of society, media images of violence, poor enforcement of legal provision, unabashed consumerism and erosion of traditional values have all added to it.

The issue of violence against women has been the most pervasive themes of the new women's liberation movement in India since its rise in 1974-75. First, it was the horrifying rising toll of fire in the growing number of dowry deaths, then from 1980 with the cases of Mathura, Maya Tayagi and Rameeza Bi, the problem of rape burst out of the shadows to stand as the symbol of women's oppression. Finally, the last few years have seen dramatic revivals of the ancient customs of Sati as well as female infanticide and female foeticide.[15]

Violence against women is an important force that helps to keep the structure of patriarchy intact. It makes gender discrimination a live and terrifying experience for women, and ensures their subjugation. We have used the term gender-based violence to describe acts that cause physical, sexual or psychological harm to women. Such acts are based in the unequals relations that exist between men and women in society. The most important thing to remember about gender-based violence is that, it is all pervasive—it can occur in all kinds of situations (within the family, at the workplace, in public places, in the community, and even when in the custody of the state) and at all stages of a women's life.[16]

'Violence against women" means any act of gender-based violence that results in, or is likely to result in, physical, sexual or psychological harm or suffering to women, including threats of such acts, coercion or arbitrary deprivation of liberty, whether occurring in public or private life. Violence against women, including threats or fear of violence is a permanent constraint on the mobility of women and limits their access to resources and basic activities. Such violence are impediments to the achievement of the objectives of equality, development and peace. It violates and impairs or nullifies the enjoyment by women of their human rights and fundamental freedoms.

The term "violence against women" following the declaration of UN Commission on the Status of Women (1993), is usually defined as "any act of gender-based violence that results in or is likely to result in, physical, sexual or psychological harm or suffering to women, including threats such as acts, coercion or arbitrary deprivations of liberty, whether occurring in public or private life."[17]

Broadly, violence against women can be divided in two categories:

(a) Physical, sexual and psychological violence occurring within the community, including rape, sexual abuse, sexual harassment and intimidation at work, in educational institutions and elsewhere, trafficking in women and forced prostitution; and
(b) Physical, sexual and psychological violence occurring in the family, including bettering, sexual abuse of female children in the household, dowry-related violence and other traditional practices harmful to women, non-spousal violence and violence-related to exploitation.

The nature and forms of violence is intertwined within physical, mental and psychological levels. Prevailing forms of violence are wife beating and cruelty at home, molestation, rape, sexual harassment at workplace, etc. It occurs regardless of age, marital status, caste, relation, culture and class or income level.

Violence includes physical, sexual emotional, psychological, social and economic abuse by one member of a family/society to control or dominate women in the family/society.

Physical violence includes slapping, punching, beating, shoving with or without weapons.

Sexual violence includes rape, molestations harassment. Rape is forcing a woman to have sex against her will. It is a violation of an individual's rights over her body.

Emotional violence can include all intentional attempts to minimise the victim's concern and to make them feel bad. Humiliating the victim in public and private places.

Psychological violence is any threats that are made or carried out with the intent of financial or emotional injury, blackmail or humiliation.

Economic violence creates financial dependence.

Intimidation as a form of violence can include making women afraid by using looks, action and gestures: by destroying their property or by displaying weapons.

Isolation can be used to control and limit what woman does, whom they see and where they go.

Using privilege to control is also a form of violence. By treating a woman or child like a servant and having the last word about everything, the abuser is acting like a master. He is defining and rigidly abiding by the traditional roles of men and women.[18]

Extent

The National Crimes Records Bureau (NCRB) under Ministry of Home Affairs has been collecting and recording data about gender-based violence. The statistical data compiled by the National Crimes Records Bureau, Ministry of Home Affairs on crimes against women during the years from 1990-2001 is given in Table 7.1. State-wise incidence of crime against women during the year 2000 given in Table 7.2. Data has been given crime-wise.

Violence against women is an impediment to the achievement of the objectives of equality, development and peace. Fear of violence is a permanent constraint on the mobility of women and limits their access to resources and basic needs. The subject "Violence Against Women" is broad based and comprehensive and includes different types of violence against women, viz. domestic violence, violence at the work place, violence by the State and its functionaries, violence during war and social disturbances, sexual harassment and abuse, female foeticide, rape, trafficking, dowry-related issues, etc. The innumerable forms of violence against women are so inter-connected that there is need to understand the ways in which women become susceptible to those who prey on their socially constructed vulnerability. The Committee on Empowerment on Women have therefore taken up the subject "Violence Against Women" for detailed examination.

It is provided in Section 10 of the National Commission for Women Act, 1990 that the Commission shall "investigate and examine all matters relating to the safeguards provided for women under the Constitution and other laws (Sec. 19(1)(a)) and "look into complaints and take *suo motu* notice of matters relating to (i) depreviation of women's rights; (ii) non-implementation of laws enacted to provide protection to women and also achieve the objective of equality and development; and (iii) non-compliance of policy decisions, guidelines or instructions aimed at mitigating hardships and ensuring welfare and providing relief to women, and take up the issues arising out of such matters with appropriate authorities." (Section 10(1).

She is today not only dishonoured in Panchayats but also in the city transport buses, in the city streets and even in her own homes. It is high time that we get rid of this inequality and indignity to women in our country." Manisha Joshi in her Article, "A cry for justice" in *Social Welfare*, 2002, rightly states: The phenomenon of violence against women arises from patriarchal notions of ownership over women's bodies, sexuality, labour, reproductive rights, mobility and level of autonomy. Deep-rooted ideas about male superiority enable men to freely exercise unlimited power over women's lives and effectively legitimize it too. Violence is thus a tool that men use constantly to control women as a result of highly internalized patriarchal conditioning coupled with legitimacy for coercion to enforce compliance and increasing aspirations, frustrations and 'might is right' becoming a legitimate view and increasing need for assertion of individual egos and control. Within this context, several developments serve as a backdrop to the discussion and analysis of increased violence against women. In the wake of liberalization new modes of living are being introduced. Consumerism, unreal aspirations incited by the barrage of the advertising industry and get rich quick schemes have been increasingly influencing the thinking and behaviour. So much so that even the remote hilly areas are being affected by the market forces and are increasingly adopting the system of dowry, which was virtually non-existent earlier (Krengel, 2000). An increasingly growing gap is being witnessed between the aspirations and their fulfilment. As per woman speak this is reflected in an increased violence in human interactions and increasingly cases are being reported of small differences leading to inexplicably violent reactions. In such a situation women have become more vulnerable.[19]

Aditi Pandey in her Article, 'Violation of Human Rights' in *Social Welfare*, April 2002 states: Violence against women should be viewed as one of the most crucial social mechanisms by which they are forced into a subordinate position. It is a manifestation of unequal power relations which has led to men's domination over and discrimination against women. The term Violence Against Women can be defined as "any act of gender-based violence that results in, or is likely to result in physical, sexual or psychological harm or suffering to women including threats of such acts, coercion or arbitrary deprivations of liberty, whether occurring in public or private life and violation of human rights of women."

All women, whether they live in the rich North or the poor South, the backward East or the progressive West are subject to violence. This is a deprivation of their fundamental human rights. Any act of gender-based violence that results in physical or mental harm or suffering to a woman or the threat of such an act constitutes gender violence.[20]

Indira Gandhi, Former Prime Minister of India has stated that:

In few countries do women hold higher positions in Politics and public life than in India. But this should not lead us to think that the old inequalities and disabilities from which the women of India suffered have all ended. Ours is a country in which oppositions and contradictions thrive, and nowhere is this more so than as regards women. If we have women who are among the most progressive in the world, we also have women who are among the most backward. In law, discrimination between men and women has been abolished. Yet, we all know the social and economic hardships which our women suffer in addition to the general hardships which every individual suffers in a society so poor and still so largely medieval as ours.

Violence against women during riots with Special reference to Gujarat pose peculiar problems. These are:

(i) During riots women have suffered immensely as they have lost their husband's parents and children; and many have lost the only earning member of the family.
(ii) The women who have faced violence are totally shattered and are yet to recover from the shock. They feel traumatized and will need trauma counselling for a long period.
(iii) There have been cases where police have not registered the crimes or have registered FIRs against the entire village equating the victims with the culprits. And wherever they have registered the cases, the progress of investigation is very slow. Special efforts are needed to help those women who want to register FIRs through free legal aid services and guidance.
(iv) As regards cases of sexual assault, it was mentioned that women, though sexually abused were hesitant to speak out of fear of reprisals.
(v) While praising the media for highlighting the instances of violence perpetrated on women and children, some NGOs were of the opinion that at times of both the print and electronic reports provoked both the communities to further violence.
(vi) There was a consistent demand that cases of atrocities on women should be investigated by an unbiased independent commission not only to do justice to the affected persons but also to verify the reports published in the media.

(vii) The compensation paid for damaged/destroyed houses is too inadequate and with that it is impossible for them to repair/reconstruct their houses.

(viii) Many families have lost their earning assets. A comprehensive survey is needed to assess the extent of loss and to take steps to adequately compensate them.

(ix) Camps are being closed down even though people have not been able to repair/reconstruct their houses and the monsoon season is on.

(x) Women are reluctant to go to their respective villages on account of security concerns and threats from their old neighbours.

(xi) Comprehensive rehabilitation schemes need to be formulated and implemented for all riots affected women and children.

(xii) Special efforts must be made by the Government to provide livelihood means by way of jobs to members of those families who have lost their earning members.

(xiii) Self-employed women need to be provided marketing linkages and credit facilities, in view of the economic boycott call of the Muslims by some organizations.

(xiv) Confidence building measures need to be launched in a serious and systematic way.

(i) Majority of the women have seen/experienced violence and are still to recover from the trauma experienced by them. They continue to feel insecure and need trauma counselling for longer periods. For this, Government ought to get assistance of trained counsellors and professionals from TISS, Mumbai and NIMHANS, Bangalore.

(ii) There are complaints that police have not registered several FIRs in cases of crimes against women, and the progress of investigations where the cases have been registered, is too slow. Women are asked to identify the attackers or produce witnesses when they are in camps while on the other hand they are under threats/pressure to withdraw their complaints. Free legal aid and assistance to those women who have so far not been able to register their FIRs is an urgent need. For this the concerned police officials need to be instructed to visit relief camps which are still operating and also the riot affected areas. While women in general did not complain of sexual harassment at Lunawada and Dariakhan Ghummat camps, women in Shah Alam Camp complained of sexual harassment and attack during riots. A list of 58 women who have allegedly been sexually assaulted was given by the organisers of the Shah Alam Camp to the Committee, a copy of which was handed over to the State Police for investigation. The Committee desire that all cases of sexual harassment which have been reported and these 58 cases be properly investigated so as to do justice to the affected women, and to follow up report sent to the Committee.

(iii) Though *ex-gratia* death relief amounting to Rs. 1.5 lakh is claimed to have been paid in respect of 767 cases, most of the women the Committee met in the Ahmedabad Camps did not know anything about it. Out of 983 death cases, the payment has not been made in the balance of 216 cases, (the Committee were told) for various technical reasons like lack of proof of death, failure to identify the bodies in morgues, etc. The Committee hope that efforts would be made to complete the process of payment for the remaining cases including the cases of unidentified dead bodies.

(iv) It has been brought to the notice of the Committee by the affected women that No. *ex-gratia* payment has been made in respect of missing persons. The Committee feel that a sympathetic attitude needs to be taken in respect of these cases and after necessary affidavits are obtained from the dependents/near relatives of the victims, the compensation to them must be paid at the earliest.

(v) Another fact which was brought to the notice of the Committee was the inadequate compensation that has been paid for damaged/destroyed houses by the State Government, the upper limit of which is Rs. 50,000. Further, earning assets of many families had been destroyed during the riots and very few of them have received the compensation and those who got it said it was absolutely inadequate. Moreover, the surveys were made in an *ad-hoc* manner when the affected families were in camps. They also complained of discrimination based on the community they belonged to. In many cases the landlords had claimed the compensation and were now refusing to let the tenants return. The Committee were informed that fresh surveys are being conducted to ascertain the exact extent of damage to the houses of the victims and their earning assets.

The Committee hope that the fresh surveys in this connection would be completed soon and fair compensation to the victims paid. If the victims need more financial help over and above the compensation they are paid as per the revised surveys, the help of agencies such as Banks, HUDCO, and other Financial Institutions should be taken to extend loans on easy terms to them.

(vi) The houses of the majority of the affected persons have not yet been repaired/reconstructed so far. With the monsoon season on and the camps being closed they have No. shelter and nowhere to go. The Committee hope that the camps which are still operating would be closed only after the monsoons so that the affected persons are able to get their houses repaired/reconstructed.

(vii) Another matter of concern was that though they are eager to go back to their villages/areas, the security aspect still haunts them. Though the State Government claimed that it had taken steps to provide security to the affected persons when they move back to their localities, the Committee are of the view that the confidence building process in the affected areas has not been seriously initiated. Women complained of threats meted out to them when they returned, forcing them to take shelter in the camps again. It is necessary to ensure that victims who have left the camps and returned to their localities are provided proper security.

(viii) Many NGOs pleaded for a separate rehabilitation colony for the affected families. If the Government gave the land they are prepared to build it. The Committee feel this should be considered where there is real danger to their lives.

(ix) At Shah Alam Camp, the Committee noticed that there was lack of beddings especially for pregnant women and new born babies. There was also shortage of milk for children and lactating mothers. The Committee had pointed out this shortcoming during their discussion with the State Government officials, and hope that suitable steps would have been taken to remedy this situation.

(x) Having suffered immensely, the major problem confronting the affected people especially women, is to work out livelihood measures for the rest of their lives. The relief operations undertaken for the riot victims require provision for not only relief but also for rehabilitation, with the objective of enabling the affected women regain the courage to achieve sustainable long-term earning capacity. Programmes for meaningful resettlement of these women and their families have, therefore, to be worked out. The Committee note that Red Cross, SEWA and some NGOs have offered support to run such programmes in camps by giving sewing machines and ensuring wages for women to earn. Some NGOs have also offered help to women to upgrade their skills under NORAD with market tie ups so that they may earn their livelihood, despite the economic boycott call against them, by some religious groups.[21]

Violence against women must be seen in the socio-economic and political context of gender relations. In every country of the world where reliable, large scale studies have been conducted, including two in the South-East Asia Region, results indicate that between 16% and 52% of women have been assaulted by an intimate partner. The "silence" of violence is breaking. To listen to women's voices is the first step in making their lives safer.

Ending violence against women in our families, communities and societies remains the greatest challenge facing humanity on the eve of the 21st century. Women are attacked on the street, in the workplace, in the home, in situations of armed conflict, and while in state custody. Violence against women devastates lives, fractures communities and is a barrier to development in every nation.

Because violence against women and girls underlies all human societies, we are all the poorer for it; world development is impeded by exactly the measure of the harm dealt out to women; the common future of all of us shrinks to exactly the degree that women are impeded from nourishing themselves and their families. In 1993 alone, the World Bank estimated that violence against women was as serious a cause of death and incapacity among women of reproductive age as cancer, and a greater cause of ill-health than traffic accidents and malaria combined. The World Health Organisation estimates that at least 20 percent of women in the world have been physically or sexually assaulted by a man at some point in their lives. In the United States alone, violence against women costs businesses $100 million in lost wages, sick leave, absenteeism, and non-productivity.[22]

ASPECTS OF STRATEGIES TO PREVENT VIOLATION AGAINST WOMEN

1. Legal Strategies

Advocates in all regions have adopted law reform and advocacy in the courts as key strategies for ending violence against women. Law embodies the social contract and can catalyse social change by sending a clear message that violence against women will not be tolerated. "The criminal justice system response has clearly played a role in educating the public on what and is not acceptable in our local community." Laws that are drafted to reflect the reality of women's experiences can—if fully implemented—provide justice for women who have suffered violence and even protect against further abuse. Legal representation for women seeking remedies in the courts and support for women victims in the judicial process is a focus for ongoing NGO activity.[23]

2. Mobilization and Political Advance

Mobilization and political advocacy are the means to build political will on the part of government to take action against violence and consensus on the part of civil society that violence against women cannot be tolerated.[24]

3. Research and Documentation

Though research and documentation, the severity and scope of violence against women can be exposed to public scrutiny, its causes and consequences can be assessed, and demands for preventive and remedial action can be supported. Members of the working group emphasized the needs to assess and further develop research methodologies and to develop stringent guidelines related to ethical and security concerns. Training and capacity-building for women's groups to support their research and documentation initiatives, including training in human rights methodologies;

Research and documentation protocols to protect the security, confidentiality, privacy and other interests of women participating in the investigations;

Educational and awareness-raising components within research projects, aimed at encouraging communities and/or the women whose experiences are the subject of investigation to;

Debate violence against women; explore the reasons for and against research; and discuss how to utilize research findings and reports; and

In depth country studies to support and promote the design and implementation of multi-disciplinary programmes on violence against women.[25]

4. Media and Communication

The use of media was highlighted both as a means of enhancing the effectiveness of other strategies and as a specific focus for anti-violence advocacy. Women's groups are working with established media and creating their own media outlets to promote coverage that exposes violence against women as a human rights violation and challenges the social, cultural and political norms that support it. Media have a key role to play in stimulating public debate, exposing the severity and prevalence of violence against women, and providing a forum for exploring strategies in other areas.

5. Changing Male Behaviour

Several members in the Working Group highlighted the importance of initiative aimed at changing social and cultural norms about the gender roles of men and societal attitudes towards violence in general. In this connection they focused on solidarity campaigns by men opposed to violence against women, educational initiatives aimed at raising awareness among boys and men, and treatment programmes for men who have perpetrated violence against women. The need to alter patterns of early socialization for both boys and girls was identified as a strategy to be pursued in the family and in the schools. The experience shared by members of the Working Group in connection with interventions with males batterers suggest that these programmes can achieve significant reductions in physical violence if they are court-mandated and last for at least one year or longer and if men enter the programmes after the very first instance of violence against women. In addition, experience indicates that staff administering treatment programmes for batterers should maintain contact with the women who have been abused by the men participating in their programmes, in order to monitor the batterers' behaviour. Two notes of caution were sounded in the discussion; the resources to support treatment programmes for offenders must not be provided at the expense of programmes for women; and verbal and emotional abuse as well as marital rape continue to occur even where physical violence is reduced or eliminated.[26]

6. Training and Education

Training and education are a primary focus of NGO advocacy. Members of the Working Group reported on training activities targeted to many different audiences, including: law enforcement officers; judges; lawyers; doctors, nurses and other healthcare providers; civil servants; high level government officials; religious leaders; women's groups; girls in public schools and youth organizations; and boys in public schools and youth organisations. Elements common to the most effective approaches include: methodologies that take participants experiences and perceptions as the starting point for dialogue; content and methodologies tailored to the experiences and needs of the target audience; the support of leaders in the group being trained; effective training materials; training in a series of workshops and sessions, rather than single sessions; the participation of senior officials in trainings for government officials, particularly for law enforcement personnel; training partnerships with local groups and/or government agencies where appropriate; the integration of information and analyses about violence against women into general education and training courses; and accessible settings for trainings.

On the one hand, the government is strengthening the existing legislations and developing new institutional machineries (all women police stations, gender sensitisation of law enforcement personnel, etc.) on the other, it is running projects that provide support to vulnerable women (short-stay homes, hostels for working women, etc.) and rehabilitation of victims of violence.[27]

LEGISLATIVE MEASURES IN INDIA—LEGAL RIGHTS OF WOMEN

To uphold the Constitutional mandate, the State has enacted various legislative measures intended to ensure equal rights, to counter social discrimination and various forms of violence and atrocities and to provide support service especially to working women. The police have been given a constitutional and a legal role to play in case of violence, laws, rules and procedures have been devised for this purpose.

Although women may be victims of any of the crimes such as 'Murder', 'Robbery', 'Cheating', etc., the crimes which are directed specifically against women are characterized as 'Crimes Against Women'. These are broadly classified under two categories:

(1) The Crimes Identified under the Indian Penal Code (IPC)

(i) Rape (Sec. 376 IPC),
(ii) Kidnapping and Abduction for different purposes (Sec. 363-373 IPC),
(iii) Homicide for Dowry, Dowry Deaths or their attempts (Sec. 302/304-B of IPC),
(iv) Torture, both mental and physical (Sec. 498-A of IPC),
(v) Molestation (Sec. 354 of IPC),
(vi) Sexual harassment (Sec. 509 of IPC) (referred to in the past as Eve-teasing), and
(vii) Importation of girls (upto 21 years of age) (Sec. 366-B of IPC).

(2) The Crimes Identified under the Special Laws

Although all laws are not gender specific, the provisions of law affecting women significantly have been reviewed periodically and amendments carried out to keep pace with the emerging requirements. Some Acts which have special provisions to safeguard women and their interests are:

1. Commission of Sati (Prevention) Act, 1987 (3 of 1988).
2. Dowry Prohibition Act, 1961 (28 of 1961).
3. Indecent Representation of Women (Prohibition) Act, 1986.

4. Immoral Traffic (Prevention) Act, 1956.
5. Medical Termination of Pregnancy Act, 1971 (34 of 1971).
6. Child Marriage Restraint Act, 1929 (19 of 1929).
7. Hindu Marriage Act, 1955 (25 of 1955).
8. Hindu Succession Act, 1956 (3 of 1956).
9. Contract Labour (Regulation and Abolition) Act, 1970 (37 of 1970).
10. Equal Remuneration Act, 1976 (25 of 1976).
11. Factories Act, 1948 (63 of 1948) as amended in 1976.
12. Maternity Benefit Act, 1961 (53 of 1961).
13. Criminal Law (Amendment) Act, 1983.
14. Special Marriage Act, 1954.
15. The Family Courts Act, 1954.
16. Employees' State Insurance Act, 1948.
17. Plantation Labour Act, 1951.

The global campaign for elimination of violence against women, in the recent years indicates the enormity as well as the seriousness of the atrocities committed against women that are being witnessed the world over. Development along with its progressive changes in personal lifestyle, living standards, varied economic growth caused by urbanisation and changes in social ethos contributes to a violent attitude and tendencies towards women which has resulted in an increase in crimes against women. Such incidents are a matter of serious concern and its containment is a necessity so that the women of India attain their rightful share and live in dignity, freedom, peace and free from crimes and aspersions. The battle against crime against women, has to be waged by the various sections of society through campaigns and various programmes with social support along with legal protection, safeguards and reforms in the Criminal Justice System.

Despite all these safeguards, the women in our country continue to suffer, due to lack of awareness of their rights, illiteracy and oppressive practices and customs. The greatest problem is that women tolerate silently and suffer the maximum. There must be a mechanism where she can express her problems in confidence till such time, women may not feel these as scars on their lives. The resultant consequences are many viz. a constant fall in the sex ratio, high infant mortality rate, low literacy rate, high drop out rate of girls from education, low wage rates, etc.

INCIDENCE OF CRIMES AGAINST WOMEN

Incidence of Crimes Against Women—All India (1998-2000)

The Crime head-wise incidence of reported crimes during 1998 to 2000 alongwith percentage variation is presented below. It is observed that Crimes Against Women reported an increase of 4.1 per cent and 3.3 per cent over previous year 1999 and 1998 respectively as shown in Table 7.1

The proportion of IPC crimes committed against women towards total

TABLE 7.1

Crimes Against Women

Sl. No.	Crime Head	Year 1998	1999	2000	Percentage variation in 2000 over 1999
1.	Rape	15151	15468	16496	6.6
2.	Kidnapping and Abduction	16351	15962	15023	-5.9
3.	Dowry Death	6975	6699	6995	4.4
4.	Torture	41376	43823	45778	4.5
5.	Molestation	30959	32311	32940	1.9
6.	Sexual Harassment	8054	8858	11024	24.5
7.	Importation of Girls	146	1	64	6300.0
8.	Sati Prevention Act	0	0	0	-
9.	Immoral Traffic (P) Act	8695	9363	9515	1.6
10.	Indecent Rep. of Women (P) Act	190	222	662	198.2
11.	Dowry Prohibition Act	3578	3064	2876	-6.1
	Total	131475	135771	141373	4.1

Source: NCRB.

IPC crimes increased to 7.2 percent during the year from 6.7 percent in 1998. (see Table 7.2)

TABLE 7.2

Proportion of Crimes against Women (IPC) towards Total IPC Crimes

Sl. No.	Year	Total IPC Crimes	Crime against women (IPC cases)	Percentage to total IPC crimes
1.	1998	1778815	119012	6.7
2.	1999	1764629	123122	7.0
3.	2000	1771084	128320	7.2

Source: *Ibid.*

The available data indicates an increasing trend during the last three years for cases registered under IPC crimes such as 'Rape', 'Torture', 'Molestation' and 'Sexual Harassment' and under SLL times such as 'Immoral Traffic (Prevention) Act' and 'Indecent Representation of Women (P) Act'. The cases under 'Kidnapping and Abduction of Women and Girls' and 'Dowry Prohibition Act' however decreased during last few years.

Crime Rate (States and Uts) (NCRB, Ministry of Human Affiars, GOI, 2000)

All India Crime Rate, i.e. number of crimes per lakh population for crimes against women reported to the police worked out to be 14.1. This rate of crime which does not appear alarming at first sight may be viewed with caution, as a sizable number of crimes against women go unreported due to social stigma attached to them.

Uttar Pradesh State reported highest incidence (13.4%) of these crimes followed by Madhya Pradesh (12.7%). Rajasthan which shared 9.2 per cent of these crimes and was fifth in the order of incidence, however reported highest crime rate at 24.0 followed by Madhya Pradesh 22.3 as compared to national rate of 14.1.

Classification

(a) Rape

Incidence of rape cases reported an increase of 6.6% over the previous year. Madhya Pradesh alone reported 22.7 per cent of total rape cases in the country. UT of Delhi, which represented only 3.1 per cent cases reported third highest rate at 3.1 after Mizoram (6.0) and Madhya Pradesh (4.7).

(b) Incest

From the year 1999, information on Incest (Rape) cases is also compiled. It is observed that out of total 16,496 Rape cases, only 2.2 per cent were Incest cases. These cases decreased by 9.7 per cent over previous year.

Rape Victims

At national level, there were an equal number of 16,496 rape victims as the number of cases, compared to 15,471 in the previous year representing an increase of nearly 6.6 per cent. Of these 40% were in the age group of 19-30 years followed by 4,622 (20.8%) in the age-group 16-18 years.

Offenders were known to the victims in as many as 14,220 (87.4%) cases. Of these neighbours were involved in nearly 30.1% of cases.

Custodial Rapes

During the year, only 2 cases of custodial rape, 1 from Orissa and 1 from Madhya Pradesh were reported in the country. However, No. case resulted in the convictions during the year.

Kidnapping and Abduction

Incidence of these cases reported a decline of 5.9 per cent as compared to the previous year. Uttar Pradesh reported 18.3 per cent followed by Rajasthan sharing 17.0 per cent of these cases at national level. U.T. of Delhi with share of 6.6% cases reported highest rate at 7.1 compared to 1.5 at the national level.

Dowry Deaths

Incidence of 'Dowry Death' cases reported an increase of 4.4 per cent over the previous year. 31.8 per cent of these cases at national level were reported by Uttar Pradesh alone followed by Bihar (15.5%). The highest rate of crime (1.3) was also reported from Uttar Pradesh.

Torture (Cruelty by Husband and Relatives)

Incidence of 'Torture' cases in the country increased by 4.5 per cent over the previous year 14.8 per cent of these were reported by Maharashtra followed by Uttar Pradesh (13.2%) while the highest rate in the country at 10.1 was reported from Rajasthan compared to 4.6 at national level.

Molestation

Incidence of Molestation cases in the country reported an increase of 1.9 per cent over the previous year. 26 per cent of total such cases were reported from Madhya Pradesh state which also reported the highest rate (10.6) as compared to national average of 3.3.

Sexual Harassment (Eve-Teasing)

The number of 'Sexual Harassment' cases reported steep rise of 24.5 per cent over the previous year. Uttar Pradesh reported 28.7 per cent of cases followed by Andhra Pradesh 20.7 per cent. However, Tamil Nadu reported the highest crime rate 3.5 compared to national level rate of 1.1.

Importation of Girls

These cases reported a steep increase of 63 per cent due to reporting of 64 cases during the year as compared to only one case in the previous year. Bihar alone reported 40 cases sharing 62 per cent of cases at the national level.

Crime Trends—(Special Laws)

Sati Prevention Act

The practice of Sati is on the wane in modern times. Still sporadically, cases under this Act get reported. No. such case from any of State/UT was reported in the country during the year.

Immoral Traffic (Prevention) Act

Cases under this Act registered an increase of 1.6 per cent during the year as compared to the previous year. Nearly three-fourth (73%) cases were reported from the State of Tamil Nadu which also reported the highest crime rate of 11.2 as compared to 0.9 national average rate.

Indecent Representation of Women (Prohibition) Act

A remarkable increase of 198.2 per cent was noticed for cases under this Act as compared to cases reported in the previous year. More than half

(57.3%) cases were reported from Andhra Pradesh alone, which also reported the highest crime rate of 0.5 as compared to 0.1 national rate.

Dowry Prohibition Act Cases

These cases reported a decline of 6.1 per cent as compared to the previous year. Of these, a sizable proportion (30.2%) were reported from Bihar state followed by Andhra Pradesh and Orissa each sharing nearly 15 per cent cases at national level.

Crime against Women Cases in Cities

A total of 16,787 cases were reported from 23 mega cities sharing 11.9 per cent of the total cases at national level. Among 23 cities, Chennai city shared 24.0 per cent of these cases followed by Delhi (12.7%). The rate was also significantly higher at Chennai (59.8) compared to the national average of 17.0.

It is worthwhile mentioning that Chennai was more vigilant in curbing these crimes as more cases under Special Laws and Local Acts were booked in Chennai compared to any other City. Delhi city, which ranked 11 with rate of 17.6 among 23 cities, however, shared 34.7 per cent of Rape cases, 45.9 per cent of Kidnapping and Abduction cases, 19.9 per cent of Dowry Deaths and 23.6 per cent of Molestation cases while 77.6 per cent of cases under Immoral Traffic Prevention Act and 24.2 per cent cases under dowry Prohibition Act were reported from Chennai city.

POLICY AND PLAN OF ACTION OF GOVERNMENT OF INDIA

National Policy for the Empowerment of Women

In order to address the concerns of women in society, the Government of India has established the Department of Women and Child Development within the Ministry of Human Resource Development. A National Policy for the Empowerment of Women, 2001 provides the policy framework for addressing women's issues. The objectives of the policy are as follows:

- Creating an environment through positive economic and social policies for full development of women to enable them to realize their full potential.
- The *de-jure* and *de-facto* enjoyment of all human rights and fundamental freedom by women on equal basis with men in all spheres—political, economic, social, cultural and civil.
- Equal access to participation and decision-making of women in social, political and economic life of the nation.
- Equal access to women to healthcare, quality education at all levels, career and vocational guidance, employment, equal remuneration occupational health and safety, security and public office, etc.

- Strengthening legal systems aimed at elimination of all forms of discrimination against women.
- Changing societal attitudes and community practices by active participation and involvement of both men and women
- Mainstreaming a gender perspective in the development process.
- Elimination of discrimination and all forms of violence against women and the girls child.
- Building and strengthening partnerships with civil society, particularly women's organizations.

Programmes

In keeping with its past and present policy objectives, the government has launched a number of programmes focussed on women. In 1993 the Women in Agriculture programme were initiated which aimed at training women framers with small holdings and in allied activities such as animal husbandry, dairying, horticulture, fisheries, etc. In 1998 a scheme was started that aimed at empowering women in rural areas. It was called Swashakti-Rural Women's Development and Empowerment Project. In 2001, the government launched Swayamsidha-Integrated Women Empowerment that aims at holistic empowerment of women through awareness generation, economic empowerment and convergence of various schemes. In 2002, Swadhar is aimed at women in distress such as destitute widows, women prisoners released from jail but without a family, women survivors of natural disaster, Assistance under this programme includes food, clothing, healthcare, measures of social and economic rehabilitation through education awareness, etc.

In the international arena India has ratified the International Convention on Elimination of All Forms of Discrimination Against Women (CEDAW) 1993, and endorsed the Mexico Plan of Action, 1975; the Nairobi Forward Looking Strategies, 1985; the Beijing Declaration as well the Platform for Action, 1995.

Empowering people to take control of their livelihood resources through legislative means, participatory and co-management methods and innovative investment in people and resources constitutes a key component of India's strategy for sustainable development.[28]

Targets for Sustainable Development upto Tenth Plan

- Reduction of poverty ratio by 5 percentage points by 2007 and by 15 percentage points by 2012.
- All children in school by 2003; all children to complete 5 years in school by 2007.
- Reduction in gender gaps in literacy and wage rates by at least 50% by 2007.
- Reduction in population growth between 2001 and 2011 to 16.2%.

- Increase in literacy rate to 75% by 2007.
- Reduction of Infant Mortality Rate (IMR) to 45 per 1000 live births by 2007 and to 28 by 2012.
- Reduction of Maternal Mortality Rate (MMR) to 2 per 1000 live births by 2007 and to 1 by 2012.
- Increase in forest cover to 25% by 2007 and 33% by 2012.
- All villages to have sustained access to potable drinking water by 2007.
- Cleaning of major polluted rivers by 2007 and other notified stretches by 2012.

The Government of India has adopted a National Policy for the Empowerment of Women. Since the goal of the Policy is to bring about the advancement, development and empowerment of women by creating an environment through positive social and economic policies and programmes for development of women in all spheres of life.

Para 7.1 of the Policy lays down as under:

All forms of violence against women, physical and mental, whether at domestic or societal levels, including those arising from customs, traditions or accepted practices shall be dealt with effectively with a view to eliminate its incidence. Institutions and mechanisms/schemes for assistance will be created and strengthened for prevention of such violence, including sexual harassment at work place and customs like dowry; for the rehabilitation of the victims of violence and for taking effective action against the perpetrators of such violence. A special emphasis will also be laid on programmes and measures to deal with trafficking in women and girls.

National Plan of Action for Empowerment of Women

The Government is drafting a National Plan of Action (POA) to Implement the National Policy for the Empowerment of Women. The POA will focus on creating support infrastructure to compliment legislative efforts, creating a conducive environment to women for reporting cases related to violence against them. Gender sensitivity among the policy-makers will be strengthened alongwith awareness on the prevention of atrocities on women.

The global campaign for elimination of violence against women, in the recent years indicates the enormity as well the seriousness of the atrocities committed against women that are being witnessed the world over. Development along with its progressive changes in personal lifestyle, living standards varied economic growth caused by urbanisation and changes in social ethos contributes to a violent attitude and tendencies towards women which has resulted in an increase in crimes against women. Such incidents are a matter of serious concern and its containment is a necessity so that the Women of India attain their rightful share and live in dignity, freedom, peace and free from crimes and aspersions. The battle against crime against women, has to be waged by the various sections of society through campaigns and various programmes with social support along with legal protection, safeguards and reforms in the Criminal Justice System.

Despite all these safeguards, the women in our country continue to suffer, due to lack of awareness of their rights, illiteracy and oppressive practices and customs. The greatest problem is that women tolerate silently and suffer the maximum. There must be a mechanism where she can express her problems in confidence till such time, women may not feel these as scars as their lives. The resultant consequences are may viz. a constant fall in the sex ratio, high infant mortality rate, low literacy rate, high drop out rate of girls from education, low wage rates, etc.

CRITICAL APPRAISAL

(1) Poverty is Main Cause for Violence: Need of Containment Jointly by Men and Women

The importance of sustainability of livelihoods of the poor is a pre-condition for sustainable development. People's enterprise, micro-credits, their participation in resource management and focussed intervention in poor areas and investment in poor people have shown positive results in the nineties. The target for the end of Tenth Five Year Plan is to bring down the poverty ratio by 5 percentage points by 2007 and by 15 percentage points by 2012. Since income is only one of the dimensions of poverty, a concerted effort to invest in social sectors for improvement in the living conditions of the poor is a critical element of this strategy.

Devolution of power to people through constitutional amendments, in the nineties, is already showing remarkable results in a number of areas. By transferring management powers of 29 sectors of economy to village councils and allowing them to raise resources through taxation, the first major step in empowering people including women to manage their resources has already been taken. The steps contemplated for the future are, sharing of state and central revenue with village council and their direct involvement in management of social sector activities and village infrastructure. Moving beyond the elected representative of village councils, a number of initiatives for management of natural resources seek direct involvement of the whole village, for example, Joint Forest Management, Watershed Development Committees and Participatory Irrigation Management to mention a few. Clearly the emerging strategy is to empower people to manage their resources to establish sustainable livelihoods.

2. Empower Women and Avoid Violence against Women

The Constitution of India grants equal status to men and women and empowers the State to adopt measures of positive discrimination in favour of women. The adverse sex ratio at 933 females per 1,000 males, however points to the challenge of converting the constitutional aspirations into reality.

Gender relations in India differ from community to community and across cast, class and other criteria. Most communities also exhibit a gender bias against girl children, with the exception of tribal communities that tend to be more equitable than non-tribal communities. Often this bias is also extended to access to healthcare, nutrition, education and other social services such as water supply sanitation and housing, and other opportunities.

Many of the poverty alleviation schemes and programmes focus on the rural or urban poor as generic entities. Women's participation in these programmes is limited although in the last decade self-help groups (SHG), mostly run exclusively by women, have emerged as an institutional arrangement that provide some social and financial power to women's groups.

3. Violent Imbalances: Need of Curbs

At present, the courts, society, community, police favour men and not women when three are violence.

4. Gap between Enactment of Laws and their Implementation: Need of Sincerity in Enforcement

Only very few cases are reported. Women suffer silently. We have to make our system active so that No. man who has done violence goes unpunished. R.D. Sharma in his article, "Violent Imbalances", in *Hindustan Times,* dated 3rd May, 2001 states that the objectives of preventive laws may not be faulted, but what is of crucial importance is their enforcement. A wide gap exists between laws with high social and economic purposes and their implementation on account of police inefficiency and widespread corruption all around. In this climate, the cutting edge to laws, both as an instrument of crime prevention and of social change, is bound to get blunted. The position further gets aggravated when the culprits are seen by the populate flouting, perverting or getting round the letter and spirit of the law. So long as these laws are not accompanied by the empowerment of women at all levels and a sense of accountability in the enforcing agency, they will serve little purpose.

In any case, legal remedies alone can not cope with a regressive socio-economic set-up in the absence of radical, structural and economic reforms which can be implemented only by mass mobilisation and participation. But with the kind of bureaucracy, police and political set-up that we have, the mere passing of laws will not serve any purpose. More important than legislative reforms is the strict enforcement of rights already available to women in relation to property matters. In fact, women's plight is compounded by their reluctance to seek legal remedies even if they are aware of them. The voluntary surrender of their rights in the matter of inheritance is the single biggest reason why women suffer the ignominy of dowry that continues to make marriage an ordeal or a death trap for many of them. The objectives of preventive laws may not be faulted, but what is of crucial importance is their enforcement. A wide gap exists between laws with high social and economic purposes and their implementation. In this climate, the cutting edge of laws—both as instruments of tackling crime and of social change—is bound to get blunted. The position further gets aggravated when the culprits are seen to flout or get around the letter and spirit of the law. As long as these laws are not accompanied by the empowerment of women at all levels and accountability is instilled in the enforcing agency, they will serve a little purpose.

In any case, legal remedies alone cannot cope with a regressive socio-economic set-up in the absence of radical, structural and economic reforms which can be implemented only by mass mobilisation and participation. But with the kind of red tape, police and political set-up that we have the mere passing of laws will not serve any purpose. More important than legislative reforms is the strict enforcement of rights already available to women in relation to property matters.

In fact, the plight of women is compounded by their reluctance to seek legal remedies even if they are aware of them. The voluntary surrender of their rights in the matter of inheritance is the single biggest reason why women suffer the ignominy of dowry that continues to make marriage an ordeal or a death trap for many.[29]

5. Women Police not in Good Strength Causing Delay and Lapse of Case against Women

It has been a common occurrence that cases of violence against women are not dealt properly as women police is very less in number. Tejdeep Kaur, Inspector General of Police, Andhra Pradesh rightly points out as:

Talk about the "fair sex" not getting a fair deal is now common. Be it enactment of new social laws, creation of institutions for target groups providing reservation for them in all elected bodies. Yet, there is not better evidence of the state of women's empowerment than the revealing statistics of Crimes Against Women (CAW), their handling, the profile of the victims, the accused and the disposal of the cases.

> Even as crime against women are on the rise,
> the number of policewomen available to tackle
> these cases is woefully inadequate.

Significantly, majority of the women are between 15 and 29 years of age while male victims are between 30 and 44. Social and economic causes led most men to commit suicide while emotional and personal factors are the prime reasons with women.

All this casts heavy responsibility on women police already saddled with important tasks and issues relating to search, arrest, custody of women witness, arrestees and juvenile delinquents. But there is just one policewoman for every 45 policemen, a woefully inadequate 2.09 per cent of the entire force.

As many as 18 States have a strength of less then 1,000 each. Maharashtra is in the lead with 4,345 policewomen. The share of women in armed police is 0.39 per cent. They exist only in a few states—Madhya Pradesh, Himachal Pradesh, Jammu and Kashmir, Assam, Goa and Delhi. There are not enough policewomen for investigation.

In such a situation there is not question of policewomen being available to tackle cases where the woman is the victim rather than the offender. It is time to put on the thinking caps.

6. Girl Child Abuses on Increase: Need of Awareness among the People

Recognising that the exploitation and abuse of the girl child in India is a subject of great socio-legal significance and that the girl child abuses were increasing at a very fast rate, the National Commission for Women in association with the society for Environment and Development, Delhi, organised a three-day workshop in Jodhpur (Rajasthan) on Girl Child Abuses in Rajasthan and Role of Social Organisations. The workshop was attended by 52 participants from 18 districts of Rajasthan. Participants included multi-disciplinarians from various fields like voluntary organisations, intellectuals, academicians, advocates and also representatives from the universities of Rajasthan. The Chairperson, National Commission for Women was the Chief Guest at the workshop. Mr. A.D. Vohra, eminent academician and renowned social worker from Jodhpur presided over the function.

There were in all four technical sessions and two working groups to discuss and finalise recommendation on the issue. The main recommendations were:

(a) There is a need for more research and studies, on region-wise basis to assess the gravity of the problem, factors responsible, efforts made so far, bottlenecks, etc. in regard to girl child abuses.

(b) There is a need for Girl Charter at Rajasthan level. A committee was formed to chalk out the Character under the convenorship of Mrs. Alice Garg.

(c) Formation of Task-forces at district level comprising NGO's Advocates, Police Officers, intellectuals and other eminent persons to take stock of the situation on regular basis, suggest action and follow-up measures.

(d) Media, both print and electronic, should be persuaded to provide small space/time slot on daily basis to educate and make aware the masses about the crimes against girl child, their causes, legal aspects, etc. This can be in the form of story, poem, cartoon, etc. There should be complete and strict ban on obsence advertisements on TV channels, magazines and newspapers and serials.

(e) There is an urgent need for resource material in local languages for use by the grass-root voluntary organisations. It can be in the form of book-lets, posters, stickers, hand bills, pamphlets, etc.

(f) A platform where joint efforts could be made to tackle the problems and victims could approach easily to get justice and rehabilitation. The workshop formed "Rajasthan Balika Chetna Manch" which proposed to meet in the last week of September at Jaipur to finalise further modalities of its structure and functionings.[30]

We shall discuss in detail in next chapters about all forms violence against women as well as the methods to check this menace. All of us agree that violence against women, whatever the reason, is neither rational nor human rather a black sport on the face of humanity.

Violence against women would continue as long as the Government is lenient and indulge in favouritism when their kith and kin are involved. So, the Government has to be strong and impartial in curbing the violence against women in any form. Besides, women organisations like NCW, CSWB, women study centres in Universities and colleges have to be active to protect the interests of women. What has been seen is that influential women head these organisations to get one benefit or the other rather than taking interest in women activities. Therefore, what is important is to weed out violence against women. There is the need of selecting, nominating women on women organisations who are sincere and committed to the cause of women.

Inspite of such achievements there are serious challenges in almost all our countries with respect to the realization of the Beijing vision and commitments—

- Lack of transparent and accountable governance.
- Negative impact of structural adjustment programmes and globalization on women.
- Increased incidence of gender-based violence, acid throwing, incest, sexual abuse and sexual harassment, trafficking of women and children.
- Continuing invisibility of women in higher levels of governance, political leadership and civil service and the continuing resistance of mainstream political parties to provide space for women.
- Marginalization of the Women's Ministries: gender continuing to be seen as a "women's issue" and as responsibility of Women's Affairs Ministries only.
- Insufficient human, technical and financial resources and political will to implement national plans of action and for addressing gender concerns in particular.
- Inadequate sex disaggregated data and analysis.
- The serious lacks of co-ordination and horizontal linkages among different agencies, both governmental and non-governmental, working in the area of gender.

- Continuing gender gaps in education and health.
- Non-responsiveness of media towards gender issues.
- Lack of gender perspectives in macro-economic policies and national budgets and investment decisions.

SUGGESTIONS

1. National Council for Women has not used the powers entrusted to them. They should be strict while dealing with the complaints. They must make use of the powers vested in them. The Council has the power of the civil court and the council must make use of it to award strict punishment. The complaints should be dealt with promptly otherwise the other party manages counter evidences, etc.
2. (i) The Council should design a proforma so that filing of complaints may become easy.
   (ii) Complaints may be classified as these are to be dealt by different acts by the council.
   (iii) PRI System and Urban Local Government should be provided all these forms so that they have not to wait to go to the council.
   (iv) PRIS and urban local self-Government should foreword these complaints to National Council for Women.
   (v) Complaints may be definite and not done for extraneous reasons. Council must ascertain this. If the complainant has a litigation in the Civil Court, complaint maybe passed on to them
   (vi) National Council of Women should try to help in compromises and not confrontation.
3. The women who indulge in anti-social activities are sent in jails till their cases come before the court. It has been a common experience that women prisoners are put in jails where men are also jailed in large numbers. The women are exploited there both by prisoners and jail authorities. Many of them have become mentally wreck and become hardened criminals. The environment in jails is beyond human existence and hence they may be kept in good atmosphere in jails.
4. (i) Women in detention should be taught some income generating activities so that their outlook towards the life can be changed.
   (ii) Women should be kept in exclusive women jails to avoid their exploitation.
   (iii) There should be jail reforms as the purpose of jail is to improve the lives of inmates.
   (iv) Civil Courts should be asked to decide the cases of women in jails so that those who are not at fault maybe out of this atmosphere at the earliest.

(v) Women should be treated leniently as compared to men.
(vi) Women cases should be settled expeditiously.

5. The Government of India and State Governments have passed a number of laws to protect the women from different atrocities on them. Even amendments have been made in them to make them more stricter. However, all these have loopholes causing them infructuous on one pretext or the other Laws are not properly drafted seriously. Government Machinery must ensure strict compliance to law.
   (i) Laws must be drafted in a way that there is No. ambiguity.
   (ii) Experts from law departments of the University may be associated in drafting the laws as they have a lot of experience.
   (iii) Slackness in the implementation of laws must be dealt strongly.
   (iv) NCW must be consulted before the law is finalised.
   (v) Laws must be framed in simple and intelligible language.
   (vi) Local language version of these laws must be made available to women organisations.
   (vii) Awareness about these laws must be made among women organisations.
6. Government is not encouraging the recruitment of women police. In addition families consider a stigma to make their female members to join police. Police does not carry good image and stature in society. Moreover, women constables are not safe and recently a course has been started for them to sensitise them in their protection. The number of police-women is small as compared to requirements:
   (i) Women police strength needs to be increased keeping in view the workload.
   (ii) Only women police should deal with women cases otherwise there is a danger of sexual exploitation in police lock-up.
   (iii) Women police should be given training in gender sensitisation.
   (iv) Women police should be allowed to see the senior police IPS women to narrate their problems on the job.
   (v) Women police can bring a lot of reforms through their positive attitude.
   (vi) Women police can reduce corruption as they cannot be free with the people of underworld.
   (vii) The Government must put a positive image of women police to attract qualified women.

and specially young girls at the University level, to take a more proactive role in the battle against sexual harassment. She was speaking at a recent regional conference on sexual harassment at place of work.

> "The problem boils down to the vast and increasing contradictions in our society. What is termed as obscenity by one section is seen as art by others. Women are also a part of this contradiction which will only increase with the passage of time and exposure to TV and the wider world. The line has got blurred, but women are not helpless. They just need to take up the problem more proactively. Colleges should raise a collective voice and train to protect themselves. Proactive programmes should be started even at the school level."

Further, handling and managing sexual harassment in the unorganised sector is a huge problem which demands an approach very different from what is needed in the private and government sector. The very nature of this segment makes the task a Herculean one. There is need for legislation to cover this sector and protect the rights of the workers, as a first step, and the adoption of a reformative approach to sensitise the public to the problem.

8. Removal of Judicial Bias

Judicial bias against women is also evident. According to a survey, conducted by Sakshi, an NGO, as many as 64 per cent judges are of the view that women are themselves partly responsible for the violence they face. In criminal cases like rape, needless emphasis is often placed on the victim's character and conduct and her past scrutinised, whereas the previous history of the accused is ignored by judges. The part of the definition of rape which says, "the act of sex must be against her will and without her consent", is more than not disbelieved by courts because of a misconceived notion that rape cannot be committed without the victim's consent.[31]

9. Need of Positive Role of Press

Putting the Carriage Back

It appears that somewhere along the way the media has lost sight of the women's carriage. Women were hardly being noticed by the media in the Fifties, the baseline of our study. But by the Seventies, because of the activities on the women's science in India and abroad, they were beginning to get noticed and written about. When they took part in rallies or entered a male bastion, it was news. A woman Prime Minister in Indira Gandhi added impetus to the image of a woman was a doer, an achiever, and a thinking person.

And then, emerged the global stereotype. Beautiful and sexy, in a world of her own where nothing matters except good clothes and make-up, five star food and exercises in the gym. Propelled by the advertisers, the media trained its lenses on this creature, making her into an icon, and lost sight of the carriage carrying the real women. Where has it gone? No. one knows, for those who should be telling us have stopped looking and are silent. If the media wants to play fair, it needs to rediscover the carriage and put it back on the pages once again. Otherwise, it would have failed one half of the population it claims to serve.

The Way Ahead

- Newspapers should make a conscious effort at engendering news, its presentation and editorial comment. A democratic press must represent women and give space to them. There has to be a concerted effort at playing fair, undoing biases and breaking the stereotype. By promoting the stereotype, newspapers further the biases that prevail against women and affect them. Women are expected to look and behave in certain set patterns and this distorts their self-image and undermines their confidence.
- It is necessary to get the female perspective into stories wherever possible. For example, sometime ago there was a ruling that Delhi schools could not take in children below four years of age. How did that decision affect the women? For many middle-class women, the neighbourhood nursery schools provide a break from the tough job of looking after children and also time when they can attend to other work. For women working outside the house, the nursery schools are a substitute for day-care and crèche facilities, which are almost non-existent. Papers will have to make more of an effort to involve women in their stories.
- A newspaper has to be socially committed. Though a paper may be owned by a proprietor or a group of persons, it belongs to the society, for it survives off the people. The masses have to be let in on its pages. It has to mirror the expanse of voices. It needs to open its antennae to the other half of the population it seeks to serve—the women. Their concerns and attention, and aspirations need to be voiced. None of the papers carried a single article on women's health —it is an area that receives little attention. The poor, Dalit and rural women are rarely written about.
- It is strange that newspapers presume that women are only interested in soft stories, and issues like war and conflict, politics or foreign affairs are beyond their comprehension. Papers should write as if women mattered, and address them like intelligent, thinking, human beings.
- Women are entering the profession, but they still do not have equal access to challenging assignments. Newspaper management and editorial teams should ensure that there is No. discrimination between men and women when it comes to assignments.

- Women, especially women's groups, need to be more active in voicing their opinion on issues that impact them and on the way women are portrayed in the media. This would mean writing to the editors, organising press conferences, issuing press releases, being active instead of a passive readers.

If Indian papers themselves do not make a conscious effort to engender news but leave it to outside influences, at the present rate of change it will take at least a couple of centuries for women to catch up with men in terms of equal space in the paper. That will be the time when women will regularly feature on business pages and their comments sought; when sportsmen will get the same coverage as sportsmen; when women will have their concerns addressed on the edit page and female by lines equal the male in different sections of the paper.

However, the media would have rid itself of biases only when a woman dying in childbirth gets the same coverage as a man who is knocked down dead by a speeding vehicle. And when the fact that about 80 per cent of Indian women are anaemic will merit a banner headline on the Front Page and edits advocate a national health emergency. But to get to that stage calls for some concerted action.[32]

We must not allow these violations of human rights to go unrecognized and unchallenged. We must open our eyes to all forms of violence against women and combat them on all fronts: behind the doors of family homes; in the community; on the streets of our villages and towns; at work and in the political and economic institutions that govern our societies. Let us use the occasion of World Health Day, 1993 to speak out strongly against this abuse of human rights and take strong measures to put an end to all forms of violence against women.

Over 21 million people died in the 150 wars that have taken place, mostly in the Third World, since the Second World War. The majority of those who died were civilians; in fact the proportion of civilian deaths to the military ones has been rising over this period and in the most recent conflicts has been well over 80%.

The consequences of armed conflict on a population's health are so drastic that the international community must look beyond the effects of war and examine its root causes. This will call for simultaneous action at several levels—

- Doing every thing possible to settle political and economic differences by means other than violence.
- Insisting on respect for the Geneva Convention's rules governing the protection of non-combatants, which 174 signatory governments have accepted.
- Training the civilian and military health services to cope with a sudden influx of injured and to ensure their speedy transport to first-aid stations.

- Teaching as widely as possible the principles of first-aid and wartime surgery.
- Rehabilitating those very seriously injured in war so as to reintegrate them into society and restore their dignity and self-reliance.

Only by taking this global approach to the problem shall we be able to combat that most murderous of human scourges—collective violence and war.

EDUCATION AND VIGILANCE: THE NEED OF THE HOUR

The root cause behind large-scale physical violence is the social discontentment/disharmony among various population groups/communities. Besides these, political rivalries, religious and ethnic conflicts have also been responsible for its genesis as is evident from the past and current global scenario in may parts of the world. Eruption of violence (date and time) remains unpredictable in most cases where it is of sudden onset, although in certain situations such as ongoing rivalry/conflict, it may be anticipated with high degree of certainty. However, in order to tackle the situation and its consequences effectively, adequate prior preparation on all fronts, including medical and health, is required. It therefore, calls for keeping an adequate vigilance at all times and at all places, playing particular attention to those areas/regions which have already been recognized as "violence prone" in the light of past experience. It also calls for an effective monitoring/information system for timely warning to all concerned—including medical and health authorities—about its anticipated/actual eruption and subsequent progress. Police/intelligence department should be competent to play this role and bear this responsibility. This is one area where inter-sectoral cooperation is of crucial importance.

Suggestions

A. To believe in the maxim "love one another" and other basic ethical tenets of the world's religious philosophies and a belief in the worth of an individual and of human survival.

B. To believe, in the present context, that recourse to violence of any kind is not the answer to sort out disputes of various nature, at various levels since violence is not only an anti-social but an inhuman act. History has made it amply clear that the final outcome of violence is always unpredictable. The need of the hour is therefore to settle all disputes and rivalries in a peaceful manner, in a humane way, through talks/negotiations across the table, rather than resort to violence.

C. Not to fall prey to alcoholism which is also associated with

> automobile accidents and violence. In the USA, it was found associated with over 50% of all deaths and major injuries due to automobile accidents, about 50% all murders, 40% of all assaults, 35% or more of all rapes and 30% of all suicides. About 1 out of every 3 arrests in US results from abuse of alcohol. Due to rising trend of alcoholism among teenagers during 1970s, it was called the "teenage tragedy of the seventies.

Teachers' role is important in preaching non-violence to their students. They should however practice what they teach and never resort to violence in any form as punishment to a student at fault.

The United Nations observed 1986 as the International year of peace. There is a perpetual necessity of having similar campaigns and observe "International Year/Decade of Non-violence." Public opinion should also be mobilized through the UN in the endeavour to put an end to all types of conflicts, wars and building up of nuclear and biochemical arsenals. Lastly, it is worthwhile to recollect what late John F. Kennedy had to say in this respect. . . . "Each man can make a difference, and each man should try."

CONCLUSION

In the ultimate analysis, there can be No. two opinions about the need for stringent laws, sensitive judiciary, effective law and enforcement machinery and vigilant women's groups to deal with such atrocious crimes against women. But what is needed more than anything else is a total revolution in the thinking of our society that always blames the woman for the crime of which she is the victim, not the perpetrator.

The problem of violence against women has its roots in a socio-economic order that is heavily biased against women. A woman having an identity of her own is a concept alien to Indian culture.

When the entire milieu is steeped in the tradition of women's utter subjugation to men, there can be little hope for a dramatic improvement in the state of women.

The Supreme Court has recently expressed its serious concern at the leniency shown by the Allahabad High Court in discharging the accused in a dowry torture case. A division bench comprising M.B. Shah and S.N. Sariava observed: "It is a matter of shame that indiscriminate attacks and violence are directed against married women and the accused being let off for various reasons. . . . The result is that violence against women continues unabated as law loses its deterrent."

More than changing laws to fight crime against women, the courts must be seen as delivering justice. Society must also radically change the way it instinctively blames the women for such crimes.

Journey has just begun and that there is a long distance to be covered to reach the far pavilions of welfare, development and empowerment for women. But we may take some satisfaction in the fact that our road map is now clearer, our team energized, our organizational resources re-grouped and our gear refurbished so that the Commission's endeavours would be more fruitful.

Mahatma Gandhi strongly feels that, "If only the women of the world would come together they could display such heroic non-violence as to kick away the atom bomb like a mere ball. Women have been so gifted by God. If an ancestral treasure, lying buried in a corner of the house unknown to the members of the family were suddenly discovered, what a celebration it would occasion. Similarly, women's marvellous power is lying dormant. If the women of Asia wake up, they will dazzle the world. My experiment in non-violence would be instantly successful if I could secure women's help."

Preventive and Educational Measures

The programme of Action, 1992 has comprehensively given the below mentioned parameters of empowerment of women:

- Enhance self-esteem and self-confidence in women.
- Build a positive image of women by recognizing their contribution to the society, polity and economy.
- Develop in them an ability to think critically.
- Foster decision-making and action through collective process.
- Enable women to make informed choices in areas like education, employment and health especially reproductive health.
- Ensure equal participation in the development process.
- Provide information, knowledge and skill for economic independence.
- Enhance access to legal literacy and information related to their rights and entitlements in the society with a view to enhance their participation on an equal footing in all areas.

The special attention given to the needs and problems of women to enable them to enjoy and exercise their Constitutional equality of status, along with other specific provisions relating to the hitherto suppressed sections of our society have led many scholars to describe the Indian Constitution as a 'social' document embodying the objectives of a social revolution. There is No. doubt that the Constitution contemplates attainment of an entirely new social order by making deliberate departures in norms and institutions of democratic governance from the inherited social, political and economic systems. In doing so the Constitution assigns primacy to law as an instrument of directed social change. It thus demands of the legislature, the executive and the judiciary, continuous vigilance and responsiveness to the relationship between law and social transformation in contemporary India. (See Chart 7.2)

We Believe

1. that equality of women is necessary, not merely on the grounds

CHART 7.2

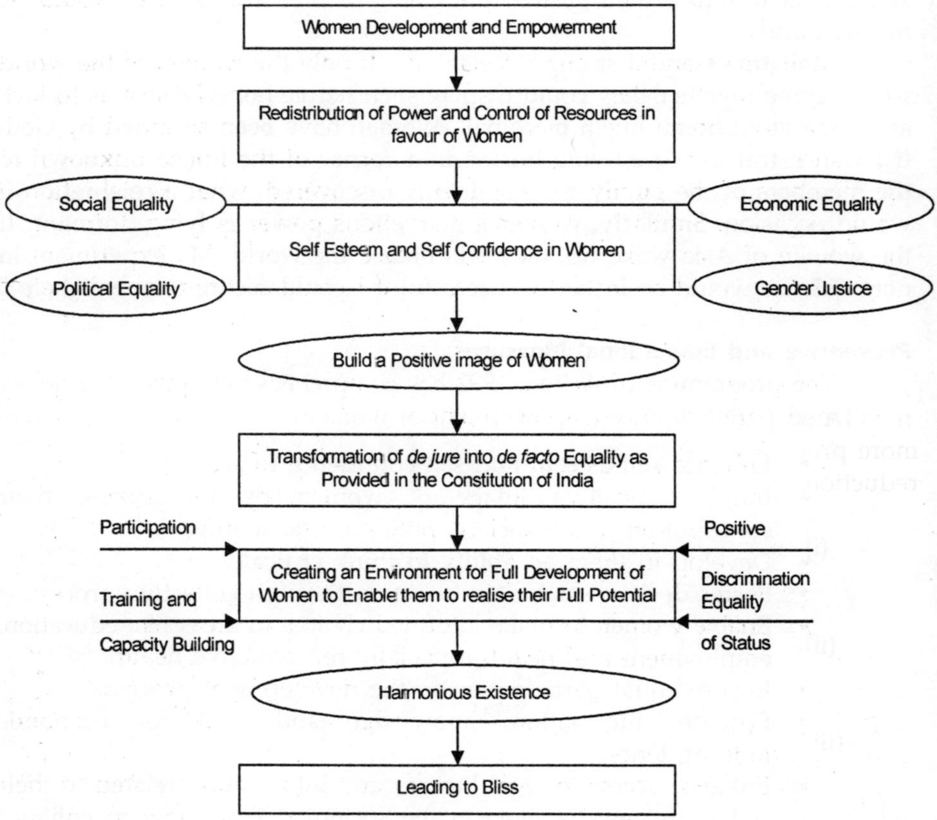

of social justice, but as a basic condition for social, economic and political development of the nation;

2. that in order to release women from their dependent and unequal status, improvement of their employment opportunities and earning power has to be given the highest priority;
3. that society owes a special responsibility to women because of their child-bearing function. Safe bearing and rearing of children is an obligation that has to be shared by the mother, the father and the society;
4. that the contribution made by an active housewife to the running and management of a family should be admitted as economically and socially productive and contributing to national savings and development;
5. that marriage and motherhood should not become a disability in women's fulfiling their full and proper role in the task of national development. Therefore, it is important that society, including women themselves, must accept their responsibility in this field;

6. that disabilities and inequalities imposed on women have to be seen in the total context of a society, where large sections of the population—male and female, adults and children—suffer under the oppression of an exploitative system. It is not possible to remove these inequalities for women only. Any policy or movement for the emancipation and development of women has to form a part of a total movement for removal of inequalities and oppressive social institutions, if the benefits and privileges won by such action are to be shared by the entire women population and not be monopolized by a small minority; and
7. that if our society is to move in the direction of the goals set by the Constitution, then special temporary measures will be necessary, to transform *de jure* into *de facto* equality.

A safe life is the basic right of everyone. Safe life leads to a longer and more productive safe community. Safe community can participate in injury reduction programmes. Community participation can be sought at:

(i) Workplaces through labour unions minimizing or preventing hazards at workplaces by providing better amenities to the workers;
(ii) Academic institutions, students and faculty participations through curricular development and providing safer environment; and
(iii) Religious functions through free talks by religious leaders and people to come forward and participate in safety programme in day-to-day life supported by media in the form of newspapers, radio, T.V. and published material.

Violence against women occurs in every country and in every social and economic class, wife-beating is considered a man's right. All too often, routine beating and rape of women and girls are considered "private matters" that do not concern others—whether the legal authorities or health personnel.

A Major Health Problem

In today's world, violence against women constitutes a major public health problem. In the US, nearly two million women a year are beaten in their homes and it is a fair assumption that many more such cases go unreported. Cases of rape are even more numerous and even less frequently reported; it has been estimated that only one rape is reported to the US authorities for every ten actually committed. Many other countries do not even have data on these crimes, since frequently it is not socially or culturally acceptable for women to reveal that they have been beaten or raped, nor are such revelations recognized.

Although our studies do not prove that men who watched sexually

TABLE 7.3

State-wise Percentage Contribution to Total Crimes Committed against Women during 2000

Sl. No.	State/City	Total		
		I	R	P
1	2	3	4	5
1.	Andhra Pradesh	14299	18.9	10.1
2.	Arunachal Pradesh	143	11.9	0.1
3.	Assam	3732	14.2	2.6
4.	Bihar	6299	6.3	4.5
5.	Goa	100	6.2	0.1
6.	Gujarat	6140	12.7	4.3
7.	Haryana	3311	16.6	2.3
8.	Himachal Pradesh	842	12.5	0.6
9.	Jammu and Kashmir	1642	16.4	1.2
10.	Karnataka	5852	11.2	4.1
11.	Kerala	4982	15.4	3.5
12.	Madhya Pradesh	17902	22.3	12.7
13.	Maharashtra	13177	14.4	9.3
14.	Manipur	74	2.9	0.1
15.	Meghalaya	69	2.8	0.0
16.	Mizoram	133	13.9	0.1
17.	Nagaland	22	1.3	0.0
18.	Orissa	4717	13.1	3.3
19.	Punjab	2156	9.1	1.5
20.	Rajasthan	12942	24.0	9.2
21.	Sikkim	21	3.7	0.0
22.	Tamil Nadu	13732	22.2	9.7
23.	Tripura	330	8.7	0.2
24.	Uttar Pradesh	19820	11.0	13.4
25.	West Bengal	7043	8.9	5.0
	Total States	138572	14.1	98.0
26.	A and N islands	45	11.6	0.0
27.	Chandigarh	161	18.0	0.1
28.	D and N Haveli	17	8.9	0.0
29.	Daman and Diu	6	4.3	0.0
30.	Delhi	2439	17.3	1.7
31.	Lakshadweep	1	1.4	0.0
32.	Pondicherry	132	11.8	0.1
	Total	2801	16.6	2.0
	Total (All India)	141373	14.1	100.0

1	2	3	4	5
33.	Ahmedabad	510	11.9	3.0
34.	Bangalore	1255	11.0	7.5
35.	Bhopal	320	19.0	1.9
36.	Chennai	4037	59.8	24.0
37.	Coimbatore	283	21.8	1.7
38.	Delhi (City)	2122	17.6	12.6
39.	Hyderabad	1227	17.2	7.3
40.	Indore	372	25.6	2.2
41.	Jaipur	804	36.4	4.8
42.	Kanpur	659	38.6	5.7
43.	Kochi	125	6.8	0.7
44.	Kolkata	558	4.3	3.3
45.	Lucknow	683	25.3	4.1
46.	Ludhiana	289	16.7	1.7
47.	Madurai	380	29.6	2.3
48.	Mumbai	888	4.7	5.3
49.	Nagpur	443	21.2	2.6
50.	Patna	212	16.3	1.3
51.	Pune	352	9.8	2.1
52.	Surat	243	10.0	1.4
53.	Vadodara	240	14.5	1.4
54.	Varanasi	206	15.7	1.4
55.	Vishakhapatnam	282	15.8	1.7
	Total (Cities)	16787	15.8	100.00

Source: NCRB.

raped, nor are such revelations recognized.

Although our studies do not prove that men who watched sexually violent films will commit rape as a result, they do show that these men will find rape and violence against women more acceptable. As men, husbands and fathers ourselves, we are personally and morally deeply offended by media depictions of women that lead to such attitudes. We hope that film-makers everywhere—for this problem is in No. way confined to the United States or even to the "western" world—will recognized the damaging effects that such films have on society in general and on women in particular, and will begin to show themselves capable of exercising a greater degree of social responsibility.

Notes and References

1. *Swasth Hind*: World Health Day Number, March-April, 1993, p. 61.
2. WHO: Editorial, World Health Day, 1993, January-February 1993, p. 3.
3. Claude J. Romer: Violence: A preventable disease, *World Health*, January-February 1993, p. 4.

4. WHO: Dinesh Mohan, Avoidable dangers on the farm, *World Health*, January-February 1993, p. 13.
5. *Ibid.*, pp. 12-13.
6. WHO: I.G. Badram, Accidents in the developing world, *World Health*, January-February 1993, p. 15.
7. WHO: Mrs. Suzanne Mubrarak, First Lady of Egypt: *World Health*, January-February 1993, pp. 16-17.
8. WHO: Anthony Zwi and Antonio Ugalde: Victims of War, January-February 1993, p. 26.
9. WHO: Remi Russbach, Warfare and health, *World Health*, January-February 1993, p. 28.
10. P.A. Samoya, Physical Violence and Health—An area of Growing Concern, Swasth Hind, New Delhi, CHEB, March-April, 1993, pp. 61-63.
11. WHO: Daniel Linz and Edward Donnerstein, *World Health*, April-May, 1990, p. 26.
12. WHO: Michie Gitau, Discrimination hurts, *World Health*, April-May, 1990, p. 27.
13. NCW—Report of the Workshop on Gender and Law Enforcement held at Bangalore on 21-22 April, 2001, p. 5.
14. UNIFEM and Institute of Development Studies, Jaipur, Support Services to Counter Violence against Women in Rajasthan, A Resource Directory, Jaipur, 2002.
15. UNIFEM and Mary, Support Services to Counter Violence against Women in Haryana, A Resource Directory, New Delhi, 2003.
16. UNIFEM and Sanhito, Support Services to Counter Violence Against Women in West Bengal, Kolkata, 2002, p. 13.
17. UNIFEM and Sakhi, Support Services to Counter Violence Against in Kerala, A Resource Directory, 2002, p. 15.
18. *Ibid.*, pp. 15-16.
19. Manisha Joshi, Violence Against Women, A Cry for Justice in *Social Welfare*, April 2002.
20. Aditi Pandey, Vision of Human Rights, *Social Welfare*, April 2002.
21. Lok Sabha Secretariat, Committee on Empowerment of Women, 2002-03, Violence against Women During Riots, Ministry of HRD, Deptt. of Women and Child Development and Ministry of Home Affairs, Ninth Report, Thirteenth Lok Sabha, August 2002, pp. 5-7, 74-75.
22. R.D. Sharma, Crime Against Women, *The Hindu*, Chennai, 15 May, 2001.
23. UNIFEM, Women a work against violence voices in Cyberpace, New York, 1999, Foreward, p. 2.
24. *Ibid.*, p. 8.
25. *Ibid.*, p. 10.
26. *Ibid.*, p. 14.
27. *Ibid.*, p. 14.
28. GOI, Ministry of Environment and Forests, Empowering People for Sustainable Development, 2002, pp. 8-9, 19-21.
29. R.D. Sharma, Crime against Women, *The Hindu*, Chennai, 15 May, 2001.
30. R.D. Sharma, Violent Imbalances, *Hindustan Times*, New Delhi, 3rd May, 2001.
31. NCW, 2000-01, pp. 74-75.
32. Shree Venkatraman, Women in Prying, A Study for UNIFEM, pp. 62-63.

CHAPTER 8

DISASTER: WITH SPECIAL REFERENCE TO EARTHQUAKE

"The objective of Disaster Management is to reduce loss of life, property damage and social and economic disruption, health of the people. Since people develop fear psychosio, there is a need of protecting not only physical health but also mental health through a well designed health education system."

—*Author*

8

CHAPTER

Disaster

With Special Reference to Earthquake

R.K. Celly and T.N. Gupta in their article, "Dimensions of Natural Disaster Management in India" in *Shelter* (Oct. 12, 1999) observe: "a natural hazard is an event of nature, which causes sudden disruption to the normal life of a society and casues damage to life and property, to such an extent that normal, social and economic mechanisms available to the society are inadequate to restore normalcy. Viewed in this manner, a host of natural phenomena causes disasters to a society, whether they are related to an occurrence in micro-environment or not. In macro terms, the hazards, which cause widespread damage and disruption in India, are floods, cyclones, earthquakes and landslides.

The past decade has witnessed an extraordinary increase in the number and extent of natural disasters. As Kofi Annan, Secretary General of the United Nations, point out, "The facts are starting. The costs of weather-related disasters in 1998 exceeded the costs of all such disasters in the decade of the 1980s. In the Caribbean, the hurricanes designated George and Mitch Milled more than 13,000 people, with Mitch being the deadliest Atlantic storm in 200 years. Major floods hit India, Nepal, Bangaldesh and much of East Asia, with thousands killed. Two-thirds of Bangladesh was inundated for months, leaving millions homeless. There were three times as many great natural hazards in the 1990s as in the 1960s, while disaster costs increased more than nine-fold in the same period.[1]

"The humanitarian community does a remarkable job in responding to disasters. But the most important task in the medium and long-term is to strengthen and broaden programmes which reduce the number and cost of disasters in the first place." While we should continue to improve and strengthen our response capacity, we need to engage in working together to build a "global culture of prevention." This means greater efforts to reduce vulnerability to natural hazards in the first place.

As we approach the beginning of a new millennium, the IDNDR is proved to have contributed with all its partners' worldwide to fostering a "global culture of prevention" for the 21st Century. To build on the progress achieved during the IDNDR, we have to act decisively, so that disaster reduction becomes an essential element of government policies. Recalling the Geneva Mandate adopted at the IDNDR Programme Forum, we have to adopt and implement policy measures at the international, regional, national and local levels aimed at reducing the vulnerability of our societies to natural disasters. These measures should have as main objectives the establishment of hazard resistant communities, the protection of people from the threat of disasters, and the safeguarding of our natural and economic resources and of our social well-being.[2]

K. Rajan, Adviser, Planning Commission, in his Article, "Natural Disaster Management in National Development—An Indian Perspective" suggests the following adversities which befall on people and the area:

- Loss of crops and availability of essentials like food and agricultural commodities;
- Loss of employment opportunities in the area where natural disaster occurs and particularly on rural employment;
- Problems of health and diseases arising both from insufficient availability of the basic necessities causing malnourishment, hunger, etc. or on the availability of good and hygienic drinking water;
- Financial distress caused to the farming community and those dependent on land which affect their ability to withstand hard conditions immediately following the occurrence of the natural disaster but also importantly, their ability to recover well enough before the next cropping season and take full advantage of normal conditions which may prevail;
- Impact on industrial sector due to loss of production of raw materials, reduce generation of power, etc; and
- Lastly, the impact of the disaster on the cattle wealth.[3]

V. Suresh has rightly summed that Natural disasters, which damage national economies and produce hardships for large sections of the population, are one of the single largest concerns for most nations. Human settlements are frequently affected by natural disasters—earthquake, floods, hurricanes, cyclones, landslides, sea erosions—which take a heavy toll on human lives, destroy buildings and infrastructure and have far reaching economic and social consequences for communities.[4]

Ashok Pahwa, Secretary, Ministry of Urban Development has rightly said, "Natural hazards are not new to the earth system. Like natural resources, they have been, and are, a part of biosphere and eco-systems. It is the human interventions, its endeavours towards development that these hazards turn into disasters, causing enormous devastation to the life and property of the nations. . . . The extent and frequency of damage, that is being caused by these extreme events, has raised concerns all over the world resulting into declaration of present decade (199s) as International Decade for Natural Disaster Reduction."[5]

CHART 8.1

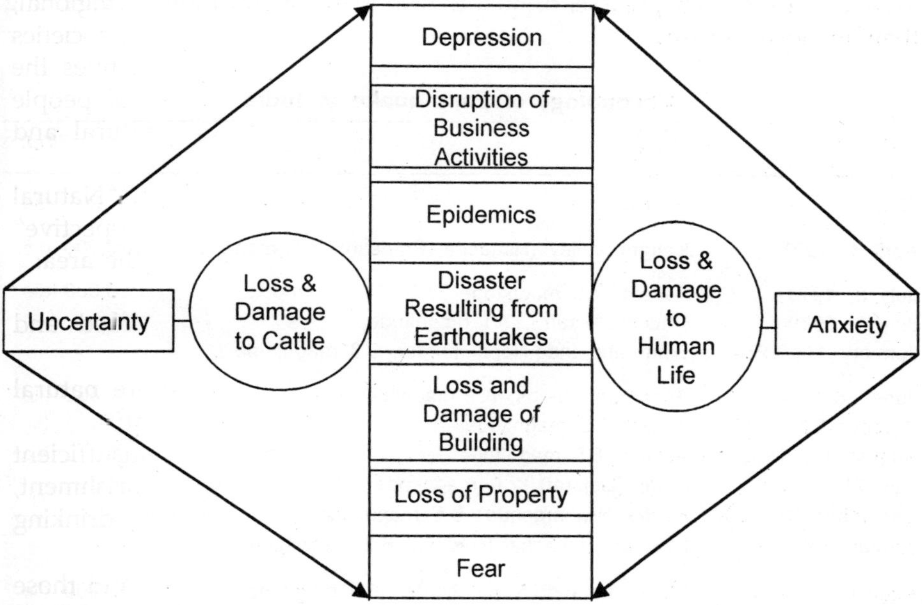

Bhagat Singh, Additional Secretary, Ministry of Agriculture has suggested the ways to reduce its serious effects while occurrence of these natural disasters cannot be prevented altogether, their adverse impact can be reduced substantially—by undertaking various preparedness and mitigation measures by community involvement. Minimizing the loss of precious human life is the first priority in disaster management. Significant achievement has been made in designing of disaster resistant houses and inventing quality-building materials to withstand the fury of natural disasters. It is gratifying to note that HUDCO has given a lead by taking a number of initiatives to propagate these designs as well as materials among the vulnerable community besides imparting training to the artisans and masons through their building centers.[6]

Earthquakes, floods, draught, cyclones, accidents, AIDS are major types of disaster phenomenon-occurred in the Region. India is a large country and has had more than its share of major natural hazards like drought, floods, earthquakes and cyclones throughout its history of civilization. Naturally, the country developed its own practices and strategies for coping with the various natural calamities. Since independence in 1947, India has developed a nationwide relief administration where a lead role of the State Governments is envisaged.[7]

American geo-physicist James. N. Brunes visited India in March 1997. He made a clear-cut observation that there was a high probability of a great earthquake of magnitude 8.5 on the Richter Scale in the northern Indian subcontinent any time within the next 100 years. He warned planners, engineers and contractors involved in the building of dams and houses in areas above the Gangetic plains in the north. He predicted that damage expected after such great earthquakes would be much more devastating than in normal cases.

Chronology of Earthquake in India

Date	*Place*	*Toll*
1803	Garhwal	200 die
April 4, 1905	Kangra Valley (Himachal Pradesh), 8.0 magnitude	20,000 die
July 8, 1918	Assam, 7.6 magnitude.	10,000 die
July 2, 1930	Dhubri (Assam), 7.1 magnitude.	
January 15, 1934	Bihar and Indo-Nepal border, 8.3 magnitude.	
June 26, 1941	Andaman islands, 8.1 magnitude.	532 die
October 23, 1943	Assam 7.2 magnitude.	
August 15, 1950	Assam, 8.5 magnitude.	
July 21, 1956	Anjar (Gujarat), 7.0 magnitude	
December 10, 1967	Koyna (Maharashtra) 6.5 magnitude.	
January 19, 1975	Kinnaur (Himachal Pradesh) 6.2 magnitude.	
August 21, 1988	Bihar and Indo-Nepal border, 6.5 magnitude.	1000 die
October 20, 1991	Uttarkashi (Uttar Pradesh) 6.6 magnitude.	1500 die
September 30, 1993	Latur and Osmanabad (Maharashtra) 6.3 magnitude.	7928 die
May 22, 1997	Jabalpur (Madhya Pradesh) 6.0 magnitude.	40 die
March 29, 1999	Chamoli (Uttar Pradesh) 6.8 magnitude.	150 die

Source: Ministry of Agriculture, GOI, New Delhi.

R.D. Sharma, quoting James N. Brunes, has rightly mentioned the grantee of Earthquakes in India. (*Tribune,* 31 January, 2001)

Earthquakes, the very name of it send shock waves. Earthquakes cannot be predicted by any method available so far. On of the one hand, we enjoy pleasures living on mother earth while on the other, we face its fury in the form of floods, fire, earthquakes, etc.

Earthquakes Occur in All Parts of the World

We mention here earthquake parameters :

Epicentre

The point on the surface of the earth below which earthquake has occurred.

Magnitude

Measure of the energy released by an earthquake, expressed in Richer Scale.

Intensity

Measure of how an earthquake is felt.

Extent of Damage (as per the Report of Ministry of Agriculture)

Loss of Human life	14241
Injured	30467
Population affected	3.5 crores
Houses damaged	73142 (completely)
	142180 (partial)
Estimated Loss of Property :	13,500 crores.
Damage of Private Property	Rs. 6000 crores
Damage of Public Property	Rs. 1000 crores
Damage to Utilities (Power, Water and other Utilities)	Rs. 1000 crores
Impact on Trade and Industry	Rs. 2000 crores
No. of Districts Affected	17
Worst Affected Districts:	
Kutch	12871 (Lives lost)
Ahmedabad	738
Rajkot	337
Jamnagar	114
Surendarnagar	89

Finance made available:

- Rs 500 crores financial assistance announced by Prime Minister.
- Rs 20 crores sanctioned from PM Relief Fund.
- 100% deduction for Income Tax purpose on donations made to charitable institutions.
- 100% deduction on donation under PM/CM Relief Fund.
- Relief material exempted from customs/excise duty.

When all over India people were celebrating their Republic day, Gujarat experienced its worst natural calamity after independence. The earthquake which struck on 26th January 2001 at 8.46 hours measuring 8.1 on the Richer Scale, hit certain regions of Gujarat state very hard. The tremor left behind huge devastation of life and property, both private and public, and created utter panic, chaos and trauma among the people.

It has been 50 years since Gujarat witnessed an earthquake and therefore most of the people did not know what to do, except that those who could rush out of their houses in whatever state they were in. It was only after getting over from the terror and shock of the earthquake tremor that the people began to think about the situation of neighbours, other cities, and other areas of the state and the country. Gradually the disaster sinked, the cries of the injured and bodies trapped inside the debris began to be heard by others.

Let us now mention the member of Districts, Talukas, Villages and families affected: Let us now briefly mention about some of the calamities in brief.

The Territory of India

(i) India covers an area of 32,87,263 sq. km. extending from snow covered Himalayan heights in the North to the tropical rain forest of the South. In the North, the territory is bounded by the Great Himalayas and stretches southwards tapering off into the Indian ocean between the Bay of Bengal and the Arabian Sea. The main land extends between latitude 8⁰4 and 37°6′ North and longitudes 68°7′ and 97°25′ East, measuring about 32,000 km from North to South and West to East. The vast land frontier of 15,200 km and coastline of 7,500 km. also has group of islands located both in the Bay of Bengal and the Arabian Sea. Hardly any other country has such a large land mass with such a diverse range of geo-agro-climatic zones.

(ii) The main land of India comprises of four regions, namely, the Great Mountain Zone, Plains of the Indus, Ganges and the Brahmaputra; the Desert Region, and the Southern Peninsula. The Himalayan range comprises three almost parallel ranges interspread with large plateaus and valleys. The mountain wall extends over a distance of 24,000 km. with a varying width of 240 to 320 km. The plain about 2,400 km. long, are formed by basins of three distinct river systems, viz. the Indus, the Ganges and the Brahmaputra. The desert region is clearly delineated in two parts—Sindh Frontier while the little desert extends between Jaisalmer and Jodhpur upto Punjab. The desert region is inhabited by local communities which have developed their own coping and recovery mechanisms. Between the two deserts is a zone of absolutely sterile region, consisting of rocky land cut up by limestones ridges.

(iii) According to 1991 census, India had a population of 843.93 million with 195.02 million housing units. The literacy rate as per 1991 census was 52.2 percent, 64 percent for male and 39 percent for female. To protect such a large population with low levels of education from the fury of natural hazards is not an easy task. However, local initiatives and the government efforts combined over the years, have tried to reduce risks and build community capacity to deal with emergencies.

NATURAL HAZARDS AND DISASTER

Because of the large geographical size of the country, India often faces natural hazards like floods, cyclones and drought occurring frequently in different parts of the country. At times, some area normally subjected to drought situation have got flooded in certain years. Hazards like earthquakes, hailstorms, avalances, landslides, etc. occur quite suddenly but they are restricted in their impact in terms of time. The extent of the impact of an earthquake depends on its magnitude, season and time of occurrence.

Indeed, as Kofi Annan started at the Programme Forum of the International Decade for Natural Disaster Reduction (IDNDR) held in Geneva in July of this year, "The humanitarian community does a remarkable job in responding to disaster. But the most important task in the medium and long-term is to strengthen and broaden programmes which reduce the number and cost of disasters in the first place." While we should continue to improve and strengthen our response capacity, we need to engage in working together to build a "global culture of prevention." This means greater efforts to reduce vulnerability to natural hazards in the first place.

Let us discuss briefly about some different disasters (For details see Appendix I and II about concepts of Hazards and Vulnerability Analysis and Guidelines For Hazards Assessment and Vulnerability Assessment)

1. Earthquake

Earthquakes, the most feared or natural hazards as they occur without any recognizable warning, are unpredictable in space and time and inflict heavy losses in less than a minute duration. A UNESCO study indicates that on an average 10,000 people die each year from earthquakes and losses amounting to billions of rupees.

The Indian subcontinent in general and India in particular is the region facing the maximum number of natural disasters. The phenomenon of occurrences of an earthquake is also very common in this region due to the continuous movement of the Indian plate and its striking the Eurasian plate as well as the location of the youngest mountain chain in the form of the Himalayas. Thus the earthquake is a regular feature of the subcontinent and may result in the severe damage of life and property.

The effective earthquake disaster management can be achieved through the adequate preparedness, effective emergency management and by rehabilitating the affected communities by disasters. The entire approach of the earthquake management should be interlinked by connecting the various phases of management and administration with each other. The preparedness phase should be linked to the rehabilitation of the community while we should start the preparation to face the next earthquake in the rehabilitation/reconstruction stage itself.[8]

Special precautions are needed for quake-prone zones. Devices are provided to help buildings survive earthquakes. One is a damper unit, which is similar to a car shock absorber. Another is to isolate the building from the ground with thick rubber pads.

Countries having quake-prone zones have uniform building codes updated annually and published worldwide every three years. Such codes focus mainly on the safety of the building occupants and emphasize on factors such as resistance to fire and structural failure. The higher the seismic activity the tougher the building regulations. In seismic belts regular official guidelines are issued for protection against earthquakes. Some governments have even lower the property taxes and insurances premiums in quake-prone areas. Incentives are also given to upgrade old buildings.

With the increasing frequency of earthquakes we have to learn lessons from the countries, which have taken such precautions. In India people care less about the structure of the building and spend much more on decoration.

Let us illustrate the losses in Gujarat due to earthquake in important sectors.

ROAD TRANSPORT AND HIGHWAYS[9]

Out of 650 kms. of national highways damaged 100 kms. severely damaged. Most of the minor/major bridges damaged. Surajbari Bridge damaged—repaired on war footing and restored. National highways made traffic worthy.

Telecommunication

Telecommunication disrupted. Number of exchanged damaged was 147 and total lines damaged 82,000. Optical Fibre system Bhuj-Bachau-Rajkot 140 Mbps damaged. Exchanges started choking due to heavy traffic. Estimated cost of damages was nearly Rs. 200 crores.

Railways

Costs

Track	25 crores
Signal and Tele	15 crores
Electrical	7 crores
Misc.	3 crores
Total	60 crores

Track:

- Viramgam—Gandhidham Broad Gauge
- Gandhidham—Bhuj
- Viramgam—Okha
- Palanpur—Gandhidham Metre Gauge
- Heavy damage to station buildings, station cabins, residential quarters, bridges in the affected sections.
- Signalling equipments at 25 stations and control communications on Viramgram—Gandhidham section damaged.

2. Floods

Floods are not a new phenomenon-in India. Severe floods occur almost every year in one part of the country or the other causing loss of life, large scale damage to property and untold misery to millions of people. Besides, extensive destruction of forests, reclamation of more and more lands even within the reverine areas, have caused changes in the river regime over the years. All these have led to increase flood damage to various flood control measures undertaken in the country.

About 40 m hectare of land area in the country is flood prone, where floods are annual phenomena and emerge as the most destructive natural hazard. It is evident from the available data that the frequency and intensity of floods is increasing regularly. As per the Central Water Commission data, the average annual losses due to flood damages amount to Rs. 938.56 crores.

Even though the problem of floods has been receiving increasing attention and inspite of substantial investments in flood sector during the last few decades, it is observed that the flood damage in the country has continuously been showing a rising trend. It was in this context that the National Flood Commission (RBA) was set-up in July 1976 by the Government of India to examine and advise on various aspects relating to floods. The RBA, in its report submitted in 1981, *inter-alia,* laid great stress on proper flood plain management without diluting the importance of structural measures for specific situation. Subsequently, the specific problems of Ganga and Brahmaputra basins were also studied by high-level committee of exert.[10]

Flood Forecasting and Warning System

Flood forecasting and flood warning system in a scientific way was commenced in the year 1958 by Central Water Commission (CWC). At present the flood forecasting and warning network of CWC covers 62 major interstate river sub-catchments which includes 132 water level forecasting stations and 25 inflow forecasting stations for important reservoirs. Hydrological and hydrometeorological data from nearly 700 stations in these rivers are being collected and analyzed, and flood forecasts and warning messages are issued, generally 24 hours to 48 hours in advance. In case of very large incoming floods, advisory forecasts 72 hours in advance or more are also issued which predicts the incoming floods at the downstream locations. Coordination between neighbouring districts, states and countries is being promoted to reduce loss of livelihood and life.[11]

3. Cyclones

The most destructive of weather systems, severe Tropical Cyclones (TC) brings worst disasters when it strikes coast in the preferred locations of the earth. Tropical cyclones are intense low-pressure areas with fierce winds blowing anti-clockwise manner in the Northern Hemisphere extending on an average 500 to 1000 km laterally (over the Indian seas) and surface to 14.16 km vertically. They are classified according to wind speed in their circulation. The associated winds often exceeding 200 kmps, rainfall exceeding 50 to 100 cm in 24 hours and worst of all, very high storm tide (storm surge combined with astronomical tide) often exceeding 5-6 meters brings disaster over the coastal areas in the wake of a cyclone. In extreme cases, wind speed of 320 kmph gusting to 360 kmph, rainfall 120 cm in 24 hours and storm surge of 13-14 meters have been recorded in association with tropical cyclones. Out of these three destructive elements viz. strong winds, heavy rainfall and storm tide, the storm tide is responsible for 90 percent of the loss of life in the case of cyclone disasters.[12]

The India Metrological Department (IMD) has a well-established organizational set-up for observing, detecting, tracking and forecasting cyclones and issuing cyclone warnings whenever a cyclonic storm develops in the Bay of Bengal and the Arabian Sea. It is tracked with the help of INSAT satellite, powerful cyclone detection radars with a range of 400 km. installed at Calcutta, Paradip, Vishakhapatnam, Machilipatnam, Madras, Karaikal on the east cost; and Goa, Cochin, Bombay and Bhuj along the west coast. The present cyclone surveillance system in the country is such that No. cyclone in the region can escape detection any time in its life cycle.

Cyclone warnings are provided through six cyclone warning centers located at Calcutta, Bhubneswar, Vishakhapatanam, Madras, Bombay and Ahmedabad. These centers have distinct responsibilities area-wise covering both the east and west coasts of India and the oceanic areas of the Bay of Bengal and the Arabian Sea, including Andaman and Nicobar Islands and Lakshadweep. The cyclone waring bulletins are issued to All India Radio and Doordarshan for broadcasting/telecasting them in different languages on all India basis. The cyclone warning division at Headquarter office, New Delhi also provides warning information to the Control Room and Crisis Management group set-up in the Ministry of Agriculture, Government of India which is finally responsible for coordination with various Central Government agencies. Cyclone Warnings Division at New Delhi also caters to the needs of international responsibilities such as issue of cyclone advisories to the neighbours countries.[13]

4. Drought

Drought is a slow onset natural hazard and it offers time and opportunity to mitigate its impact. The droughts can be grouped on the basis of physical characteristics and their impact on socio-economic system both in time and space:

- Meteorological drought: A situation arising from inadequate and mal-distribution of rainfall;
- Hydrological drought: Conditions denote reduced stream flow and inadequate filling of reservoirs, tanks or drying up of water in the surface water storage structures;

- Soil moisture drought: Inadequate soil moisture particularly in rainfed areas which may not support crop growth;
- Agricultural drought: Characterised by low soil moisture levels and shortage of water resulting in crop failures;
- Socio-economic drought: The reduction of availability of food and income loss on account of crop failures endangering food and social security of the people in the affected areas;
- Famine: When large scale collapse of access to food occurs which without intervention, can lead to mass starvation; and
- Ecological drought: When the productivity of a natural eco-system fails significantly as a consequence of distress induced environmental damage.[14]

In order to find solutions many conferences and symposia are arrange and literature published. Some of these are:

1. Symposium on Preparedness Mitigation and Management of Natural disasters organized by Central Water Commission, New Delhi, August 2-4, 1989.
2. 9th Symposium on Earthquake Engineering organized by DEQ-UOR and ISET, November 1990.
3. National Policy Analysis—Workshop on Natural Disaster Reduction organized by Administrative Staff College of India, Hyderabad, December 16-20, 1991.
4. Workshop on Uttarkashi Earthquake organized by DEQ-UOR, December 1991.
5. World Congress on Natural Hazard reduction organized by The Institution of Engineers (India), New Delhi, January 10-14, 1992.
6. 4th Session of the Scientific and Technical Committee of IDNDR, organized by Ministry of Agriculture, Government of India, Febuary 1-5, 1993, New Delhi.
7. National Seminar on Hydrological Hazards—Prevention and Mitigation, organized by DH-UOR, March 1993.
8. Workshop on Natural Disaster Reduction in the South Asia Region, New Delhi, March 30-April 2, 1994.
9. 10th Symposium of Earthquake Engineering, organized by DEQ-UOR and ISET, November 1994.
10. Seminar on comprehensive Flood Loss Prevention and Management organized by ESCAP hosted by Government of India, 28-29 September 1994, New Delhi.
11. International Conference on Wind Engineering, organized by Indian Society for Wing Engineering, Roorkee, at New Delhi, January 9-13, 1995.
12. IDNDR-Day celebrations on given theme on regular basis since 1995, on Second Wednesday of October every year, organized by NCDM.

13. Workshop on Himalayan Eco-Development and Natural Disaster Reduction organized by NCDM, New Delhi, November, 1995.
14. International Seminar on Mathematical Modeling of Atmospheric and Oceanic Processes, organized by Department of Mathematics, Berhampur University, Berhampur, December 18-21, 1995.
15. International Conference on Disasters and Mitigation, organized by Anna University, Chennai, January 19-22, 1996.
16. Workshop on Safety from Forest Five: Courses and Remedies, organized by Uttar Pradesh Academy of Administration, Nainital and Forest Panchayat Training Institute, April 16-17, 1996.
17. PIARCG2 Group Seminar, Natural Disaster Reduction for Roads, organized by Central Road Research Institute, New Delhi, January 29-31, 1997.
18. International Seminar on Coping with Natural Disasters: Aspects of Risks, Crisis and Development, organized by Natural Disasters Management Cell, Agri-Economic Research Centre, Visva Bharati, Shantiniketan, February 28-March 2, 1997.
19. Workshop on Earthquake Disaster Mitigation, organized by DEQ-UOR, October, 1997.
20. Seminar on Natural Hazards in Urban Habitat organized by Central Building Research Institute, Roorkee at New Delhi, November 10-11, 1997.
21. International Symposium on Asian Monsoon and Pollution over the Monsoon Environment, organized by Indian Meteorological Society, New Delhi, December 2-5, 1997.
22. Third Annual Convention of Indian Building Congress on Built Environment and Natural Hazards, New Delhi, February 7-8, 1998.
23. International Conference on Disaster Management, organized by Tezpur University, Guwahati, Assam, April 23-26, 1998.
24. Workshop on Geohazard and Related Societal Issues, organized by Indian Society of Engineering Geology, Lucknow, November 26, 1998.
25. 11th Symposium on Earthquake Engineering, organized by DEQ-UOR and ISET, December, 1998.
26. Policy Forum on Future of Mitigation of South Asian Disasters, organized by Disaster Management Institute and Duryog Nivaran, New Delhi, February 5-6, 1999.
27. National Symposium on Tropical Meteorology, organized by Indian Meteorological Society, Regional Meteorological Centre, Chennai, February 16-19, 1999.
28. National advisory Group Meeting on Managing and Measuring the Vulnerability, organized by Disaster Management Institute, New Delhi, June 12, 1999.

SOME RESOURCE PUBLICATIONS

1. Uttarkashi Earthquake, October 20, 1991, special Publication No. 30, Geological Survey of India, 1992.
2. Disaster Management, V.K. Sharma, NCDM, New Delhi, 1993.
3. Impact of Natural Disasters on the Environment and Development: Examples from Himalaya and Eastern and Western Ghats, 1994, Chandi Prasad Bhatt, Himalayan Research Centre, Dehradun.
4. Applicability of Long Range Forecast of South-West Monsoon rainfall in different parts of India with special Reference to Andhra Pradesh, 1994, B.V. Ramana Rao *et. al.*, Central Research Institute for Dryland Agriculture, Santoshnagar, Hyderabad.
5. Killari Earthquake, September 30, 1993, Special Publication No. 37, Geological Survey of India, 1996.
6 Current Science, Volume 62, Numbers 1 and 2, Special Issue: Seismology in India—An Overview.
7. Current Science, Volume 67, Number 5, Special Issue: Strong Ground Motions and Engineering Specifications.

The purpose of Disaster Management is to mitigate sufferings as well as find their causes and solutions. International Decade For Natural Disaster Reduction (IDNDR), (See Appendix III) has set the following objectives and goals in this direction.

When the UN General Assembly adopted resolution 44/236 in 1989 and formally decided on the IDNDR, the following objectives and goals were established:

1. The Objective of the decade is to reduce through concerted international action, especially in developing countries, the loss of life, property damage and social and economic disruption caused by natural disasters, such as earthquakes, windstorms, tsunamis, floods, landslides, volcanic eruptions, wildfire, grasshopper and locust infestations, drought and desertification and other calamities of natural origin.
2. The goals of the Decade are:
   (a) To improve the capacity of each country to mitigate the effects of natural disasters expeditiously and effectively, paying special attention to assisting developing countries in the assessment of disasters damage potential and in the establishment of early warning systems and disaster-resistant structures when and where needed;
   (b) To devise appropriate guidelines and strategies for applying existing scientific and technical knowledge, taking into account the cultural and economic diversity among nations;
   (c) To foster scientific and engineering endeavours aimed at

closing critical gaps in knowledge in order to reduce loss of life and property;

(d) To disseminate existing and new technical information related to measures for the assessment, prediction and mitigation of natural disasters; and

(e) To develop measures for the assessment, prediction, prevention and mitigation of natural disasters through programmes of technical assistance and technology transfer, demonstration projects, and education and training, tailored to specific disasters and locations, and to evaluate the effectiveness of those programmes.

There is also a need of Legislation to manage disasters (See Appendix IV for model Law for Disaster Management).

EDUCATIONAL AND PREVENTIVE MEASURES

Need to keep up the Morale of the Community so that they can take care of themselves

The will power of the community is the backbone to sustain any calamity like earthquake. Will power gives extra-energy to the community as well to the administrator. *The Times of India,* News Service (dated February 7, 2001) indicates that the District Collector of Kutch, Anil Mukim, is equally impressed by the spirit of the Gujarat people. I know that if such a thing had happened anywhere else, there would have been complete chaos. . . . People would have been after each other's blood . . . but out here, we are flooded with all the help we can get. There is some inner strength in the people, which is so reassuring. Rajeev Topno, the District Development Officer of Kutch, says: "Even though in the first few days the government machinery was buckling under pressure, it was heartening to note that the community at large had not collapsed. Kutch has shown a tremendous fighting spirit, which is a triumph in adversity."

The administration, through its sincere efforts, has to ensure that the morale of the community is not dampened. There is a need of constant counselling, guidance and advice. The strengthening of democracy in its social and economic aspect has to be attained through the participation on the part of the people.

We have to have three pronged attacked to contain the ill-effects of earthquake. Hardarshan S. Walia in his article, "Bhuj Quake from a Geologists Perespecive" in *The Tribune,* dated March 8, 2001 suggested the following:

(a) During an Earthquake

(i) If you are indoor: Follow the rule of DUCH (Duck, Cover and Hold under a strong piece of furniture). If there is No. furniture, stand under a doorway. If you are in a high-rise building and away from a furniture, move against an interior wall and protect your head with your arms. Don't use electrical, gas equipment.

(ii) If you are outdoor: Move away as far as possible from the building, tall structure, power lines, etc.

(iii) If you are driving: Slow down, move to clear area (if possible) stop and stay inside until shaking stops.

(b) After Earthquake

(i) Wear Safety gears (specially heavy shoes).

(ii) Check for hazards (fire, gas, electric water, spills, etc.) shut-off all the valves.

(iii) Provide first-aid.

(c) Before Earthquake

(i) Plan earthquake preparedness with family, neighbours, and friends (Talk about a meeting place to reunite and assign an out of town phone number of a relative to inform status).

(ii) Keep emergency supplies in a plastic container (example: canned food, water blanket, first-aid kit, flashlight with extra batteries and bulbs, fire extinguisher, portable radio, etc.)

(iii) Know where gas, electricity, water main shut-off valves are.

(iv) Fasten structures inside the house that may fall during earthquake (e.g. refrigerator, furniture, bookshelves, etc.)

(d) Build Earthquake Resistant Structures

One cannot construct a dwelling completely earthquake proof but it can be made earthquake resistant. Also an older building can be retrofitted to resist an earthquake.

Process is followed in two steps:

(i) Know the hazard map of the area: Obtain a hazard map from the Regional Geological survey office. A hazard map shows geologic problems, soil and bedrock conditions which will determine the behaviour of building during shaking.

(ii) Incorporate earthquake resistant design.

Action Plan

(a) Initiate earthquake awareness.

(b) Build earthquake-resistant structures in seismic zone area.

(c) Force builders to adopt earthquake resistance code for structures.

(d) Strengthen the existing structures.

(e) Ask law-makers to develop a strong programme of earthquake disaster preparation, mitigation and management programmes.

A.S. Arya in his article, "Action Plan for Earthquake Disaster Mitigation" rightly suggests the following steps to mitigate the effects of earthquake.

Preventive Phase Before Disaster

This phase should involve the following actions:

(i) Preparation of earthquake catalogues and epicenter and geologic-tectonic maps;
(ii) Analysis of seismic risk and seismic zoning for general purposes;
(iii) Development of anti-seismic codes of design and construction of various structures;
(iv) Education and training of engineers and architects in earthquake engineering principles and use of codes;
(v) Promulgation of laws and bye-laws for providing earthquake resistance features in all new construction according to the codes;
(vi) Development of methods for seismic strengthening of existing structures, particularly in the structures considered critical for the community;
(vii) Development of simple methods for upgrading the seismic resistance of traditional non-engineered construction and their dissemination to the common builders and owners by mass communication techniques, demonstrations, extension work, etc.;
(viii) Earthquake insurance for the buildings and structures to reduce the economic impact on individuals; and
(ix) Installation of seismological observations for monitoring seismic activity with a density of instruments capable of recording and locating all earthquakes bigger than a selected magnitude.

Emergency Phase just after Occurrence of Disaster

This phase will include the following actions:

(i) Maintenance of law and order;
(ii) Evacuation of people;
(iii) Recovery of dead bodies and their disposal;
(iv) Medical care for the injured;
(v) Supply of food and water and restoration of water supply lines;
(vi) Temporary shelters like tents, metal sheds;
(vii) Restoring lines of communication and information;
(viii) Restoring transport routes;
(ix) Quick assessment of damage and demarcation of damage areas according to grade of damage;
(x) Cordoning-off severely damaged structures liable to collapse during aftershocks;

(xi) Temporary shoring of certain precariously standing buildings to avoid collapse and damage to other adjoining buildings;

(xii) Immediate actions to prevent certain chain-reactions from developing; such as release of water from the reservoir behind a damaged dam to avoid flooding of the areas if the dam fail, emptying of containers of toxic or inflammable liquids and gases, treatment of environment for preventing spread of diseases, etc.;

(xiii) Collection of scientific data from field observations as well as from instrumentation specially deployed in the affected areas to monitor the aftershocks; and

(xiv) Preparation of proposals about the reconstruction requirements and strategy to be adopted and whether reconstruction opportunity could also be utilized for affecting socio-economic development of the damaged areas.

An effort needs to be made in the emergency phase, to involve the affected people to the maximum extent so as to create a feeling of self-reliance. They need to be encouraged to start following economic pursuits as quickly as possible so that the period of relief is minimized.

Consolidation and Reconstruction Phase

The phase will involve the following phase:

(i) Detailed survey of buildings for assessment of damage and decision regarding repair, restoration and strengthening or demolition;

(ii) Repair, restoration and seismic strengthening or demolition;

(iii) Selection of sites for new settlements;

(iv) Adoption of strategy for new construction, such as, through contractors, through self-help construction or core houses only, or supply of construction materials only, etc.;

(v) Execution of the reconstruction programme;

(vi) Preview of existing seismic zoning maps and risk maps;

(vii) Review of the seismic codes and norms of construction;

(viii) Training of personnel, engineers, architects, builders and artisans; and

(ix) Statistical studies regarding the earthquake.

Relief at a Glance

- Quick administrative response from Centre and State levels.
- Visit of Prime Minister and Cabinet Ministers to support relief efforts.
- Immediate deployment of Defence and Pra-Military forces.
- Spontaneous public response with overwhelming generosity in terms of relief assistance.

- Rapid transportation of Relief materials, food items, medical supplies/equipments.
- Rs. 500 crore assistance announced by the PM, besides financial aid from many government and non-governmental organizations.
- Overwhelming international response with personnel and material.

There is a need to develop holistic approach and need of integration of disaster management plan with normal plans. A good administration in normal times can easily take care of disaster management as well. We must introduce administrative reforms, which can keep the administration efficient.

Administrative improvement means the act or the process of improving the administration. As stated in a United Nations Report: "Management improvement comprised the planning, implementation and evaluation of various measures conducive to the increase of organizational effectiveness and efficiency."

Simple commitment by management is not enough. The improvement process must become basic and continuous. There is No. magic approach or solution to be gleaned from either a textbook or a consultant, although either of these can help management discover an effective programme for carrying out its required responsibility.

The Indian Express editorial: "The Ugly the Beautiful" over the private initiatives in relief and rehabilitation (January 31, 2001) stresses that the magnitude of the death and destruction of quivering of the earth caused, it is neither desirable nor feasible to leave the work of relief and rehabilitation entirely to the government. The situations calls for better private initiatives. It would be pertinent to recall how long before the term privatization came into common parlance, the great Bihar Earthquake of 1934 brought the entire state under the banner of a relief committee headed by Dr Rajendra Prasad. It not only coordinated all the relief and rehabilitation work but also published a 400-page report listing every cash contribution received from the public. The report bore the signature of J.C. Mumarappa, a chartered accountant and disciple of Mahatma Gandhi, and it is even today cited as an epitome of transparency. Such relief bodies need to be replicated by the dozen to meet the challenge in Gujarat.

Karuna M. Johan in his article, "Gujarati Samaj cautions donors" rightly pointed that the Shree Delhi Gujarati Samaj has appealed to residents of the Capital to be careful while donating money for quake relief programme. The 104 year old Gujarati Samaj that acts as an umbrella organization for all major Gujarati associations in the city has warned that the tragedy in Gujarati is being used by unscrupulous people for one-upmanship.

A number of temporary 'collection centres' have sprung up in residential and commercial areas across the city. Many stop passers-by and ask them to 'donate' money for Gujarat. However, the Shree Delhi Gujarati Samaj warns that many of these centers may not be genuine.

According to Gujarati Samaj President Prafull Joshi, the umbrella association has already received some complaints from harassed donors. "We appeal to the people to donate money only to authorized agencies", he said. The Samaj, he added will issue valid receipts against any donations.

Ela R. Bhatt in his article, "Reconstructing Gujarat" in *The Hindu,* dated February 2001 rightly thinks that Gujarat will have to be rebuilt. But in whose image and on whose ideas? Given the scale of death and destruction, the answer is obvious: Gujarat will have to be reconstructed in the image of its common people. And who can be a better guide in this endeavour than Gandhiji, whose name Gujarat proudly uses. Let us not forget that his vision of a free India was abolition of poverty, misery and fear. How do we translate Gandhiji's concepts into practical lessons for reconstruction of destroyed villages and towns today? Three major principles can be recalled here. First is the centrality of rural India and the balanced rural-urban growth. Second is the removal of economic poverty and third the principle of trusteeship.

We need a holistic approach. Water, health, food, shelter, livelihood, child care are all closely integrated in human life that has clearly come out of the current relief work being done in Kutch. The earthquake has also showed us the strong spirit of voluntary work, of helping others, of community ties in Gujarat. Let us build on our community spirit to make these dreams into reality.

CONCLUSION

There is a Need of Transparency, Good governance, accountability and responsiveness. It has been reported in the press, T.V. and other platforms that disaster management programmes become haven of unscrupulous people. Money is collected and used for personal purpose. Therefore, there is a need for good account keeping, good governance and responsive administration to keep rogues out of this noble cause. Only the people with faith in ethics should be associated with such work. It is a challenging task, which requires hard work, sincerity, loyalty and spirit of service. They should believe in social service, as advised by Swami Vivekanand;

It is a great privilege,
  For all of us,
To have been altered,
  To do anything for the world,
In helping the world,
  We really help ourselves.

V. Suresh and Taranjot K. Gadhok in their article, "Disaster to

Development (*Shelter*, Oct. 13, 1999) rightly suggest that it is high time that the thinking process is brought to a turn around from "actions to pre-action." It requires strong political will to put knowledge base to work, to use the forces of legislation, education, public awareness and policy-making on development and relief to make disaster reduction measures part of our everyday consciousness and planning activities.

Whenever disasters strike, they do not discriminate or differentiate between men and nations, poor or rich, young or old. They do not negotiate or listen and they do not wait, they simply come, kill and destroy, irreparable losses are irrecoverable. And when these hazards strike, it is the communities who are first to react, it is the communities irrespective of their profession, status, cast or culture who need to react. Therefore, it is important that capacities of communities are built to observe, understand and prepare themselves for worst impact. It is important to allow transparency of actions of the nodal agencies working towards mitigation measures to encourage communities to get involved, so that at the time of occurrence of disasters, they do not wait for help they can stand on their own feet and mobilize self-help, before rescue and relief reaches them. This may require coordination with NGOs, which are trained to handle such situation.

In the rapidly changing scenario, the real wealth will lie in knowledge, innovation and speedy action. It would mean discarding the bureaucratic apparels and getting into the space suit of the 21st century. The road ahead is bumby, but exciting being totally in an uncharted territory. It is up to us to use our intellectual prowess and negotiate the road with bold imagination, and deep urge to succeed.[15]

Notes and References

1. Phillips and Boulle, Message, in *Shelter*, Dec. 13, 1999.
2. *Ibid.*
3. K. Rajan, Natural Disaster Management in National Development—An Indian Perspective quoted in Vinod K. Sharma, *Disaster Mangement*, IIPA, New Delhi, 1999, p. 26.
4. V. Suresh, Message Towards a Safer Millennium in *Shelter*, Dec. 13, 1999
5. Ashok Pahava, *Ibid.*
6. Bhagat Singh, *Ibid.*
7. IDNDR, *op. cit.*, p. 3.
8. Vinod Kumar Sharma and Amir Ali Khan, Earthquake Disaster Management and Administrative Issues, Training of Trainees Programmes in Distance Management, NGO, IJPA, 1999, p. 1.
9. R.O. Sharma, *The Tribune*, January 31, 2001.
10. B.S. Ahuja, Dimensions of the Problem—Floods, *Shelter*, *op. cit.*, p. 5.
11. IDNDR, *op. cit.*, p. 13.
12. G.S. Mandal, Cyclones, The Problem Size, *Shelter*, *op. cit.*, p. 6.
13. IDNDR, *op. cit.*, p. 13.
14. A.R. Subbiah, Drought Management Through Anticipatory Multidimensional Approaches, A Case Study, in Vinod Sharma, *op. cit.*, p. 92.
15. V. Suresh and Taranjot K. Gadhok, *Shelter*, Dec. 13, 1999, p. 110.

APPENDIX I

GUIDELINES FOR HAZARD ASSESSMENT AND VULNERABILITY ANALYSIS

I. Hazard Assessment

A process of analysis which attempts to specify the "hazard occurrence probability" of an event of a given proportion occurring in a certain area within a stated time period (type/intensity/space/time).

The process of identifying and assessing the relative properties and direct effects of hazards with reference to time is based on the collection of historical and scientific data able to be presented in scales, maps or other means of comparison for analysis. The accuracy and degree of sophistication possible or desirable will depend on the extent of perceived risk and the detail of available information, determined by the human, financial, decretal and temporal resources available.

A. Types of Hazards

1. Earthquake
2. Landslide
3. Tsunami
4. Volcanic eruption
5. Tropical cyclone (typhoon, hurricane)
6. Flood
7. Drought
8. Environmental desertification, etc.)
9. Biosphere (wildfire)
10. Civil conflict
11. Population displacement degradation (pollution)
12. Prepared by ADPC, Bangkok
13. Epidemic, biological
14. Technological hazard (industrial accident)

B. Physical Characteristics of Hazard Occurrence

1. Identity—knowledge of hazard, its development and behaviour.
2. Nature—types of forces associated with the hazard.
3. Intensity—capacity, or potential destructive forces, effects.
4. Extent—geographical distribution, range of impact.
5. Scope—community, sectoral extent, range(s) of impact.
6. Predictability—consequence of temporal properties.
7. Manageability—consequence of primary causes, properties.

C. Temporal Characteristics of Hazard Occurrence

1. Frequency—how often the event occurs.
2. Duration—expected time of lasting impact.
3. Speed of onset—rapidity of arrival of impact.
4. Forewarning—time between identification/warning and impact.

D. Hazard Assessment Considerations

1. History.
2. Probability of various intensities.
3. Maximum credible threat.
4. Necessary to consider secondary hazards, or 'knockon' effects of primary forces or main triggering event (e.g., earthquake causes dam burst/landslide causes flash/impounded flood, causes building collapse, causes population displacement, etc.).
5. The more rare hazards are in a given area, the less historical or statistical information there is to work with. Therefore, they present a less confident opportunity for prediction or common awareness and they can be a greater liability.

E. Elements at Risk to the Effects of Hazards

(Direct consequences of the forces of hazards): Those elements, people, property or environment, processes or systems affected by the forces of a hazard if it occurs:

1. People, loss of life.
2. Personal health, injury or disease.
3. Damage, destruction of property.
4. Damage, destruction of infrastructure, public service systems.
5. Damage, destruction of environment.
6. Damage, destruction of crops.
7. Disruption, loss of production.
8. Disruption, loss of livelihood.
9. Disruption, loss of essential services.
10. Disruption, loss of national infrastructure.
11. Disruption to governmental process, systems.
12. Loss to national, local economies.
13. Disruption, loss of community or lifestyle.
14. Sociological and psychological consequences.

II. Vulnerability Analysis

A process which results in an understanding of the types and levels of exposure of persons, property, and the environment to the effects of identified hazards at a particular time.

Vulnerability = People + Condition + Place + Time + Event

The process to identify physical, social and economic conditions susceptible to the effects of hazards of a given intensity by focusing on the types of risk to which they are exposed. Different elements vary significantly in their susceptibility to damage of disruption and vulnerability also differs according to intensity of the hazard.

A. Types of Vulnerability

1. Physical Vulnerability, pertaining to matters of location, proximity, structural and infrastructural conditions, frequently including agricultural assets as representing physical 'plant'.

(a) Building—considering their use, site, design, shape, proximate locations, materials used, state of maintenance, construction techniques and quality.

(b) Infrastructure—structurally-based systems and related processes necessary for the social and economic functioning of a society or a community, which in terms of their essentiality are sometimes referred to as 'lifelines'.
1. Transportation systems and component elements.
2. Telecommunication system (external and internal).
3. Public utilities services (water, electricity, drainage).
4. Essential public or community services and related facilities (health, public administration, emergency or security services and facilities, essential economic structures, official civil protection systems or measures, etc.).

(c) Agricultrual—primarily considering physical assets-related, but opportunity loss potential of essential natural resources, crops, trees, livestock, fisheries, also should be recognised.

2. ***Economic Vulnerability,*** determined by evaluating the direct loss potential of economic assets and processes, indirect loss potential, and consequent secondary effects, generally derived from previous historical data applied to current conditions affected by a variety of disaster scenarios. As the direct disaster assistance seldom exceeds a small fraction of total assets loss, it is in terms of net opportunity cost that economic vulnerability must be measured.

Any complete assessment of economic vulnerability must be linked to studies of physical and social vulnerability.

(a) Direct Loss Potential

1. Damage, destruction of buildings, plants, facilities, raw material, products
2. Replacement costs
3. Loss of employment
4. Crop losses
5. Damage to means of production

(b) Indirect Loss Potential

1. Impact of lost production
2. Impact of lost employment
3. Destructions of savings
4. Loss of markets
5. Loss of opportunity
6. Loss of vital services
7. Loss to consequential income-earning activities

(c) Secondary Effects

1. Inflation
2. Indebtedness
3. Income disparities
4. Labour migration
5. Reorientation of capital allocation
6. Frustration of developmental investment
7. Economic isolation of affected areas

3. Social Vulnerability, determined by the perception of risk and the ability of people to take measure to reduce that risk. Social vulnerability is more difficult to measure than either physical or economic vulnerability, but efforts can be made to identify those elements of society or social behaviour which may reflect a greater risk of adverse affect.

(a) Critical indicators of perceived risk, ability of response:

1. Poverty, limitation of resources, reserves or options,
2. Degree of public awareness about the immediate social and physical environments as they relate to hazards and effects, and
3. Prior personal experience of specific risk,

Vulnerability Analysis Considerations

1. Need to focus on degrees of loss, damage,
2. Focus attention on important elements, concentrate analytical resources on critical or significant items:
   (a) people, concentrated populations,
   (b) lifelines,
   (c) economic activity, resources,
   (d) areas of developmental importance, and
   (e) production;
3. Essential to consider relationships of factors that determine social and economic systems and processes, over time.

III. Risk

Risk is the expected loss from a given hazardous event for a given element of vulnerability over a specified time period. It is a function of:

- the probability of a hazard of a particular magnitude occurring,
- the elements susceptible to potential loss or damage ('at risk'),
- the nature of vulnerability of those elements, and
- a specified future time period.

A. Risk Management

Risk Management is the process of analysis which leads to the estimation of the magnitude of a given risk and the determination of how important such a risk is to matters of 'our' concern. It includes an evaluation of all the elements that are relevant to an understanding of existing or contemplated hazards and their effects on a specific environment. When this evaluation is considered in social or political terms, it enables the determination of appropriate hazard prevention, or vulnerability reduction, or mitigation strategies.

(b) Demographic Considerations

1. Magnitudes, total population,
2. Concentration densities,
3. Demographic distinctions, vulnerable groups of socially disadvantaged people or those requiring special attention:
   (a) children,
   (b) disabled or physically/mentally impaired people,
   (c) single parent families,
   (d) elderly people,
   (e) women, particularly if pregnant or lactating,
   (f) remotely located, isolated groups of people, and
   (g) seasonal, temporary or migrant populations.
4. Socio-political or cultural attributes affecting social vulnerability:
   (a) Educational and literacy levels,
   (b) Leadership, extent of coherent and effective governance,
   (c) Political viability, integrity, public confidence,
   (d) Extent of self-reliance, community organisation capabilities,
   (e) informed, practiced, local or traditional coping mechanisms, and
   (f) Nature of belief systems, people's view of themselves and their own abilities.

B. Capabilities

When conducting vulnerability analysis, special note should be taken of positive attributes able to be identified that may contribute to an enhanced ability to prevent or mitigate the effects of a disaster, or which may strengthen a community's ability to respond effectively to the hazard.

1. Risk Assessment

The scientific quantification of risk determined from data and an understanding of the processes involved. Determines the magnitude of the risk consequence.

2. Risk Evaluation

The social, economic and political judgements of the importance of various risks faced by those exposed to them.

Determines the accepted importance of the risk.

3. Conditional Elements

(a) Importance of amount and type of information and a careful understanding of the nature of the hazard and its associated forces. Prevailing ignorance constitutes a major risk factor.
(b) There is a need to balance rigorous scientific or rational analysis against other "belief factors" of social or personal importance:
   1. people respond to risks which they perceive, which may be affected by media exposure, previous experience, or judgemental bias. Perceptions may be altered by vividness or frequency of exposure, dread or imagination, and
   2. variation of voluntary and involuntary exposure and presumed ability effective response (prevention and controllability).
(c) Relative costs and benefits associated with specific options of risk reduction:
   1. affordable risks, literal costs *vs.* benefits,
   2. acceptable risks, personal, social or political choices, and
   3. degree of risk over time, relative probability of risk.

C. Policy Options for Risk Reduction

1. Decision-making

Essential to have commitment:

(a) priority needs of attention,
(b) time and resource allocation, and
(c) decide relative effects of intervention.

2. Importance of Information

(a) for policy determination, and
(b) for public knowledge.

3. Hazard Prevention

(a) man-made hazards offer much potential for prevention, and
(b) natural hazards offer less potential for prevention.

4. Vulnerability Reduction

5. Mitigation of Effects

(a) structural measures of mitigation, and
(b) non-structural measures of mitigation.

APPENDIX II

CONCEPTS OF HAZARDS AND VULNERABILITY ANALYSIS

Compiled by:
TERRY JEGGLE, and ROB STEPHENSON

I. Introduction

A. Definitions—hazard, vulnerability, risk, analysis
B. Nature of Hazards
C. Hazard Assessment Process
D. Nature of Vulnerability (and Capabilities)
E. Vulnerability Analysis F. Sources

II. Definitions

A. Hazard

An event or occurrence that has the potential for causing injury to life or damage to property or the environment. The magnitude of the phenomenon, the probability of its occurrence and the extent and severity of the impact can vary. In many cases, these effects can be anticipated and estimated.

B. Vulnerability

A set of prevailing or consequential conditions composed of physical, socio-economic and/or political factors which increase a community's susceptibility to calamity or which adversely affect its ability to respond to events. The community and its members may or may not be willing participants in contributing to or tolerating the conditions. Taken together, they create a dynamic mix 01' variables, each of which results from a continuous process. Vulnerabilities can be physical, social, or attitudinal and can be primary or secondary in nature. If there are positive factors, that increase ability to respond to needs effectively or which reduce susceptibility, they are considered to be capabilities.

C. Risk

A probability that injury to life or damage to property and the environment will occur. The extent to which risk is either increased or diminished is the result of the interaction of a multitude of causation chains of events.

D. Hazard Assessment, Vulnerability Analysis

Risk Analysis Structured analytical procedures to identify hazards and to estimate the probability of their occurrence and the consequences in light of conditions. Taken together with a similar structured analysis of actual or potential vulnerabilities these estimations are then to be compared with a standard or criterion in order to decide whether or not action is desirable, to reduce the probabilities or to protect the people, property, or environment. Realistically, it is necessary also to consider to what extent perceived constraints of time, resources, or effect may impede the application of desirable counter-measures indicated.

III. Nature and Conditions of Hazards

A. Example Cyclone Hazards

1. Primary:
   - (a) Wind
   - (b) Water
     1. Rain
     2. Flood
        - (a) Marine
        - (b) Riverine
        - (c) 'Run-off'
        - (d) Low-lying
     3. Wave and tidal
     4. Storm surge
   - (c) Land
     1. Slips, slides
     2. Erosion
     3. Alteration of river course
     4. Marine encroachment
2. Multiple (or Sequential) Hazards:
   - (a) Multiple examples
   - (b) Cascade examples
3. Secondary:
   - (a) Health Risks
   - (b) Economic Loss
   - (c) Loss of Shelter, Infrastructure
   - (d) Destruction of Food Supply
   - (e) Destruction of Water Supply
   - (f) Erosion, Destruction of Land, Natural Resources
   - (g) Destruction of Community

B. Characterisation of Hazards

1. Frequency
2. Duration
3. Speed of onset

4. Scope
5. Intensity
6. Predictability
7. Forewarning time
8. Controllability

C. Factors Affecting Magnitude of the Physical Effects of Hazards

1. Geographical pattern of severity
2. Number, spatial distribution and density of population
3. Vulnerability of people, things to a given force
4. Effect of local conditions in modifying severity of effects

IV. Hazard Assessment Process

A. The Hazard Assessment Process

1. Hazards-Community-Environment-Consequences-Policies
2. Sequence of assessment:
   (a) Identification of hazards
   (b) Collection of information
      1. About the hazard
      2. About the community
      3. About the environment
   (c) Analysis of information
   (d) Application of the analysis to policy, planning, management
3. Assessment Process:
   (a) Overview:
      1. History
      2. Probability
      3. Vulnerability
      4. Maximum threat to protect against
   (b) Factor Analysis:
      1. Frequency
      2. Duration
      3. Speed of onset
      4. Scope
      5. Intensity
      6. Predictability
      7. Forewarning
      8. Controllability
   (c) Cross-Hazard Analysis:
      1. Management requirements that are common to two or more hazards:

(a) Awareness programme
(b) Information and communications
(c) Operations (procedures, centres)
(d) Evacuation or rescue (procedures, service functions)
(e) Coordination
(f) Resources
(g) Time sequencing

2. Requirements specific to individual hazards.

4. Conceptual Model of Hazard Analysis:
   (a) History
   (b) Technological analysis
   (c) Pre-requisite to vulnerability analysis

V. Nature and Conditions of Vulnerability

A. Types of Vulnerability

1. Physical (material):
   (a) Geographical, geophysical (location and exposure)
   (b) Poverty—Poor suffer more, fewer resources, No. reserves, on influence, little political power of influence. Overall, limited means and fewer options (if any). If not a Consequence of Ignorance, the Vulnerability to Natural Hazards is Essentially Determined by Conditions of Poverty.
   (c) Capital Resources—Cash, property, land, personal capital goods, reserves (and the nature of their allocation)
   (d) Basis of livelihood, economic activities, options, multiples
   (e) Occupational tools, equipment, goods (land, boat ownership)
   (f) Skills, labour
   (g) Environmental (locale, situational, prevailing practice)
   (h) Climatic
   (i) Infrastructural (access, protection)
   (j) Strength, health (food+nutrition, clean water, etc.)
   (k) Domestic (shelter, access to food, water)
2. Social (organizational)
   (a) Community organization, its cohesiveness, commitment. Extent of social, ethnic, economic, political, religious divisions.
   (b) Leadership, the governance of a community, how decisions are taken. What internal conflicts? How they are addressed?
   (c) Resource possession and control, degree of access, application to common or individual benefit.
   (d) Information, where, when, and how the community gets it and how it contributes to common knowledge and decisions.

3. Attitudinal (motivational, cultural)
   (a) How people view themselves (and are encouraged to view themselves) particularly in terms of capacities. Perception of limitations and capabilities to affect their own environment.
   (b) Traditional belief systems, degree of indigenous, historical coping mechanisms.

B. Characterizations of Vulnerability

1. Location of population groups in relation to hazard.
2. Population densities, rate and distribution of growth.
3. Special population groups (aged, women, disabled, children).
4. Location, value, access to economic and material resources.
5. Location, value, 'capacities' of vital facilities.

C. Recurrent Elements Contributing to Vulnerability

1. Rural Areas:
   (a) unequal access to land,
   (b) inability to produce a surplus,
   (c) absence of other income earning opportunities,
   (d) No. access to credit,
   (e) forced migration,
   (f) ecological damage, degradation,
   (g) reduction of natural or essential local resources.

2. Urban Areas:
   (a) low income settlements sited or able to squat only in vulnerable areas,
   (b) subsistence income levels.
   (c) inadequate personal, social, infra structural, or transport services.
   (d) population in-migration, compressing risks.

D. Why do People Live in Conditions of Vulnerability?

1. Ignorance of the vulnerability or limited perception of risk:
   (a) *Antidote*: education, communication, awareness.
2. Limited interest, authority, ability to change it:
   (a) *Antidote*: attitude, motivations, capabilities.
3. Poor, ineffectual leadership to alter conditions:
   (a) *Antidote*: political or community alteration.
4. Few, if any, alternate options (physically, socially, economically, politically)—No. choice:
   (a) *Antidote*: empowerment (generally economic or political).

VI. Vulnerability Analysis

A. Process of Risk Analysis

1. Identify the nature, extent, and risk of threat.
2. Determine the existence and degree of vulnerabilities.
3. Identify the capacities and resources available.
4. Determine acceptable levels of risk, cost-benefit considerations.
5. Set priorities relative to time, resource allocation, effectiveness of results.
6. Develop methods to protect people and key resources and reduce overall losses.
7. Design effective and appropriate management systems to implement and control.

B. Factors Determining the Magnitude of Physical Vulnerability

1. Geographical pattern of the severity of the hazard(s):
   (a) Pattern of highest wind, direction, relative timings, and
   (b) Location, extent, depth, direction, timing, tidal circumstances to storm surge.
2. The number, density, spatial distribution, special characterization of population groups exposed to the effects of the various hazards.
3. The degree of vulnerability of the elements at risk to a given force (e.g., wind, water, sea, land) or to a combination of these forces. Consideration of primary and secondary or consequential effects.
4. The effect of local conditions, capabilities, in modifying the severity of effects:
   (a) natural topographic features,
   (b) degree of awareness and foreknowledge,
   (c) state of preparedness abilities, and
   (d) mitigation practice (non-structural and structural).

C. The Vulnerability Analysis Process

1. Key elements:
   (a) Persons-Place-Time-Event
   (b) Risk-probability of threat actually occurring
   (c) Rates-risk over time
2. Conceptual Model:
   (a) Overview
      1. Historical
      2. Community experience
   (b) Nature and extent of hazards

(c) Nature and extent of vulnerabilities
(d) Determination of relative risks and benefits
(e) Map areas of risk ANALYSIS/RESPONSE
(f) Planning
(g) Nature of intervention
(h) Education
(i) Preparedness
(j) Mitigation
(k) Response
(1) Management structures

3. Factors:
   (a) Data (information)—for a purpose:
      1. Availability
      2. Quantity
      3. Quality
      4. Structure
   (b) Designated group responsible:
      1. Understanding of purpose
      2. Authority
      3. Needs
      4. Knowledge
      5. Skills
      6. Technical access
   (c) Resources:
      1. Time
      2. Money

D. Strategies for Improved Application of Analysis

1. Include analysis of natural hazard risk as part of ongoing natural resource evaluation and development strategy formulation.
2. Identify and formulate mitigation measures for development investment projects.
3. Make information on natural hazards and community vulnerability more widely available, more accessible to emergency response and development planning departments.
4. Train planning technicians and decision-makers in hazard assessment, vulnerability analysis, and disaster mitigation appreciation and techniques.

E. Special Considerations for Further Emphasis

1. Review risk perceptions of different economic groupings, (e.g., farmers, fishermen, small business community, labourers, etc.).
2. Coastal zone storm surge risk assessment.

3. Special emphasis on 'lifeline systems' vulnerability analysis.
4. Energy sector vulnerability in relation to natural hazards.
5. Flood hazard assessment and early flood alert systems as part of integrated development (or agricultural) projects.
6. Include hazard assessment and vulnerability reduction measures as a part of provincial capitals/towns' urban development plans.
7. Include landslide hazards and vulnerability assessments in metropolitan areas and on critical transportation routes (viz., Baguio conditions).
8. Use of geographical information systems in national, sub-national, and metropolitan level analysis of natural hazards, resources, populations, critical facilities and infrastructure.

CHAPTER 9

STRESSES AND STRAINS

From the Heart of God
Let the entire earth be blessed with
Loving-Kindness.
Let the entire earth be blessed with great joy,
Happiness and divine peace
Let the entire earth be blessed with
Understanding, harmony, goodwill and
Will-to-do good. So be it!

—*Choa Kok Sui*

9
CHAPTER

Stresses and Strains

STRESS AND HEALTH MANAGEMENT

Remain in bliss in this world,
Fearless, pure in heart,
Wake up in bliss every morning,
Carry out all your duties in bliss,
Remain in bliss in weal and woe,
In criticism and insult,
Remain in bliss unaffected,
Remain in bliss pardoning everybody.

—*Rabindranath Tagore*

MEANING, NATURE, CAUSES AND EFFECTS OF STRESS

According to ancient texts, health is the harmony between body and mind, harmony between mind and knowledge, harmony between the members of the family, harmony in the neighbourhood and with every other person. Thus, disease is the disharmony between all of the above.

If we want a healthy body we have to make our mind healthy. With physical health, mental health has to improve. The nature, personality, psychological and psychic framework has to change. Aim of all is to get freedom from all bondages and from vagaries of mind. Health is an equipoise state of body, mind, sense—organs, and soul. This is the harmonious vibration of the elements of human body. This is the state of ease. Contrary to this is disease.

In order to understand the different manifestations of life first of all know the mind. It is through the mind that we experience traumas, obsessions and conflicts. Through the practice of meditation you can

CHART 9.1

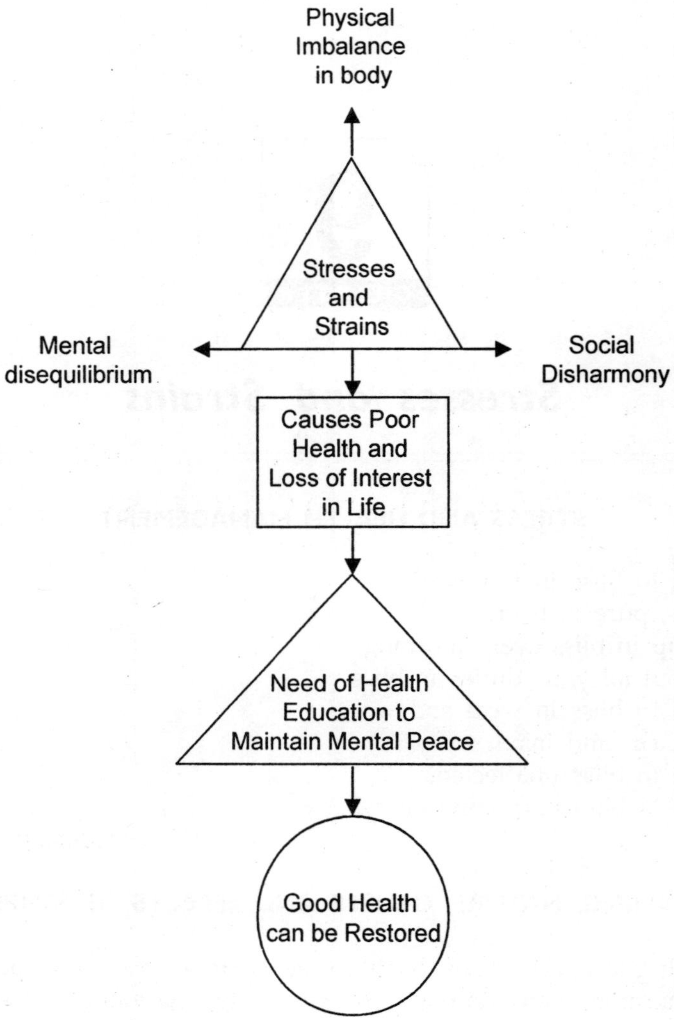

learn to smile at circumstances, you can learn to see every stressful situation as a challenge, or an opportunity to learn, give, serve and love. Meditation is a process of knowing the mind, which can happen anywhere at any time. You will find that with the change in our perspective, you will work more efficiently in whatever you do.

—*Vyasa*

INTRODUCTION

Stress is a common occurrence among people causing health hazards, laziness, uninterestedness and lack of physical and mental vitality. Stress in elementary form may not be dangerous but its prolongation for long causes worry, loss of interest in life and tendency to do No. work.

Medical Science has progressed but failed to treat people suffering from mental and spiritual problems. Many people visiting the hospitals constantly turn to doctors without showing any sign of physical disorder. Most of the doctors do not bother to diagnose their problems and administer to them sleep inducing drugs which are ultimately harmful. Tranquillizers and barbiturates are being dispensed on a large scale. "It is because medicine has become so accustomed to searching for technical answers to its dilemmas that quests for answers on the behavioural side continue to be deferred."

What can be done to make the doctors understand all this? The situation can be improved by providing courses in anthropology, sociology, psychology, yoga to the doctors. According to Maureen A. Bailey, "In the face of a virtual epidemic of behavioural disorders, modern healthcare must place a new emphasis on solving the human side of medicine."

Swami Brahmeshananda[1] in his book, Health, Medicine and Religion feels that just as physical suffering leads to anxiety and mental stress, so also worry, anxiety and psychological tensions affect the body and cause disease. These are called psychosomatic diseases. Peptic ulcer, asthma, diabetes, hypertension, neuorder matosis and others are sometimes caused and sustained by worry, anxiety, fear, frustration, jealousy, etc. The fast pace of modern life with its rigid fixation with the clock is causing tremendous stress, leading to hypertension reactions not only consume lot of psychic energy, but they can also precipitate serious problems, like the perforation of a peptic ulcer. A greedy person is more liable to develop diabetes than a contented one. An over-ambitious person is more liable to develop diabetes than a contended one. An over-ambitious person is more prone to hypertension, and an emotionally high-strung one runs greater risk of having an attack of stroke.

These observations have led to rapid growth and popularity of psychiatry and psychotherapy. But more than palliative and superficial psychiatric help, what more patients with psychosomatic disease need is a healthy way of living and a right attitude towards life, which religion can provide. Relgion teaches how not to become a prey to greed and anger and thus helps one to avoid psychosomatic problems. This is the reason why Yoga is becoming extremely popular, not only as a treatment for diseases like diabetes, asthma and hypertension, but also as a way to a healthy tension—free life.

That none can be truly healthy without a healthy mind was the opinion of Plato in ancient times. "No. attempt should be made to cure the body without the soul", he said, "and if the head and body ought to be healthy, you must begin by curing the mind."

A major cause of mental ill-health is not faulty reaction to persons and situations, which is often tarnished by envy, anger, jealousy or hatred. This must be avoided by cultivating friendship towards the happy and prosperous, compassion towards those who suffer, a feeling of positive joy towards the virtuous and indifference towards the wicked. This four-fold mental attitude conduces to mental peace and health, and is the basis for all sane social conduct health. According to Hindu psychology, the pranamaya-kosha is situated between the annamaya and the manomaya-kosha and is therefore affected by, and in turn influences, both the koshas. In other words, breathing is influenced by mental and physical states, and it influences both mind and body. Hence, its regulation by practice of rhythmic breathing conduces to physical and mental health.

Though mental health has been in existence, since times immemorial, but in the modern civilization, it has its serious effects on the health of the people. Urbanisation, over-population, competition, stresses and strains of modern life are adding to the mental health problems. We have studied in this book as to how our environment has been creating stresses and strains. The need is to make environment harmonious through efforts at various levels.

Swami Jagdatmananda feels "What is the state of the inner environment which consists of the mind, intellect, ego and the soul, the inner environment which is actually at the root of all men's activities. Is the pollution of this inner environment declining? In other words, are we able to control this inner environment? Are there any principles that can help us gain this control? If so, what are they? When the six notorious internal waves (lust, anger, greed, sensuality, pride and envy) leading to arrogance, selfishness, greed and licentiousness rise high and lash upon the shore of the human mind, is it ever possible to decrease the resulting violence and misery, however technologically developed we may be in the outside world?"

There is No. guarantee that there will be progress within man's mind if the progress only results in discoveries about the external world. To understand the principle of the progress within, we have to grasp the nature and structure of the interior of the mind. We should get acquainted with the precious stones hidden in the ocean of each man's mind.

Dr. Alexis Carrel, the renowned Nobel Prize Winner for his research on biology, who gave evidence of his superior intellectual powers in his book, 'Man, the Unknown', says, "The mind is hidden within the living matter, completely neglected by physiologists and economists, almost unnoticed by physicians. Yet it is the most colossal power of this world." Smily Blanton, the American psychologist holds a similar view, "In the deeper levels of the mind are resources of power, strength, and courage hardly imagined. To each person himself is given the task of these levels, with what assistance he can muster. There are, fortunately, untold resources in each of us if we will only find and utilize them."[2]

We have devoted one chapter on how mind wrongly trained can influence personality of human beings through lust, greed, etc.

Suskreeta Tatre in his article, "Concept of health, disease and treatment in text of Yoga and spiritual love" feels that according to ancient texts, health is the harmony between body and mind, harmony between mind and knowledge, harmony between the members of the family, harmony in the neighbourhood and with every other person. Thus, disease is the disharmony between all of the above.

If we want a healthy body we have to make our mind healthy. With physical health, mental health has to improve. The nature, personality, psychological and psychic framework has to change. Aim of all is to get freedom from all bondages and from vagaries of mind. Health is an equipoise state of body, mind, sense-organs, and soul. This is the harmonious vibration of the elements of human body. This is the state of ease. Contrary to this is disease.[3]

Begin to change your attitude and your vision of the world will change. Everything will be peaceful and good. This is the non-dualism of the vedantic vision. This is the supreme knowledge.

The question is how to control the stresses and strains. Yoga, meditation, Pranayama, etc. dealt in this book in great detail can help in control of inner problems. Dr. H.R. Nagendra and T. Mohan feel that Yoga, the ancient science of India, is a conscious process for gaining mastery over the mind and thereby grow faster from the animal level to become normal human beings and reach heights of greatness, super-human levels and ultimately attain divinity or perfection itself. This conscious process of gaining mastery helps us to manifest the innate potentialities dormant in all of us and blossom into men with the five-fold personality development mentioned above. Yoga harmonises our five-fold personality development mentioned above. Yoga harmonises our growth and through balance helps in total development. Such growth brings the divine qualities like love, affection, sacrifice, service, etc., which are at the base of the four-fold consciousness. In this sense, Yoga is a science of holistic living and is synonymous with basic or real education. Hence, Yoga is being introduced in the educational system.[4]

Yoga deals with the problems of human nature and human exigencies through a vast repertory of practical methods, which aim towards purification, regulation and awakening of human potential. At present, yoga is passing through a momentous period of growth and expansion with its rapid integration to modern society. At many levels we can see changes and new developments as yoga is being applied in different facets of life in a variety of new ways, such as a form of therapy, a technique of health and stress management.

Bhagavad Gita in Sloka 23 of Chapter 5 defines Yogi thus: He alone who is able to stand, in this very life before casting off this body, the urges of lust and anger is a Yogi, and he alone is a happy man.

Everybody in the world seeks happiness. But very few know what is real happiness and how to attain it. Due to this ignorance they run away with the wrong idea that happiness consists only in enjoying the objects of senses. That is why they hanker after them and strive to attain them. And when they find themselves balked in their efforts, they are seized with anger.

But as a rule one who is habitually under the sway of lust and anger can never be happy. One who is under the sway of desire and the one who is under the sway of anger, both betake themselves to all sorts of mischiefs and vices—the former for the sake of a wife, progeny, wealth and honour, etc. and the latter with view to harming others. They thereby expose themselves to illness, grief, ignominy, infamy, perturbation, unrest, anxiety and various kinds of agonies in this world. He alone is a real 'Narah' or man, who having thus subdued his evil propensities like lust and anger and developed dispassion and quietism attains. God, the embodiment of Truth, Knowledge and Bliss. The word, 'Narah' signifies such a person, No. matter to which sex he belongs.[5]

Part III deals with stress control education. There is a need of ethical and moral values which need be taught so that people in young age builds a good character. Swami Vivekananda observes: Today, man is subjected to a large number of stressful situations in the modern fast way of life and his balance is frequently disturbed. The system is constantly kept under sympathetic stimulations without enough time for the parasympathetic to do its job. This repeated sympathetic stimulations lead to intermittent upsurges of heart rate, blood pressure, poor digestion, elevated blood glucose, etc. When this happens over a number of years it becomes a habit for the heart and the blood vessels to remain in a stimulated state and they lose the capacity to come back to the resting levels. This is the main cause for the increasing incidence of high blood pressure and diabetes among people today.

In understanding stress we have been looking at one segment of the population of the world namely the highly developed sector, for whom issues such as the usefulness, advantages as well as the problems and challenges of scientific progress and technological advancements, are at the fore-front. The fast, sensitive, sharp mind of modern man is demanding its physical system to cope with the rush. Unable to meet the challenges, the physical system is collapsing and problems of hyper-sensitivity and stress are on the ascent.

Whatever problems we find at the global level, hyper-activity in the developed parts and hypo-activity predominantly in the underdeveloped, are also the two-fold problems at the individual level. In fact, both these aspects are found in each part of the globe, and in each mind but they may be in different proportions. For example, during sleep even the hyper-active mind is drowsy, lazy and lethargic. Man does not want to get up early in the morning. Similarly, a lazy village man will also have times of excitement and over-activity during the day. Thus, each mind is featured by both these facets of hyper and hypo-activity.

Yoga has the ability to fill the vacuum in modern education which is essentially left brain-oriented. As Swami Vivekananda had envisioned, we should not be satisfied with information-gathering and bread-earning education. He said, 'Education is the manifestation of perfection already in man'. To build an all-round (4-fold) personality—physical, mental, emotional and intellectual with a spiritual basis and 4-fold consciousness—civic sense, patriotism, service zeal and spiritual urge, should be the goal of education.[6]

According to Sathya Sai Baba, "Education must instil the fundamental human values—Truth, Right conduct, Peace, Love and Non-violence and these should constitute the life and breath of students. Development of these correspond to the five domains of human personality—intellectual, physical, emotional, psychic and spiritual— leading to holistic and integrated development. The five human values are the pillars on which stands the entire approach.

Swami Tejomayananda in his book, "Right Thinking" beautifully mentions that when a person works with inspiration, he never gets tired or exhausted. When man works only for himself, there is perspiration; but when he works for a noble goal there is inspiration. In cases where a man cannot dedicate his actions to the Lord, even if he works for some ideal or goals he will derive tremendous strength from his chosen altar of dedication. The nobler the goal, the greater will be the strength he gains. This is the beauty of love and dedication, which brings efficiency in life.

In Sanskrit there is a beautiful verse which says, "He really lives in whose living countless people live." What is there to say about a man when even his death becomes an inspiration? He laughs at death. Death cannot destroy him. One who has fulfilled his life and has blessed and inspired many others alone can be called a successful person. He alone is proficient and he alone can be called efficient. Such is the success from which we get great happiness and the strength to face whatever situations confront us. This is where sorrow ends. Such a life is an inspiration to others.[7]

In addition just to overcome, temporary problems like Arjuna in the battlefield of Kurukshetra. Lord Krishna motivated Arjuna from despair, stress and depression and made him mentally prepared to fight. We have tried to discuss the methods of motivation by which individuals can be saved from temporary set backs caused by temporary stresses and strains.

We can say in brief that stress cannot be cured by medical gadgets, it requires the action at the level of mind and spirit which poses unlimited potentialities. Science of Yoga, meditation, pranayama, ethical and moral values have great scope in dealing with the problems of stress.

Inspite of the proliferation of health institutions both in public and private sector, health problems are on the increase. An interesting phenomenon-of health problems is rising cases of diseases caused by stresses and tensions for which medical treatment is inadequate as the medical science deals mostly on physical plane. This has also led to the consumption of medicines on a large scale causing side-effects. It is being realized that the existing health system has failed to provide quality health services and that is why new institutions dealing in the science of Yoga, medication, are coming up in a big way to strike at the root causes of ill-health. We may keep in mind that these institutions also failed in treating patients suffering from diseases arising from stress as the first requirement of such institutions is to change the mind set of the people under stress from the present values borne out of affluence to mental equanimity which is a Herculean task. It has been rightly said that it is easy to destroy the mountains than to change the minds of the people. These institutions appear from outside attractive but a depth analysis of these institutes would reveal that these institutes are also charging huge money and are simply engaged on physical aspects of Yoga.

Selye and Levi have defined stress as a non-specific, conventional and phylogenetic-based response pattern, the primary function of which is to prepare the body or physical activity such as resistance or flight (called Eustress). If, however, the subject lacks the means of restoring either to fight or flight, i.e. of relieving the stress reaction, stress gives rise to distress which manifests itself in the form of psychosomatic symptoms or disorders.[8] Ivancevich and Matteson define stress simply as "the interaction of the individual with the environment" but then they go on to give a more detailed working definition, as follows: "an adaptive response, mediated by individual differences and/or psychological processes, that is a consequence of any external (environmental) action, situation, or event that places excessive psychological and/or physical demands upon a person." Beehr and Newman define stress as "a condition arising from the interaction of people and their jobs and characterized by changes within people that force them to deviate from their normal functioning." High levels of stress may be accompanied by anger, anxiety, depression, nervousness, irritability, tension, and boredom. One study found that stress had the strongest impact on aggressive actions, such as sabotage, interpersonal aggression, hostility, and complaints.[9]

Stress according to Yoga is imbalance. Imbalance is misery. At the mental and physical levels, it is excessive speed and thus a demanding situation which causes pain and leads to ailments and diseases. Imbalances at the emotional level manifest as upsurges which are caused by strong likes and dislikes. At the psychological level the imbalances lead to conflicts and often manifest as petty and narrow ego-centric behaviour. Lack of holistic knowledge and a balanced outlook, at the subtle levels are responsible for imbalances found at gross levels.[10]

One of the implicit functions of HR is the responsibility of overall organizational health . . . they need to step up to the plate, recognize the signs and proactively introduce preventative stress management to reduce or mitigate potential stressors and resultant strains.

According to researchers, Jex, Beehr and Roberts (1992), stress is an overarching umbrella concept that is comprised of stressors and strain; or the processes where a stressor leads to strain. In other words, a stressor is the physical or psychological stimulus present in the environment (e.g., work overload due to shortage of staff, poor lighting on the shop-floor, unclear job expectations or role ambiguity). A strain, also known as distress, is the negative reaction to the stressor (i.e., job burnout, substance abuse, violence, depression, anxiety). Not all stressors produce strain. An individual may also have a positive response to a stressor, and this is known as eustress. Eustress, or good stress, occurs when the individual constructively manages their response to a stressor.[11]

Stress is a state of mind which reflects certain biochemical reactions in the human body and is projected by a sense of anxiety, tension and depression and is caused by such demands by the environmental forces or internal forces that cannot be met by the resources available to the person. The intensity of such demands that require a readjustment of resources or operational styles would determine the extent of stress. Such environmental events or conditions that have the potential to induce stress are known as "Stressors."

The stress created by desirable and successful effects is called "eustress" and the stress created by undesirable outcomes is known as "distress." It is primarily the distress form of stress which requires examination and steps to cope with it.[12] It is important to deal with stress at an early stage. Early warning signs such as headaches, back pain, irritability, insomnia, absenteeism from work or alcoholism should be taken seriously. Otherwise they could lead to serious emotional disorders as well as physiological problems such as ulcers and heart diseases. When stress is left untreated for a long time, it can develop into anxiety and depression.

"Selye" postulated a 'general adaptation syndrome' of somatic systems caused by 'non-specific stress'. It involved three stages:

(a) Alarm reaction—When an initial shock phase of lowered resistance is followed by counter-shock during which an individual's defence mechanisms are activated.
(b) Resistance—It is a stage of maximum adaptation when the individual restores the equilibrium.
(c) Exhaustion—If the stress continues or the defence mechanism falters, the individuals moves to this stage.[13]

Feeling stressed is a danger signal: a sign that you are reaching the limits of your resources. Stress is bad for health as well as a cause of increasing inefficiency and worsening relationships. The danger is that when under stress we ignore our health, and put our relationships under increasing strain. This sets up a vicious cycle because poor health and poor relationships then add to the stress. It is important, therefore, to focus not only directly on the stresses but also to look after one's health and relationships.

This idea is clearly enunciated in the Katha Upanishad where the God of Death tells Nachiketa that human beings have been created in such a way that they cannot but want to enjoy the outside world. Only in rare moments of inner awareness we are conscious of a divine spark in us. Even then our biological urges pull us down towards the mundane things of the physical plane. This results in a situation where a person is aware of the presence of perfection within and is eager to reach it but is hindered by powerful urges. Obviously, the result of this conflicting pull is tension.[14]

In modern society there are different kinds of diseases and nervous tension which can also be counted as one of them. But it is different from most other diseases because there is No. germ or virus causing it. It is the result of the malfunctioning of the body-mind interaction. In other words, we can say that nervous tension is a psychosomatic disease in the true sense of the term. The word "psyche" means the mind and "soma" means the body. Nervous tension is the result of the way we have consciously or unconsciously chosen to live. When we speak of tension we should understand that the primary need of the mind and the body is that the mental and physical functioning be regulated.[15]

Nervous tension is a kind of recurring imbalance resulting in the daily wear and tear of the body. The two aspects of it which we need to understand are how it occurs and how we give expression to it. It comes in different guises, so to say. It may take the form of emotional or mental stress which is generated by our personality as it interacts with the environment everyday. This can also be called "social stress." In addition, there is another form of stress called the "digestive stress." It is the tension which results due to our poor eating habits. Therefore, it would be a mistake to think that the causes of stress are merely external: at home or in the place of work, that overwork alone causes stress. There are many other causes, such as poor eating habits.

Apart from these we have another common form of stress called environmental stress in the present times. It may be the result of many factors such as smog, noise and air pollution.

Each of us thus has a psychophysical system in the body which reflects our state of mind through physical diseases. If we suffer from nervous tension, fatigue or tremendous strain at the mental level, it is sure to come out in the form of aches and pains or more serious diseases such as hypertension, ulcer, stroke, cancer, heart attack and others. In fact, the doctors and psychologists are strongly of the opinion that most diseases are closely linked with a state of sustained nervous tension which has become an invariable component of our daily routine.

Sustained nervous tension is therefore a common phenomenon-today. It stems directly from different kinds of frustration, worry and despondency. Each day we have to meet various forms of challenges at home, in our place of work or even at play. These are in addition to the ordinary demands imposed on our mind and body by the process of living. The result of this is acute nervous tension which shows itself in the form of impatience, anger, anxiety or fear. If we take an unhealthy diet, or if we have the habit of smoking, drinking or an addiction to drugs, they too result in different kinds of tension. In short, we can say that we are living in a world of tensions.[16]

Janina Gomes in his Article, "Still the Chattering of the Mind States."[17]

All of us in life experience moments of disharmony. We find we are often at cross-purposes with life, with events, with daily happenings, with others. Out of all this disorder and disharmony, if we can build lives of harmony and orderliness, we will succeed if not at all times, at least in the most crucial moments in stilling the chattering of our minds.

Ever since the dawn of civilization, man has been constantly engaged in the pursuit of unraveling mystery of nature with a view to arriving at the fundamental values of life. Today, the world is in a state of turmoil, the causes of which seem to be beyond man's comprehension and capabilities. Paradoxically enough, man seems to be lost in the world of plentitude. It's soul is starved in the midst of unbounded materialistic pleasures and comforts that science and technology of today have placed at his disposal. The harder he strives to extricate himself out of the web of these problems, the more he is caught and involved in it. Underneath the morass of conflicting values lies man's quest for the real meaning of life and the destiny to which it leads. Science does not help us to find answers to the fundamental moral and spiritual values of life or "how to live" and here we see that the advancement of science has led to mankind, is lopsided growth and development. Sanskrit Literature is full of details as to how to lead our lives decently without causing tensions, stresses and depression. Since we have forgotten our ancient literature and its value, such problems are on the rise.

Human being is the best creation of God and is endowed with logic, perception and capacity to verbalize his experiences. He can make his life pleasurable depending upon how does he use his own resources and experiences. He can induce tension and stress in others by imparting wrong information and can also lesson his worries by imparting correct information.

Present day society is highly competitive. Every one strives for power, prestige and possession to excel over one's own fellow being. This competitive process obviously poses many challenges for the society and the susceptible individuals and may cause anxiety, stress and tension. These are the related terms having almost similar genesis and outcome and are often used to denote hardship of life. Scientifically, however, they are different.

Anxiety refers to a fear reaction in which the cause of the fear is not a specific object. Stress refers to a condition resulting from disturbances to physical or psychological well-being. Tension is readiness for action generally with No. action possible and often refers to the strain resulting from stress. Under these situations, logical process is constricted, slowed down and emotional process took up the individual's control.

D.R. Kaarthikeyan suggests the need of harmony to avoid problems—Physical, mental, social, spiritual. To quote him:

Revered Shri Vethathiri Maharishi says, 'Harmony is a precious treasure of human life'. Real success and satisfaction, happiness are the different facets of harmony. If one is to enjoy the benefits of life to the fullest, it is necessary to develop and maintain harmony; and for this understanding the philosophy of nature is required

Harmony should be maintained in all spheres of life, and these are:

Between body and life;
Between wisdom and habits;

Between self and society;
Between the purpose of life and the method of living; and
Between will and nature.

The more one understands life, the more one will achieve harmony; and success will be proportionate to that. No. doubt, harmonizing life is a difficult task, but it is worth all the striving, for it is the only way to equip oneself to enjoy life to the fullest extent and to reach the goal of life, which is the perfection of consciousness. By the development of knowledge man comes to understand the Cause and Effect system, which is a Law of Nature.

The greatest wealth is to live content with life for there is never want where the mind is satisfied and save oneself from stress and mental tensions. Richard Howell in his article, "The importance of spirituality in our lives" in *Hindustan Times* (Aug. 13, 2002) rightly emphasizes that Medical Profession paid a great price when it detached itself from all religious and philosophical references in order to obey only laws of science. There are so many human problems created by technical progress that in great industrial firms, psychologists and moralists occupy prominent places alongside technical experts and economists.

We should clearly understand that the problems is rooted in the minds and therefore stress management is to be managed at mental level though we may take physical help as a sound mind is in a sound body.

Swami Chaitanya Keerti in his Article, "In Search of Eternal India" (*Hindustan Times*, Aug. 14, 2002) rightly feels: The rise of consciousness, the light of enlightenment, the blossoming of flowers of meditations and their fragrance in the form of love and compassion that has blessed this part of the earth has never been experienced so much anywhere else.

For almost ten thousand years, thousands of people have reached the ultimate explosion of consciousness. Their vibration is still alive, their impact is in the very air, you just need a certain receptivity, a certain capacity to receive the invisible that surrounds this strange land, says the Master in Osho Upanishad.

The Upanishads declared: Amritasya Putrah! O Sons of the Eternal and Immortal! Wake Up:" Osho says that only those who have heard this clarion call and are on this amrit path—the eternal path, are the real citizens of India. People accidentally born here are not the real citizens.

Physical ailments form but one tribe of hordes that barbarously attack us; even more relentless and cruel are our mental sufferings. As we progress in our knowledge of the curative processes for ameliorating the physical sufferings, we observe that the mind's ill health affects the body much more than what one could imagine; and this kind of suffering proves all the more difficult to deal with. Mental disintegration is more dangerous, for, it brings about not only misery to the sufferer but a kind of dangerous disharmony in and excruciating intolerance with the surroundings of such an individual.

On the whole, it means each one of us who is suffering (and is there anyone who is not?) from this inner malady is an unhappy centre spreading all around him unhappiness and restlessness. A solution to these problems, very complicated and extremely confusing to the average mind, is what we seek individually and collectively. The results of such investigations conducted by the ancient enquiries and the data collected from their personal experiences constitute the bulk of our scriptures.

Today instead of searching for any radical solution and specific cure for this problematic disease and consequent suffering in life, what man actually does in society is to collect around him various kinds of "escape-distractions" and compromise-dopes, through all kinds of foul methods. He vainly hopes to drown his sorrows in ever so many unhealthy indulgences. By these methods at best man succeeds in turning his mind away from the actual facts of life as they are. To analyse scientifically and to observe closely the nature and behaviour of our outer world-of-objects and the inner instruments-of-experience in us, are the methods employed in the Upanishads, by which the Seers have discovered a happy solution for the great problems of man and his life.

Vedanta is the Science of life. It explains the art of living.[18]

People, who thus follow religion as an escape from themselves, ultimately come to gain nothing except perhaps a lingering sorrow, dulled by a blind faith that benumbs the very capacity to perceive their own tragedies of life! Scientific detachment, honest observation, logical conclusions and heroic decisions alone can help an individual to come away from his own life's fallacies.[19]

Thus, stress management is a very complex problem as it involves mind whose control is very difficult. Until and unless, we learn to control the mind, stress would continue. Stress management requires change of existing value system based on materialism to spiritualism. There is a rat race for material comforts and possessions of material resources resulting into recoiling on such persons in the form of stresses, tensions, depression and many other ailments. From those material possesions, they wanted to lead a life of quality and peace but what has been the result? They spend the physical resources in getting treatments in nursing homes without getting peace. Thus, the stress requires overhauling our existing value system and change it with our old value system enshrined in our sacred literature—Shrimad Bhagvad Geeta, Vedas, Mahabharata, etc. if we follow the values as given in our ancient wisdom we would be getting many benefits like—

(1) Mental peace, which every body requires but does not work for it in practice.
(2) Enjoying a life of quality with vigour and vitality.
(3) Creating more centres of Yoga as there would be No. need of such a big health infrastructure causing more problems than solutions.
(4) Less expenditure on health services and thus less material requirements.

(5) Creating a stimulating physical, social and spiritual environment radiating peace.
(6) Avoiding tensions among nations as stated in UNESCO preamble that war begins in the minds of men, it is the minds of men that are to be reformed.
(7) Creating harmonious interpersonal relationships.
(8) At home, society, nations and international level, there will be peace and spiritual prosperity.

CLASSIFICATION

Many scholars are writing and producing literature on stress management for special categories of individuals like stress management for executives, stress management among police personnel, political elite, bureaucracy, students, women, etc. However, such classification is of No. use as stress is the same in all. Stress does not differ in different categories of personnel. Stress may, however, differ in severity and to deal with people in stress, we have to understand the level and severity of stress. It may be stressed that stress management in this book is for all without any distinction in status.

APPROACH

Approach to stress is understood wrongly. We are seeing today that every third shop is of a chemist as we think that medication can cure stress which is totally fallacious. We also find the opening of many gyms, religious institutes, training institutions for stress management which is also not a right approach. Stress is mental and need be dealt on mental level. Until and unless we do not purify our minds, there can be No. mental peace. We shall discuss various approaches to control stress.

CAUSES

There are many causes responsible for stress:

(1) Wrong use of mind for greed, lust, manipulation causing turbulence in mind and disturbing the mental equanimity.
(2) Filling the mind with impurities responsible for stress like hatred, lack of service to humanity, self-centred.
(3) Always planning harassing other people and disturbing the peace and tranquility of mind.
(4) Lack of right thinking causing destructions of mind causing mental turbulations.
(5) Lack of practices leading to mental purity like yoga, meditation, etc.

Effect of Stress

1. Poor health leading to many health problems—depression.
2. Low productivity/efficiency at work.
3. Lack of interest in life and work.
4. Absence of harmony in social life.
5. Absence of right thinking.
6. Degenerated mental environment.

Today, man is subjected to a large number of stress situations in the modern fast way of life and his balance is frequently disturbed. The system is constantly kept under sympathetic stimulations without enough time for the parasympathetic to do its job. This repeated sympathetic stimulations lead to intermittent upsurges of heart rate, blood pressure, poor digestion, elevated blood glucose, etc. when this happens over a number of years it becomes a habit for the heart and the blood vessels to remain in a stimulated state and they lose the capacity to come back to the resting levels. This is the main cause for the increasing incidence of high blood pressure and diabetes among people today.[20]

Mental Health

There is very close relationship between mental equanimity, peace and happiness of an individual and his physical health and efficiency. A mentally tense, anxious and sick person has a tendency to develop various symptoms of organic disorders. Thus, other conditions remaining equal a normally serene and cheerful person may be expected to have various pathological symptoms in his body.

Consciousness shrinks in a mentally abnormal person, and his shrunken consciousness finds expression through his pathological organic disorders. The consciousness of a diseased person has a trend towards continuous contraction. The domain of consciousness of a mentally and organically sick person becomes narrow, clouded and depressed. The ancient Indian seers used the conception of 'mental equanimity' instead of the concept of 'mental health'. Sri Aurobindo used the concept of mental serenity in the same sense as the concept of 'mental equanimity' of ancient Indian seers. The concept of 'mental equanimity' is more satisfactory than the concept of mental health because the former alone can produce spiritual development in an individual.[21] Swami Vishnu Devananda states:

Tad everthamatra-nirbhasam svarupa-sunyam iva samadhih

When consciousness of subject and object disappears and only the meaning remains, it is called samadhi.

Samadhi is a merging of the mind into the essence of the object of meditation. Nothing exists but that pure awareness.[22]

Let us take the role of mental health in Government. Mind is the most powerful part of the human system. It is a Super Computer. We don't realize its potential or devise ways and means to harness this most important source. We can achieve excellence, provided we know the secret of tapping human mind. We generally notice that most of us are not mentally positive as one or the other problem concerning us continuously bogs us down. Many of us become mental wrecks and a liability. The health institution, instead of solving their problems, cause further deterioration. 25 percent of people in every organization are a liability and the other 75 percent are not contributing as per their potential. We should try to create positive mental attitudes among them. Positive mental attitude is a state of mind that reflects among the people. Positive mental attitude is a state of mind that reflects the strength of one's belief in what we do. It generates inner and voluntary emotions, which enhances motivation, resulting in positive thoughts. Positive thinking is the key to development and is result-oriented.

Ethical behaviour is considered as a blend of moral qualities and mental attitudes. The requisite moral qualities include not only the willingness to serve the public but also the willingness to behave competently, efficiently, honestly, responsibly, objectively, fairly, and accountably. Mental attitudes include awareness of moral dilemmas inherent in policies and conflicting claims on the substantive and procedural aspects of policy, an empathy for divergent views held not only by some members of the public but also by professional colleagues, and a sensitivity to paradoxes of rules that may lead to frustrating and unkind actions. Thus, an appropriate blend of moral qualities and mental attitudes become an essential ingredient for moral government and administration. Such a mixture strengthens the basis of legitimate and effective government, which is founded on public trust and confidence.

We get a moral government by creating those conditions within which a moral government can operate. This is done by making it possible for officials to acquire the necessary traits and by practicing the same. An exemplary public servant is not simply the one who obeys and behaves within the confines of law but is also one who strives for a moral government. Such is the duty of those who wish to be involved in the difficult and complex world of government. This is the essence and basis of a moral state.[23]

Public life is in a desperate state today, with vice regal regalia dominating it with its fierce ferocity and crushing criminality, sounding the death knell of ethics, morality, and value system. There is dire need to save it. Public men, at whatever station of life they function—must be 'men' for the public; leaders must lead; and most importantly, politicians must stop 'politicking'. Public opinion which is often branded as meaning neither public nor opinion—must be built up against acceptance and tolerance of unethical behaviour and action by anybody, howsoever high and mighty he may be. Crisis of confidence—which admittedly is a function of culture—must be restored in public life; otherwise, the ancient civilization that we boast of, will be No. more; there will remain No. public, No. life, worth living, without ethics.[24]

The ancient Indian philosophers laid stress on mental equanimity for the general well-being of individuals. The mind of an ordinary person is usually very restless. Myriads of desire produce upheavals in the mind of an individual. Over and above this, the mind of an ordinary person is affilicated by several tensions.

The ancient Indian philosophers maintained that if the mind of an individual usually remains in a disturbed state, he is very likely to develop pathological symptoms. An individual with pathological mental symptoms quite often develop certain pathological organic symptoms because there is very close relationship between the body and the mind of an individual. The mind of an individual becomes free from anxiety and miseries, if there is peace in his mind.[25]

The mind is a reservoir for numerous powers. By utilizing the resources which are hidden within it, one can attain any height of success in the world. If the mind is trained, made one-pointed and inward, it also has power to penetrate into the deeper levels of our being. It is the finest instrument that a human being can ever have.[26]

SPIRITUAL HEALTH

Individuals can have perfect health only when they are able to ascend from the lower to the higher states of consciousness, and remain perfectly poised in the higher plane of consciousness for a considerable duration of time. Perfect health is a comprehensive concept which includes mental equanimity, physical fitness and spiritual development of an individual.

The most crucial problem with which mankind is faced at present is the problem of health in its comprehensive sense. Health in its comprehensive sense means perfect physical fitness, mental serenity and vivid comprehension of the higher planes of consciousness in an individual. Healing means restoration of an individual to his normal state of physical efficiency, mental equanimity and clear comprehension of the higher planes of consciousness.

Health has its base in spiritual powers. We can arrange different lectures on spiritually which can keep the health of the people in good shape as well move them to positive action. J.L. Gupta in his article "Power of Prayer" in the *Daily Tribune*, dated August 31, 2000 stated that, "Today, we care for what we eat, but not for what is eating us. We worry about what we wear, not what is wearing us out. We build houses and furnish them at considerable cost to make them comfortable. Then we look for the fastest cars to get away from our homes. We get every place air conditioned so that we do not sweat at work or on the road of life. Then we spend more—we buy a treadmill or join a gym, even to go to a health-club all to be able to sweat out."

Such indeed is the dichotomy in our lifestyle. In the new millennium we are moving fast, at a rather rapid pace, but we are not aware of the direction. We are rudderless. No. wonder, we have problems —of body and mind—All tension and lot of stress. There is not a moment of peace and rest. No. time to stand and stare. Resultantly, the medicos claim a substantial share of our earnings, regularly.

Shirish Joshi rightly stresses the need of spiritual health. To quote him: that the notion that religious faith can promote physical well-being is not new. Most of us have heard of cases in which someone, by sheer faith and will have, miraculously recovered from a terminal illness or survived far longer than doctors thought possible. What is new that such rewards of religion are becoming the subject of study by scientists. A study found that religious folks had lower blood pressure, less depression and anxiety, stronger immune system and generally spent less money on medicines than people who did not believe in the existence of God and were less involved in religious activities in temples.

Scientists cannot prove that God heals, but they can now prove that belief in God has a beneficial effect. There is little doubt that healthy religious faith and practices can help people get better.

As a result of many studies, which say that prayer can help people feel better and live longer, many medical schools in the USA are offering courses in spirituality, religion and health.

Man without divine knowledge wanders in darkness. He is like a tree without fruits, flowers without fragrance, a stream without water. Such a life is absolutely barren and worthless.

S.K. Kiran Kumar and K.A. Geetha have rightly summed up: Holistic approach to health represents a revisioning of the human endeavour to restore order in the organismic functioning, that has occurred in the past several centuries within the medical profession. The holistic health movement is the reflection of the growing dissatisfaction among the professionals as well as lay people about the capacity of modern medicine in delivering the healthcare. A shortcoming of modern medicine is its failure to recognize the interactive nature of the different aspects of human existence viz., physical, psychological, social and spiritual in the etiology of illnesses and in the maintenance of health and well-being.

Since modern medicine is itself a development within the framework of science, many have argued that the change needs to be brought about in the very framework. Thus, holistic movement is viewed as a by-product and manifestation of the contemporary thrust on the revision of the scientific framework. One can find this trend in the works of behavioural, natural and social scientists which are contributing for major change in the world view. It involves a fundamental shift in cognition leading to radical alternations in the belief and assumptions about the nature of the universe, about the human nature, about organism environment interaction, and about the nature of consciousness. The newly emerging worldview is described as holistic paradigm (Krippner, 1991).

In the final analysis, the physical, social, mental and spiritual balance is the most desirable for holistic health. Unless a person is physically fit and active; he cannot perform at his best level. On the other hand, it is the mind, which accounts for 80 percent of physical and social problems. These are called psychosomatic diseases. Lastly, it is the spirit which ultimately directs the mind and through it to the body. We should devise ways and means to ensure synergy of the physical, social, mental and spiritual capabilities, which would release the infinite potential powers and generate efficiency and happiness in the society.

The secret of right action in reality is not a secret. It does not lie in any formula that we repeat. There is No. magic by means of which we can follow the path of idleness and yet make our life productive. No.! The secret lies in our own motives, in our power of application. It is not the strong physical vehicle which makes the productive human being; it is skillfulness in action, knowing how to adjust ourselves quickly, how to perform a task with the least expenditure of energy. This is what gives immediate success. We should take action in time to solve problems before they become violent and result in destruction and unpleasant atmosphere.

Gita has given us some thoughts which if followed can remove tensions and stresses.

Man has a right to action alone, not to the renunciation of action. If out of egoism he forcibly tries to renounce all action, he will not succeed in the attempt (III.5); for his nature will compel him to act (III.33; XVIII.59, 60). In this way he will be abusing his authority, and by refusing to perform an obligatory duty he will also have to bear the evil consequences of violating the commands of the scriptures.

Arjuna, perform your duties established in Yoga, renouncing attachment, and even-tempered in success and failure; evenness of temper is called Yoga (48).

The word 'Yoga' bears a peculiar meaning in the Gita and the Lord conveys that peculiar meaning by defining it as equanimity. The Lord thus establishes identity between Yoga and equanimity, and shows that one can become a Yogi by attaining equanimity through any discipline whatsoever.

By declaring action with a selfish motive as far inferior to the Yoga of equanimity, the Lord has shown that the fruit of actions prompted by desire is the attainment of fleeting and momentary pleasure whereas the fruit of Karmayoga is realization of God. Thus, there is No. comparison whatsoever between the two. The word 'Karma' in this verse cannot be interpreted in the sense of prohibited action, for such action is altogether worth renouncing and its fruit is nothing but untold misery and suffering. Therefore, it cannot be cited as a fit subject of comparison to bring out the glory of the Yoga of Equanimity.

Endowed with equanimity, one sheds in this life both good and evil. Therefore, strive for the practice of this Yoga of equanimity. Skill in action lies in (the practice of this) Yoga.

We should avoid favouring some at the cost of others. Our actions should be fair and impartial.

"Many people confuse attachment with love. But in attachment you become selfish, interested in your own pleasure, and you misuse love. You become possessive and try to gain the objects of your desires. Attachment creates bondage, while love bestows freedom. When yogis speak of non-attachment they are not teaching indifference, but are teaching how to genuinely and selflessly love others. Non-attachment, properly understood, means love. Non-attachment or love can be practiced by those who live in the world as well as those who are renunciates."[27]

Kaibara Ekken, the Japanese sage has nicely put it as: If by study, enquiry or thought, we have learned the truth, we should then put it into practice in both our speech and action. Let what we say be true and what we do discreet. Regulate the emotions, and suppress anger and selfish desires. Shake off evil and cling to good. Discovering our faults, let us not hesitate to correct them. Towards others let us be considerate. All this is the way of true action. . . . Without putting what we have learned into practice, it bears No. fruit.

All these would divert the energy in positive channels and thus reduce stress or lead stress free life.

A few remedies for overcoming fatigue are to increase our interest in whatever work we undertake and to perform it joyfully. Often our daily duties become monotonous resulting in boredom and fatigue. This can be relieved if we make the atmosphere of our place pleasant.

Monotony can be cured by genuine love for our work.

Of the innumerable techniques prescribed by the rishis for self-development, the most popular ones are the path of selfless dedicated service (karma yoga), the path of discriminative knowledge (jnana yoga), and the mystic path of self-development through disciplined contemplation (raja yoga).

According to Sage Narada, true devotion for the Lord is superior and nobler to all these, because devotion is the final outcome of all other methods of self-development.

This supreme devotion is indeed, as a technique, even superior to the path of action, the path of knowledge, and the path of disciplined contemplation. (Narada Bhakti Sutra II:I:25).

All the other paths are the means that take the seekers to the final goal of spiritual experience, but in devotion there is very little difference in essence between the means and the end, between way and the goal. Love alone is love's own end and fulfilment. Devotion is both the means and the end. As long as residual *vasanas* (inherent tendencies) are still lingering in the devotee's personality, so long is devotion only the path. But when, as a result of his love for the Lord, his *vasanas* disappear totally, a stage comes when his supreme love itself becomes the Lord of love Superme.

Than all other paths, devotion is the one most readily available and most easily attainable. (Narada Bhakti Sutra VI:1:58)

Having dedicated all activities unto Him, the devotee should turn all desire, anger, pride and so forth toward him alone. (Narada Bhakti Sutra VI: 2:65).

Having gained this supreme devotion, the devotee attains perfection and immortality and becomes extremely satisfied. (Narada Bhakti Sutra I:1:4).

Because Love is of the nature of peace; it is of the nature of Supreme Bliss. (Narada Bhakti Sutra VI:1:60).[28]

CONCLUSION

Techniques of Stress Management

Uma Arulnidhi stated, Meanwhile, over all his years in his pursuit of spiritual truth, he had found that certain techniques of physical exercise and meditation were useful, even necessary, tools—in that exercises served to keep the body sufficiently healthy so that one could pursue one's spiritual search without the worry, loss of energy and suffering of disease; and meditation served to quiet the mind to enhance insight, sharpen awareness and enable deeper, subtler spiritual enlightened persons of the past and present, when he wanted to convey his philosophy to the world he felt that it must be conveyed along with such practices as he had personally found efficacious and felt confident of transmitting to others so as to be useful and practical for them. He realized that there are books full of eternal Truth always available for anyone to open and read: the problem is that we cannot seem to fully grasp those truths through books, No. matter how well written they may be, or how many times we read them! A personal dedication and systematic, persistent practices of body and mind should be the best way to fully realize and integrate spiritual knowledge in one's life.[29]

When we face life's problems and are confronted with turbulent or worrying events, we often get so obsessed with the problem that our minds chatter and weave round and round the problem to No. avail. This chattering of the mind disturb our mental poise and ease and makes us compulsively obsessed with the happenings. The result—a loss of equilibrium and balance.

Deep down inside us is a felt need for a still mind. In fact, there are ways to experience this stillness in the thick of the battles of our lives. In the midst of confusion and conflict, we can retain a stillness that quietens us and creates a certain distance between us as experiencing selves and our circumstances.[30]

To maintain calm in situations of threat, hazards, disorder and conflict is not easy. It is a life-long lesson we have to learn. It comes through practice, through trial and error, through many failed efforts, through the process of human growth and evolution.

Stillness is a divine gift. The human heart has divine treasures which unfold through patient effort and calm. Stillness is not passivity but experiencing calm in the midst of trials. It is the ability to respond to life with courage and the ability to stand the test without turbulence.

But to be still is not to be frozen in one's mindset or state of mind. Those who are frozen in a certain state do not move and are not evolving or growing. Those who move and flow with life are, however, those who like the ripples in a still pond, experience movement but maintain an underlying stillness that makes life a movement of grace and harmony.[31]

All of us in life experience moments of disharmony. We find we are often at cross purposes with life, with events, with daily happening, with others. Out of all this disorder and disharmony, if we can build lives of harmony and orderliness, we will succeed if not at all times at least in the most crucial moments in stilling the chattering of our minds.

Follow the heart. A pure heart sees beyond the intellect; it gets inspired; it knows things that reason can never know, and whenever there is conflict between the pure heart and the intellect, always side with the pure heart, even if you think what your heart is doing is unreasonable.

When it is desirous of doing good to others, your brain may tell you that it is not expedient to do so, but follow your heart, and you will find that you make less mistakes than by following your intellect.

The pure heart is the best mirror for the reflection of truth, so all these disciplines are for the purification of the heart. And as soon as it is pure, the truth will flash upon it in a minute; all truth in the universe will manifest in your heart, if you are sufficiently pure.

Louis Lavelle states that the meaning of holiness. Love transports us beyond ourselves; it is like an inspiration that is constantly being renewed, a power that is always present, sustaining us. Louis Lavelle the meaning of holiness.

Rediscovering ourselves and trying to build a new life from the wreckage of the earlier one which has been causing depression and despair are effective strategies to overcome the problem of tension. With strong determination we can resolve the trouble which may at first sight seem insurmountable. Bringing about effective changes is totally up to us as long as we are prepared to accept the responsibility for our behaviour, actions and attitudes. As a good General can inspire his soldiers to move forward fearlessly, fight boldly and win glorious victories against the most invincible enemies so also is an answering determination able to inspire an individual to achieve remarkable feats of courage in the battle of life.

Individuals can thus determine the course of their own lives if they have sufficient confidence and unshakeable faith in themselves. It is not right to just sit back and wait for fortune or luck. One should depend rather on one's own acts, thoughts, efforts, skills and values. These induce positive thought currents that we have to make our own life significant. Nothing else or No. one else can do this for us. It is for us to formulate a workable strategy of meaningful existence and carry it throughout life. Then we should have No. time to indulge in our predilection for being depressed.[32]

Stress as the author feels is caused by lack of control over mind which becomes susceptible to senses and impulses. Mind is quickly influenced by selfish motives and lust for worldly pleasures. When there is No. control over mind, the individual is engulfed by lust, greed, anger, attachments and manipulations. The result of all these is stress and strains which cannot be cured simply by medicines and physical exercises. For this we have to control our mind.

When non-acquisitiveness is established, an understanding of the purpose of birth is gained. When the yogi No. longer desires to have possessions he frees himself from the material world. This gives him a perspective of the purpose of his birth, both in this life and in past ones. He gains comprehension of the law of Karma and understands what lessons remain to be learned before attaining Realization.[33]

Let us have a great ideal, an ideal that will startle us with its greatness. That is the only kind of an ideal to hold before our mind's eye and to work for. Little by little our imperfections and difficulties will vanish and instead of regarding life as a drudgery, instead of shirking from it, we shall bless this life which offers so many opportunities. We shall find joy even in the little daily tasks and wherever we are placed we shall know happiness.[34]

This inscription means that the order of Karikala, who is the kaala (death) of enemies, is that those who follow the vedic path should be protected and those who pursue evil paths should be punished.

There are many diseases for which modern medical science has not discovered a remedy, but these mountaineers do not even suffer from these. Perhaps fresh food, fresh air, and, above all, free thinking with No. anxiety is responsible for their health. Millions of patients all over the world who suffer from psychosomatic diseases can be helped through right diet, juices, relaxation, breathing, and meditation. Preventive and alternative medicine should not be ignored.[35]

Notes and References

1. Swami Brahmeshanand, "Health, Medicine and Religion," Shri Ramakrishna Math, Chennai, 2004, pp. 79-80, 85-86 and 155-56.
2. Swami Jagadatmananda, Learn to Live, Vol. I, Sri Ramakrishna Math, Chennai, Oct. 7, 2000, pp. 142-47.
3. VYASH, Annual Report, 2003-04, Bangalore, p. 104.
4. H.R. Nagendra and Sri T. Mohan, Yoga in Education, Swami Vivekananda, Yoga Prakashna, 1986, p. (iii)
5. Jayadayal Goyanka, Shrimd Bhagavad Gita with Sanskrit Text and English Translation, Gita Press, Gorakhpur, 1976, pp. 262-63.
6. VYASH, Annual Report, 2002-03, Bangalore, p. 4.
7. Swami Tejomayananda, Right Thinking, Central Chinmaya Mission Trust, Mumbai, 2002, pp. 29-30.
8. Dr. H.R. Nagendra, New Perspectives in Stress Mangement, Swami Vivekanand Yoga Prakashan, Bangalore, 2003, p. 9
9. Peter Y. Chen and Paul E. Spector, "Relationship of Work Stressors with Aggression, Withdrawal, thief and substance use: An exploratory Sudy, *Journal of Occupational and Organisational Psychology*, Rand MC Nolly, Chicago, 1976.
10. Dr. H.R. Nagendra and R.P. Nagarthma, *op. cit.*, p. 41.
11. Ritu Kappula, Under the Influence of Stress, in *Human Capital*, Vol. 7, No. 10, March 2004, pp. 36-37.

12. Jito Chandan, Organizational Behaviour, Vikas, New Delhi, 1994, pp. 182, 192.
13. H. Seyle, The General Adaptation Syndrome and the Disease of Adaptation, *Journal of Clinical Endrocology*, 1946, p. 117.
14. Swami Gokulananda, How to Overcome Mental Tension, Ramakrishna Mission Institute of Culture, Calcutta, 1997, pp. 20-21.
15. *Ibid.*, p. 1.
16. Swami Gokulananda, How to overcome Mental Tension, Ramakrishna Mission Institute of Culture, 2000, pp. 1-3.
17. *The Daily Tribune*, Sept. 12, 2002.
18. Swami Chinmayananda, Atma Bodha, Central Chinmaya Mission Trust, Mumbai, 2001, pp. (ii) and (iii).
19. *Ibid.*, p. 2.
20. Dr. H.R. Nagendra and R. Nagarathama, New Perspectives in Stress Management, Swami Vivekananda Yoga Prakashna, 2002, p. 27.
21. A.K. Sinha, Science and Tantra Yoga, 1993, p. 9.
22. Swami Vishnu Devananda, *op. cit.*, p. 185.
23. O.P. Dwivedi, "Reflections on Moral Government and Public Services as a Vocation, in *IJPA*, July to Sept. 1995, p. 297.
24. O.P. Dwivedi, "Conclusion: A comparative Analysis of Ethics, Public and Public Service", James, S. Bowman and F.A. Elliston (eds.) Ethics, Government and Public Policy, New York, Greenwood Press, 1988, p. 318.
25. Bata K. Dey, Ethics, Maladies and Remedies, in *IJPA*, July-Sept. 1995, p. 461.
26. Swami Rama, Living with Himalayan Masters, The Himalayan Institue Press, Pennsylvania, 1999, p. 313.
27. *The Sunday Tribune*, Sirish Joshi, August 19, 2000.
28. Swami Rama, Living with Himalayan Masters, The Himalayan Institute Press, Pennsylavania, 1999, p. 58.
29. *The Tribune*, Nov. 24, 1980.
30. Alliyar, 2000, *op. cit.*, p. 128.
31. Aliyar, 2002.
32. R.H. Singh, "Yoga and Heath", Science and Philosophy of Indian Medicine, Baidyanath Bhawan, Pvt. Ltd., Nagpur, 1978.
33. Swami Gokulananda, How to overcome Mental Tension, Ramakrishna Mission Institute of Culture, 2002, pp. 224-25
34. Swami Vishnu Devananda, Meditation and Mantras, Delhi, Motilal Banarsi Das, 1978, p. 179.
35. Swami Rama, *op. cit.*, p. 348.

APPENDIX

TABLE I

National AIDS Control Programme, India
AIDS Cases in India (Reported to NACO)

(As on 30th April, 2004)

Sl. No.	*State/UT*	*AIDS Cases*
1.	Andhra Pradesh	7198
2.	Assam	171
3.	Arunachal Pradesh	0
4.	A and N Islands	33
5.	Bihar	155
6.	Chandigarh	861
7.	Delhi	894
8.	Daman and Diu	1
9.	Dadra and Nagar Haveli	0
10.	Goa	418
11.	Gujarat	4233
12.	Haryana	350
13.	Himachal Pradesh	149
14.	Jammu and Kashmir	2
15.	Karnataka	1945
16.	Kerala	267
17.	Lakshadweep	0
18.	Madhya Pradesh	1131
19.	Maharashtra	11726
20.	Orissa	128
21.	Nagaland	417
22.	Manipur	1238
23.	Mizoram	52
24.	Meghalaya	8
25.	Pondicherry	302
26.	Punjab	261
27.	Randasthan	978
28.	Sikkim	8
29.	Tamilnadu	29782
30.	Tripura	5
31.	Uttar Pradesh	1307
32.	West Bengal	930
33.	Ahmedabad Mun. Corp.	267
34.	Mumbai M.C.	4342
	Total	69559

TABLE I (*Contd.*)

Surveillance for AIDS Cases in India
(as reported to NACO as on 30th April 2004)

AIDS Cases in India	*Cumulative*	*This Month*
Males	50900	558
Females	18659	192
Total	69559	750

Risk/Transmission Categories

	No. of cases	*Percentage*
Sexual	60008	86.27
Perinatal transmission	1964	2.82
Blood and blood products	1687	2.43
Injecting Drug users	1389	2.00
History not available	4511	6.49
Total	69559	100.00

Age group	*Male*	*Female*	*Total*
0-14 yrs.	1619	1025	2644
15-29 yrs.	15178	8485	23663
30-44 yrs.	30234	8186	38420
>45 yrs.	3869	963	4832
Total	50900	18659	69559

TABLE I (*Contd.*)

State-wise List of Voluntary and Counselling Testing Centres

Sl. No.	District	Name of the V.C.T.C	Address	Phone No.
1.	Srikakulam	Dist. Head Qrts. Hospital,	Srikakulam, 532001	08942-222158,223033 223073 Fax
2.	Srikakulam	Area Hospital,	Tekkali, Srikakulam, 532201	08945-244262 249661 (R)
3.	Srikakulam	Area Hospital,	Palakonda, Srikakulam, 532440	08942-263130
4.	Vizianagaram	Dist. Head Qrts. Hospital,	Vizianagaram, 535202	08922-263130, 222124
5.	Vizianagaram	Area Hospital,	Parvathipuram, Vizianagaram, 532501	08944-261088, 261212
6.	Visakhapatnam	Indian Naval Hospital Services, Kalyani	Visakhapatnam, 530001	0891-573586, 578000
7.	Visakhapatnam	Dept. of Microbiology Andhra Medical College,	Visakhapatnam, 530001	0891-2352960, 2563345, 2564892
8.	Visakhapatnam	Area Hospital, Narsipatnam	Visakhapatnam	531160
9.	Visakhapatnam	Area Hospital, Anakapalli	Visakhapatnam, 531001	08924-223340, 222143
10.	East Godavari	Dept. of Microbiology Rangaraya Medical College, G.G.H. Campus,	Kakinada, East Godavari, 533001	0884-2376206, 2375831 2358474 Fax
11.	East Godavari	Dist. Head Quarter Hospital,	Rajahmundry, East Godavari, 533101	0883-2444415
12.	East Godavari	Area Hospital,	Amalapuram, East Godavari, 533201	0883-231103
13.	East Godavari	Area Hospital,	Ramachandrapuram, East Godavari,	08857-533255 262303
14.	East Godavari	Area Hospital,	Tuni, East Godavari, 533401	
15.	West Godavari	Dist. Head Qrts. Hospital, Eluru	West Godavari 534001	08812-230403, 230401(BB)
16.	West Godavari	Area Hospital, Tanuku	West Godavari	534211 08819-222175, 223501 Fax
17.	West Godavari	Area Hospital, Tadepalligudem	West Godavari 534101	08818, 221144
18.	Krishna	Siddhartha Medical College,	Dept. of Microbiology, Vijayawada, Krishna-520001	0866-2450390, 2451657 Fax
19.	Krishna	Dist. Head Quarter Hospital,	Machilipatnam, Krishna-521001	08672-223328 223328 Fax

20. Krishna	Area Hospital,	Nuziveedu, Krishna, 521201	08656-232732
21. Krishna	Area Hospital,	Gudivada, Krishna, 521301	08674-245040
22. Guntur	Guntur Medical College	Dept. of Microbiology, Guntur, 522002	0863-2234625, 2320908 Fax
23. Guntur	Dist. Head Quarter Hospital,	Tenali, Guntur, 522201	0864-228850
24. Guntur	Area Hospital,	Bapatla, Guntur, 522101	086432-224038
25. Guntur	Area Hospital,	Narsaraopet, Guntur, 522601	08647-223232
26. Prakasam	Dist. Head Qrts. Hospital,	Ongole, Prakasam, 523001	08592-236712, 234300
27. Prakasam	Area Hopital,	Chirala, Prakasam, 523125	08594-232373
28. Prakasam	Area Hospital,	Markapur, Prakasam, 523316	08596-223041
29. Prakasam	Area Hospital,	Kandukur, Prakasam, 523105	
30. Nellore	Dist. Head Qrts. Hospital,	Nellore, 524001	0861-2326833, 2328500
31. Nellore	Area Hospital, Gudur	Nellore, 524101	08624-251804
32. Nellore	Area Hospital, Kavali	Nellore, 524201	08626-243524
33. Chittoor	S.V. Medical College, Tirupati	Dept. of Microbiology, Chittoor, 517501	0877-2287368, 2286666
34. Chittoor	District Hospital,	Chittoor, 517001	0857-2229324
35. Chittoor	Area Hospital,	Kuppam, Chittoor 517425	08570-255011
36. Chittoor	Area Hospital,	Madanapalli, Chittoor, 517325	08571-262087
37. Chittoor	Area Hospital	Srikalahasti, Chittoor, 517644	0578-2222530
38. Ananthapur	Govt. Medical College,	Dept. of Microbiology, Ananthapur, 515002	08554-20666, 20667
39. Ananthapur	Area Hospital,	Kadiri, Ananthapur, 515591	08494-24144
40. Ananthapur	District Head Quarters Hospital,	Hindupur, Ananthapur	08554-20666, 20667
41. Ananthapur	Area Hospital,	Guntakal, Ananthapur, 515801	08552-247105
42. Cuddapah	Dist. Head Qrts. Hospital,	Cuddapah, 516001	08562-26074, 242152
43. Cuddapah	Area Hospital,	Pulivendula, Cuddapah, 516390 516360	08568-266156
45. Kurnool	Kurnool Medical College	Dept. of Microbiology, Kurnool, 518001	08518-255160, 255158

46. Kurnool	Dist. Head Quarter Hospital,	Nandyal, Kurnool, 518501	08514-242575
47. Kurnool	Area Hospital,	Adoni, Kurnool, 518301	08512-253566
48. Mahabubnagar	Dist. Head Qrts. Hospital,	Mahabubnagar, 509001	08542-242431
49. Mahabubnagar	Area Hospital,	Gadwal, Mahabubnagar 509125	08546-262111
50. Mahabubnagar	Area Hospital,	Narayanpet, Mahabubnagar, 509201	08506-282354
51. Mahabubnagar	Area Hospital,	Nagarkurnool, Mahabubnagar, 509209	
52. Mahabubnagar	Area Hospital,	Wanaparthy, Mahabubnagar, 509103	
53. Medak	Dist. Head Quarter Hospital,	Sangareddy, Medak, 502001	08452-276409
54. Medak	Area Hospital,	Medak, 502110	08452-21271
55. Medak	Area Hospital, Siddipet	Medak, 502103	08457-22525
56. Nizamabad	Dist. Head Qrts. Hospital,	Nizamabad, 503001	08462-21603, 20937
57. Nizamabad	Area Hospital, Kamareddy	Nizamabad, 503111	08468-24933
58. Nizamabad	Area Hospital, Banswada	Nizamabad, 503187	08466-277070
59. Nizamabad	Area Hospital, Bodhan	Nizamabad, 503185	084672-272146
60. Adilabad	Dist. Head Qrts. Hospital,	Adilabad, 504001	08732-26474
61. Adilabad	Area Hospital,	Bhainsa, Adilabad, 504103	08752-231086
62. Adilabad	Area Hospital,	Mancherial, Adilabad, 504208	08736-252028
63. Karimnagar	Dist. Head Qrts. Hospital,	Karimnagar, 505001	0877-2240337
64. Karimnagar,	Area Hospital, Jagityal	Karimnagar, 505327	0877-221028
65. Karimnagar,	Area Hospital, Sircilla	Karimnagar, 505301	
66. Karimnagar	Area Hospital,	Ramagundam, Karimnagar, 505208	
67. Warangal	Kakatiya Medical College,	Dept. of Microbiology, Warangal, 506002	0870-2446888 2450390
68. Warangal	Area Hospital,	Mahaboobabad. Warangal, 506101	
69. Warangal	Area Hospital,	Jalgaon, Warangal, 506167	08716-22546
70. Khammam	Dist. Head Qrts. Hospital,	Khammam, 507001	08742-24815, 24175
71. Khammam	Area Hospital,	Kothagudem, Khammam, 507101	08744-242490
72. Khammam	Area Hospital,	Bhadrachalam, Khammam, 507111	08743-232455
73. Nalgonda	Dist. Head Qrts. Hospital,	Nalgonda, 508001	08682-232350
74. Nalgonda	Area Hospital,	Suryapet, Nalgonda, 508213	08684-220059

75.	Nalgonda	Area Hospital,	Nagarjunasagar Nalgonda	08680-276570
76.	Nalgonda	Area Hospital,	Miryalaguda, Nalgonda, 508207	08689-262050
77.	Nalgonda	Area Hospital,	Bhongir, Nalgonda, 508116	08685-242535
78.	Hyderabad	Gandhi Medical College,	Department of Microbiology, Hyderabad, 500003	040-23226221, 27502856
79.	Hyderabad	Osmania Medical College,	Department of Microbiology Hyderabad, 500012	040-24656992
80.	Hyderabad	Institute of Preventive Medicine,	Narayanaguda, Hyderabad, 500143	040-27567892, 27567893
81.	Hyderabad	Govt. General and Chest Hospital,	Hyderabad, 500038	040-23814424 23814939
82.	Hyderabad	Area Hospital,	Vanasthalipuram, Hyderabad, 500070	040-24240593
83.	Hyderabad	Area Hospital,	Nampally, Hyderabad, 508373	040-23214424
84.	Hyderabad	Area Hospital,	Malakpet, Hyderabad 500036	040-24527320
85.	Hyderabad	Dist. Head Quarters Hospital,	King Koti, Hyderabad, 500095	040-24753474 24752086
86.	Hyderabad	Area Hospital,Golconda	Hyderabad, 500008	040-23513776
87.	Ranga Reddy	Dist. Head Quarter Hospital,	Tandur, Ranga Reddy, 501141	08411-272700
88.	Ranga Reddy	Area Hospital,	Kondapur, Ranga Reddy, 502110	

Ahmedabad

Sl. No.	*Voluntary Counselling and Testing Centers*	*Address*	*Phone/E-mail/Fax*
1.	V.S. Gen. Hospital	Ellisbridge, Ahmedabad.-6	079-6577621/622/623 vshospad1@sancharnet.in
2.	New Civil Gen. Hospital	Asarwa, Ahmedabad-16	079-2683721/73/742
3.	L.G. Gen. Hospital	Maninagar, Ahmedabad-8	079-5461380/1384
4.	SCL Gen. Hospital	Saraspur, Ahmedabad-18	079-2164261/4264

Andaman and Nicobar Islands

Sl. No.	*District*	*Name of the VCT Centre*	*Address Contact Person/ Phone/Fax No./E-mail*
1.	Andaman	G.B. Pant Hospital Port Blair-744104 Dr. R. Thulasi Dasan,	230628, 236555, 237941, 231176 (Fax)
2.	Andaman	CHC Medical Officer I/C	Rangat-744205 274241, 274242(Fax)

3. Andaman	Dr. R.P. Hospital Medical Officer I/C	Mayabunder-744204 273215, 273999 (Fax)
4. Andaman	CHC Medical Officer I/C	Digilipur-744202 272244, 272236 (Fax)
5. Andaman	PHC Medical Officer I/C	Hutbay-744207 284209, 284209 (Fax)
6. Nicobar	B.J.R. Hospital Medical Superintendent	Car Nicobar-744301 265280, 265234 (Fax)
7. Nicobar	CHC Medical Officer I/C	Nancowrie-744303 263221, 263242 (Fax)
8. Nicobar	PHC Medical Officer I/C	Katchal-744304 262335, 262335 (Fax)
9. Nocobar	PHC Medical Officer I/C	Campbell Bay-744302 264214, 264214 (Fax)

Arunachal Pradesh

Sl. No.	*District*	*Name of the VCT Centre*	*Contact Person/ Address*	*Phone No.*
1.	Papum Pare	General Hospital	Dr. S. Tawsik, Pathologist, Naharlagun, Pin: 791110	0360-1097
2.	East Siang	General Hospital	Dr. B. Apum, Microbiologist, Pasigha-791102	0368-2222249
3.	Lohit	District Hospital	Dr. S. Chai Pul, Medical Officer, Tezu Lohit-792001	03804-1097
4.	West Kameng	District Hospital	Dr. T.C. Khrime, Bomdil, West Kameng-790001	03782-2222174

Assam

Sl. No.	*District*	*Name of the VCT Centres*	*Address*	*Phone/Fax*
1.	Guwahati	Gauhati Medical College Hospital,	P.O. Bhangagarh, Indrapur, Guwahati 781005	0361-2460014 0361-2529457
2.	Nalbari	Nalbari Civil Hospital	P.O. Nalbari-781335	03624-22305
3.	Dhubri	Dhubri Civil Hospital	P.O. Dhubri-783301	03665-230011
4.	Goalpara	Goalpara Civil Hospital,	P.O Goalpara-783101	03663-243800
5.	Nagaon	B.P Civil Hospital,	P.O. Nagaon-782002	03672-233931
6.	Jorhat	Jana Nayak Debeswar Sarma Civil Hospital,	P.O Jorhat-785001	0376-2372283
7.	Dibrugarh	Assam Medical College Hospital,	P.O. Assam Medical College-786002	0373-2301613 0373-2300088
8.	Karimganj	Karimganj Civil Hospital	P.O. Karimganj-788710	03843-62565
9.	Cachar	Silchar Medical College Hospital,	P.O. Ghungur-788014	03842-241712 03842-233000
10.	N.C. Hills	Haflong Civil Hospital	P.O: Haflong-788819	03673-236555

11.	Karbi-Anglong	Diphu Civil Hospitals,	P.O. Diphu-782460	03671-272437
12.	Lakhimpur	North Lakhimpur Civil Hospital.	P.O. North Lakhimpur 787001	03752-244114
13.	Dhemaji	Dhemaji Civil Hospital Blood Bank,	P.O. Dhemaji-787057 037532-24252	
14	Sonitpur	Kanak Lata Civil Hospital Blood Bank,	P.O. Tezpur-784001	03712-221494
15	Golaghat	Kushal Konwar Civil Hospital .	P.O. Golaghat-788710	0376-2480505, 248037

Bihar

Sl. No.	*District*	*Name of the Voluntary Counselling and Testing Centres*	*Address*	*Phone No. Fax/Email*
1.	Patna	Patna Medical College,	Ashok Rajpath, Patna Pin-800004	0612-2300343
2.	Patna	Nalanda Medical College Hospital,	Agamkuan, Patna Pin-800007	0612-2631159
3.	Patna	Rajendra Memorial Research Inst. of Med. Sciences,	Agamkuan, Patna-800007	0612-2645465
4.	Patna	Indira Gandhi Institute of Medical Sciences,	Sheikhpura, Patna-800014	0612-2287631/ Fax-2287225
5.	Patna	Kurji Holy Family Hospital,	Sadaquat Ashram, Patna, Pin-800010	0612-2262540
6.	Rohtas	Sadar Hospital,	Sasaram, Dt. Rohtas-821115	06184-222039
7.	Bhojpur (Ara)	Sadar Hospital,	Ara, Dt. Bhojpur-802231	06182-224737
8.	Kaimur Bhabua	Lok Nayak Jay Prakash Narain,	Mohania-821109	06189-233250
9.	Gaya	Anugrah Narain Magadh Medical College,	Gaya-823001	0631-2241407
10.	Gaya	Pilgrim Hospital	Gaya Pin-823001	0631-2220303
11.	Aurangabad	Sadar Hospital,	Aurangabad 824101	06186-223183
12.	Jahanabad	Sadar Hospital,	Jahanabad Pin-804408	06114-222426
13.	Muzaffarpur	Srikrishna Medical College,	Umanagar, Muzaffarpur 842004	0621-2220866
14.	Muzaffarpur	Sadar Hospital,	Muzaffarpur Pin-842001	0621-2249113
15.	Vaishali	Sadar Hospital,	Hajipur, Dt. Vaishali-844101	06224-2261742
16.	East Champaran (Motihari)	Duncan Hospital,	Raxaul Dist. East Champaran Pin Code-845305	06255-220653
17.	East Champaran (Motihari)	Indian Red Cross Society,	Hospital Road, Motihari-845401	06252-222711
18.	East Champaran (Motihari)	Sadar Hospital,	Motihari, Dt. East Champaran Pin-845401	06252-235372

19.	West Champaran (Bettiah)	M.J.K. Hospital,	Bettiah, Pin-845438	06254-232278
20.	Sitamarhi	Sadar Hospital,	Sitamarhi Pin-843301	06226-257375
21.	Bhagalpur	Jawahar Lal Nehru Medical College,	Bhagalpur-812001	0641-2401078
22.	Darbhanga	Darbhanga Medical College	Laherisarai, Darbhanga-846003	06272-233228
23.	Samastipur	Sadar Hospital,	Samastipur Pin-848101	06274-220484
24.	Saran	Sadar Hospital,	Chapra-841301	06152-228377
25.	Siwan	Sadar Hospital,	Siwan, Dt. Siwan Pin-841226	06154-222782
26.	Gopalganj	Sadar Hospital,	Gopalganj Pin Code-841428	06156-224685
27.	Munger	Sadar Hospital,	Munger- Pin-811201	06344-222213
28.	Begusarai	Sadar Hospital,	Begusrai, Dt. Begusarai-851101	06243-245512
29.	Saharsa	Sadar Hospital,	Saharsa, Dt-Saharsa Pin-852201	06478-223431
30.	Supaul	Sadar Sub-Divisional Hospital,	Supaul-852131	061473-224073
31.	Purnea	Sadar Hospital,	Purnea Pin-854301	06454-222965
32.	Araria	Sadar Hospital,	Araria Pin-854311	06453-222171
33.	Kishanganj	Sadar Hospital,	Kishanganj, Dt. Kishanganj-855107	06456-222966
34.	Katihar	Indian Red Cross Bhawan,	Katihar, Dt. Katihar. Pin-854105	06452-222583

Chandigarh

Sl. No.	*Name of The VCT centre*	*Address*
1.	Department of Immunopathology, Sector-12, PGIMER, City-Chandigarh District-U.T. Pin Code-160012	STD Code-0172 Phone-747585, Ext. 6088, 5191,5192 Fax No. 0172-744401,745078 Email ID-immuno@emmtel.com
2.	Department of. Microbiology, Government Medical College and Hospital, Sector-32 B, City-Chandigarh District-U.T. Pin Code-160030	STD Code-0172 Phone-665252-59,Ext-1060/1061 Fax No. 0172-609360, E-Mail ID-mailto:jchander@cha.191.net
3.	Microbiology Department, Pathology Lab General Hospital, Sector-16 City-Chandigarh District-U.T. Pin Code-160016	STD Code-0172 Phone-768311 Fax No. 780781

Chattisgarh

Sl. No.	District	Name of VCT Centres	Address	Phone/Fax
1.	Raipur	J.N. Medical College,	Jail Road Raipur 492001	0771-2525602
2.	Durg	District Hospital	Durg, 491001	0788-2322808
3.	Rajgaon	District Hospital Rajnandgaon,	Basant Pure, 491441	07744-223587
4.	Bilaspur	Sardar Patel District Hospital,	Bilaspur, Gol Bazar Road, 495001	07752-230910
5.	Raigarh	District Hospital	Sarangarh Road, 496001	07762-222979
6.	Surguja	District Hospital	Surguja, 497001	07774-220070
7.	Jagdalpur	Maharani District Hospital	Jagdalpur, 494001	07782-222367 07782-222281
8.	Kanker	District Hospital	Kanker, 494834	07868-241036
9.	Korba	District Hospital	Korba, 495684	07759-221044 07759-226766

Chennai

Sl. No.	Zone No.	Address	Contact Person Name and Phone No.
1.	Chennai	Stanley Medl. College, Chennai 600001	Dr. Shanta, Prof. of Immunology, 91-44-25214941
2.	IandII	Director, Communicable Diseases Hospital, Handiarpet Chennai-600081	Dr. Janartanan, 25952686
3.	III	Medical Officer, 40, Thiruvenkadam Street, Pulianthope, Chennai, 600012	Dr. Larunakaran, 26670476
4.	IV	Medical Officer, 29, United India Nagar, Ayanavaram	Dr. Kalaiselvi, 26449758
5.	V	Medical Officer, 17, Sherfudeen Street, Choolaimedu, Chennai, 600094	Dr. Pushpa, 24802908
6.	VI	Professor STD/AIDS, Govt. Royapettah Hospital, Chennai-600014	Dr. Usman, 28533056 28533051

7.	VII	Medical Officer, 30, Kariyappa Street, Purasaiwakkam, Chennai-600007	Dr. Dharini, 26422106
8.	VIII	Medical Officer, 4, Sivagnanam Road, T. Nagar, Chennai-600017	Dr. D. Sita, 24342300
9.	IX	Medical Officer, 51, Jeenis Road, Saidapet, Chennai-600015	24358465
10.	X	Medical Officer, 2, Venkatarathinam Street, Adyar, Chennai-600020	Dr. Vijayachamundeswari, 24413427
11.	Chennai	Department of Microbiology, Madaras Medical College, Chennai and Govt. General Hospital, Chennai-600003	Dr. Shameem Banu, 25363131/43

Dadra and Nagar Haveli

Sl. No.	*Name of the VCT Centre*	*Address*
1.	Shri. Vinobha Bhave Civil Hospital	DNH, 396230

Daman and Diu

Sl. No.	*Name of the VCT Centre*	*Address*
1.	Government Hospital Campus	Marward, 369210

Delhi

Sl. No.	*District*	*Name of the VCT Centres*	*Address*	*Name of Incharge*	*Phone No.*
1.	North	National Institute of Communicable Diseases (NICD)	Department of Microbiology, Dt.-22, Sham Nath Marg Dist.: North Delhi-110054	Dr. Usha Baweja	011-23934517
2.	East	Lal Bahadur Shastri Hospital	Department of Microbiology, Lal Bahadur Shastri Hospital, Khicripur, Delhi	Dr. Sunita Upadhyaya	91-11-2774145-46
3.	New Delhi	NDMC Poly Clinic	Department of Microbiology, Shaheed Bhagat Singh Marg-110001	Dr. Ravindra Verma	011-23362882
4.	South	Safdarjung Hospital	VCTC, Regional STD Teaching, Training and Research Centre, 5th Floor (C-Wing), New OPD Complex, Ring Road, New Delhi-110029	Dr. Krishna Ray	011-26196740

5.	South West	AFTC (Armed Forces Transfusion Center)	Department of Microbiology, Delhi Cantt, 110010	Col. P.S. Dhot 011-25666145
6.	South	All India Institute of Medical Science	Department of Microbiology, Ansari Nagar, Ring Road, New Delhi 110029	Dr. Pradeep Seth 011-26593288
7.	Central	Lady Harding Medical Collage and S.K. Hospital	Panchkuian Road, 110001	Dr. Geeta Mehta 011-23363728
8.	Central	Maulana Azad Medical College	Bahadur Shah Zafar Marg 110002	Dr. V.K. Sharma 011-23239272
9.	North East	University College of Medical Science	Shahdara 110095	Dr. V.G. Rama Chandran 011-2582971-72, 73
10.	North	RBTB Hospital	Kingsway Camp, Delhi	Dr. Praveen Kumar 011-27113491
11.	West	Guru Govind Singh Hospital	Room No. 17 Raghubir Nagar, New Delhi	Dr. B.B. Kachru 011-25114548, 25114532
12.	North-west	Ambedkar Hospital	Room No. 1034 Sector-6 Rohini	Dr. Soma Roy 011-27055585
13.	New Delhi	G.L. Maternity Hospital	Azmari Gate	Dr. Jyotsna Malik 011-23232224
14.	West	Deen Dayal Upadhya Hospital	Hari Nagar	Dr. Anupama 011-25494328
15.	West	Hindu Rao Hospital	G Block, IIIrd floor, Malkaganj	Dr. Sanjay Jain
16.	South	Lala Ram Sarup Institute of Tubercolosis and Respiratory Diseases	Sri Aurobindo Marg (Near Qutab Minar) 110030	Dr. Sushil Munjal 011-26854922, 26854929
17.	New Delhi	Dr. Ram Manohar Lohia Hospital	Baba Kadak Singh Marg, New Delhi-110001	Dr. Charu Haus 011-23365525
18.	North	Kasturba Hospital	Jama Masjid 110006	Dr. Pushpa Bhatia 011-23275022

Gujarat

Sl. No.	*District*	*Name of VCT Centres*	*Address*	*Phone/Fax*
1.	Ahmedabad	B.J. Medical College,	C/O—Medical Superintendent, B.J. Medical College, Asarwa, Civil Campus, Ahmedabad-16	079-2683721, 2681379, Fax :2683067
2.	Ahmedabad	V.S. General Hospital,	C/O—Medical Superintendent V.S. General Hospital, Ellisbridge, Ahmedabad	079-6577621-25
3.	Surat	New Civil Hospital,	C/O—Medical Superintendent, New Civil Hospital, Out side Majura gate, Surat	0261-3479311, Fax : 3479175

4. Baroda	S.S.G Hospital,	C/O—Medical Superintendent, S.S.G Hospital, Baroda	0265-24248[illegible]48, 2421594
5. Jamnagar	Guru Govind Singh Hospital, Bedi Road, Jamnagar	C/O—Medical Superintendent, Guru Govindsing Hospital, Bedi Road, Jamnagar	0288-2553[illegible]15, 2554629 Fax: 2221 5
6. Bhavnagar	Sir. T. Hospital,	C/O—Medical Superitendent, Sir. T. Hospital, Bhavnagar	0278-2423[illegible]50 Fax : 24[illegible]2011, 2432883
7. Rajkot	Civil Hospital and Govt. Medical College,	C/O—Medical Superintendent Civil Hospital and Govt. Medical College, Rajkot	0281-2479[illegible]15
8. Valsad	General Hospital,	C/O—Chief District Medical Officer-*Cum*-Civil Surgeon General Hospital, Valsad	02632-251[illegible]11, 251046, 251019
9. Navsari	General Hospital,	C/O—Chief District Medical Officer-Cum-Civil Surgeon General Hospital, Navsari	02637-257[illegible]01, Fax : 25[illegible]265
10. Bharuch	General Hospital,	C/O—Chief District Medical Officer-Cum-Civil Surgeon General Hospital, Bharuch	02642-241[illegible]59, 243515 Fax : 24[illegible]17559
11. Panchmahal	General Hospital,	C/O—Chief District Medical Officer-Cum-Civil Surgeon General Hospital, Godhra, Dist. Panchmahal	02673-242[illegible]559 Fax : 2[illegible]2559
12. Banaskantha	General Hospital,	C/O—Chief District Medical Officer-Cum-Civil Surgeon General Hospital, Palanpur, Dist. Banaskantha	02742-26[illegible]083
13. Mehsana	General Hospital,	C/O—Chief District Medical Officer-Cum-Civil Surgeon General Hospital, Mehsana	02662-25[illegible]217 Fax : 2[illegible]1784
14. Sabarkantha	General Hospital,	C/O—Chief District Medical Officer-Cum-Civil Surgeon General Hospital, Himmatnagar, Dist. Sabarkantha	02772-24[illegible]1892, 246618 Fax : 2[illegible]18
15. Surendranagar	General Hospital,	C/O—Chief District Medical Officer-Cum-Civil Surgeon, General Hospital, Surendranagar	02752-2[illegible]2052 Fax : [illegible]34815
16. Porbandar	General Hospital,	C/O—Chief District Medical Officer-Cum-Civil Surgeon, General Hospital, Porbandar	0286-22–2910
17. Junagadh	General Hospital,	Voluntary Counselling and Testing Centers, C/O—Chief District Medical Officer-Cum-Civil Surgeon, General Hospital, Junagadh	0285-26[illegible]0090 Fax : [illegible]651436
18. Nadiad	General Hospital,	C/O—Chief District Medical Officer-Cum-Civil Surgeon, General Hospital, Nadiad Fax : 255210	0268-2[illegible]10744

19.	Patan	General Hospital,	C/O—Chief District Medical Officer-Cum—Civil Surgeon, Patan	02766-233311 Fax : 233055
20.	Gandhinagar	General Hospital,	C/O—Chief District Medical Officer-Cum-Civil Surgeon, General Hospital, Gandhinagar	079-3221931, 3221932 Fax : 3222733
21.	Gandhinagar	Civil Hospital,	C/O—Chief District Medical Officer-Cum-Civil Surgeon, Civil Hospital, Gandhinagar Sarkhej Highway Road, Nr. Gujarat High Court, Sola, Ahmedabad	079-7474359, 7474355 Fax : 7474355
22.	Gandhinagar	General Hospital,	C/O—Chief District Medical Officer-Cum-Civil Surgeon, General Hospital, Nr. Bus Stand, Amreli	02792-222587, 223416 Fax : 222115
23.	Vadodara	Jamnabai General Hospital,	C/O—Chief District Medical Officer-Cum-Civil Surgeon, Jamnabai General Hospital, Vadodara	0265-2517400,
24.	Anand	General Hospital,	C/O—Chief District Medical Officer-Cum-Civil Surgeon, General Hospital, Petlad, Dist. : Anand	02697-224645, 224722
25.	Dahod	General Hospital,	C/O—Chief District Medical Officer-Cum-Civil Surgeon, General Hospital, Dahod	02673-230548
26.	Dahod	General Hospital,	C/O—Chief District Medical Officer-Cum-Civil Surgeon, General Hospital, Rajpipla, Dist.- Narmada	02640-222163
27.	Surat	Old Civil Hospital,	C/O—Chief District Medical Officer-Cum-Civil Surgeon, Old Civil Hospital, Surat	0261-3479311
28.	Dang	General Hospital,	C/O—Chief District Medical Officer-Cum-Civil Surgeon, General Hospital, Ahwa, Dist. Dang	02632-220205 Fax : 220294
29.	Jamnagar	General Hospital,	C/O—Chief District Medical Officer-Cum-Civil Surgeon, General Hospital, Jamkhambhalia, Dist. Jamnagar	02833-234704
30.	Rajkot	P.K. General Hospital,	C/O—Chief District Medical Officer-Cum-Civil Surgeon, P.K. General Hospital, Rajkot	02822-230203, 2227136
31.	Kutch	G.K. General Hospital,	C/O—Chief District Medical Officer-Cum-Civil Surgeon, G.K. General Hospital, Bhuj, Dist. Kutch	02832-250150 Fax : 250150

Goa

Sl. No.	*District*	*Name of VCT Centres*	*Address*	*Contact person*	*Phone/Fax*
1.	Goa	Goa Medical College	Department of Microbiology, Bambolim, Tiswadi 403202	(Dr. Savio Rodrigues)	2458712/3 Ext. 2220
2.		Hospicio Hospital	Margao, Goa 403601	(Dr. N.V. Markande)	2705754/ 2705664

Haryana

Sl. No.	Name of the VCT Centre	Address
1.	General Hospital,	Faridabad
2.	General Hospital,	Gurgaon
3.	General Hospital,	Hissar
4.	General Hospital,	Karnal, 132001
5.	General Hospital,	Sector-6, 134109
6.	Pt. B.D.S.P.G.I.M.S.	Rohtak, 124001

Himachal Pradesh

Sl. No.	District	Name of the VCT Centre	Address/Pin Code	Phone
1.	Bilaspur	Zonal Hospital, (Dr. M.L. Gupta)	Bilaspur-174001	01978-224979
2.	Hamirpur	Zonal Hospital, (Dr. K.C. Kaushal)	Hamirpur-177001	01972-222223
3.	Kangra	Zonal Hospital, (Dr. Kuldeep Sharma)	Dharamsala, Kangra-176215	01892-224874
4.	Mandi	Zonal Hospital, (Dr. Hemant Kapoor)	Mandi-175001	01905-222177
5.	Shimla	IGMC Shimla (Dept. of Microbiology), (Dr. Vijay Kumar Sharma)	Shimla-171001	0177-2883313
6.	Kullu	Zonal Hospital, (Dr. Sat Parkash)	Kullu-175101	01902-223068
7.	Kinnaur	Zonal Hospital, (Dr. Ajit)	Kalpa, Dist. Kinnaur-171107	01786-222213
8.	Sirmour	Zonal Hospital, (Dr. Sanjay Sharma)	Nahan, Sirmour-173001	01702-222526
9.	Solan	Zonal Hospital, (Dr. Bhupinder Bhardwaj)	Solan-173212	01792-221099
10.	Chamba	Zonal Hospital, (Dr. Ram Kamal)	Chamba-176310	01899-222223

Jharkhand

Sl. No.	Name of the VCT Centre	Address	Phone No.
1.	Rajendra Institute of Medical Science (RIMS)	Bariatu, Dist. Ranchi	
2.	MGM Medical College,	Jamshedpur	
3.	Patliputra Medical College and Hospital	Dhanbad	0326-2204730

Jammu and Kashmir

S. No.	Name of the VCT Centre	Address	Phone No.
1.	S.M.H.S. Hospital	OPD Complex, S.M.H.S. Hospital, Karan Nagar, Srinagar	0194-2477378
2.	Sher-e-Kashmir Institute of Medical Sciences	OPD Complex, Soura, Srinagar	0194-2400348
3.	Govt. Medical College	OPD Block, Main Entrance, Bakshi Nagar, Jammu	0191-2584290

Kerala

Sl. No.	District	Name of the VCT Centre	Address	Phone No.
1.	Trivandrum	Regional Public Health laboratory	Red Cross Road, Trivandrum 695035	0471-2467438
2.	Eranakulam	Regional Public Health laboratory	Eranakulam 68201	0484-2361932
3.	Palakkad	District Hospital	Palakkad 678001	0491-233327
4.	Kozhikode	Dept. of Microbiology, Medical College	Kozhikod 673008	0495-2356530

Karnataka

Sl. No.	District	Name of the VCT Centre	Address	Phone No.
1.	Bangalore (Urban)	Dept. of Neurovirology, National Institute of Mental Health and Neuro Sciences,	Hosur Road, Bangalore	080-6995126, 6995128, 6564830/6562121
2.	Bangalore (Urban)	Dept. of Mircrobiology, Victoria Hospital/Bangalore, Medical College,	City Market, Bangalore	080-6701950/ 6705031, 6703267 (fax)- Dept. of Microbiology, 6704342 (fax)- Principal
3.	Chitradurga	District Hospital,	Chitradurga,	08194-434710/ 435464, 434710 (Telefax)
4.	Davangere	C.G. Hospital,	Davangere,	08192-259610/ 259050, 259610/233743
5.	Kolar	S.N.C. Hospital,	Kolar ,	958152- 222035 (Telefax)
6.	Shimoga	Mc. Gann Hospital,	Shimoga,	0-8182-271566
7.	Tumkur	District Hospital,	Tumkur,	095816-257404, Fax:257404 (Telefax)
8.	Mysore	Sri Vivekananda Memorial Trust Hospital, Saragur,	H D Kote Tq, Mysore Dt.	095821-245877, 433898 (Fax) 095821-563192/ 563845 Extn.354
9.	Mysore	Dept. of Microbiology, Govt. Medical College,	Mysore-4,	Off: 520512, Fax: 520803
10.	Mysore	Dept. of Microbiology, JSS Hospital	Ramanuja Road, Mysore	91-821-447928, 563843, 563845

11. Mandya	The District Surgeon, District Hospital,	Mandya	0958232-224040 (Telefax)
12. Mangalore	Kasturba Medical College Hospital, Attavar	Mangalore, Dakshina Kannada District.	0824-421771/ 428379 Fax:428379/ 442946, EPABX: 445858, Mobile: 98451 49368
13. Chickmagalur	M.G. Hospital,	Chickmagalur	08262-235213/ 234876/231163, 91-8262220329
14. Chamarajanagar	District Hospital,	Chamarajanagar	0821-722067/ 724197 Mobile: 94480 61950
15. Coorg District.	District Hospital,	Kodagu (Madikeri)	08272-223442/ 223444, 223445 (D.S)
16. Hassan	SC Hospital,	Hassan,	0958172-250330 (Telefax)
17. Belgaum	District Hospital,	Belgaum,	0831-420173 (Telefax),420320
18. Bagalkot	District Hospital,	Navnagar, Bagalkot	08354-420444/ 436261, 436260 (Telefax)
19. Bagalkot	Sub-Divisional Hospital,	Jamkhandi Taluk,	08350-320066/ 320068
20. Bagalkot	KEM General Hospital,	Mudhol Taluk, Bagalkot District	08350-380038
21. Bijapur	District Hospital,	Bijapur,	08352-270173/ 270009 (Telefax)
22. Dharwad	District Hospital,	Dharwad,	0836-278606, 373724 (fax) Director: 278097 (fax) Principal-741277 (fax)
23. Dharwad	Dept. of Microbiology, Karnataka Institute of Medical Sciences (KIMS)	Hubli,	0836-278606, 373724-(Fax) Director-370057- Ext. 279, 278097- Principal(Fax) 278095 (Fax) 370745-(Resi.)
24. Gadag	District Hospital,	Gadag,	0836-530933 (Telefax) Hospital, 521496 (Resi), Mobile: 94480 27296

25. Haveri	District Hospital,	Haveri,	0836-832222, 853360 (Telefax)
26. Karwar,	District Hospital,	Uttara Kannada (Karwar)	08382-226319 (Hospital), 226731
27. Gulbarga	District Hospital,	Gulbarga,	08472-421922, 438768 (Resi.)
28. Koppal	District Hospital,	Koppal,	0853-430444/ 430626 (Telefax)
29. Bidar	District Hospital,	Bidar,	08482-225474/ Fax: 225474
30. Raichur	District Hospital,	Raichur,	08532-235855, 91-8392-235201/ 235202, Fax: 235201
31. Bellary	Dept. of Microbiology, Vijayanagar Institute of Medical Sciences,	Bellary	Mobile: d9448073965, 235288 (Dir)

Manipur

Sl. No. *District*	*Name of the VCT Centre*	*Address*	*Phone No.*
1. Imphal West	RIMS	Lamphelpat, Imphal 795004	0385-2301629/ 2310411/2310750
2. Imphal West	Telephone Counselling Meitei Leimarol Sinaisang	Khoyathong, Imphal	795001 0385-2413836
3. Imphal East	J.N. Hospital	Porompat, Imphal	795001 0385-2223516
4. Bishnupur	District Hospital	Bishnupur	795126
5. Churachandpur	District Hospital	Churachandpur	795128
6. Thoubal	District Hospital	Thoubal	795138
7. Tamenglong	District Hospital	Tamenglong	795141
8. Senapati	District Hospital	Senapati	795106
9. Ukhrul	District Hospital	Ukhrul	795143

Mizoram

Sl. No. *District*	*Name of the VCT Centre*	*Address*
1. Aizawi	Civil Hospital Aizawi	P.O Aizawi-796001
2. Lunglei	Civil Hospital Lunglei	P.O Lunglei-796701
3. Champhai	Civil Hospital Champha	P.O Lunglei, Champhai-796321
4. Aizawi	Presbyterian Hospital Civil Hospital Durtlang	P.O Durtlang, Aizawi-796025
5. Kolasib	Civil Hospital Kolasib	P.O Kolasib-796061

6. Serchhip	Civil Hospital Serchhip	P.O Serchhip-796181
7. Chhimtuipui	Civil Hospital Saiha	P.O. Saiha, Chhimtuipui-796901
8. Mamit	Civil Hospital Mamit	P.O. Mamit-796441

Tamilnadu

Sl. No.	*District*	*Name of the VCT Centres*	*Address*	*Phone No.*
1.	Chennai	Madras Medical College	Chennai 600003	044-25392889
2.	Chennai	Stanley Medical College	Chennai 600001	044-25214941
3.	Chennai	Siddha Medical College	Chennai 600106	044-26281563
4.	Chennai	National Institute of Epideomiology Chetpet	Chennai 600031	09265425-8265403
5.	Chennai	Govt. Hospital for Thoracic Medicine	Tambaram Sanatorium, Chennai 600047	044-2368899
6.	Chennai	Coimbatore Medical College Hospital	Cimbatore 641018	0422-2300871
7.	Chennai	Govt..Head Qrs. Hospital	Tiruppur 641601	0421-2421201
8.	Cuddalore	Govt. Head Qrts..Hospita,	Cuddalore 607001	04142-220058
9.	Dharmapuri	Govt. Head Qrts. Hospital	Dharmapuri 636701	04342-32852
10.	Dindigul	Govt. Head Qrts. Hospital	Dindigul 624001	04514-30066
11.	Erode	Govt. Head Qrts. Hospital	Erode 638001	0424-258355
12.	Erode	IRT Medical College, Hospital	Perundurai 638052	
13.	Kancheepuram	Govt. Head Quarters Hospital	Kancheepuram 631501	0411-222307
14.	Kancheepuram	Govt. Chengalpattu Medl. College Hospital	Chengalpattu 603001	04114-231909
15.	Thiruvallur	Govt. Head Qrts. Hospital	Thiruvallur 602001	0954116-666620
16.	Vellore	Govt. Medical College Hospital	Vellore 632001	0416-229401
17.	Salem	Govt. MKM College Hospital	Salem 636001	0427-2210964
18.	Salem	Govt. Head Qrts. Hospital	Mettur dam 636401	04298-244046
19.	The Nilgiris	Govt. Head Qrts. Hospital	Ootacamund 643001	0423-442212
20.	Namakkal	Govt. Head Qrts. Hospital	Namakkal 637001	04286-21203

21.	Namakkal	Kolli Hills	Namakkal 637001	04286-21203
22.	Thiruvannamalai	Govt. Head Querters Hospital	Thiuvannamalai 606601	0954175-236080
23.	Villupuram	Government Head Qrts. Hospital	Villupuram 605602	04146-222566
24.	Karur	Government Head Qrts. Hospital	Karur 639001	04324-30280
25.	Perambalur	Government Head Quarters Hospital	Perambalur D-186, 621212	04328-77128
26.	Trichy	KAP Viswanthan Govt. Medical College Hospital	Trichirappalli 620001	0431-771465
27.	Thanjavur	Thanjavur Medl. College	Thanjavur 613001	04362-340854
28.	Kumbakonam	Government Head Qrts. Hospital	Kumbakonam 612001	0435-430002
29.	Thiruvarur	Government Head Qrts. Hospital	Thiruvarur 610001	04366-22354
30.	Nagapattinam	Government Head Qrts. Hospital	Nagapattinam 611001	04365-42379
31.	Pudukkottai	Govt. Head Qrts. Hospital	Pudukkottai 622001	04322-421775
32.	Madurai	Madurai Medical College Hospital	Madurai 625001	
33.	Madurai	Govt. Hqrs. Hospital	Usilampatti 625532	04552-53334
34.	Sivagangai	Government Headquarters Hospital	Sivagangai 630561	04575-4040
35.	Theni	Govt. Headquarters Hospital	Theni	04546-42600
36.	Virudhunagar	Govt. Hqrs. Hospital	Virudhunagar 626001	04562-344722
37.	Ramanathapuram	Govt. Hqrs. Hl.	Ramanathapuram 623501	04567-20340
38.	Thoothukudi	Govt. Medl. College Hospital	Thoothukudi 628001	0461-2321051
39.	Thoothukudi	Government Head Qrs. Hospital	Koilpatti 628501	04632-20040
40.	Tirunelveli	Tirunelveli Medical College Hospital	Tirunelveli 627001	0462-2572911
41.	Tenkasi	Govt. Head Qrs. Hospital	Tenkasi 627811	04633-22309
42.	Palayamkottai	Siddha Medl. College	Palayamkottai 627002	
43.	Kanyakumari	Govt. Head Qrs. Hospital	Nagercoil 629001	04562-245176/ 244158

Maharashtra

Sl. No.	Division	Name of the VCT Centre	Contact Person/ Incharge VCTC	Telephone Number
1.	Thane	Civil Surgeon, Civil Hospital, Thane	Dr. S.S. Mohanalkar	(022) 25471409
2.	Thane	Civil Surgeon, Civil Hospital, Raigad	Dr. Sonavane	(95214) 222667
3.	Thane	Civil Surgeon, Civil Hospital, Ratnagiri	Dr. S.T. Wandule	(02352) 223206
4.	Thane	Indira Gandhi Hospital, Bhiwandi	Dr. Sontakke,	(952522)-256186
5.	Thane	Navi Mumbai Municipal Corporation	Dr. Pattiwar,	(022) 27573028
6.	Thane	Kalyan Dombivali Municipal Corporation	Dr. Borvankar,	(95251) 2204304
7.	Nasik	Civil Surgeon, Civil Hospital, Nasik.	Dr. P.J. Bardapurkar	(95253) 2576368
8.	Nasik	Dean, Bhausaheb Hire G.M. College, Dhule	Dr. Mrs. M.N. Dravid	(02562) 239407
9.	Nasik	Civil Surgeon, Civil Hospital, Nandurbar	Dr. J.D. Borse	(02564) 226225
10.	Nasik	Civil Surgeon, Civil Hospital, Jalgaon.	Dr. Nitin Bharambe	(0257) 2226611
11.	Nasik	Civil Surgeon, Civil Hospital, Ahmednagar.	Dr. P.P. Pargaonkar	(95241) 2430785
12.	Nasik	Rural Hospital, Malegaon.	Dr. R.B. Sonavane	(0255)-2417151
13.	Pune	Dean, BJMC, Pune.	Dr. A.V. Bhore	(9520) 6128000/ 6126010
14.	Pune	Commandant, AFMC, Pune.	Lt. Col. A.K. Sahni	(9520) 2673290/ 26306037/38
15.	Pune	Civil Surgeon, Civil Hospital, Satara.	Dr. Kodre	(952162) 230051
16.	Pune	Dean, Dr. VMMC Solapur.	Dr. Kannale	(0217) 2319448
17.	Pune	Chest Hospital Aundh, Pune.	Dr. Ulhas Jadhav, Superintendent	(9520) 7280603/ 7280237
18.	Pune	Cottage Hospital, Karad.	Dr. Pawar, Medical Superintendent	(02162)-221020
19.	Pune	Rural Hospital, Pandharpur.	Dr. S.N. Padalkar, MO	(02186)-223181
20.	Pune	Pimpri Chinchwad Municipal Corporation.	Dr. Iyer, Medical Director	(9520) 7477777
21.	Kolhapur	Civil Surgeon, CPR, Kolhapur	Dr. S.V. Salokhe	(0231) 2644233
22.	Kolhapur	Dean, GMC, Miraj, Sangli.	Dr. Mrs. Vanita Kulkarni	(0233) 2231959
23.	Kolhapur	Civil Surgeon, Civil Hospital, Sindhudurg.	Dr. Sanjay Sawant	(02362) 228900
24.	Kolhapur	Rural Hospital, Ichalkaranji.	Dr. Vivekanand Patil	(0230) 2420311/ 2420312
25.	Kolhapur	Rural Hospital, Islampur.	Dr. Shedge	(915) 223158
26.	Aurangabad	Dean, GMC, Aurangabad.	Dr. Rajesh Karyakarte	(0240) 2402028
27.	Aurangabad	Civil Surgeon, Civil Hospital, Parbhani.	Dr. R.R. Kulkarni	(02452) 220182
28.	Aurangabad	Civil Surgeon, Civil Hospital, Jalna.	Dr. J.G. Matsawar	(02482) 224381
29.	Aurangabad	Civil Surgeon, Civil Hospital, Hingoli.	Dr. D.L. Gaikwad	(02456) 223086
30.	Aurangabad	Rural Hospital, Vaijapur.	Dr. M.L. Dongalikar	
31.	Latur	Civil Surgeon, Civil Hospital, Latur.	Dr. S.A. Sudke	(02382) 249183
32.	Latur	Dean, SRTR MC, Ambejogai.	Dr. A.N. Bagate	(02446) 247060
33.	Latur	Dean, GMC, Nanded.	Dr. Sanjay More	(02462) 234118
34.	Latur	Civil Surgeon, Civil Hospital, Osmanabad.	Dr. A.D. Diwan	(02472) 234118

35.	Latur	Civil Surgeon, Civil Hospital, Beed.	Dr. S.V. Mukhare	(02442) 222618
36.	Latur	Rural Hospital, Udgir.	Dr. Patil, MD Medicine	(02385) 256336
37.	Akola	Civil Surgeon, Civil Hospital, Akola.	Dr. K.B. Gadhave	(0724) 2434918
38.	Akola	Civil Surgeon, Civil Hospital, Amravati.	Dr. A.S. Pimpalkhare	(0721) 2663340
39.	Akola	Civil Surgeon, Civil Hospital, Buldhana	Dr. K.D. Rathi	(07262) 242423
40.	Akola	Dean, GMC, Yavatmal.	Dr. K.V. Ingole	(07232) 242456
41.	Akola	Civil Surgeon, Civil Hospital, Washim.	Dr. U.B. Jadhav	(07252) 235720
42.	Nagpur	Dean, GMC, Nagpur.	Dr. R.P. Fule	(0712) 2743588
43.	Nagpur	Dean, IGMC, Nagpur.	Dr. S.V. Jalgaonkar	(0712) 2725274
44.	Nagpur	Civil Surgeon, Civil Hospital, Chandrapur.	Dr. A.K. Hazarey	(07172) 253992
45.	Nagpur	Civil Surgeon, Civil Hospital, Wardha.	Dr. B.A. Dongre	(07152) 243895
46.	Nagpur	Civil Surgeon, Civil Hospital, Bhandara	Dr. Ku. Shaila Maidamwar	(07184) 252532
47.	Nagpur	Civil Surgeon, Civil Hospital, Gadchiroli	Dr. Suvarna Hubekar	(07132) 233320
48.	Nagpur	Civil Surgeon, Civil Hospital, Gondia.	Dr. K.K. Tripathi	(07182) 221495
49.	Nagpur	Rural Hospital, Kamathi.	Dr. D.K. Gedam	
50.	Nagpur	Rural Hospital, Warora.	Dr. Baraputre, MO	(07176) 281370

Madhya Pradesh

Sl. No.	*District*	*Name of the VCTC*
1.	Barwani	District Hospital, Barwani
2.	Balaghat	Near CMHO Office, Balaghat
3.	Betul	District Hospital, Betul
4.	Bhind	District Hospital, Bhind
5.	Bhopal	Department of Microbiology, Gandhi Medical College, Bhopal
6.	Chhatarpur	District Hospital
7.	Chhindwara	District Hospital, Chhindwara
8.	Damoh	District Hospital, Damoh
9.	Datia	District Hospital
10.	Dewas	District Hospital, Dewas
11.	Dhar	District Hospital, Dhar
12.	Dindori	District Hospital
13.	Guna	District Hospital, Guna
14.	Gwalior	Department of Microbiology, G.R. Medical College, Gwalior
15.	Harda	District Hospital
16.	Hoshangabad	District Hospital, Hoshangabad
17.	Indore	Department of Microbiology, M.G.M. Medical College, Indore
18.	Indore	Department of Microbiology, Choithram Hospital and Research Centre, Manik Bagh Road, Indore
19.	Jabalpur	R.M.R.C. Jabalpur, RMRC Complex, Garha, Nagpur Road, Jabalpur
20.	Jabalpur	Department of Microbiology, N.S.C.B. Medical College, Jabalpur
21.	Jhabua	District Hospital, Jhabua
22.	Katni	District Hospital

23. Khandwa	District Hospital, Khandwa
24. Khargone	District Hospital, Khargone
25. Mandla	District Hospital, Mandla
26. Mandsour	District Hospital, Mandsaur
27. Morena	District Hospital
28. Narsinghpur	District Hospital
29. Neemcuh	District Hospital, Neemuch
30. Panna	District Hospital
31. Raisen	District Hospital, Raisen
32. Rajgarh	District Hospital, Rajgarh (Biaora)
33. Ratlam	District Hospital
34. Rewa	Department of Microbiology, S.S. Medical College, Rewa
35. Sagar	District Hospital, Sagar
36. Shahdol	District Hospital, Shahdol
37. Satna	District Hospital, Satna
38. Sehore	District Hospital, Sehore
39. Seoni	District Hospital, Seoni
40. Shajapur	District Hospital, Shajapur
41. Sheopur	District Hospital
42. Shivpuri	District Hospital, Shivpuri
43. Sidhi	District Hospital
44. Tikamgarh	District Hospital
45. Ujjain	T.B. Hospital, Ujjain
46. Umaria	District Hospital
47. Vidisha	District Hospital

Mumbai

Sl. No.	*Name of the VCT Centre*	*Address*	*Phone No.*
1.	J.J. Hospital,	Near Skin and VD Dept., Byculla, Mumbai-400008.	23735555 Ext.2351/ 2276
2.	B.Y.L. Nair Hospital	3rd Floor, Dept. of Microbiology, Bombay Central, Mumbai-400008	23081490/99 Ext. 151
3.	STD Clinic Ground Floor	Belasis Road, Opp. Alexandra Cinema, Nagpada, Mumbai-400008.	23007643/ 23074216
4.	Savera Counselling Centre, Cell of AIDS Research Action and Training (CARAT) TISS	17, Old OPD, Ground Floor, Shatabdi Hospital, Govandi, Mumbai-400088.	25563289 Ext. 322
5.	Rajawadi Hospital	Ground Floor, OPD No. 4 Ghatkopar (E), Mumbai-400077	25115066/ 25094149/53 Ext.133
6.	Dr. R.N. Cooper Hospital,	Ground Floor, OPD No..17A, North South Road No. 1, Juhu-Vileparle (W), Mumbai-400056	2620 7254/5892 Ext. 325.
7.	G.T. Hospital	2nd Floor, CST, Mumbai-400 001.	2262 1467/65/64/66 Ext. 352/351
8.	V.N. Desai Hospital	1st floor Room No. 34, 11th Rd., Golibar Rd., Opp. Roof Talki, Santacruz (E), Mumbai-400 055.	26182081/26183018

9. K.B. Bhabha Hospital	1st Floor OPD No. 102, Bandra (W), Mumbai-400 050.	26422541/42 Ext. 4206.
10. K.M.J. Phule Hospital,	Ground Flr, Pathology Dept., Room No. 18 Kannamwar Nagar No. 2, Vikhroli (E), Mumbai-400 083.	2578 2253
11. S.V.D. Savarkar Mun. Hospital,	Mahatma Phule Rd. Mulund, Mumbai 400 081.	2568 6225
12. St. George's Hospital	Near G.P.O., Dr. P. D'Mello Rd., CST, Mumbai-400 001.	
13. Shatabdi Hospital,	Ground Floor, Dept..of Obstetrics and Gynaecology, Govandi, Mumbai 400088	5564069-71
14. ESIS Hospital,	Worli, Mumbai	
15. M.W. Desai Mun. Gen. Hospital	Haji Bapu Road, Malad (E), Mumbai-400097	
16. KEM Hospital, Dept. of Microbiology	5th Floor, Multistoreyed Building, Parel, Mumbai-400 012.	2413 6051/1763 Ext. 2525
17. Lokmanya Tilak Municipal General Hospital	4th Floor, Dept. of Microbiology, Sion, Mumbai-400022.	24076381/82-89 Ext. 329/340
18. The Humsafar Trust	Old BMC Building, 2nd floor, Nehru Rd., Vakola, Santacruz (E), Mumbai-400 055	26187476
19. Sarvodaya Hospital	O.P.D.Room No..12,Rifle Range, L.B.S. Marg, Ghatkopar (W), Mumbai-400 086	25152237/2332 Ext. 230
20. Siddhartha Nagar Hospital	1st Floor, Room No. 112, Goregaon (W), Mumbai-400104.	2876 6886/5
21. Kasturba Hospital	Pathology Dept. Sane Guruji Marg,. Arthur Road, Mumbai-400 011	23083901/4 Ext. 239
22. Group of TB Hospitals	P.F.L. Dept., Room No. 10, Sewree, Mumbai-400 015.	2414 6993 Ext. 523
23. H. Bhagawati Hospital	O.P.D. No. 5, Tulsi Baug, S.V.P. Road, Borivali (W), Mumbai-400 092.	28932461/62/63 Ext. 409
24. K.B. Bhabha Hospital	Ground Floor, OPD No. 35 Kurla (W), Mumbai-400070.	26500241/26503145 Ext. 245
25. Sant Muktabai Mun. Gen. Hospital,	Dept. of Obstetrics and Gynecology Barve Nagar, Ghatkopar (W), Mumbai-400 084.	25126088/2515 3771
26. Oshiwara Maternity Home	Ajit Glass Lane, Near Oshiwara Dumping Ground, Jogeshwai (W), Mumbai-400 102.	26781443
27. Cama and Albless Hospital	Mahanagar Palika Marg, CST, Mumbai-400001	
28. K.J. Somaiya Medical College	Dept. of Obstetrics and Gynecology, Somaiya Ayurvihar Complex, Eastern Highway, Sion, Mumbai-400022	
29. LandT Hospital		

Meghalaya

Sl. No.	Dist.	Name of the VCT Centre	Address	Phone No.
1.	Shillong	VCTC Shillong Civil Hospital	E.K. Hills	0364-2223889/ 2224100

Pondicherry

Sl. No.	District	Name of the VCT Centre	Address	Phone No.
1.	Odiansalai	The microbiologist I/C Voluntary Counsellind and Testing Centre	Anna Square Odiansalai 605001	0413-2221144
2.	Pondicherry	The Medical Officer I/C, Voluntary Counselling and Testing Centre, Dept. of Microbiology, JIPMR	Gorimedu, Pondicherry 605006	0143-2272380
3.	Karaikal	The Medical Officer I/C, Voluntary Counselling and Testing Centre, Govt. General Hospital	Kamaraj Salai, Karaikal	04368-222450 609602

Punjab

Sl. No.	Name of VCTC and Address	Name of the Area/Street	District/ Pin code	Telephone No. Office	Residence
1.	Dr. Mrs. Aruna Aggarwal, Professor and Head, (I/C VCTC) Microbiology Deptt., Govt. Medical College, Amritsar	Majitha Road	Amritsar-143001	0183-2426353 0183-242630 2426918 (PBX)	220090 506699
2.	Dr. (Mrs.) Amarjit Kaur Gill, Professor and Head, (I/C VCTC) Microbiology Deptt., Govt. Medical College, Patiala.	Sangrur Road	Patiala-147001	0175-5000125	200795
3.	Dr. P.K. Jain, Professor and Head, (I/C VCTC) Microbiology Deptt., Govt. Medical College, Faridkot.	Sadhik Road	Faridkot-151203 Near Central Jail	9815578061 (M)	254187
4.	Dr. Davinder S. Bhimbra, I/C VCTC, Civil Hospital, Jalandhar	G.T. Road	Jalandhar-144001	0181-2460822	98141-18345(M)
5.	Dr. Chaman Lal, I/C VCTC, Civil Hospital, Kapurthala.	Sultan Road	Kapurthala-144601	01822-231237	98143-19206(M)
6.	Dr. Khem Raj Bansal, I/C VCTC, Civil Hospital, Bathinda.	Mansa Road Opposite Police Line	Bathinda-151001	0164-2212221	2252831
7.	Dr. Ravinder Pal Kaur, I/C VCTC, Civil Hospital, Ropar.	Baila Chowk	Ropar-142001	01881-221141	0172-65103

8. Dr. Surinder Pal Kataria, I/C VCTC, Civil Hospital, Ferozepur.	Near Housing Board Colony	Ferozepur-152002	246761 (t.w. CH.) 2422964 (PP SMO Office)	220987
9. Dr. Jasbir Singh I/C VCTC, Civil Hospital, Ludhiana.	Near Old Jail	Ludhiana-	0161-665003 0161-665874 0161-643577	0161-2451597
10. Dr. Meena Mahajan I/C VCTC, Civil Hospital, Gurdaspur	G.T. Road	Gurdaspur-145321	01874-240025 01874-232153	01874-246221 98141-26799(M)
11. Dr. Jasbir Singh, I/C VCTC, Civil Hospital, Sangrur	Barnala Kanchiana Dhuri Road	Sangrur-161605	01672-2200113	01672-89374
12. Dr. A.K. Sood I/C VCTC, Civil Hospital, Hoshiarpur	Jallandhar Road	Hoshiarpur-143001	01882-250700	01882-221647
13. Dr. APS Gill, I/C VCTC, Civil Hospital, Moga	Main Bazar	Moga-142001	229221 283012	98140-36869(M)

Uttaranchal

Sl. No.	*District*	*Name of the VCT Centre*	*Address*	*Phone/Fax*
1.	Dehradun	District Hospital	Dehradun.	0135-2659355
2.	Dehradun	Himalayan Institute Hospital Trust	Swami Ramnagar Jolly Grant, Dehradun	0135-2412081
3.	Almora	District Hospital	Almora	05962-236558
4.	Champawar	Community Health Centre	Lohaghat, Champawar	05965-222312
5.	Pauri	District Hospital	Pauri	01368-23102
6.	Chamoli.	Dsitrict Hospital	Gopeswar, Chamoli.	01372-52245
7.	Tehri.	Suman Hospital	Narendra Nagar, Tehri	01376-32093
8.	Pithoragarh	District Hospital	Pithoragarh	05964-25687
9.	Udham Singh Nagar	J.L.N. District Hospital	Rudrapur	05944-241422
10.	Uttarkashi.	District Hospital	Uttarkashi	01374-22103
11.	Haridwar	Har Milap Govt., District Hospital	Haridwar	01334-222210
12.	Nainital	S.S.J.Bose Hospiatl	Haldwani, Nainital	04946-251088

West Bengal

Sl. No.	*District*	*Name of VCC Centre*	*Address*	*Phone*	*Name of the Contact Person*
1.	Bankura	Bankura Sammilani Med. College and Hospital	PO: + D: Bankura		Prakriti Ranjan Bandopadhyay 03242-240550
2.	Kolkatta	Calcutta Medical College			Debarati Chatterjee 2577-1673

3.	Kolkata	Nil Ratan Sarkar Med. College,	133A PC Rd. Kolkata-14,	Dr. Krishna Roy 033-2244 3213	Aparna Majumdar 25283390, 25578051
4.	Kolkata	R. G. Kar Medical College,	Kolkata		Tanusree Rakshit 25303274
5.	Kolkata	Calcutta National Medical College and Hospital,	24, G.C Rd., Kolkata-700014		Surabhi Chakraborty 25421167/8015
6.	Kolkata	S.S.K.M. Hospital	Ajc Bose Rd., Kolkata-700020	Dr. D · Roy 033-22239735 (F) 222333	Debasmita De 26538179, 38992919
7.	Kolkata	M.R. Bangur Hospital	Deshpran Sasmal Road, Kolkata-33,	Dr. Tapas Chakraborty 033-24901188 Dr. Nivedita Basu 033-24786419 Dr. Bhupali Saha 033-24410598	Sangita Kundu 23353178
8.	Kolkata	School of Tropical Medicine			Anurita Mukherjee 25715646
9.	Darjeeling	Darjeeling District	Dr. A K Mukherjee	0354 2256790	Rita Sharma
10.	Darjeeling	North Bengal Med. College Hospital (Regional)	Shsrutnagar, Darjeeling	Dr. Mrinmoy Das 053-2585225/ 2551342 Dr. U. Dutta (M) 09434121152	Sampa Sarkar 0353-253092
11.		BHR District Hospital			Kakoli Mondal 03482-230351
12.	Purulia	District Hospital	Dr. Gautam Ghosh	03252-222474	Dr. Siba Kr. Patra
13.	Durgapur	Durgapur	Dr. Chhabi Nandi	(O)0343-2537163 ® 0343-537168	Dr. Meghnath Mondal 0342-2716019
14.	Burdwan	Burdwan Medical College		Dr. Tamal Ghosh 558641-43 Extn 228,0342-2563915/ 2566486/2565228	Jugabrata Majumder 03463-255475
15.	Suri	Suri District Hospital		Dr. B B Gupta 03462 55483 ® 03462 55834	Nityananda Roy 03463-264661
16.	Suri	District Hospital	MDP		Shukla Mukherjee 03222-274512
17.	Krishna-nagar	Krishnanagar District Hospital	Krishnanagar Kumar Huri	Dr. Swapan 0347252872 Extn 219	Paulavi Majumder

18. Malda	Malda District Hospital	District Hospital	Dr. Manilal Das 035122221427	Arup Mukherjee

Tripura

Sl. No.	District	Name of VCT Centres	Address	Phone/Fax
1.	Agartala	G.B. Hospital	Agartala, PO Kunjaban, Tripura West	91-381-2353112 (Telefax) GB PBX-2356388 2355512, Extn.-430

Lakshadweep

Sl. No.	Name of the VCT Centre	Address
1.	I.G. Hospital	Kavaratti, Lakshdweep 682555
2.	Govt. Hospital	Minicoy, Lakshadweep 682559

Sikkim

Sl. No.	District	Name of the VCT Centre	Address	Phone/Fax No.
1.	Gangtok	STNM Hospital	Gangtok, East Sikkim	03592-228104
2.	Singtam	District Hospital	Singtam, East Sikkim	03592-233645/233757
3.	Namchi	District Hospital	Namchi, South Sikkim	91-3595-263849

Orissa

Sl. No.	Name of the VCT Centre	Contact Person	Address
1.	S.C.B. Medical College	Prof. and HOD, Microbiology Dept.	P.O. and Dist.: Cuttack
2.	V.S.S. Medical College	Prof. and HOD, Microbiology Dept.	P.O.: Burla Dist.: Sambalpur
3.	M.K.C.G. Medical College	Prof. and HOD, Microbiology Dept.	P.O.: Berhampur, Dist.: Ganjam
4.	District Head Quarters Hospital	Chief District Medical Officer	P.O. and Dist.: Balasore
5.	Capital Hospital,	Chief Medical Officer	P.O.: Bhubaneswar, Dist.: Khorda
6.	District Head Quarters Hospital	Chief District Medical Officer	P.O. and Dist.: Bolangir
7.	District Head Quarters Hospital	Chief District Medical Officer	P.O. and Dist.: Koraput
8.	District Head Quarters Hospital	Chief District Medical Officer	P.O. and Dist.: Puri
9.	District Head Quarters Hospital	Chief District Medical Officer	P.O. and Dist.: Sundargarh
10.	District Head Quarters Hospital	Chief District Medical Officer	P.O. and Dist.: Jharsuguda

11.	District Head Quarters Hospital	Chief District Medical Officer	P.O. and Dist.: Angul
12.	District Head Quarters Hospital	Chief District Medical Officer	P.O. and Dist.: Bhadrak
13.	District Head Quarters Hospital	Chief District Medical Officer	P.O. and Dist.: Jajpur
14.	District Head Quarters Hospital	Chief District Medical Officer	P.O. and Dist.: Phulbani
15.	District Head Quarters Hospital	Chief District Medical Officer	P.O. and Dist.: Nuapada
16.	District Head Quarters Hospital	Chief District Medical Officer	P.O. and Dist.: Rayagada
17.	District Head Quarters Hospital	Chief District Medical Officer	P.O. and Dist.: Sambalpur
18.	Government Hospital	Chief Medical Officer	P.O.: Rourkela Dist.: Sungergarh
19.	District Head Quarters Hospital	Chief District Medical Officer	P.O.: City Hospital, Berhampur, Dist.: Ganjam
20.	District Head Quarters Hospital	Chief District Medical Officer	P.O. and Dist.: Kendrapara

Uttar Pradesh

Sl. No.	*District*	*Name of the VCT Centre*	*VCTC Incharge*	*Phone/Fax No./E-mail* *Office*	*Residence*
1.	Agra	Deptt. of Microbiology, S.N. Medical College	Dr. B.M. Aggarwal	0562-2260353	0562-2210888(R) 9837074933
2.	Agra	Dept. of Immunology, Cenrtral Jalma Institute for Leprosy	Dr. T. Hussain	0562-2331751-4 Ext: 214, 287 0562-2331755 (Fax)	0562-2231143 tahziba-hussainjalma @zybenway. comtahziba-hussain@ hotmail.com
3.	Agra	Dept. of Pathology, District Hospital	Dr. R.C. Joshi		0562-2264487
4.	Mainpuri	Dept. of Pathology, District Hospital	Dr. P.K. Shukla	05672-234252	05672-234932
5.	Mathura	Major Blood Bank	Dr. R.K. Chaturvedi	0565-2502078	0565-2424135
6.	Etah	Dept. of Pathology, District Hospital	Dr. Arun Upadhyaya		05742-233865
7.	Ferozabad	Dept. of Pathology, District Hospital	Dr. S.C. Gupta	05612-244245	05612-258158
8.	Aligarh	Dept. of Microbiology, J.N.Medical College	Dr. Abida Maloik	0571-2700731	0571-2701388
9.	Aligarh	Dept. of Pathology, District Hospital	Dr. Saheed Mohammed	0571-252338	0571-2523338
10.	Allahabad	Dept. of Pathology, K.N.M. Trust Hospital	Dr. J.K. Gupta	0532-2466672 0532-2466673 (fax)	
11.	Allahabad	Dept. of Microbiology,	Dr. Anudita Bhargava	0532-600882	

11.	Allahabad	Dept. of Microbiology, M.L.N. Medical College	Dr. Anudita Bhargava	0532-600882	
12.	Fatehpur	Dept. of Pathology, District Hospital	Dr. B.K. Sharma	05172-224788	
13.	Pratapgarh	Dept. of Pathology, District Hospital	Dr. Dilip Kumar	05342-220666	05342-222738
14.	Etawah	Dept. of Pathology, District Hospital	Dr. S.K. Agarwal	05688-255526	
15.	Kanpur	Dept. of Pathology, G.S.V.M. Medical College	Dr. A.K. Gupata	0512-2214215	0512-2294175
16.	Kanpur Nagar	Dept. of Pathology, District Hospital	Dr. U.K. Srivastava	0512-2311144	0512-2214920
17.	Farrukha-bad	Dept. of Pathology, District Hospital	Dr. P.K. Gupta	05692-240256	05692-240282
18.	Faizabad	Dept. of Pathology, District Hospital	Dr. N.K. Mehrotra	0527-225225	0527-220329
19.	Sultanpur	Dept. of Pathology, District Hospital	Dr. C.P. Tewari	0536-222241	0536-223510
20.	Barabanki	Dept. of Pathology, District Hospital	Dr. I.S. Srivastava	05248-223602	
21.	Ambedkar Nagar	Dept. of Pathology, Combined Hospital	Dr. Ram Dhirendra	05271-244545	
22.	Gorakhpur	Major Blood Bank, District Hospital	Dr. R.S. Mishra	0551-2202898/ 0551-2202898 Fax	
23.	Deoria	Dept. of Pathology, District Hospital	Dr. S.C. Singh		05568-221891
24.	Kushi Nagar	Dept. of Pathology, Male and Eye Hospital	Dr. G.K. Barnwal		05564-242542
25.	Maharaj-ganj	Community Health Centre	Dr. P. Kanosia	05523-222081	05523-223464
26.	Jalaun (Orai)	Dept. of Pathology, District Hospital	Dr. Mohini Saxena	05162-252203	
27.	Jhansi	Dept. of Microbiology, M.L.B. Medical College	Dr. R.K. Agarwal	0517-2320858	0517-2320640
28.	Jhansi	Dept. of Pathology, District Hospital	Dr. Satyandra Kumar	0517-2444183	0517-2320552
29.	Lalitpur	Dept. of Pathology, District Hospital	Dr. M.K. Chowdhury	05176-272343	
30.	Banda	Dept. of Pathology, District Hospital	Dr. S.K. Bajpai	0519-286597	0519-285750
31.	Hamipur	Dept. of Pathology, District Hospital	Dr. V.K. Srivastava	05282-222055	
32.	Mahoba	Dept. of Pathology, District Hospital	Dr. M.S. Rajput	05281-244202	

33.	Hardoi	Dept. of Pathology, District Hospital	Dr. Ravindra Singh	05852-234713	05852-220120
34.	Lakhimpur-Kheri	Dept. of Pathology, District Hospital	Dr. Ram Nath	05872-252903	
35.	Lucknow	Deptt. Microbiology, C.S.M. Medical College	Dr. S.K. Agarwal	0522-2257569	0522-2255571
36.	Sitapur	Dept. of Pathology, District Hospital	Dr. Ashwani Kumar	05862-242217	
37.	Unnao	Dept. of Pathology, District Hospital	Dr. Sanjeev Ahuja	0515-2823900	
38.	Rae Barelly	Dept. of Pathology, District Hospital	Dr. T.N. Puri	0535-2202101	0535-2203636
39.	Gautam Nagar	National Institute of Biologicals	Dr. C. Sokhey	0118-2400015-17 0118-4587089	0118-26413503 nbindia@now-india.net.in j_sokhey@hotmail.com
40.	Meerut	Deptt. of Microbiology, L.L.R.M. Medical College	Dr. Anil Agarwal	0121-2760888 0121-2760666 (fax) 0121-2760444	
41.	Bulandshar	Dept. of Pathology, District Hospital	Dr. D.P .Baidhya	05732-254633	
42.	Ghaziabad	Dept. of Pathology, District Hospital	Dr. Chiranjee Lal	0120-4730038	0575-2730038
43.	Meerut	Dept. of Pathology, District Hospital	Dr. G.D. Goel	0121-2531147	0121-2526474
44.	Gautam Buddha Nagar	Dept. of Pathology, District Hospital	Dr. Daya Prakash	0120-2456174	0120-26413504
45.	Bagpat	Dept. of Pathology, Community Health Centre	Dr. Ram Gopal Verma		0120-2220886 0120-2221961
46.	Muzaffar Nagar	Dept. of Pathology, District Hospital	Dr. Vipin Chandra Gupta		0131-2440509
47.	Sharanpur	Dept. of Pathology, District Hospital	Dr. D.C. Saxena	0132-2725408	0132-2723636, derix@sancharnet.in
48.	Barelly	Major Blood Bank	Dr. N.K. Jhingran	0581-2550009	
49.	Badaun	Dept. of Pathology, District Hospital	Dr. Neeta Chandel	05832-224613	
50.	Shahjahan-pur	Major Blood Bank	Dr. R.C. Ashthana	05492-240209, 05482-240209(fax)	05482-225583
51.	Pilihbhit	Dept. of Pathology, District Hospital	Dr. Yogendra Singh	05882-255874	05882-252758
52.	Bijnore	Dept. of Pathology, District Hospital	Dr. Narendra Kumar	01342-63279	
53.	Morada-bad	Dept. of Pathology, District Hospital	Dr. (Mrs). Nutan Khare	0591-2419225	0591-2435728
54.	Rampur	Dept. of Pathology, District Hospital	Dr. R.S. Saini	0595-2324689	0595-2342040

55.	Ghazipur	Dept. of Pathology, District Hospital	Dr. Balram Thakur	0548-2220231	0548-2222993
56.	Jaunpur	Dept. of Pathology, District Hospital	Dr. M.K. Mallik	05452-269102	
57.	Varanasi	Dept. of Microbiology, L.M.S, B.H.U	Dr. A.K. Gulati	0542-2307516 0542-2367568(Fax) akgulati@banaras.ernet.in	0542-2318540
58.	Varanasi	Dept. of Pathology, District Hospital	Dr. Y.N. Pande	0542-2214723	
59.	Chandauli	Dept. of Pathology, District Hospital	Dr. V.K. Verma	05412-262164	05412-2222
60.	Azamgarh	Dept. of Pathology, District Hospital	Dr. Surendra Mishra	05462-265172	05462-265287
61.	Ballia	Major Blood Bank	Dr. S.N. Sinha	05494-220420	05494-220970
62.	Mau	Dept. of Pathology, District Hospital	Dr. Ashok Kumar	0547-2220875	0547-2227578
63.	Mirzapur	Dept. of Pathology, District Hospital	Dr. K.K. Jain	05442-252795	05442-252498
64.	Sonbhadra	Dept. of Pathology, District Hospital	Dr. A.K. Singh	05444-223352	05444-222558
65.	Sant Ravidas Nagar (Vadohi)	Dept. of Pathology, District Hospital	Dr. S.N. Gupta		05414-2369424
66.	Basti	Dept. of Pathology, District Hospital	Dr. R.B. Singh	05542-283773	05542-282111
67.	Siddharth Nagar	Dept. of Pathology, District Hospital	Dr. Jai Prakash Singh	05542-222011	
68.	Baharaich	Dept. of Pathology, District Hospital	Dr. R.S. Mishra	05252-232000	05252-235722
69.	Gonda	Dept. of Pathology, District Hospital	Dr. S.K. Kapoor	05262-222355	05262-224846
70.	Balaram-pur	District Hospital	Dr. Deepak Kumar	05263-232024	05263-234662

Nagaland

Sl. No.	*Name of the VCT Centres*	*Address*	*Phone No.*
1.	Naga Hospital Kohima	Kohima-797001	(0370)2222916
2.	Civil Hospital Dimapur	Dimapur-797112	(03862) 227444
3.	Civil Hospital Mokokchung	Mokokchung-798601	(0369) 2226216
4.	Civil Hospital, Tuensang	Tuensang-798612	(03861) 20320
5.	Civil Hospital, Zunheboto	Zunheboto-798620	(03867) 220344
6.	Civil Hospital, Phek	Phek-797168	(03865) 223115
7.	Civil Hospital, Wokha	Wokha-797111	(03860) 222255
8.	Civil Hospital, Mon	Mon-798621	(03869) 221360
9.	Impur Christian, Hospital	Impur-798615 Mokokchung	226220

Sl. No.	*Name of the VCT Centre*	*Address*
1.	J.L.N Medical College	Ajmer
2.	S.P.M.C.	Bikaner
3	S.M.S. Medical College	Jaipur
4	Dr. S.N. Medical College	Jodhpur
5	M.B.S. Medical College	Kota
6	R.N.T. Medical College	Udaipur

Bibliography

Anita, N.B. and Bhatia, Kavita, Peoples Health in People's Hand-A model for Panchayati Raj, FRCH, Mumbai. 1993.

Basch, P.E., Vaccines and World Health, New York, Oxford University Press, 1994.

Bhatnagar, S. and Goel, S.L., Development Planning and Administration. New Delhi. Deep & Deep Publications (P) Ltd., 1992.

Bhattacharjee P.J. and G.N. Shashtri, Population in India, A Study of Interstate Variation, New Delhi, Vikas, 1976.

Bosh, Ashish, From Population to People, Delhi, B.R. Publication, 1988.

Brown, Esther, Newer Dimensions of Patient Care, Russell Sage Foundation, New York, 1961.

Cartwright, A., Patients and their Doctors, A Study of General Practice, Routledge Kegan Paul, London, 1961.

Chanawongse Krasal, Rural Development Management, Research and Development Institute, Khon Kaen University, Thailand.

Chandra, R.C., A Geography of Population, Concepts, Determinants and Patterns, New Delhi, Kalyani, 1987.

Chauhan, Devraj, Anaita, N.H. and Ramdan, Sangita, Healthcare in India: A Profile, FRCH, Mumhai, 1996.

Das, K., Civil Service Reforms and Structural Adjustment, Oxford, Delhi 1998.

Duggal, R., Nandaraj, S. and Shetty, Sahana, State Sector Health Expenditure-A Database All India, FRCH, Mumbai, 1992.

P. Jurfelds, G. and Lindbergs, Pills against Poverty—A Study of Introduction of Western Medicine in a Tamil Village, Curzon Press, London, 1975.

FRCH, Panchayati Raj Information Resource Book, Mumbai, 1996.

Ghai, Sandhaya, Bursing Services Administration: A Case Study of Nehru Hospital, PGI, Chandigarh (Doctoral Thesis, Panjab University, 1998).

Ghosh, Brindra Nath, A Treatise on Hygiene and Public Health, Scientific Publishing Company, 1970, Calcutta.

Gill, Sonya, Health Status of the Indian People, FRCH, Mumbai, 1987.

Goel, S.L., Healthcare Administration Policy-making and Planning, Sterling, Delhi, 1981.

———, Healthcare Administration Levels and Aspects, Sterling, Delhi, 1981.

Goel, S.L., Healthcare Administration Ecology, Principles and Modern Trends, Sterling, Delhi, 1981.

———, Family Planning Programme and Beyond, New Delhi, Deep & Deep Publications Pvt. Ltd., New Delhi, 1990.

———, International Administration: WHO, South-East Asia Regional Office, Sterling, New Delhi, 1977.

———, Modern Management Techniques, Deep & Deep Publications Pvt. Ltd., New Delhi, 1987.

———, Public Health Administration, Sterline, New Delhi, 1984.

———, Public Personnel Administration, Sterling, New Delhi, 1984.

———, Hospital Administration and Management, Deep & Deep Publications Pvt. Ltd., New Delhi, 1903.

———, Distance Education in 21st Century, Deep & Deep Publications Pvt. Ltd., New Delhi, 2000.

Hanlon, John, Principles of Public Health Administration, C.V. Mobsy, Sthouis, 1969.

ICSSR & ICMR, Health for All-an Alternative Strategy—Report of a Study Group set-up Jointly by ICSSR & ICMR, Pune, Indian Institute of Education, 1981.

Govt. of India, Annual Reports of the Ministry of Health and Family Welfare, Delhi.

———, Committee on Multi-purpose Workers under Health and Family Welfare Programme (Kartar Singh Report), Delhi, Ministry of Health and Family Welfare, Delhi, 1973.

———, Govt. of India, Health in Independent India (G. Borkar Report), Delhi, 1961.

———, Health Survey and Development Committee (Bhore Committee), Delhi, 1946.

———, Lok Sabha Secretariat, Estimates Committees and Public Accounts Committees Reports.

———, Planning Commission, Five Year Plans, New Delhi.

———, Report of Health Survey and Planning Committee, (Mudaliar Committee) Ministry of Health, August-October, 1961.

———, Ministry of Information and Broadcasting, India, 1999, A Refresher Manual, New Delhi, 1999.

———, Initiatives and Best Practices of Government of India for Effective and Responsive Administration, New Delhi, Ministry of Personnel, Public Grievances, and Pensions, 1997.

———, Deptt. of Family Welfare, Reproductive and Child Health (World Bank Component), Vols. I and II, New Delhi, 1997.

———, Report of the Working Group on Health for All by 2000 A.D., New Delhi Ministry of Health and Welfare, 1981.

Gunaratne Herat, V.T., Challenges and Response Health in South-East Asia Region, New Delhi, McGraw Hill, 1977.

Hardon, A., et. al., Monitoring Family Planning and Reproductive Rights, A Manual for Empowerment, London, Zed Books, 1997.
Indian Society of Health Administrators, Bangalore.

Annual Conference Reports

Health for all by 2000 (AD 1980).
The Role of Hospitals in Healthcare (1981).
Health Manpower Requirements for 2000 (1982).
Role of the Health Administrator in India (1983).
On Growing Needs of Urban Health Management (1985).
Cost Reduction in Hospitals and Healthcare (1986).
Health of the High Risk Groups Mothers, Children and Elderly (1985).
Health of Women and Children for Development (1988).
Healthcare for the Villages and Urban Slums (1989-90).
Health of the Youth and the Female Child.
Role of Voluntary Organizations in Healthcare in India (1992).

Books

Stress and Health of Executives and Professionals.
Hospital and Health Administration.
Modern Technology for Hospitals and Healthcare.
Management for Nursing Administrators.
Community Participation in Health and Family Welfare-Indian Experiences.
Health of the Metropolis-Bangalore-A Guide to Health Planning and Development of Urban Cities in India.
Leadership and Human Resources Development for Healthcare.
Managerial Effectiveness for Organizational Excellence.
Computer Applications to Hospitals, Healthcare and Medical Education.
Health and Development of the Tribal People in India-A Guide for Professionals and Administrators.
Retirement Planning, Adjustment and Health.
Janovsky, K., Health Policy and Systems Development on Agenda for Research, WHO/SHS/NHP/96.1, Geneva, 1996.
Jesani, Amar & Ganguly, Shilpi, Some Issues in Community Participation in Health Services, FRCH, Mumbai, 1993.
Khandewale, Shreekant V., Health Administration and the Weaker Sections in an Indian Metropolis, Devika Publications, Delhi, 1996.
Klinoboul Krienkrai, Health and Family Welfare Administration in Thailand—A Case Study of Lampang Province (Doctoral Thesis).
Kumar, R., Child Development in India, Ashish, New Delhi, 1988.
———, Environment Pollution and Health Hazards in India, Ashish, New Delhi (Year not mentioned).
———, Youth Health, Problem, Planning and Development, Deep and Deep Publications Pvt. Ltd., New Delhi, 1986.
Lane, S.D., From Population Control to Reproductive Health: An Emerging Policy Agenda, Social Science and Medicine, 1994.

Lush, L., Integrating Services, from Rhetroic to Action, Development Research Insights, 1997.

Mattoo, P.K., Project Formulation in Developing Countries, Macmillan, Delhi, 1978.

Meher, C. Nanavaty and P.D. Kulkarni, NGO's in the Changing Scenario, New Delhi, Uppal, 1998.

Miller, George E. and Tamas Fulop, Educational Strategies for the Health Professionals, Geneva, WHO, 1974.

Mishra, R.P., Medical Geography of India, NBT, Delhi, 1970.

Murray, C.J.L., Lopez, A.D., The Global Burden of Diseases, WHO, Geneva, Switzerland, 1996.

Myrdal Gunnar, Asian Drama, An Enquiry into the Poverty of Nations, Vol. III, Penguis, London, 1968.

Naik, J.P., An Alternative System of Healthcare Service in India Some Proposals, Allied, Bombay, 1988.

National Institute of Health and Family Welfare, New Delhi

Management Training Modules for District Health Offices.

Management Training Modules for Health Offices.

Management Training Modules for Health Assistants (Male and Female).

Management Training Modules for Health Workers (Male and Female).

Management Training Modules for TBA.

Management Training Modules for Health Guide.

Park, J.E. and K. Park (1990), Textbook on Preventive and Social Medicine, Banarasidas Bhanot Publishers, Jabalpur.

Pai Panadiker, V.A., et. al., Organizational Policy for Family Planning, New Delhi, Uppal, 1983.

Pathak, Shankar, Social Welfare, Health and Family Planning in India, Marwah Publications, Delhi, 1979.

Rao, C. Hayavandana, Mysore Gazetteer, Vol. IV, B.R. Publishing Corporation, Delhi, 1984.

Ramanathan, S. (ed.), Landmarks in Karnataka Administration, New Delhi, Uppal, 1998 (Published for Indian Institute of Public Administration, Karnataka, Regional Branch, Bangalore).

Rafei, Dr. Uton M., Primary Healthcare in Changing World South-East Asia Regional Perspectives, WHO Regional Office for South-East Asia, Delhi, India, 1993.

Ranga, R.K., Admn. of Family Planning Programmes in India—A Case Study of Haryana (Doctoral Thesis, Panjab University, 1998).

Rao, V.K.R.V., Food, Nutrition and Poverty in India, Vikas, New Delhi, 1982.

Rifikin, S.B., Health Planning and Community Participation, Crown Helm, London, 1985.

Sahni, Ashok, The Third Force in Healthcare—Voluntary Sector, Bangalore Indian Society of Health Administrators (1992).

Scott-Samuel A., Total Participation, Total Health, Scottish Academic Press, 1990.

Sarjivi, K.S., Planning India's Health, Orient Longman, Delhi, 1971. Shenoi, P.V. (ed.), Contours of Social and Economic Development Political Issues, Concept, New Delhi, 1997.

Sharma, R.D., Advanced Public Administration, New Delhi, H.K. Publishers, 1994.

Singh, Sarabjit, Management Information System in a Hospital—A Case Study of General Hospital, Chandigarh (Doctoral Thesis, Panjab University, 1991).

Taori, Kamal, People's Participation in Sustainable Human Development (A Unified Approach), New Delhi, Concept, 1998.

Vaeth, R.M., A Theory of Medical Ethics, New York, Basic Books, 1981.

Vettivel, S.K., People's Participation in Social Development, Role of NGO, New Delhi, Vetri Publishers, 1992.

World, Health Organisation Alma Ata Revisited, WHO/SHS/CC/ 94.2, WHO, Geneva, 1994.

Werner, D., Where there is No. Doctor?, The Voluntary Health Association of India, Delhi, 1984.

World Bank Financing of Health Services in Developing Countries, Washington, 1987.

World Bank, Development Report, 1993, New York, Oxford University Press.

World Bank, World Development Report, 1997, New York, Oxford University Press, 1997.

World Health Organisation, Annual Report of South-East Asia Regional Office, Delhi, 1997.

———, Bulletin of Regional Health Information, Regional Office for South-East Asia, Delhi, 1980, 1981, 1982, 1983, 1984-85, 1986-87, 1988-90, and 1991-93.

World Health Organization, Collaboration in Health Development in South-East Asia, 1948-88, Fortieth Anniversary Volume (Revised), Delhi, 1992.

———, Community Action for Health, SEA/HSD/185, Regional Office for South-East Asia, Delhi, 1993.

———, Development of Indicator for Monitoring Progress Towards Health for all by the Year 2000, Geneva, 1981.

———, Eighth General Programme of Work—Covering the Period 1990-95, Geneva, 1987.

———, Evaluation of the Strategy for Health for All by the year 2000, Regional Office for South-East Asia, Delhi, 1986.

———, Formulating Strategies for Health for all by the year 2000, Geneva, 1979.

———, Global Strategy for Health for all by the year 2000, Geneva, 1981.

———, Health in Development—Prospects for 21st Century, WHO! DGH/ 94.5, Geneva, 1994.

World Health Organization, Health Situation in the South-East Asia Region, 1991-93, Regional Office for South-East Asia, Delhi, 1995.

———, Implementation of the Global Strategy for Health for All by the year 2000, Second Evaluation, Regional Office for South-East Asia, Delhi, 1993.

———, Inter-sectoral Action for Health in South-East Asia Region, SEA/HSD/107, Regional Office for South-East Asia, Delhi, 1987.

———, Monitoring of Strategies for Health for All by the year 2000, WHO/SEA/RC41/15 Rev. 1, Regional Office for South-East Asia, Delhi, 1988.

———, National Decision-making for Primary Healthcare, Geneva, 1981.

———, New Challenges for Public Health, WHO/HRH/96.4, Geneva, 1996.

———, Ninth General Programme of Work—Covering the Period 1996-2001, Geneva, 1994.

———, Primary Healthcare, Geneva, 1978.

———, Regional Health Report, 1996, Regional Office for South-East Asia, Delhi, 1996.

———, Regional Summary of Progress, Impediments and Further Actions Needed in Implementing National HFA Strategies, WHO/SEA/RC47/20, Regional Office for South-East Asia, Delhi, 1994.

———, Renewing the Health for All Strategy, WHO/PAC/95.1, Geneva, 1995.

———, Report on Monitoring of Progress in Implementing Strategies for Health for All by the year 2000 in the South-East Asia Region, WHO!SEA/RC36/14, Regional Office for South-East Asia, Delhi, 1983.

———, Strategies for Health for All by the year 2000, SEA/HSD/43, Rev. 1, Regional Office for South-East Asia, Delhi, 1983.

———, The World Health Report, 1995, Geneva, 1995.

———, The World Health Report, 1996, Geneva, 1996.

———, The World Health Report 1997, Geneva, 1997.

———, Declaration on Health Development in the South-East Asia Region in the 21st Century, WHO, Delhi, 1997.

———, WHO Quality Assurance in Healthcare, Report of a WHO, Introductory Meeting, Surabaya, Indonesia, 16-20 Dec., 1996, WHO, Delhi.

———, WHO Health Sector Reform, Delhi, 1997.

———, South-East Asia Regional Committee Report, WHO, Delhi, 1997.

———, Sixth Consultative Committee on Organization of Health Systems Based on Primary Healthcare, Geneva, 7-10 November, 1994.

———, Role of Health Centres in the Development of Urban Health Systems, Report of a WHO Study Group on Primary Healthcare in Urban Areas, WHO Technical Report Series, No. 827, 1992, (42 pages).

World Health Organization, Community Involvement in Health Development Challenging Health Services. Report of a WHO Study Group, WHO Technical Report Series, No. 809, 1991 (56 pages).

World Health Organization, Coordinated Health and Human Resources Development. Report of a WHO Study Group, WHO Technical Report Series, No. 801, 1990.

World Health Organization, Health System Decentralization. Concept, Issues and Country Experience, A. Mills, J.P. Vaughan, D.L. Smith, I. Tabibzadehg, eds., 1990.

———, Information support for New Public Health action at district-level, Report of a WHO Expert Committee, WHO Technical Report Series, No. 845, 1994.

———, Strengthening Health Management in districts and provisions. Handbook for facilitators, A. Cassels and K. Janovsky, 1991.

———, Towards a healthy district, Organizing and managing district health systems based on primary healthcare, E. Tarimo, 1991.

———, Integration of Healthcare Delivery, Report of a WHO Study Group, WHO Technical Report Series, No. 861, 1996.

———, Primary Healthcare Reviews, Guidance and Methods, A. El Bindari-Hammad and D.L. Smith, 1992.

———, Health Promotion and Community Action for Health in Developing Countries, H.S. Dhillon and L. Philip, 1994.

———, Achieving Health for All by the year 2000, Midway Reports of Country Experiences, E. Tarimo, A. Creese, eds., (1990).

Young, Paul V., Scientific Social Surveys and Research, Englewood Cliffs, New Jersey, 1966.

Books by the Same Author

1. International Administration: WHO South East-Asia Regional Office, (New Delhi, 1977), Sterling Publishers.
2. Principles, Problems and Prospects of Co-operative Administration, New Delhi (1979), Sterling Publishers, (Co-Author Dr. B.B. Goel).
3. Administration of Personnel in Co-operative, (New Delhi, 1979), Sterling Publishers (Co-Author Dr. B.B. Goel).
4. Health Care Administration: Ecology, Principles and Modern Trends, (New Delhi, 1980), Sterling Publishers.
5. Health Care Administration: Policy-making and Planning (New Delhi, 1980), Sterling Publishers.
6. Health Care Administration: Levels and Aspects, (New Delhi, 1980), Sterling Publishers.
7. International Civil Service: Principles, Problems and Prospects, (New Delhi, 1984), Sterling Publishers.
8. Public Health Administration, (New Delhi, 1984), Sterling Publishers.
9. Public Personnel Administration, (New Delhi, 1984), Reprint 1987, Sterling Publishers.
10. International Civil Services—Principles, Problems and Prospectives, (New Delhi, 1984), Sterling Publishers.
11. Social Welfare Administration, Vols. I and II: Theory and Practice, (New Delhi, 1988), Deep & Deep Publications Pvt. Ltd.
12. Hospital Administration and Management (ed.) Co-Author Dr. R. Kumar in 3 volumes (New Delhi, 1989), Deep & Deep Publications Pvt. Ltd.
13. Policy and Administration: Family Planning & Beyond (New Delhi, 1990), Deep & Deep Publications Pvt. Ltd.
14. Modern Management Techniques, (New Delhi, 1990) Deep & Deep Publications Pvt. Ltd. (Revised & Reprinted).
15. Development Planning and Administration (ed.) S. Bhatnagar (Co-editor), (New Delhi, 1992), Deep & Deep Publications Pvt. Ltd.
16. Financial Administration and Management, (New Delhi, 1993), Sterling Publishers.
17. Advanced Public Administration, (New Delhi, 1993), Sterling Publishers.
18. Personnel Administration and Management, (New Delhi, 1994), Deep & Deep Publications Pvt. Ltd.

19. Educational Policy and Administration, (New Delhi, 1994), Deep & Deep Publications Pvt. Ltd.
20. Slum Improvement Through Participatory Urban Based Community Structures, (New Delhi, 1999), Deep & Deep Publications Pvt. Ltd.
21. Distance Education in 21st Century, (New Delhi, 2000), Deep & Deep Publications Pvt. Ltd.
22. Health Care System and Management: Organization and Structure, (New Delhi, 2000), Deep & Deep Publications Pvt. Ltd.
23. Health Care System and Management: Policies and Programmes (New Delhi, 2000), Deep & Deep Publications Pvt. Ltd.
24. Health Care System and Management: Management and Administration (New Delhi, 2000), Deep & Deep Publications Pvt. Ltd.
25. Heath Care System and Management: Management and Administration, (New Delhi, 2000), Deep & Deep Publications Pvt. Ltd.
26. Management Techniques: Principles and Practices, (New Delhi, 2001), Deep & Deep Publications Pvt. Ltd.
27. Encyclopadeia of Disaster Management in 3 Volumes, (New Delhi, 2001), Deep & Deep Publications Pvt. Ltd.
28. Management of Hospitals: Hospital Core Services, (New Delhi, 2002), Deep & Deep Publications Pvt. Ltd.
29. Management of Hospitals: Hospital Supportive Services, (New Delhi, 2002), Deep & Deep Publications Pvt. Ltd.
30. Management of Hospitals: Hospital Preventive and Promotive Services (New Delhi, 2002), Deep & Deep Publications Pvt. Ltd.
31. Management of Hospitals: Hospital Managerial Services, (New Delhi, 2002), Deep & Deep Publications Pvt. Ltd.
32. Public Personal Administration, (New Delhi, 2002), Deep & Deep Publications Pvt. Ltd.
33. Public Financial Administration, (New Delhi, 2002), Deep & Deep Publications Pvt. Ltd.
34. Urban Development and Management, (New Delhi, 2002), Deep & Deep Publications Pvt. Ltd.
35. Public Administration: Theory and Practices, (New Delhi, 2003), Deep & Deep Publications Pvt. Ltd.
36. Advanced Public Administration, (New Delhi, 2003), Deep & Deep Publications Pvt. Ltd.
37. Panchayati Raj in India, (New Delhi, 2003), Deep & Deep Publications Pvt. Ltd.
38. Encyclopedia of Higher Education in 21st Century, Organisation and Structure, (New Delhi, 2004) Deep & Deep Publications Pvt. Ltd.
39. Encyclopedia of Higher Education in 21st Century, Quality and Excellence, (New Delhi, 2004), Deep & Deep Publications Pvt. Ltd.
40. Encyclopedia of Higher Education in 21st Century, Extension Education Services (New Delhi, 2004), Deep & Deep Publications Pvt. Ltd.

41. Stress Management and Education : An Indian and Perspective, (New Delhi, 2004), Deep & Deep Publications Pvt. Ltd.
42. Human Values and Education, (New Delhi, 2004), Deep & Deep Publications Pvt. Ltd.
43. Public Health Policy and Administration, (New Delhi, 2004), Deep & Deep Publications Pvt. Ltd.
44. Administration and Management of NGO's Text and Caste Studies, (New Delhi, 2004), Deep & Deep Publications Pvt. Ltd..
45. Nursing Services: Management and Administration (New Delhi, 2005), Deep & Deep Publications Pvt. Ltd.
46. Population Policy and Family Welfare Administration (New Delhi, 2005), Deep & Deep Publications Pvt. Ltd.
47. Human Resource Development in 21st Century (New Delhi, 2005), Deep & Deep Publications Pvt. Ltd.
48. Encyclopaedia of Disaster Management, 3 Volumes, (New Delhi, 2006), Deep & Deep Publications Pvt. Ltd.
49. School Health Education, (New Delhi, 2007), Deep & Deep Publications Pvt. Ltd.
50. Health Education : Theory and Practices, (New Delhi, 2007), Deep & Deep Publications Pvt. Ltd.
51. Good Governance : An Integral View, (New Delhi, 2007), Deep & Deep Publications Pvt. Ltd.
52. Right to Information and Good Governance, (New Delhi, 2007), Deep & Deep Publications Pvt. Ltd.
53. Disaster Management: Text and Case Studies, (New Delhi, 2007), Deep & Deep Publications Pvt. Ltd.
54. Hospital Administration : Theory and Practices (New Delhi, 2007), Deep & Deep Publications Pvt. Ltd..
55. Environmental Health Values and Education, (New Delhi, 2008), Deep & Deep Publications Pvt. Ltd.
56. Administrative and Management Thinkers: Revelvance in New Millennium, (New Delhi, 2008), Deep & Deep Publications Pvt. Ltd.
57. Principle and Practice of Human Values, (New Delhi, 2008), Deep & Deep Publications Pvt. Ltd.
58. Distance Education: Principles, Potentialities and Perspectives, (New Delhi, 2008), Deep & Deep Publications Pvt. Ltd.
59. Educational Administration and Management : An Integral View, (New Delhi, 2008), Deep & Deep Publications Pvt. Ltd..
60. Women Health Education, (New Delhi, 2008), Deep & Deep Publications Pvt. Ltd.
61. Health and Hospital Care Administration and Management, Vol. 1, Organizational Structure, (New Delhi, 2008), Deep & Deep Publications Pvt. Ltd.
62. Health and Hospital Care Administration and Management, Vol. II, (*Resources* : Human, Finance and Material), (New Delhi, 2008), Deep & Deep Publications Pvt. Ltd.

63. Health and Hospital Care Administration and Management, Vol. III, (Policy-Making and Programmes), (New Delhi, 2008), Deep & Deep Publications Pvt. Ltd.
64. Health and Hospital Care Administration and Management, Vol. IV, (Emerging and Thrust Area) (New Delhi, 2008), Deep & Deep Publications Pvt. Ltd.
65. Health and Hospital Care Administration and Management, Vol. V, (Primary and Rural Health Care) (New Delhi, 2008), Deep & Deep Publications Pvt. Ltd.
66. Health and Hospital Administration and Management, Vol. VI, (Secondary and Teritary Hospital) (New Delhi, 2008), Deep & Deep Publications Pvt. Ltd.
67. Health and Hospital Administration and Management, Vol. VII, (Management Techniques and Good Governance) (New Delhi, 2008), Deep & Deep Publications Pvt. Ltd.
68. Education of Life Style and Life Time Disease—In Press.
69. Health Education Administration—Process International Level to Village Level—In Press.
70. Health Education for Healthy Cities—In Press.
71. 383

Rural Health Education—In Press.

Index